HOCKEY
Challenging Canada's Game
Au-delà du sport national

Edited by
Jenny Ellison and Jennifer Anderson

MERCURY SERIES
HISTORY PAPER 58

CANADIAN MUSEUM OF HISTORY
AND UNIVERSITY OF OTTAWA PRESS

Co-published by
the Canadian Museum of History
and the University of Ottawa Press

The University of Ottawa Press gratefully acknowledges the support extended to its publishing list by the Government of Canada, the Canada Council for the Arts, the Federation for the Humanities and Social Sciences through the Awards to Scholarly Publications Program and the University of Ottawa.

Copy editing: Robbie McCaw/Émilie Pelletier
Proofreading: MichaelWaldin/Sabine Cerboni
Typesetting: Édiscript enr.
Cover design: Édiscript enr.

Library and Archives Canada
Cataloguing in Publication

Hockey (2018)

Hockey: challenging Canada's game = au-delà du sport national / edited by Jenny Ellison and Jennifer Anderson.

(Mercury series, 0316-1854; 58)
Includes bibliographical references.
Issued in print and electronic formats.
Includes some text in French.
ISBN 978-0-7766-2599-7 (softcover)
ISBN 978-0-7766-2600-0 (PDF)
ISBN 978-0-7766-2771-7 (EPUB
ISBN 978-0-7766-2594-2 (Kindle)

1. Hockey—Social aspects—Canada. I. Ellison, Jenny, 1977-, editor
I. Anderson, Jennifer, 1972-, editor III. Title. IV. Series: Mercury series; 58

GV848.4.C3H627 2018   796.9620971   C2018-901273-0
                                        C2018-901274-9

The Mercury Series

Strikingly Canadian and highly specialized, the *Mercury Series* presents research from the Canadian Museum of History and benefits from the publishing expertise of the University of Ottawa Press. Created in 1972, the *Mercury Series* is the Canadian Museum of History's primary vehicle for the publication of academic research, and includes numerous landmark contributions in the disciplines of Canadian history, archaeology, and anthropology. Books in the series are published in either English or French, and all include a second-language summary.

La Collection Mercure

Remarquablement canadienne et hautement spécialisée, la *Collection Mercure* réunit des ouvrages portant sur des recherches effectuées au Musée canadien de l'histoire, et elle s'appuie sur le savoir-faire des Presses de l'Université d'Ottawa. Mise sur pied en 1972, la *Collection Mercure* est le principal véhicule qu'utilise le Musée canadien de l'histoire pour publier ses recherches scientifiques. Elle comprend plusieurs contributions remarquables à l'histoire, à l'archéologie et à l'anthropologie. Les ouvrages de la série sont publiés en français ou en anglais, et ils comportent un résumé dans l'autre langue officielle.

How To Order

All trade orders must be directed to the University of Ottawa Press:

> **Web:** www.press.uottawa.ca
> **Email:** puo-uop@uottawa.ca
> **Phone:** 613-562-5246

All other orders may be directed to either the University of Ottawa Press (as above) or to the Canadian Museum of History:

> **Web:** http://www.historymuseum.ca/shop/#publications
> **Email:** publications@historymuseum.ca
> **Phone:** 1-800-5550-5621 (toll-free)
> or 819-776-8387 (National Capital Region)
> **Mail:** Mail Order Services
> Canadian Museum of History
> 100 Laurier Street
> Gatineau, QC K1A 0M8

Pour commander

Les libraires et autres détaillants doivent adresser leurs commandes aux Presses de l'Université d'Ottawa :

> **Web :** www.presses.uottawa.ca
> **Courriel :** puo-uop@uottawa.ca
> **Téléphone :** 613-562-5246

Les particuliers doivent adresser leurs commandes soit aux Presses de l'Université d'Ottawa (voir plus haut), soit au Musée canadien de l'histoire :

> **Web :** http://www.museedelhistoire.ca/magasiner/#publications
> **Courriel :** publications@museedelhistoire.ca
> **Téléphone :** 1-800-5550-5621 (numéro sans frais) –
> 819-776-8387 (région de la capitale nationale)
> **Poste :** Service des commandes postales
> Musée canadien de l'histoire
> 100, rue Laurier
> Gatineau (Québec) K1A 0M8

Canada Council   Conseil des arts
for the Arts   du Canada

Abstract

For Canadians, hockey is *the* game. Shared experiences and memories—lacing up for the first time, shinny on an outdoor rink, historic goals, and heartbreaking losses—make hockey more than just a game.

Hockey reflects Canada's social history. Through it we see how Canada has become more inclusive, but also the ongoing need to address inequities and exclusions between groups of people. Essays in this volume express skepticism, not about hockey itself, but about some of the mythologies around the game.

Where does the game fit into our understanding of multiple, diverse Canadian identities today? Because hockey is so closely identified with Canada, asking questions about the gender and ethnic politics of the sport means troubling concepts of Canada. This interdisciplinary book considers hockey, both as a professional and amateur sport, and both in historical and contemporary contexts, in relation to larger themes in Canadian Studies. It includes essays on gender, race/ethnicity, ability, sexuality, business, geography, and other aspects of hockey in Canadian life.

Going forward it will be necessary to reconcile Canada's past hockey identity with contemporary hockey identities. Dealing with these questions is part of the process of re-evaluation and reconciliation necessary to the next 150 years of hockey in Canada and throughout the world.

This interdisciplinary scholarly collection is an extension of the *Hockey: More Than Just a Game* exhibition presented by the Canadian Museum of History.

Résumé

Aux yeux des Canadiens, le hockey constitue *le* sport national. Du fait d'expériences vécues et de souvenirs partagés — qu'il s'agisse de la première fois où on lace nos patins, d'une partie disputée sur une patinoire extérieure, de buts historiques ou de défaites crève-cœurs —, le hockey en est venu à représenter beaucoup plus qu'un simple jeu.

Le hockey reflète l'histoire sociale du Canada. Par son entremise, il est possible de voir de quelle façon le Canada s'est ouvert à la diversité, mais aussi de constater le besoin, toujours présent, de résoudre les problèmes d'inégalité et d'exclusion qui marquent parfois les relations entre communautés. Les essais qui se trouvent dans cet ouvrage expriment un certain scepticisme, non pas à l'égard du hockey lui-même, mais à propos de certains mythes qui entourent ce sport.

Où se situe le hockey dans notre compréhension des multiples et diverses identités qui constituent le Canada d'aujourd'hui ? Puisque ce sport demeure étroitement associé au Canada, poser des questions sur les politiques liées aux genres et aux origines ethniques du hockey risque, par le fait même, de nous amener à remettre en question les concepts qui définissent le Canada. Cet ouvrage interdisciplinaire, qui traite de la pratique professionnelle et amateur du sport tout en abordant les réalités historiques et contemporaines qui le caractérisent, examine aussi le hockey en le plaçant en relation avec d'autres grands thèmes associés aux études canadiennes. Les divers essais se penchent sur toutes les dimensions que peut revêtir le hockey dans la vie des Canadiens, notamment en abordant des questions de genre, de race et d'ethnicité, d'habiletés, de sexualité, d'affaires et de géographie.

Pour aller de l'avant, il sera nécessaire de parvenir à réconcilier l'identité traditionnelle du hockey et les identités qui le caractérisent aujourd'hui. Réussir à manœuvrer à travers ces questions fera partie des défis entourant les processus de réévaluation et de réconciliation essentiels à l'épanouissement des 150 prochaines années de hockey au Canada et dans le monde.

Ce recueil interdisciplinaire de contributions érudites s'inscrit dans le prolongement de l'exposition *Hockey : plus qu'un simple jeu*, présentée par le Musée canadien de l'histoire.

Table of Contents

PART II
Childhoods

PART III
Whose Game?

PART IV
Reporting Hockey

Document 5
Hockey in New Media

Chapter 9
O Canada, We Stand On Guard For Thee: Representations of Canadian
Hockey Players in the Swedish Press, 1920–2016

Chapter 10
The *Hockey Night in Canada* Punjabi Broadcast:
A Case Study in Ethnic Sports Media

Chapter 11
Taking Slap Shots at the House: When the Canadian Media
Turn Curlers into Hockey Players

Chapter 15
Whiteness and Hockey in Canada: Lessons from Semi-Structured Interviews with Retired Professional Players

List of Figures

Acknowledgements

We are grateful to the contributors for the thoughtfulness they put into their research and the ways in which their work challenged us to expand the exhibition in new directions.

We benefitted from the expertise and resources of our colleagues at the Canadian Museum of History. Dean Oliver, Director of Research, and Bianca Gendreau, Manager of Canada and the Contemporary World, worked with us in the exhibition development process and encouraged us to broaden our work to include this edited collection. From the publishing team, Pascal Laplante, Lee Wyndham, and Pascal Scallon-Chouinard guided the manuscript through development and production. Erin Gurski navigated us through the copyright permissions process with grace. John Willis, Editor for the Mercury Book Series, provided critical support and ensured we delivered the project on schedule.

Inside and outside the museum, many other people contributed to this project. Thank you to Geneviève De Mahy, Xavier Gélinas, and Tanya Anderson. Thanks to Library and Archives Canada for supporting our work on this book project. A huge thank you to the organizers of the 2016 Hockey Conference, for allowing us to launch the call for papers in Fredericton, and to learn from their panelists while we were in exhibition development. In particular, some scholars responded to our requests for more context at the drop of a puck: thanks to Michael Robidoux, Andrew Holman and J. Andrew Ross for being such great team players.

A debt of gratitude is owed our anonymous peer reviewers.

Thank you to the whole team at the University of Ottawa Press.

We would particularly like to thank our families, particularly Pat, Rick, Ben and Jeremy, and Duncan, Piper and Sebastian, for the value they bring to our lives and the intangible ways they have influenced our work.

We were brought together by chance and circumstance at the Canadian Museum of History, and thrust into a complex exhibition project. Collaboration can be challenging, and yet it is tremendously rewarding. So, the editors wish to thank each other, for demonstrating unrelenting flexibility, for collegial critiques when required, and mostly, for all the hard work.

Préface

CHANTAL MACHABÉE

Le 28 septembre 1972. Je suis en classe, à l'école primaire. Je sens une certaine fébrilité, mais je n'ai aucune idée de sa raison. L'enseignante allume le téléviseur et ne dit rien. Elle poursuit sa leçon, mais jette régulièrement un coup d'œil à l'écran, qui diffuse un match de hockey. C'est le tout premier que je vois, car à la maison, personne ne s'intéresse au hockey. Mon père déteste tous les sports ; c'est le cinéma qui occupe une place de choix dans sa vie. Je fixe l'écran. J'ai un coup de foudre. Je viens de découvrir le hockey sans en comprendre quoi que ce soit. J'aime la vitesse du jeu et la description endiablée de René Lecavalier. Le Canada gagne et les enseignants sortent de leur classe respective en criant de joie. On entend des clameurs dans les autres salles. C'est la fête !

J'ai eu la chance de découvrir le hockey dans les années 1970, des années glorieuses pour les Canadiens de Montréal : pensons à ses quatre coupes Stanley consécutives, ainsi qu'à Guy Lafleur et à ses coéquipiers du Temple de la renommée. Puis, dans les années 1980, ce fut au tour des Islanders de Mike Bossy et des Oilers de Wayne Gretzky, et la venue de Mario Lemieux, que j'ai eu la chance de voir jouer quotidiennement avec son équipe junior, les Voisins de Laval, car j'étais relationniste et statisticienne pour l'équipe. Je n'avais ni le talent ni les ressources pour jouer au hockey. Les ligues de filles n'existaient pas, à l'époque, dans mon voisinage. J'ai alors décidé, très jeune, que j'allais devenir journaliste sportive et couvrir le hockey.

Quarante-cinq ans plus tard, ma passion dure encore, comme c'est le cas pour des millions de Canadiens.

Le hockey a changé au cours de ces années. Il a évolué. Les joueurs de l'époque ne portaient pas de casque ! Guy Lafleur était spectaculaire avec ses montées à l'emporte-pièce, les cheveux au vent. C'était presque poétique… mais pas très sécuritaire !

On a certes travaillé fort pour améliorer la sécurité des joueurs, mais on a aussi voulu présenter du hockey plus offensif. Certains règlements ont été modifiés : on a ainsi aboli la ligne rouge, réduit l'équipement du gardien, appliqué la fusillade et aboli les matchs nuls.

Un des plus grands changements concerne sans aucun doute le hockey féminin. Je me rappelle très bien lorsque RDS m'a demandé de décrire le championnat mondial à Ottawa, en 1990. J'étais tellement impressionnée ! Toutes les équipes, la canadienne et l'américaine en particulier, avaient livré des performances de haut calibre et les 10 000 spectateurs étaient complètement ébahis devant un jeu collectif aussi enlevant.

Au cours des années, le progrès a été tel que depuis 1998, à Nagano, nos hockeyeuses participent aux Jeux olympiques et sont admises au Temple de la renommée du hockey. C'est un honneur pleinement mérité pour ces pionnières.

Et qu'en est-il du métier de journaliste sportif? Il a lui aussi évolué. Nous avons aujourd'hui beaucoup plus d'outils qu'il y a 20 ou 30 ans. La venue d'Internet a simplifié notre travail. Plus besoin d'appeler constamment les relationnistes des équipes pour obtenir les nouvelles : une recherche rapide sur le Web nous renseigne en quelques secondes. Maintenant, la nouvelle est instantanée. Nous la publions sur Twitter dès que nous l'avons. Il n'est plus nécessaire d'attendre les bulletins sportifs pour communiquer les actualités de nos équipes. La technologie a également grandi. Nous sommes en mesure de faire des reportages en direct à toute heure du jour, peu importe l'endroit, grâce au système de transmission mobile Dejero.

Quant à la présence des femmes en journalisme sportif, le progrès s'est fait lentement, mais sûrement. Nous sommes de plus en plus nombreuses et c'est tant mieux. On ne nous juge plus aussi sévèrement, quoiqu'on pourrait encore faire mieux. Nous sommes bien acceptées et pouvons travailler à notre guise sans subir les regards condescendants et les remarques désobligeantes de certains, ce qui était monnaie courante à mes débuts, dans les années 1980.

Oui, le hockey a évolué au fil des ans, mais une chose demeure : nous aimons ce sport, nous le jouons, nous l'analysons. Il est encore et toujours le sujet de discussions enflammées avec les amis et la famille ou dans les tribunes téléphoniques. Mais connaissons-nous vraiment son origine et son histoire? Je vous invite à les découvrir à travers ce livre fort bien documenté. Vous en ressortirez non seulement mieux informé, mais encore plus passionné par ce sport qui fait partie de nos vies depuis plus de cent ans.

Introduction
Challenging Hockey

JENNY ELLISON AND JENNIFER ANDERSON, EDITORS

More Than Just A Game

For many Canadians, hockey is *the* game. Hockey animates conversations at work and school. Fine art, popular culture, and books explore hockey's role in everyday life. Communities use hockey to teach children teamwork and to advance social causes. The year 2017 marked several important anniversaries for Canada and hockey: the 150th anniversary of Confederation, the 125th anniversary of the Stanley Cup, and the 100th anniversary of the National Hockey League (NHL). Rather than merely celebrate these milestones, this book uses them as a starting point to critically evaluate hockey's place in Canada.

This book project grew out of the *Hockey* exhibition we co-curated at the Canadian Museum of History, which opened in March 2017. The museum wanted to join the conversation about hockey by considering the history of Canada's national winter sport. Hockey is often called "Canada's game," but how, and why, does it matter to Canadians? We addressed this question in eight thematic zones at the museum, beginning with the cross-cultural origins of hockey in Canada, origins which featured diversity among teams and players. After that, exhibition-goers moved through sections that explored other elements of the game: equipment, fan culture, coaches and other members of the "team behind the team," sports broadcasting, hockey in popular culture, community activism, and business/labour relations.

Through artifacts, photographs, and art, our goal was to show that hockey is "more than just a game." Memorable goals and games were highlighted alongside community experiences and culture. Our premise was that hockey also lives off the ice, in the everyday experiences of Canadians. Making this case required a different approach than writing an academic article on hockey. Visitors do not necessarily read all text on every display panel. For that reason, the selection and placement of artifacts, the *mise-en-scène,* and the sound were as important as the text in our storytelling. Entering the exhibition, visitors first encountered a video of contemporary players talking about hockey. They were met with the sounds of an arena, of a game, and of fans. Inside, the space had the look and feel of a hockey arena. Visitors entered a dressing room, stood behind a bench, came onto the rink, and into a corporate board room, and a broadcasting booth. Diverse aspects of hockey were highlighted in each section—in terms of geography, ethnicity, gender, and also the types of artifacts displayed. Para hockey and women's and men's hockey were featured side by side. By intentionally placing these objects together, we made an argument about hockey history:

women, non-white, and Indigenous players of the past were not just a side story, they were integral to the history of the game.

As professionally-trained historians working in collecting institutions, we are aware that there are gaps in the material history of hockey. Collecting institutions' practices, much like the game of hockey, are racialized and gendered. Of archives in general, Rodney Carter has argued, "there are distortions, omissions, erasures, and silences . . . Not every story is told" (2006, 215). Collection decisions have resulted in the magnification of some voices in hockey's history, like those of professional teams, and gaps in the material record of amateur, non-white, and women's teams. Such silences can have a negative impact on marginalized groups (ibid., 220). Contemporary efforts to fill these silences can been challenging. Marginalized communities are sometimes reluctant to share their histories with collecting institutions. For example, Naomi Norquay (2016) found some reluctance in talking about the history of racism in her efforts to construct an archive of an early Canadian Black settlement. Some people she approached felt shame about their biracial ancestry, others felt that Black settlement was too brief a part of the community's history to merit much mention. A community's reluctance to share archives and artifacts might equally reflect mistrust of collecting institutions and their colonial pasts. As both Norquay and Karina Vernon have noted, many treasures likely remain in private collections because of the perception that donating items to an archive is tantamount to "turning…over" community heritage to "white people" (Vernon 2012, 199). Museological theorists have also acknowledged and responded to these tensions. Tony Bennett identified the power nexus occupied by museums, and the ways exhibitions traditionally went beyond public education to discipline social values and norms. More recently Viv Golding has explored the power of museums to build visitor-centred exhibitions that include difficult histories and embrace diversity with the intention of offering informal learning opportunities (Bennett, 1995; Golding, 2009). Our exhibition research gave us cause to reflect on these theories.

Some stories and individuals were left out of the exhibition. Sometimes this was because we did not have artifacts; at other times, we did not have the space to tell their stories. Making choices was difficult. There are inherent challenges in trying to fill holes in the historical record: instead, we drew attention to gaps, to engage the visitor in historical critical thinking. The record was sometimes fleeting. There is plenty of documentary evidence on the Coloured Hockey League of the Maritimes (c. 1895–1930), for example, but we were unable to locate artifacts. Photos of lesser-known but impactful teams—like the Coloured Hockey League's Halifax Eurekas (Figure I.1) or the Alkali Lake Braves, one of the first, if not the first, Indigenous men's teams in British Columbia—were included in the exhibition, but this section is not as artifact-rich as we had hoped. Photo panels were included to tell personal stories of hockey personalities when artifacts could not be located. In a few cases we were lucky and found artifacts to tell these stories. Part way through planning the exhibition we found a 1938 uniform from the Preston Rivulettes (Figure I.2), which allowed us to bring to life the story of the Dominion Women's Amateur Hockey Association of the 1930s. Rather than letting silences remain, we wanted to address gaps through artifacts and images that invited visitors to consider lesser-known hockey stories.

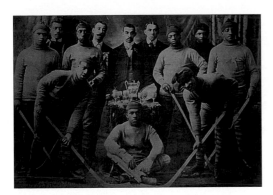

Figure I.I Halifax Eurekas, Coloured Hockey League Champions Halifax, N.S., 1904.
Courtesy of George and Darril Fosty, Black Ice (2004).

Our goal was to tell a diverse story—in terms of geography, ethnicity, gender, and also the types of artifacts displayed. To do this we borrowed about 180 (of 280) artifacts from fifty museums and private lenders. Reaching out to private collectors and other museums allowed us to bring new perspectives on the game. Some objects, like Sidney Crosby's 2010 Olympic jersey, reflect moments that visitors expect and are excited to encounter. Others, like the graffitied plywood hoarding walls erected after the 2011 Vancouver Stanley Cup riots or Jim Logan's 1991 painting *National Pastimes* (Figure I.3) about hockey on Indigenous reserves and at residential schools, where Indigenous children were forcibly assimilated, might be unexpected. Some visitors might find the insertion of hockey's darker moments difficult, but we felt it was important to show the complexity of the game.

We chose to organize the exhibition thematically, around places and spaces. Hockey fans may quibble with our choice of memorable moments and people, but we embraced this element of debate in the game. Why Paul Henderson but not Phil Esposito? Why Foster Hewitt and not Bob Cole? Scholars will note that the project is not organized around themes of class, gender, and race that normally animate academic work on such subjects. These issues are addressed explicitly (and implicitly) in our selection and juxtaposition of artifacts, but they are not overarching themes. We also decided against a chronological exhibition. Visitors won't find a survey of every great coach or media personality. Through choice and circumstance, the exhibition tells the hockey story differently than would an academic or a journalist.

Figure I.2 The Preston Rivulettes
The Rivulettes captured four national championships, and attracted huge paying audiences in the 1930s. Team member Hilda Ranscombe was the best player of the era. She wore this sweater during the 1938 hockey season.
Hilda Ranscombe Preston Rivulettes Jersey, 1930s
Canadian Museum of History, 2015.95.2,
IMG2017-0036-0013-Dm

This book grew out of our efforts to ensure the exhibition touched on contemporary issues. It came from a deep passion for hockey, a strong intellectual engagement with the history of the game, and a desire to inspire positive responses to current and historical challenges. Seeking new hockey stories and re-evaluations of existing narratives of the game, we invited scholars to contribute new research. As a public history

Figure I.3 *National Pastimes*

In *National Pastimes*, Jim Logan has drawn on personal experience to critique the way the game can divert attention from the painful social and economic realities affecting Indigenous communities. Logan's piece includes seven separate paintings, the largest of which is shown here.

Jim Logan (1955–)
Cree Sioux Métis
1991
Acrylic on canvas
Collection of Indigenous and Northern Affairs Canada, 407209 A-G

project, the exhibition presented short, accessible ideas about hockey in Canada. This book expands on the exhibition's themes and delves deeper into experiences of class, gender, race/ethnicity, language, ability, sexual orientation, and region. We also sought papers that reflected upon fandom, sports media, popular culture, and community activism through hockey. Many of the contributors participated in the 2016 Hockey Conference at the University of New Brunswick in Fredericton.

Alongside the academic papers, we have included six brief experiential accounts related to hockey. These primary documents reflect our orientation toward combining academic analysis with personal experience and community perspectives. Some, like the excerpts from the *Final Report of the Truth and Reconciliation Commission of Canada*, are first-person experiential perspectives on hockey. Other papers reflect more celebratory perspectives on the role of hockey in Canadian life. The fun of hockey and Canadians' love for the game can be difficult to reconcile with the more challenging questions raised in this book. As historians and fans, our love of hockey coexists with our knowledge of inequities and problems in the sport. We too have both emotional and critical responses to the sport. Instructors might use these contributions to explore such tensions, which are indeed part of the game in Canada.

Canada's Game?

Many Canadian communities lay claim to being the birthplace of hockey, but evidence shows stick-and-ball and puck games were played by Indigenous people and in England long before it was taken up by Canadian settlers (Culin [1907] 1975; Giden, Houda, and Martel 2014; Heine 1997; Morrow, 2009). Versions of hockey were played in the territory we now call Canada before European settlement. Early settler accounts mention "shinny," a word they used to describe a version of hockey played by Indigenous people of the northwest plains and in the western subarctic. While skates were not used, shinny games of the Han, Deg Hit'an and Gwi'chin people were played on ice or open plains. Using a "hide-covered ball or a puck," players used a stick to score goals (Morrow 2009, 11). Dene communities in northeastern Canada probably played these games at gatherings, like those associated with a successful hunt (Heine, 1997). In 1976 Gwich'in Elders told anthropologist Michael Heine that Elders usually supervised shinny. There were no time limits on the game. Elders recalled that shinny was a rare example of a game where players could lose their temper. Fights sometimes broke out in the heat of a match (M. Heine, 1997). Anthropological research suggests that shinny was a men's and women's game, which was different from the earliest versions of hockey described in England and pre-Confederation Canada (M. Heine 1997; Culin [1907] 1975; Morrow 2010). Other names for hockey-like sports include *Gontl* from Nisga communities (Culin [1907] 1975, 628), *smuk* in Songish communities, and *aiyutalugit* or *patkutalugit* in the far North (ibid., 629). In eastern Canada, hockey was *Oochamkunutk,* the Mi'kmaq stickball game. On ice and with whites, they called it *Alchamadijik* (Vaughan, 1996). Like the sport European people variously called hurly, bandy, and ricket, Indigenous versions of hockey were not played on ice. The games shared a common objective with the sport that evolved into hockey: moving a ball, puck or "bung" down a playing area and scoring a goal on an opposing team. Another common feature is that the game was played in cooler temperatures. Skates, probably first adopted in England around 1775, were popularized by the Starr Manufacturing Company of Halifax, Nova Scotia. Starr developed an affordable blade that could securely attach to one's boot. Skates made the game faster and trickier. "Hockey" became the common term for the sport in the late 1800s (Culin [1907] 1975; Giden, Houda, and Martel 2014).

Giden, Houda, and Martel take on the origins of hockey in their 2014 book of the same name. Aimed at investigating various claims about the Canadian origins of hockey, the book concludes that the sport has European origins. Indigenous influence on the game is not explored in the text, which instead focuses on the various versions of hockey that settlers may have imported into the territory that is now Canada. Using newspaper accounts, they found references to versions of hockey in English sources that predated almost all others; they concluded that the origins of hockey are likely European. We did not take up this debate in the exhibition because we felt focusing on the famous firsts of hockey obscured the longer, cross-cultural history of the game in Canada. Our view is that there is no single origin for hockey; the game evolved and was influenced by diverse groups.

In addition to the game itself, the material history of hockey in Canada has Indigenous influences. Oral history accounts and Indigenous and Northern Affairs Canada documents show that Indigenous people were carving sticks for sale to Settlers as early as 1898. Given the longer history of hockey-like games in these communities, it is likely that Indigenous and Settler versions of the game co-mingled (Indian Affairs Annual Report, 1898; Wicken 2012; Vaughan 1996). Initially, sticks were hand-carved. For instance, the stick pictured here, popularly called "the Moffatt stick," was made for W. M. "Dilly" Moffatt (b. 1829), whose initials are engraved on the blade (Figure I.4). Scientific evidence confirms the wood is from the 1830s. Based on the differences between this stick, which has an elongated blade, and European sticks used in Canada that had a shorter, field-hockey blade, we suggest that this stick is made in a Mi'kmaq style (Vaughan, 1996). The Moffatt stick therefore illustrates the cross-cultural and transnational evolution of hockey in Canada: crafted in a Mi'kmaq style but owned by a Euro-Canadian child. A Mi'kmaq carving knife (Figure 1.5) was exhibited next to the Moffatt stick to emphasize the connection between Indigenous carving and the object. The Moffatt Stick shows the influence of Indigenous people on European settlers before Confederation, and this distinguishes the stick from others found in Canada. Through the stick we can see the exchange of ideas, activities, and technology between cultures.

Although evidence shows that many different groups have played ice hockey, not everyone played together. Hockey history reveals longstanding divisions along racial, class, and gender lines. In addition to the previously mentioned Coloured Hockey League of the Maritimes, archival photographs and documents provide evidence of numerous other teams organized around ethnic identity. Vancouver's Japanese-Canadian Asahi Athletic Club had an ice-hockey team (Figure I.6). Little is known about this club, but an image of the players is evidence that diverse groups were among Canada's earliest players. In Toronto, the King Clancy Hockey League had an "all-Chinese team" in 1949. CBC Radio reported (1949) that the "unusual" team included Canadian-born men of Chinese

Figure I.4 Early Hockey Stick
Dated to the 1830s, this stick is carved in a Mi'kmaq style. The initials of its owner, William "Dilly" Moffatt, appear on the blade.
1835–1838
Canadian Museum of History, 2014.27.1,
IMG2016-0253-0027-Dm

Figure I.5 Mi'kmaq Knife
In hockey's earliest days, the Mi'kmaq of Eastern Canada used crooked knives such as this to make superb hockey sticks from the tough, naturally curved roots of young trees.
Eastern coast of Canada
Around 1900
Canadian Museum of History, III-F-163,
IMG2017-0036-0006-Dm

descent who decided it was time to learn the sport. More research is necessary to understand where and how these teams formed. Reproducing and perhaps even reinforcing ethnic and class divisions in Canadian society, hockey crossed communities and cultures.

Hockey: Challenging Canada's Game is not the first and will not be the last effort to find new ways to talk about the game. It builds on a continual re-evaluation of hockeys. There is now a lively field of sports scholarship about hockey's place in Canadian society. Researchers have criticized the politics and power dynamics of hockey. Richard Gruneau and David Whitson's *Hockey Night in Canada: Sports, Identities, and Cultural Politics* was a foundational text in this genre. Like them, we seek to analyze, rather than romanticize, "hockey's enduring link to the idea of 'Canadianness'" (Gruneau and Whitson 1993, 7). Michel A. Robidoux's work influenced our thinking on Indigenous hockey for the exhibition and inspired our desire to rethink hockey. In *Stickhandling Through the Margins*, Robidoux (2014) shows that hockey is part of Canada's history of colonialism. European reshaping of traditional stick-and-ball games and the residential-school system were examples of the ways that Indigenous people were pressured to "assume qualities and customs of the empire" (ibid., 4). And yet, as Robidoux shows, Indigenous people passionately embrace hockey, and it has been a source of cultural pride. The game is a form of "cultural expression" within a larger national sports system (6).

Figure I.6 The Vancouver Asahi Hockey Club
Vancouver B.C.
1919-1920 season
Library and Archives Canada
e011184878

Imagined community and invented tradition are two theoretical concepts that have interested hockey researchers, and have inspired many contributors to this collection. "Imagined community," a term coined by political scientist Benedict Anderson, has been widely taken up by Canadian scholars. Most agree on the basics of the concept. Anderson argues that nations are constructs. They are formed first in the minds of their citizens, brought together by common bonds, composed of symbols and events. Tim Elcombe argues (2010, 1292) that hockey is an example of imagined community, as it serves as "a source of pride that brings citizens together and reveals a culture's values." Hockey, many scholars agree, is one of the few mythologized images of Canadian life. Canada's perceived dominance at international events, the ubiquity of the sport for players and spectators, and its connection to the nation's northern mythology make it an important marker of imagined community (Elcombe, 2010).

Himani Bannerji has been critical of the way some scholars have employed the notion of imagined community. Bannerji argues (1996, 110) that nations require ideologies of "unification and legitimation," they are not just imagined into being. In order to address inequities, she says it is necessary to address power differences within cultures. Like Bannerji, historian Gillian Poulter argues (2009, 5) that Canada's northern mythology was not simply passively "imagined" but actively envisioned by settlers seeking to articulate a Canadian identity. Using snowshoeing and lacrosse as examples, Poulter shows how the sports' "Canadian-ness" was taken up by settlers of pre-Confederation Montreal who wanted to distinguish the nation from England and the United States (ibid., 7). Representations and practices, like sports, became a way for settlers to assert a particular white and European vision of Canada.

Several of the contributors to this collection examine the significance of hockey to Quebec culture. As Amy Ransom earlier argued in *Hockey PQ: Canada's Game in Quebec's Popular Culture* (2014), the Québécois see hockey as a part of their national identity. Hockey is central to how Quebec represents itself in popular culture. Three of the documents included in this book reflect this Quebec-centred view of hockey. Marc Durand, Benoit Melançon, and John Willis show that Quebec has a hockey mythology all its own. Whether and how to connect these histories are subjects for debate. Harold Ramos argues that the idea of "two solitudes" remains relevant to Canada's history to the present day. Reviewing media coverage of Maurice "Rocket" Richard, Ramos (2002) observed that francophones and anglophones had different interpretations of the meaning and legacy of the player. Our approach to this question was influenced by the seemingly innocent representation of English- and French-Canadian relations in Roch Carrier's (1984) *Le chandail de hockey* (*The Hockey Sweater*). Carrier's children's classic is centred on a miscommunication between a French-speaking woman in a rural community in mail-ordering a hockey sweater from an urban, Anglo-Canadian department store. His book reveals not only the power imbalance between French- and English-Canadians, but, through the character of the local priest, the overwhelming power of the church in rural Quebec life. Carrier's book uses hockey to reveal the complexity of Québécois society before the Quiet Revolution of the 1960s. Using one boy's horror over being forced to wear a rival NHL team's hockey sweater, *Le chandail* situates hockey in the broader story of Canada. Charming and challenging aspects of Canada's history are presented together.

"Invented tradition" is a concept related to imagined community, used by scholars to challenge or add complexity to the idea that hockey is Canada's game. British historian Eric Hobsbawm used invented traditions to describe rituals that might "appear or claim to be old are often quite recent in origin and sometimes invented" (1983, 1). Some contributors to this collection see hockey as an example of such a tradition, because of the accent placed on "Canada" or "Canadian traditions" in some accounts of the game. Efforts to establish Canada's ongoing hockey dominance often leave out major gaps and failures in that record. Canada's fifty-one-year Olympic-hockey medal drought, for example, is rarely mentioned in public celebrations of the nation's hockey dominance. Hockey also fits Hobsbawm's typology of an invented tradition in that it is often taken to symbolize social cohesion "as Canadians" even though, historically, teams have been formed based on ethnic, gender and religious alliances, and presumably some Canadians may not follow the sport. Hockey is also said to symbolize Canadian values, but which ones? A hallmark of an invented tradition is one that is "quite unspecific and vague as to the nature of the values, rights and obligations of the group membership they inculcate" (ibid., 10). Looking at hockey through the lens of invented tradition and imagined community reveals the game has been an important element of Canadian nationalism. The notion that hockey is "Canada's game" universalizes and diminishes the differences within the game.

Scholars have pointed to declining hockey enrollment as a way to question the importance of hockey in Canadian life. Since 2006, soccer has consistently ranked ahead of hockey in terms of number of registrations per year (Jedwab 2007, 201). Canadian Heritage's 2010 survey (2013) indicated that 42 per cent of Canadian children play soccer, while only 27 per cent play hockey. This shift is likely the result of several factors, including the relative high cost of hockey. A number of efforts have been made to recruit new constituencies to hockey (Jedwab, 2007; Canadian Heritage 2013; Institute for Canadian Citizenship 2014). Women's hockey registration dramatically increased in the 1990s in spite of the downward trend in overall enrollment. This is attributed to the higher profile of the national women's team, in domestic and international circles (Reid and Mason, 2015). This finding is echoed in Carly Adams and Jason Laurendeau's chapter in this volume. In 2012, Hockey Canada launched a Grow the Game initiative to try to add one million new players to the game worldwide by 2022.

Registration numbers are only a starting point for a discussion about the future of hockey. There remain troubling questions about the culture of hockey, including the persistence of homophobia, hyper-masculinity, and violence in the game. In 2011, the You Can Play Project was founded with the goal of ending homophobia in all sports, although the project's roots lie in hockey. NHL players starred in the first You Can Play public-service announcement that year. We included it in the *Hockey* exhibition as a positive example of activism in contemporary hockey. The message was simple: "If you can play, you can play" (You Can Play Project 2012). Presented alongside other game changers, You Can Play is an example of players challenging stigmas in hockey. By 2014, one player from each team on the NHL had joined the You Can Play Project (2014). You Can Play has had an impact, but questions still exist about homophobia in hockey. While there are high-profile "out" players in women's elite hockey, the NHL is the only North American sports league where an athlete has not come out as gay during or after professional career (C. Hine, 2016). In her contribution to this collection, Cheryl A. MacDonald suggests the culture of hockey contributes to such silences on sexuality.

Hockey, by its nature, is a physical sport. How can it not be when players rapidly traverse an ice surface on metal blades? Dangers inherent in playing a sport on ice are made worse by physical violence within the game. Player equipment, rules, and officiating have evolved to make hockey safer for players, but balancing the game's speed and energy with the physicality that erupts in the game remains a problem. Aggression is part of the spectacle of hockey, as Russell Field (2008) has shown. Varda Burstyn (1999) argues that aggression is not unique to hockey, of course, but to a naturalization of male violence in Canadian (and North American) culture. As Tobias Stark's contribution to this collection shows, historically, Canadian hockey players have had a reputation for violence. Such historical perspectives are essential to unpacking the culture of hockey and preventing personal injury, particularly concussions, in the future. Aggression has physical and mental consequences that are still being analysed.

The concepts of imagined community and invented tradition also need to be considered in light of the history of racism within hockey. Who, exactly, gets to be imagined as Canadian? The NHL never had an official colour bar, and Black players have enjoyed success in the league, but non-white and Indigenous players are still highly underrepresented in the professional and amateur game. As Joseph, Darnell, and Nakamura argue (2012, 7) in their path-breaking book on race and sport in Canada, whiteness is the norm: "Whiteness does not refer directly to white people but rather to the myriad social and political processes by which hierarchies and privileges are codified and normalized along lines of race." Non-white players are celebrated as examples of Canadian inclusion, but in the process they are also codified as "other" within a predominantly white sport (ibid.).

While women's hockey has grown considerably in the past thirty years, the process has been rife with internal debates about how women and girls play and who they can play with. After the heyday of women's hockey in the 1930s (see Adams, 2008), girls and women's hockey teams nearly disappeared. From the 1950s to the 1970s, girls who wanted to play had limited options. In that time, there were two controversial cases where girls joined boys' teams. Abby Hoffman famously disguised herself to play on a boys' team in Toronto in the 1950s. In 1976, Gail Cummings filed a complaint with the Ontario Human Rights Tribunal when she was not allowed to join a boys' team. Cummings lost. This type of gender discrimination was legal at the time because section 19(2) of the Ontario Human Rights Code allowed sports associations to limit teams to people of the same gender. Less than ten years later, Justine Blainey successfully challenged this limitation (Figure I.7). A 1986 Ontario Court of Appeal ruling determined that the Ontario Hockey Association's rule preventing girls from playing with boys contravened the equality provisions (section 15) of the Canadian Charter of Rights and Freedoms (Hall 2002; Findlay and Corbett, 2009).

Scholars of women's hockey have documented the feminist debates that shaped the Blainey case, as well as the gendered experience of hockey. M. Ann Hall's *The Girl in the Game* (2002), Nancy Theberge's *Higher Goals: Women's Ice Hockey and the Politics of Gender* (2000), and Linda Baril's *Nos glorieuses: plus de cent ans de hockey féminin au Québec* (2013) document the ways that gender has shaped hockey norms and experiences. Carly Adams's research (2008, Adams and Stevens 2013, Adams and Leavitt 2016) shows that gender continues to shape how girls see themselves in hockey. Women have played hockey since at least the 1890s, so it is troubling that women sometimes continue to feel less important in the game. It is important to note, however, that female players have not accepted secondary status. In 2016, members of the United States women's hockey team went public with a dispute with USA Hockey. Unlike their male counterparts, female players were earning little-to-nothing in the years between Olympic Games. The women were successful. Under

Figure I.7 Justine Blainey, 13, after winning her bid to play hockey on a boys' team. Toronto, Ont., 1986. Photo by Andrew Stawicki/Toronto Star/Getty Images

their new deal, players will receive a monthly training stipend, bonuses for winning medals, and financial compensation (Svrluga 2016; Zirin 2017). Change is possible within hockey. It has been (and will be) achieved when players, fans, and organizations work to make hockey more accessible, safe, and equitable.

Challenging Hockey

Hockey's past and present is explored in the five thematic sections of this book.

"Debating Hockey's Origins" examines hockey's apparent Canadian roots. Andrew Holman argues that hockey is a metaphor for Canada but not in the ways you might expect. Hockey unites and divides Canadians, according to Holman. It is both a symbol for a nation that "desperately and continuously" seeks unity and divides Canadians along lines of region, race, language, and gender. Hockey helps us to understand why Canadians often struggle to articulate an identity because there are so many different lived experiences of the game. Paul Bennett takes on the origins-of-hockey debate, about whether hockey was first played in Canada. Bennett argues that the debate reflects efforts to promote an official past for Canada that emphasizes social cohesion. Indigenous forms of hockey are erased in favour of an "invented tradition" that credits settlers of the 1830s (through to the 1890s) with creating hockey. Picking up on these themes, Michael Robidoux's research on hockey has addressed the troubling relationship between national identity and sport. His 2001 article looking at hockey and lacrosse, reprinted here, remains relevant today. Both games flourished in a period of nation-building. Situating hockey in relation to other sports helps link it to other themes in Canadian society. Rhetoric and representation around both games combined Indigenous stereotypes with elements of nineteenth-century nativism to assert Canada's national strength. Canada's strength on the field and ice was a metaphor for a rough-hewn, settler, masculinity. Robidoux offers insight into the bases of the relationship between hockey and whiteness, which is explored in other sections of the book.

The "Childhoods" section looks at the mythic and sometimes troubling place of hockey in the lives of young people. Excerpts from the Final Report of the Truth and Reconciliation Commission of Canada show that, while hockey was often fondly remembered by survivors, it was not exclusively a good-news story. Numerous children reported being beaten with hockey sticks. Some hockey programs were also abusive, with players reportedly punished for failings on the ice. In this book, Sam McKegney and Trevor Phillips demonstrate the ways Richard Wagamese, in his novel *Indian Horse*, reflected on the deeply disturbing underpinnings of the game, rooted in white settler colonialism, while simultaneously offering a decolonized alternative view of hockey. Residential-school stories are a stark contrast to the myth of the outdoor rink examined by Robert Rutherdale. Rutherdale examines how Canadian boyhood and hockey are inextricably linked in representations of outdoor rinks. Such representations obscure the dominant forms of hockey in this country, such as the indoor competitive leagues examined in Carly Adams and Jason Laurendeau's contribution. Adams and Laurendeau argue that hockey was intended to be a form of physical and moral development for young (white) men. Competitive sport was seen as a way to build a stronger nation.

"Whose Game?" asks about inclusivity in Canadian hockey. Short accounts by Hayley Wickenheiser and Emily Sadler offer positive examples of the growth of the game among women and athletes with disabilities. Sadler's piece also suggests the role of the media in inspiring upcoming athletes. Julie Stevens and Denyse Lafrance Horning evaluate the contemporary state of the women's game in their scholarly articles. Canadian women's hockey is thriving, as these authors persuasively show, but the growth of the game has not always been smooth. Canadian women's hockey dominance internationally is particularly explored by Stevens. She argues that Canadian players' cultural diplomacy and leadership is essential to growing women's hockey internationally. Horning looks at the player profiles of recreational programs. Not unlike the national women's team, recreational teams rely on informal mentorship among players and coaches to thrive.

The section on sports media reflects on how hockey is imagined by, and communicated to, Canadians. The press has helped to construct hockey narratives. Representations of hockey in sports media are analyzed in three very different contributions to this collection. Tobias Stark examines Swedish press accounts of Canadian hockey players from 1920 to 2010. Swedes were fascinated by Canadian hockey players, but they were also horrified by the violence in the Canadian style of game. Kristi Allain looks at hockey as a metaphor for masculinity in her article on men's curling. Men's hockey bodies have become a standard by which media evaluate curlers. Rather than deconstructing masculinity or allowing for different ways to be a man, certain curlers are celebrated for being like, or looking like, hockey players. Lastly, Courtney Szto and Richard Gruneau look at *Hockey Night in Canada*'s Punjabi-language broadcast. Celebrated as an example of Canadian inclusion, the show also raises questions about the racialization of some groups within hockey. Cheryl A. McDonald examines the persistence of homophobia and sexism among teenage male hockey players. Interview and social-media data show troubling attitudes among such players, who continue to use social media as an informal space to share "locker room talk," despite high-profile efforts to change the culture of hockey.

In "Rethinking the Pros," the focus is on elite hockey and the NHL. Andrew Ross and Laurent Turcot re-evaluate two key moments in NHL history. Ross sheds light on the internal debates that led to the first incarnation of the National Hockey League Players' Association, which was short-lived. While contemporary audiences may not think of professional hockey players as labourers, Ross shows that a paternalistic and sometimes abusive management system existed well into the 1950s. Laurent Turcot revisits Eric Lindros's controversial decision to reject the opportunity to play in the NHL after being selected first overall in the NHL entry draft by the Quebec Nordiques. Seen at the time as an example of poor French-English relations, Turcot considers other possible interpretations of these events, which saw the Nordiques trade the future hall of famer after a yearlong holdout. Nathan Kalman-Lamb looks at racism in the professional leagues; Kalman-Lamb's research shows that white and non-white players have different interpretations of racism in elite hockey.

Together, the essays in this collection reflect current debates about hockey in Canada. They address issues of violence, sexuality, inclusion, indigeneity, race, gender, and representation. Changes in Canadian society and culture continue to raise new questions about the game, from the role of social media to the inclusion of lesbian, gay, and transgendered athletes. Debates about masculinity and femininity in the game likewise continue to evolve. Identifying "hockey masculinities" helps us to deconstruct aggression and violence in the game. We also find it heartening that new research on women's hockey addresses the state of the game itself, and not just the problem of discrimination. These are signs of positive change.

Hockey is important to many people but there is an inherent tension in claiming it is Canada's game. Hockey reflects Canada's social history. Through it we see how Canada has become more inclusive, but also that there is an ongoing need to address inequities and exclusions between groups of people. Each author expresses skepticism, not about hockey itself but about some of the mythologies around the game. Because hockey is so closely identified with Canada, asking questions about the gender and ethnic politics of the sport means troubling the very notion of Canadian identity. A critical question going forward will be to reconcile Canada's claim to being the birthplace of hockey with Indigenous histories, experiences, and perspectives in that regard. Dealing with these questions is part of the process of re-evaluation and reconciliation necessary to the next 150 years of hockey in Canada.

Bibliography

Adams, Carly. 2008. "'Queens of the Ice Lanes': The Preston Rivulettes and Women's Hockey in Canada, 1931–1940." *Sport History Review* 39 (1): 1–29.

Adams, Carly, and Julie Stevens. 2013. "'Together we can make it better': Collective action and governance in a girls' hockey association. *International Review for the Sociology of Sport* 48 (6): 658–72.

Adams, Carly, and Stacy Leavitt. 2016. "'It's just girls' hockey': Troubling progress narratives in girls' and women's sport." *International Review for the Sociology of Sport*. Online first.

Bannerji, Himani. 1996. "On the Dark Side of the Nation: Politics of Multiculturalism and the State in 'Canada.' *Journal of Canadian Studies* 31 (3): 103–28.

Baril, Lynda. 2013. *Nos Glorieuses: Plus de Cent Ans de Hockey Féminin au Québec*. Montréal: Les Éditions La Presse.

Bennett, Tony. 1995. *The Birth of the Museum: History, Theory, Politics*. London and New York: Routledge.

Burstyn, Varda. 1999. *The Rites of Men: Manhood, Politics and the Culture of Sport*. Toronto: University of Toronto Press.

Canadian Heritage. February 2013. *Sport Participation 2010: Research Paper*. Ottawa: Queen's Printer. http://publications.gc.ca/collections/collection_2013/pc-ch/CH24-1-2012-eng.pdf.

Carrier, Roch. 1984. *Le chandail de hockey*. Montréal: Livres Toundra.

Carter, Rodney. 2006. "Of things said and unsaid: Power, archival silences and power in silence." *Archivaria*. 61: 215–233.

CBC (Canadian Broadcasting Corporation). 1949. CBC Radio, *News Roundup*, February 10. http://www.cbc.ca/archives/entry/a-chinese-hockey-team-in-toronto.

Culin, Stewart. [1907] 1975. *Games of the North American Indians*: Don Mills, ON: General Publishing Company Ltd.

Dominion of Canada Annual Report of the Department of Indian Affairs for the Year Ended 30 June 1898. Ottawa: Queen's Printer, 1898. http://www.bac-lac.gc.ca/eng/discover/aboriginal-heritage/first-nations/indian-affairs-annual-reports/Pages/introduction.aspx

Elcombe, Tim. 2010. "Hockey New Year's Eve in Canada: Nation-Making at the Montreal Forum." *International Journal of the History of Sport* 27 (8): 1287–312.

Field, Russell. May 2008. "Constructing the Preferred Spectator: Arena Design and Operation and the Consumption of Hockey in 1930s Toronto." *The International Journal of the History of Sport* 25 (6): 649–77.

Findlay, Hilary, and Rachel Corbett. 2009. "Sex Discrimination in Sport: An Update." Ottawa: Canadian Association for the Advancement of Women and Sport and Physical Activity. http://www.sportlaw.ca/wp-content/uploads/2011/03/em-Sex-Discrimination-in-Sport-An-Update...-for-CAAWS-2009-full-report.pdf.

Golding, Viv. 2009. *Learning at the Museum Frontiers: Identity, Race and Power*. New York: Routledge.

Giden, Carl, Patrick Houda, and Jean-Patrice Martel. 2014. *On the Origin of Hockey*. Stockholm and Chambly, QC: Hockey Origin Publishing.

Gruneau, Richard, and David Whitson. 1993. *Hockey Night in Canada: Sport, Identities and Cultural Politics*. Toronto: Garamond Press.

Hall, M. Ann. 2002. *The Girl and the Game: A History of Women's Sport in Canada*. Peterborough, ON: Broadview Press.

Heine, Michael. 1997. *Dene Games: A Culture and Resource Manual*. Yellowknife: Sport North Federation.

Hine, Chris. 2016. "Gary Bettman says NHL is ready for its first openly gay player." *Chicago Tribune*, June 29. http://www.chicagotribune.com/sports/hockey/blackhawks/ct-bettman-nhl-gay-players-spt-0630-20160629-story.html.

Hobsbawm, Eric. 1983. "Introduction: Inventing Traditions." In *The Invention of Tradition*, ed. Eric Hobsbawm and Terence Ranger. Cambridge: Cambridge University Press.

Holman, Andrew. 2009. *Canada's Game: Hockey and Identity*. Kingston, ON: Queen's Policy Studies.

Institute for Canadian Citizenship. July 2014. "Playing Together – New Citizens, Sport and Belonging." Toronto: ICC Insights. https://www.iccicc.ca/en/insights/docs/sports/PlayingTogether%20Full%20Report.pdf.

Jedwab, Jack. 2007. "Giving Hockey's Past a Future: Identity Meets Demography in Canadian Sports. *International Journal of Canadian Studies* 35:191–214.

Joseph, Janelle, Simon Darnell, and Yuka Nakamura, eds. 2012. Introduction: The Intractability of Race and Sport in Canada. In *Race and Sport in Canada*, ed. Janelle, Darnell, and Nakamura, 1–26. Toronto: Canadian Scholars Press.

Morrow, Don, and Kevin B. Wamsley. 2009. *Sport in Canada: A History*. Don Mills, ON: Oxford University Press.

Norquay, Naomi. 2016. "An Accidental Archive of the Old Durham Road: Reclaiming a Black Pioneer Settlement." *Archivaria* 81:1–22.

Poulter, Gillian. 2009. *Becoming Native in a Foreign Land: Sport, Visual Culture and Identity in Montreal, 1840–85.* Vancouver: University of British Columbia Press.

Ramos, Howard, and Kevin Gosine. 2002. "'The Rocket': Newspaper Coverage of the Death of a Québec Cultural Icon, A Canadian Hockey Player." *Journal of Canadian Studies* 36 (4): 9–31.

Ransom, Amy. 2014. *Hockey, PQ: Canada's Game in Quebec's Popular Culture.* Toronto: University of Toronto Press.

Reid, Pat, and Daniel S. Mason. 2015. 'Women Can't Skate that Fast and Shoot that Hard!' *International Journal of Sport History.* 32 (14): 1678–96.

Robidoux, Michael A. 2012. *Stickhandling Through the Margins: Hockey in Canada.* Toronto: University of Toronto Press.

Svrluga, Barry. 2016. "The U.S. Women's Hockey Team Fights the Good Fight – and Wins." *Washington Post,* March 29. https://www.washingtonpost.com/sports/olympics/the-us-womens-hockey-team-fights-the-good-fight--and-wins/2017/03/29/28bce0ce-1432-11e7-ada0-1489b735b3a3_story.html?utm_term=.2e7d45ac2373.

Theberge, Nancy. 2000. *Higher Goals: Women's Ice Hockey and the Politics of Gender.* Albany: State University of New York Press.

Vaughan, Garth. 1996. *The Puck Starts Here: The Origin of Canada's Great Winter Game Ice Hockey.* Fredericton, NB: Goose Lane Editions.

Vernon, Karina. 2012. "Invisibility Exhibit: The Limits of Library and Archives Canada's Multicultural Mandate." In *Basements and Attics, Closets and Cyberspace: Explorations in Canadian Women's Archives*, editors Linda M. Morra and Jessica Schagerl. Waterloo, ON: Wilfred Laurier University Press, 193–206.

Wicken, William. *The Colonization of Mi'kmaw History and Memory, 1794–1928: The King v. Gabriel Sylliboy.* Toronto: University of Toronto Press, 2012.

You Can Play Project. 2012. "The Faceoff." YouTube video, 1:00 min. Posted March 4. https://www.youtube.com/watch?v=SXoTRTAw6Dc. <<CITED IN TEX

———. 2014. "You Can Play – 2014 Year in Review." YouCanPlayProject.org. http://youcanplay-project.org/news/entry/you-can-play-2014-year-in-review.

Zirin, Dave. 2017. "How to Win a Sports Strike." Edge of Sports Podcast. http://www.edgeofsportspodcast.com/post/159191905735/how-to-win-a-sports-strike

Hockey: More Than Just a Game

Images from the Canadian Museum of History Exhibition, March-October 2017

Figure H1 Hallway Entrance of *Hockey: More than Just a Game*
Visitors enjoyed this wall treatment, climbing on the letters for photographs.
Canadian Museum of History, IMG2017-0136-0021-Dm

Figure H2 Zone 1: Earliest Players
A sweeping overview of hockey history, from its origins on the outdoor rink to the modern game, started the exhibition. Using large archival images that literally drew the visitor onto the ice, we presented important artifacts from the game's past, attesting to its diversity, and its rootedness in communities.
Canadian Museum of History, IMG2017-0136-0058-Dm

Figure H3 Zone 2: A Team Sport
As historians, we wanted to make the evolution of hockey equipment a major exhibition theme, but since we were telling this story in a social history museum, we chose to angle the display towards players' stories. With a wink at arena dressing rooms, we designed this space to suggest continuity and change, and to highlight some major names in the game.
Canadian Museum of History, IMG2017-0136-012-Dm

Figure H4 Zone 3: The Team Behind the Team
Behind players, even amateur ones, there is a vast team of coaches, trainers and families. Larger-than-life coaches Roger Nielson, Jacques Demers and Pat Burns pop out of the scenery in this zone, which also features a physiotherapist, scorekeeper and referee.
Canadian Museum of History, IMG2017-0136-0015-Dm

Figure H5 Zone 4: For the Love of Hockey
We had a lot of fun bringing together fans' memorabilia, presented in this zone by decade. Whether it is a framed jersey, a hand-knit sweater, gloves worn by the kid who skated on his driveway, or the home-made tool box, fans have never been shy about showing their colours.
Canadian Museum of History, IMG2017-0136-0052-Dm

Figure H6 Zone 5: Memorable Moments
On ice, visitors saw Team Canada jerseys representing diverse players: Hayley Wickenheiser, Sidney Crosby, Manon Rhéaume, Paul Henderson, Jean Labonté and Wayne Gretzky. Women, men and sledge hockey players shared the space, evoking our core idea, that all hockey matters.
Canadian Museum of History, IMG2017-0136-0032-Dm

Figure H7 Zone 6: Hockey Inc.
Visitors looked behind the scenes of the NHL in this section, which told the story of the expansion of the league, contracts, drafts, trades, strikes and lock-outs. On the right, the interactive map allowed visitors to identify changing logos (and home bases) of NHL teams through the ages.
Canadian Museum of History, IMG2017-0136-0041-Dm

Figure H8 Zone 7: Hockey Makes Headlines

Hockey is big news! Preparing for the exhibition, the team swapped newspaper articles and followed the media closely. In the exhibition, visitors could read newspaper articles on the interactive screen, and hockey news stories were posted on a bulletin board. Broadcast personalities from *Hockey Night in Canada* and *La Soirée du hockey* also contributed artifacts for this space. The contributors included Foster Hewitt, Claude Quenneville, Cassie Campbell Pascal, Don Cherry and Harnarayan Singh.

Canadian Museum of History, IMG2017-0136-0065-Dm

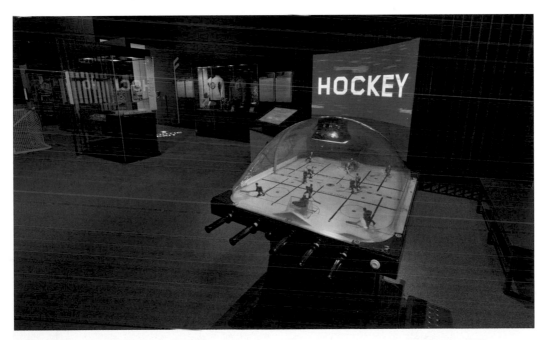

Figure H9 Zone 8: Passion for the Game

Today hockey is played around the world, but its influence in this nation is why it is known as Canada's game. Popular culture is filled with hockey themes and references. Sometimes art, movies, books and songs celebrate the game. At other times, hockey is used to build community, such as with the "You Can Play" initiative featured in this section. Hockey's importance is illustrated by the variety of cultural forms it inspires.

Canadian Museum of History, IMG2017-0136-0049-Dm

PART I
Debating Hockey's Origins

Chapter 1
A Flag of Tendons:
Hockey and Canadian History[1]

Andrew C. Holman

"Sport is a form of culture recognized by all Canadians," Don Morrow and Kevin Wamsley begin their book, *Sport in Canada*, even among "those who dislike participating in or watching sport" (2009, 1). Sport is a part of daily, weekly, and seasonal routines for many Canadians—the sort of lived experience that the German philosopher Wilhelm Dilthey would have seen as "an immediate, pre-reflective consciousness of life" (Van Manen 2016, 35). But sport is much more than that in Canada. It is also the source of nostalgic recollection and excitement, a lens for reflection that helps Canadians sort out who they believe they are. The variety of sport that is watched and played in Canada is vast and reflects the multicultural character of the country. One might find in evidence cricket, soccer, rugby, gymnastics, athletics, and boxing; bocce, Highland games, baseball, golf, tennis, and basketball. Despite this, in Canada not all sports are considered equal. Above most, a few rest higher in public estimation and participation: the quintessential *Canadian* games, lacrosse and curling, and the *national passion*, hockey. While each of these sports expresses Canadian cultural identity in profound ways, hockey stands out as by far the most prominent emblem of Canadian popular culture. For more than a century, a great many Canadians have found in hockey what they think it means to be Canadian. Hockey's meaning is an historical construct that gets reinterpreted and re-remembered with every passing generation.

The history of ice hockey is, at some level, the history of Canada. As poet Richard Harrison has argued eloquently, "hockey invented Canadians as much as Canadians invented hockey" ([1994] 2004, 16). Hockey has symbolized what it means to be Canadian for a variety of simple reasons. First, hockey was born in Canada, and the claim as its birthplace continues to resonate among the game's followers in Canada and beyond. Canadians can claim hockey as their own, many of them feel, because they *made* it. But, second, hockey remains Canadian beyond that because it expressed and continued to express the country's most important historical conditions and themes. It is a hackneyed (and perhaps too-often-repeated) expression that hockey is a "metaphor for Canadian life." Only in a very limited

---

1. This chapter was originally published in Spanish as "Una bandera de tendones: el hockey sobre hielo y la historia de Canadá" in the Mexican history journal *ISTOR: Revista de Historia Internacional* [Special Issue on Canada] XIII, 49 (July 2012) 61–89. It appears here, in slightly revised form, with permission.

sense is that true anymore, if it ever really was. But hockey is a metaphor in many respects for Canadian history and is a grand narrative that dominates the telling of Canadian history from British colony to North American nation. In short, hockey is Canadian because the game's storied past encapsulates, roughly though unmistakably, the trajectory of the nation's history. Third, and oddly, perhaps, hockey maintains its emotional strength in Canada because it possesses the power to simultaneously unite a vast, disparate country that desperately and continuously seeks unity, and divide it along familiar lines: region, race, language, and gender. In a country uniquely divided, an experimental nation, hockey is one of the few cultural constructs that possesses the nostalgic power for Canadians to conjure a better, more harmonious and united past, and project it as a possibility into the future. At the same time, hockey in Canada is a site of contestation, of conflict; a place where Canadians continue to delineate their various, contrasting lived experiences and alternative views of their collective "self," and to express why the country defies national unity.

Hockey History

In one light, it is remarkable that a sport seemingly so simple can be so complex and fraught with meaning. An encyclopedia definition might read, dryly: *Hockey: a game played on a rectangular frozen ice surface (normally 200 feet by 85 feet) pitting two sides of six skaters against one another. Equipped with long, flat-bladed sticks and padding from head to toe, the players use their sticks to propel a rubber disc (a puck) past their opponents' designated goaltender and into a goal net (4 feet high by 6 feet wide). The game takes place over three periods of twenty minutes each, and on-ice officials regulate the game according to standard rules, which prohibit excessive use of the stick or body to prevent an opponent's progress (by tripping, hooking, slashing, etc.).* But that sort of definition masks the game's characteristic dynamism. Like Canada itself, hockey's rules have evolved incrementally. Prior to the 1920s, hockey was an "onside" game (like rugby); rule changes opened up the game to forward passes and sped its pace. Fast and routinely violent,[2] the game is also one of considerable strategy: like soccer, its coaches and players employ a variety of combination plays and player positioning to create scoring opportunities. Though essentially a team game, hockey's flow also encourages specialization and individual talent. Put together, these are the bases of the game's popular appeal.

Perhaps nothing expresses the importance of hockey to Canadians more than the fact that they cannot agree upon when and where the game was first played. The heir to a variety of ball-and-stick games that were played among the First Nations, French habitants, and British soldiers and settlers, ice hockey was an amalgam of games and traditions. Like all modern sports, it went through many permutations; it evolved, then congealed. Hockey

---

2. Canadian poet Al Purdy once described the game as a "combination of ballet and murder" (Purdy [1965] 2005, 26)! Hockey's violence is a perennial problem and a staple of discussion among hockey observers and commentators. Hockey rules allow for body contact—the use of the body to separate player from puck—and the ever-increasing speed of the game has made bodychecks that were once innocuous always dangerous. Most recently, the spate of concussions suffered by players from sometimes routine, in-game contact has been a cause of alarm. Moreover, in professional, junior, and senior leagues in Canada, fistfights that emerge from rough play in the game are penalized only minimally, removing the intended deterrent effect of penalties and, de facto, encouraging the threat and use of violence as strategy. See Lorenz and Osborne 2006; Scanlan 2002; Dryden 2004.

"happened" first, its claimants declare, in a number of locations: Dartmouth, Nova Scotia; Windsor, Nova Scotia; Kingston, Ontario; and Deline, Northwest Territories, to cite a few. These "birthplaces" are rather like roots on a single tree. They came together to form a trunk, from which the modern game of hockey grew. That trunk developed in Montreal, Quebec.[3] It was there, as a 2002 report of the Society for International Hockey Research reveals (see SIHR 2017), where hockey as we know it today was codified and standardized, between 1875 and 1879, and it was that city's version which became the basis for the sport in the following decades. From that trunk, we can trace direct lineage to the sport we know today.

The modern sport of hockey was the product of a "re-invention" of on-ice ball-and-stick games by Halifax native James Creighton and a group of his Montreal friends, largely former students at McGill University in 1875, less than a decade after Canada had become a self-governing dominion. "At the [Victoria Skating] Rink last night," the *Montreal Gazette* reported in early March 1875, "a very large audience gathered to witness a novel contest on the ice. The game of hockey...was an interesting and well-contested affair, the efforts of the players exciting much merriment." The Montreal game was branded with regular rules that were published in the *Gazette* in February 1877. Though the article was brief and cursory, the publication of these rules is important for two reasons: first, symbolically, the act of publication asserted the Montreal game as *the* game of hockey; and second, the rules reveal how early hockey was a hybrid of other sports. In the rules' first iteration, the puck was called a "ball," a faceoff (to start play) was called a "bully," and, like rugby, a player "must always be on his own side of the ball" (*Montreal Gazette* 1877). Early hockey players' garb borrowed rugby players' pants and lacrosse players' sweaters; early sticks resembled Irish hurleys (Fitsell 1987).

The Montreal version of hockey became ascendant in the 1880s. The game spawned by Creighton and friends achieved local popularity in the immediate aftermath of the game's rules being published, but modern ice hockey was propelled and popularized beyond the city chiefly via the Montreal Winter Carnival, 1883–1889, an annual celebration of winter organized by the city's businessmen and politicians to boost the seasonally sagging local economy. "Upwards of 50,000 visitors attended the Carnival Week festivities held in Montreal in 1883, 1884, 1885, 1887, and 1889," Gillian Poulter notes (2004, 85). "They came from other Canadian cities, from across the U.S., and from as far afield as England, Germany, and Havana." Amid elaborately constructed sets, such as an ice palace (made of 500-pound ice blocks), Montrealers *performed* winter in fancy dress balls, masquerade skating parties, snowshoe tramps, and tobogganing competitions, as well as in a hockey tournament that featured teams from Montreal, Quebec City, and Ottawa (Dufresne 1983; Morrow 1996). The Montreal Winter Carnival happened at a critical time for ice hockey. It gave the game needed momentum. During those carnival years, in 1886, players of the Montreal game were emboldened to establish a perennial league, the Amateur Hockey Association of Canada, and to publish revised rules. And the carnival helped to sell the game beyond Montreal. It was here that hockey found its most famous patron: Queen Victoria's newly

---

3. The debate over hockey's birthplace is a circular one, more important for the heat it generates than the light it spreads. For a good summary of the arguments and an assessment of their merits, see SIHR 2017.

appointed representative to the Government of Canada, Frederick Arthur (Lord) Stanley, first baron of Preston. "In February 1889," archivist James Whalen writes (1994, 3), "Lord Stanley witnessed his first hockey match at the…carnival…. Expressing 'his great delight in the game of hockey and the expertness of the players,' Stanley became a regular and distinguished spectator." Three years later, he donated a challenge trophy for the amateur hockey champions of the Dominion: the hallowed Stanley Cup (Whalen 1994; McKinley 2000).

In just a few years, hockey became a national phenomenon. British visitor J. Macdonald Oxley observed in 1895: "the game of rink hockey … as played in Canadian cities to-day, is, without question, a distinctly home product" (Oxley 1895, 340). In 1899, Arthur Farrell published a compendium of the game's origins and history, tellingly titled *Hockey: Canada's Royal Winter Game*. "Like the Klondyke gold fever, the love of hockey spreads. A few years ago, the sport was known only in a few cities in the Dominion—now, from far east Halifax to frigid Winnipeg the glorious game is played" (Farrell 1899, 15, 17). By 1905, as sport historian Alan Metcalfe wrote (1987, 73), "hockey pervaded the whole country," spread by the game's evangels who, as young men, had played it in 1880s Montreal and carried it, its rules, and equipment, with them as they travelled the railways to the country's farthest reaches. Hockey, by the turn of the twentieth century, was not only broadly spread but thick on the ground. Most major cities in Canada had intra-town leagues made up of bankers and clerks, coreligionists, service-club members, and a variety of other constituencies, including, in some places, women. "In Winnipeg, by 1898–99," historian Morris Mott notes (2002), "there were well over one hundred teams…. Ten years later, by 1909, there were so many…that no person could have possibly counted them all."

The game's mercurial growth presented new, unanticipated challenges, the biggest of which was the question of control. As the number of hockey teams and players mushroomed, organizers worried about ice hockey's "brand"; specifically, that the game's rules remain uniform and that its players be respectable and gentlemanly. From the 1890s until the 1920s, hockey underwent a search for order. This organizational reckoning was most visible, perhaps, in the creation of hockey's governing bodies—the game's first bureaucratic scaffolding—the most powerful of these being the Ontario Hockey Association, created in 1890. Gradually, other provinces followed suit: Alberta (1907), Saskatchewan (1912), Manitoba (1913), and Quebec and British Columbia (1919). In 1914, a truly national organization, the Canadian Amateur Hockey Association (CAHA, known since 1994 as Hockey Canada) was created as an umbrella body, encompassing all the affiliated provincial associations. All of these organizations—with their printed constitutions, codes of ethics, executive boards, and annual meetings—asserted new, efficient, progressive control over their regions as arbiters of the game. These organizations rationalized the game, creating age-based divisions of play, sanctioning leagues and championship tournaments, and hosting trophies for winning teams (Kidd 1996a).[4]

The most pressing and prominent issue discussed in their councils was a question of ethics: who could play the game. When hockey was born, the inherited British sporting ideal of amateurism held sway in Canada. Sport was to be played by gentlemen against

---

4. Most of these associations await their historians, an exception being the Ontario Hockey Association. See Young 1989; Metcalfe 1992.

gentlemen for the purpose of building character, not for individual or collective glory, and certainly not for pay or other rewards. Pay for play could only corrupt sport, as American horseracing and baseball had plainly shown. "So long as [hockey] remains free from the taint of professionalism, it will remain dear to the hearts of all true sportsmen," the writer and famed Montreal Shamrocks player Farrell wrote in 1899, the first year in which he and the Shamrocks won the first of two consecutive Stanley Cups. "But as soon as this vice creeps in the knell will sound for its death … when a monetary consideration depends upon the result of a match … roughness, brutality, will characterize it.… When a young man sees his way clear to earn a livelihood at sports, he will … throw away on them the most valuable time of his life, by neglecting the duties that his age demands" (Farrell 1899, 42–43). Amateur hockey associations strictly forbade professionalism in hockey, adopting the Ontario Hockey Association's life-sentence penalty: once a player was declared professional, he would be considered one forever. Moreover, early amateur hockey bodies in Canada refused to consider reinstating players' amateur status, and ruled as ineligible athletes who had been paid for play in other sports (Metcalfe 1992, 7–8).

Still, like most modern sports, turn-of-the-century hockey could not resist the influence of commercialization. Fast, exciting, and vital, hockey was a dynamic game that lent itself particularly well to partisanship. Despite its laudable potential as a character builder, hockey instilled in its players and fans, from community leagues to intercity play, a desire to win. Competition—across or between towns, among occupational groupings or fraternal orders—bred rivalries, and victories on the ice soon came to be seen as badges of honour. Winning felt good, and to win consistently, teams needed to have the best players. By the 1890s, admonitions such as Farrell's began to appear in discourses about hockey, not because professionalism was an abstract evil that could be prevented by popular jeremiads on the issue, but because it was already an established practice. In these years, in many towns and cities, industrial and commercial teams adopted the practice of "shamateurism"—ostensibly claiming they were amateur organizations while secretly paying (via stipends and no-show jobs) star players to help bring home the victories. The writing was on the wall. While amateur hockey associations continued to fight against encroaching professionalism, their control over the game's elite levels of play began to slip.

An openly professional hockey league first appeared in Canada in 1907, the Ontario Professional Hockey League. Others followed soon thereafter. By the First World War, Canada had four professional leagues, which were largely regional.[5] The most competitive of these early professional leagues was the National Hockey Association (1910), which was transformed in 1917 into the National Hockey League. In the mid-1920s, through competition and merger and the collapse of other professional leagues, the NHL became (and remains) the premier professional hockey league in the world (Wong 2005; Holzman and Nieforth 2002).[6] By the 1920s, then, amateur and professional hockey in Canada coexisted uneasily, side by side. Only in the depths of the Depression, in 1936, did amateur and

---

5. In addition to the four-team OPHL, there was the Pacific Coast Hockey Association (1912), the Maritime Professional Hockey League, and the National Hockey Association (1910). See Wong 2005; Ross 2015.

6. No symbol better represented the NHL's ascendancy than the fact that, in 1926, the Stanley Cup ceased to be a challenge trophy and became the veritable property of one league, the NHL.

professional hockey organizations find peace. In that year, the NHL concluded a formal agreement with the CAHA that effectively concentrated authority over the game in Canada and swept under the rug old prejudices against the professional game. In 1936, the administration of hockey in Canada took on its modern form—a pyramid—in which, in Bruce Kidd's words (1996a, 226), "the vast network of CAHA teams and leagues [became] a tightly controlled feeder system" for the NHL. The end product of bureaucratic rationalization had been reached. The NHL became both the icon and functional nerve centre of the game. Canadians today regard the NHL first, and Hockey Canada only second, as the locus and standard bearer of their national game.

A Metaphor for Canadian History

"Hockey captures the essence of Canadian experience in the New World," renowned twentieth-century Canadian humourist and McGill University political scientist Stephen Leacock is reputed to have said. "In a land so inescapably and inhospitably cold, hockey is the chance at life, and an affirmation that despite the deathly chill of winter we are alive."[7] The idea that ice hockey reflects Canadians' "victory" over winter is a powerful one. It is a corollary to Canada's northern myth: hockey embodies the northern landscape and celebrates the country's embrace of *nordicity* (Francis 1997). Like most myths, perhaps, the closer one looks, the less true it rings. In many places, hockey's early days might have relied upon the existence of natural outdoor ice—a game played amidst the formidable elements—but, since at least the 1930s, hockey's setting has changed. Today, most (but not all) hockey in Canada is played and watched in expensive indoor arenas, using modern technology to maintain ice surfaces, equip players, and heat viewing areas, and in segmented, hour-long slots for successive users of the facilities. Hockey's nordicity is contrived, but that does not make the equation any less dear. Canadians continue to write paeans (in film, prose, and song) to the game's winter condition that repeat the mantra, "true" but no longer real, that hockey is a metaphor for Canadian life (*Shinny* 2001; *Hockey* 2011).

But if hockey is not really a metaphor for Canadian life, it may well be a metaphor for Canadian history. The story of hockey parallels the grand Canadian historical metanarrative, the orthodox version of the country's history that was written in the middle decades of the twentieth century and has, with admittedly important qualifications, maintained its central thematic hegemony ever since. Canada's history, to historians such as A. R. M. Lower, is at root the story of Canada's emergence from colony to nation, from an unsure existence as a British imperial creature composed of two "warring" ethnic factions (the "conquered" French and the ascendant English), to a confident, North American nation whose people's common need to get along, and whose continental challenge vis-à-vis its larger southern neighbour (the United States) have forged a sense of common purpose. Writing in the immediate aftermath of the Second World War, Lower could not have predicted just how daunting that American challenge would become in the Cold War context of the twentieth century. If Canada's first sixty years were focused on moving away from British control toward independence, in its second sixty years Canadians were preoccupied with the bugbear of American domination—economic, political, and cultural; or, as historian W. L.

---

7. This apocryphal attribution is more important for its widespread credence (as a simple Google search reveals) than its veracity. See, for example, Avery 2008, 110.

Morton argued, "the forces of pernicious Americanization" (as referenced in Granatstein 1989, 4). Canadian history is marked by the omnipresence of successive external "others"— first Mother Britain and then the United States—against whom Canadians measured their own distinctiveness, sovereignty, and national progress.

Hockey was created in the decade following Confederation (1867), when British Parliament passed the law (the British North America Act) that created the self-governing (but not yet sovereign) Dominion of Canada out of four adjoining colonies. In retrospect, the invention of hockey was part of a critical cultural genesis in the country—the attempt to invent patriotic spirit in a new nation. Like the nationalist intellectual movement known as Canada First and the Victorian-era project among Canadians thinkers to identify a series of distinctly Canadian symbols, myths, and mottoes (Berger 1970), hockey became a proxy of sorts, through which Canadians could express their singularity.

The first iterations of sport in modern Canada were decidedly British. The principal agents were middle-class urban anglophones—professionals and businessmen, mostly British stock—whose money and leisure time in the early days of industrialization gave them the wherewithal to play. Cricket, curling, rugby, soccer: before Confederation, British sporting transplants were the sports that Canadians played. But the reign of British sports in Canada was short-lived. In the 1860s and 1870s, amid the rhetoric of Confederation, Indigenous "Canadian" activities—such as snowshoeing and lacrosse—were championed by Canadian sportsmen and elevated in importance. In Montreal, the cradle of Canadian sport, white bourgeois anglophones appropriated First Nations' activities and turned them into Canadian games, sports in which "Canadianness" could be performed or acted out. By the 1880s, about twenty-five snowshoeing clubs existed in Montreal, each with its own distinctive uniform, membership roll, constitution, dues, and regular winter-weekend excursions. Lacrosse was snowshoeing's summer variant. In the 1850s, Montreal sportsmen began to play a version of the Aboriginal tradition of *baggataway*, the Creator's game, transforming a loosely defined seasonal ritual into a modern sport, with standard written rules, strategy, and a "gentlemanly" ethic. By the 1860s, the appropriation was complete. W. George Beers, a Montreal dentist and avid sportsman, helped to form the country's first national sports league, the National Lacrosse Association, made up of twenty-nine clubs from Quebec and Ontario. In 1869, he authored a declaratory tome on the game, *Lacrosse: The National Game of Canada*, and in the years following became the game's chief proponent (Poulter 2003). These "Canadian sports," he wrote in 1883, "have a character of their own" (quoted in West 1990).

Though the first sports to capture Indigenous culture and repackage it as Canadian culture, snowshoeing and lacrosse gradually waned in popularity. By the First World War, Gillian Poulter tells us (2003, 315), "they had lost their potency…as national signifiers…. Ice hockey,…the invention of Canadian-born colonists,…[became the] perfect expression of Canadian identity." By rejecting British cultural forms in the late nineteenth century and replacing them with sports like hockey that were new, northern, rugged, and independent, Victorian Canadians were declaring a new sense of self. According to Michael Robidoux, the subjugation of soccer, cricket, and other "garrison games" to hockey represented nothing less than a sporting declaration of independence, a "vehicle of resistance against British… hegemony" (Robidoux 2002, 220, 221). What is more, when ice hockey expanded beyond

Canadian borders, Britain was one place where the game gained early and avid followers. In 1885, students at Oxford and Cambridge began to play the Montreal game; a decade later there were five ice-hockey clubs in England and Scotland. Britain was among the European countries that met to form the Ligue Internationale de Hockey sur Glace, in 1908. Gradually, Britain's calibre of play rose. In 1936, Great Britain won Olympic gold in ice hockey (Kivinen, Mesikämmen, and Metsä-Tokila 2001). Hockey had reversed the natural imperial cultural flow. Britain's colony had become Britain's tutor. In this context, hockey became a symbol of Canada's coming of age in the early twentieth century, and, ever since, that equation (Canada = hockey) has been so regularly drawn as to become orthodoxy.

Still, history is unkind to orthodoxies. Since the 1920s, hockey has been subject to the same historical force that has challenged Canadian sovereignty and identity in politics, economics, and other realms of culture: Americanization. "Living next to you," former Canadian Prime Minister Pierre Elliott Trudeau famously quipped in a speech to the National Press Club in Washington, DC, in 1969, "is in many ways like sleeping with an elephant. No matter how friendly and even-tempered is the beast, one is affected by every twitch and grunt" (quoted in Lennox 2009, 7). Canadians have long worried that their proximity to the military and economic colossus to the south jeopardizes their independent existence (Flaherty and Manning 1993). And hockey has been seen sometimes as a sort of bulwark against unwitting American cultural imperialism, as Al Purdy's oft-cited 1965 poem "Hockey Players" plainly admits: "For years a Canadian specific / to salve the anguish of inferiority / by being good at something the Americans aren't" (Purdy [1965] 2005). But even hockey was not beyond the reach of American influence. The commercialization of the game in the early twentieth century opened it up to "continentalization." Hockey, some say, was carried away to the United States and Canadian control of their own signature sport was compromised as a result.

The Americanization of Canadian hockey is most visible in the sport's most commercial venue: professional hockey. The NHL began life as a wholly Canadian venture, with its league office in Montreal and its first member teams in Canadian cities: Montreal, Ottawa, Toronto, and Quebec City. It did not take long before the lure of American markets pushed NHL directors to seek franchises in the United States. In 1924, the NHL admitted the Boston Bruins to the league, and, in succeeding years, the New York Americans (1925) and the New York Rangers (1926) followed. By 1929, a familiar pattern had emerged: six of the NHL's ten teams were located in the United States. Even during the league's highly nostalgic "Original Six" era, 1942–1967, four of its six teams (Boston Bruins, Detroit Red Wings, Chicago Black Hawks, New York Rangers) entertained American audiences (Kidd 1996a; Hyatt and Stevens 2009). Today, only seven of the thirty-one NHL teams reside in Canadian cities. Prior to the 1980s, moreover, almost all (more than 90 per cent) of the league's players—its basic "product"—were Canadian-born and -trained, a fact that made the exportation of elite hockey to United States arenas all the more galling to Canadians. Today, Canadians compose only about 50 per cent of the NHL's team rosters, and the quandary for Canadians remains. One Toronto sportswriter wrote, in 1925, just after the NHL's American investment began, "Will U.S. cash cripple hockey?" (Good 1925). The answer to that question depended upon which side of the Canadian-American border the responder lived. Unquestionably, the NHL's American expansion has made it a continental commercial success, a "big business." Still, for many Canadian nationalists, ever since the 1920s the NHL's American dream has robbed some Canadians of their "birthright," which creates ever more resentment as the NHL chooses to locate franchises in capital-rich but tradition-poor American sunbelt cities, such as Tampa Bay, Miami, Dallas, Phoenix, and Las Vegas, and not in smaller Canadian cities, such as Saskatoon or Hamilton, which are arguably less able to attract corporate sponsorships and television contracts but immeasurably richer in local passion for the game.[8] Fan attendance is but one revenue stream in today's NHL, and, on its own, an insufficient one. The symbolism of moving the NHL's head offices from Montreal to New York in 1989 was hard to miss.[9] "What this country needs is a sport it can call its own," journalist Bob Bossin wrote acerbically in 1970 in *Maclean's*, Canada's national weekly news magazine. "We used to have one. Hockey" (Bossin 1970). Others concurred. Writing in a collection of scholarly essays titled *Close the 49th Parallel etc: The Americanization of Canada* (1970), the academic and Canadian distance runner Bruce Kidd argued for an alternative: an all-Canadian professional hockey league that would keep its product and capital at home (Kidd 1970, 270–72; Kidd and Macfarlane 1972).

The fear of the Americanization of Canadian hockey spread beyond the professional ranks. As American collegiate ice hockey took hold in the 1950s, 1960s, and 1970s, a curious demographic phenomenon took place: schools in the U.S. National Collegiate Athletic Association (NCAA) scrambled to fill their coaching and playing ranks with those who had the most talent. Often, they were Canadians. Older, hockey-playing schools, such as Harvard, Cornell, Boston, Denver, and St. Lawrence, capitalized on the flow of talent southward and wholly new collegiate hockey programs, such as those at Bowling Green State University and the University of Notre Dame, were constructed on the foundation of Canadian hockey recruits. "The supremacy of Denver [University's] Canadians, holders of last season's championship," *Time* magazine complained in 1961, "is hard enough on U.S. pride. Harder still is the fact that Denver is defending its title against other top U.S. teams manned almost entirely by Canadians" (*Time* 1961, 55). But equally angry were Canadian hockey administrators and coaches who accused American recruiters of filching Canadian talent, creating a "brawn drain" that robbed Canadian communities invested in these athletes from seeing them perform at the height of their abilities. American "raiding parties," as one journalist put it, "whip across the border, strike swiftly, then return home with the booty" (*Globe and Mail* 1969). Only after the NCAA tightened its eligibility rules in the mid-1970s did the flow of Canadian amateur talent southward ebb (Holman 2007). In any guise, the

---

8. The most prominent recent cases involved the Winnipeg Jets and the Quebec Nordiques, two Canadian-based NHL franchises that moved to seemingly more profitable American locales—the Jets to Phoenix, Arizona, in 1996, and the Nordiques to Denver, Colorado, in 1995. In 2011, a failed NHL franchise in Atlanta, Georgia, relocated to Winnipeg, where the team took on the old Jets name and mantle, and NHL hockey was welcomed back with wild enthusiasm. In 2015, the NHL decided to locate an expansion franchise in Las Vegas over calls for a renaissance of NHL hockey in Quebec City.

9. Another bellwether was the 1988 sale of Canadian star Wayne Gretzky from the Stanley-Cup champion Edmonton (Alberta) Oilers to an American "poor sister," the Los Angeles Kings, a move that was widely interpreted as a money-motivated bid to sell the NHL game in the U.S. sunbelt and a theft of Canadian national treasure (Jackson 1994).

Americanization of hockey in the twentieth century shook Canadians' faith in the game. "This is our fundamental dilemma," Hall of Fame goaltender and Canadian hockey philosopher Ken Dryden wrote in his book *The Game*: Hockey "is part of our national heritage, and pride, part of us; but we can't control it" (Dryden [1983] 1999, 231).

A Source of Unity, a Mirror of Divisions

On February 28, 2010, seven minutes and forty seconds into overtime in the Canada–United States men's hockey final, Canada's hockey superstar, Sidney Crosby, scored the sudden-death goal that won Olympic gold for his country (Figure 1.1). The goal triggered uncharacteristically loud, colourful, and lengthy celebrations of national pride among Canadians; a paroxysm of joy and relief. As with all significant historical moments, the context mattered as much as the feat. The Olympics took place in Vancouver, in hockey's home nation, and the opponent for the gold medal was the United States, a team that had beaten the Canadians in the tournament's opening round. But the stakes were higher than a home audience and neighbourly rivalry would normally produce. At another, deeper level, Canada's fortunes in hockey at the Vancouver Olympics represented to many a summary judgment about the ability of the country to maintain its claim as the sport's top nation, even as the forces of globalization and growing disinterest among youth threatened to undermine that. Though Canada's men's and women's hockey teams had won gold at the Salt Lake City Winter Olympics in 2002, and the women had repeated at Torino in 2006, Canada's performances in international hockey since the 1950s had (to that time) been anything but dominant. Crosby's goal, broadcast live to the largest audience to ever view a televised program in Canada, reasserted the Canadian myth boldly emblazoned on fans' T-shirts and banners: "Hockey is Canada's Game." Even the winning of gold by both Canada's men's and women's teams in the 2014 winter Olympics in Sochi, Russia, hasn't eclipsed the shining Vancouver moment. "Canada's collective psyche was on full display," journalist John Branch wrote in the *New York Times*. "The depth and breadth of the moment was rare, but powerful" (Branch 2010, A1).

"Rare" and "powerful," but not unique. Hockey has served this function for Canadians before—an occasional lightning rod that brings the country together. The

Figure 1.1 The Golden Goal
Sidney Crosby wore this jersey while playing for Team Canada at the Winter Olympics in Vancouver. On February 28, 2010, millions of Canadians celebrated his overtime goal, which won Canada a gold medal.
Private collection, Sidney Crosby.
Canadian Museum of History, IMG2016-0253-0049-Dm

relevance of hockey to Canadian history rests in its ability to act periodically as a sort of social glue. Hockey has been sometimes a source of unity. It has had the ability to crystallize "fellow feeling" among Canadians who play the game together and who consume it together, really and virtually. Playing hockey, in organized leagues or regular pickup games, has come to be seen as both a signature form of exercise for many Canadians, and a ritual performance of national identity. Canadians of all ages and genders and in all regions play hockey, and, for immigrant families, the sport has sometimes been held out to be a site of conscious assimilation. "In a thousand rinks, in a thousand towns," Leslie McFarlane's 1953 National Film Board of Canada documentary ode to the game begins, "from the time they're old enough to skate, youngsters in hundreds of Canadian communities play in organized leagues to learn the great Canadian game" (*Here's Hockey!* 1953). In this text, hockey games were much more than play. In performing their culture on the ice, Canadian children at the same time learned about their own identities. Occasionally, adult hockey players have articulated the same feelings. In 2004, when asked what her participation in a weekly hockey match meant to her, one Newfoundland woman had a common but telling reply: "This is being Canadian" (Loeffler and Beausoleil 2004).

Hockey brings Canadians together as consumers of the sport and partners in its nostalgia. In a limited sense, hockey arenas—the buildings themselves—perform this function. When hockey arenas were first constructed in Canadian towns and cities in the 1880s and 1890s, few could have anticipated their value as community centres—places where the anomie of modern industrial life could be counterbalanced by an hour or two of a weekly sporting diversion with neighbours and friends, usually for a small admission fee. Local hockey teams boosted civic pride and community spirit in the late nineteenth century, as they still do today. In Canada's biggest cities, professional hockey arenas performed this function on a much grander scale. Montreal's Forum and Toronto's Maple Leaf Gardens, for example, came to be seen as civic temples or secular cathedrals, where the most import ant cultural events in the city could be staged and consumed: political conventions, state funerals, military tattoos and, of course, NHL hockey games (Field 2008; Dennis 2009).

Hockey became a part of Canadian popular culture in the twentieth century beyond the rink, as well. Starting in the 1930s, it could be consumed at home, via the modern wonder of the radio. In 1931, the Canadian National Railway radio network (forerunner of the Canadian Radio-Broadcasting Corporation, or CRBC) began to air a weekly hockey program called *General Motors Hockey Broadcast*, featuring play-by-play calls of Toronto Maple Leafs games. In 1933, the CRBC's Montreal stations began to air the games of the Montreal Canadiens (in French) and Montreal Maroons (in English) (the Maroons were in the NHL from 1924 to 1938). By 1936, the CRBC had become the Canadian Broadcasting Corporation (CBC) and its hockey programs became *Hockey Night in Canada* (*HNIC*). The effect of these broadcasts was electric. *HNIC*'s first play-by-play announcer in Toronto, Foster Hewitt, soon became a wildly popular Canadian personality, known from coast to coast for his signature broadcast opening ("Hello Canada, and hockey fans in the United States and Newfoundland") and catch phrase for announcing goals ("He shoots, he scores!"). In 1952, the CBC took its program to television and the transition was a remarkable success. Saturday-night hockey games, first broadcast on radio, then on television, became a staple of Canadian culture in English Canada and in French Canada, where *La Soirée du Hockey* catered to

French-Canadian loyalties. *Hockey Night in Canada* has long maintained its place as the most-watched television program on the CBC, in any genre—news, drama, or sports (Kidd 1996a; Mellanby 2008). Moreover, it has vaulted its commentators to iconic status in Canada, foremost among whom is the bombastic and cartoonish former NHL coach, Don Cherry, who has made his intermission segment, *Coach's Corner*, a bully pulpit for pronunciations on everything from the code of violence in hockey to the want of fortitude among foreign (non-Canadian) players to the heroism of Canadian troops in Afghanistan (Podnieks 2006).

Hockey pervades Canadian culture, in forms both high and low. There is now, according to two recent academic studies, a large enough mass of serious writing about the sport to constitute a field of Canadian hockey literature (Blake 2010; Buma 2012). Still, that lofty stature has not been realized across all cultural realms. Hockey is more conspicuous in low-brow Canadian cultural ephemera: coffee-table books, pop art, beer commercials, and youth fashion (especially T-shirt) designs. Canada's 2010 and 2014 Olympic victories in both men's and women's hockey, and in the more recent World Cup of Hockey, in 2016, resulted in a market flood of memorabilia in books, DVDs, lapel pins, caps, team jerseys, and kitsch of all sorts. By collecting and wearing these things, Canadians connect themselves to a virtual, imagined community of fellow nationals, a *hockey nation*. All of this cultural work has contributed to an overwrought but palpable collective nostalgia about hockey's importance to developing community in Canada. Canadians look to hockey's past as a sort of common trust, a wellspring from which memories (real or imagined) can be drawn and employed to specific, useful ends.

Canadians' collective memories of the heroic 1972 Summit Series provide a case in point. In September 1972, an eight-game series was staged between the USSR men's national hockey team and Team Canada, a collection of NHL professional players who had been prevented from playing for their country in previous international and Olympic tournaments, where only amateurs were eligible to play and in which the Soviets (teams composed almost wholly of Red Army soldiers and, technically, amateurs) had swept the competitions. Expecting to dominate the series and reclaim hockey as Canada's game, Team Canada and the nation were shocked by the Soviets' prowess on ice. In the eighth and final game, played in Moscow with the series tied 3-3-1, Team Canada won on a goal scored in the waning seconds by Paul Henderson. That goal created a magnetic moment for Canadians, publicly feted in the press and society, and burned in the memories of thousands of school-children who remember watching the live television broadcast of Game Eight in their classrooms and auditoriums. The victory (slim though it was) confirmed a comfortable, mythic "home truth," and, since 1972, it has been a central moment in Canadian public memory. The continuing manufacture of 1972 Summit Series memorabilia and the occa-sional public appearances of Henderson and his teammates confirm and re-stoke that memory. Forty-five years on, the event lives as a lesson in perseverance and national pride. As Brian Kennedy writes (2009, 59), "Canadians' sense of who they were" was confirmed, and, ever since, they have stored the Summit Series events in "the zone of an epic past, untouchable except as symbol."[10] (Figure 1.2)

---

10. Canadians rely on more than just public memory for their hockey nostalgia, however; they also have the resource of the Hockey Hall of Fame, in Toronto, a handsome brick-and-mortar repository of the game's artifactual history; a sort of secular shrine (Kidd 1996b).

Figure 1.2 An Untouchable Symbol?
Many Canadians recall Paul Henderson's final goal in the 1972 Summit Series against the Soviet team as an iconic moment, perhaps even the iconic moment in the history of Canadian sports.
Henderson's Summit Series Jersey
Worn in Moscow, U.S.S.R.
1972
CMH IMG2016-0253-0046-Dm

Of course, one must be cautious about the power of nostalgia to whitewash the real, empirical past and Canadians' lived experiences. The history of hockey has an important purchase on Canada's past for more reasons than its origins, its external influences, and its ability to demonstrate Canadian unity, real and imagined. Hockey is and remains a meaningful cultural touchstone in Canada because it has revealed the rifts that divided and continue to divide Canadians in quintessentially Canadian ways.

Canada's history is a divided history. Though Americans (until at least the 1870s) routinely called their nation an experiment in republican liberty, in truth the most fragile national experiment on the continent was and is that of their northern neighbours. Canada's history is peppered with episodes that threatened to rend the country along the lines of region, race, class, and language. These contexts have mattered to Canadians as much or more than any national construct. "It might just be," historian J. M. S. Careless noted in 1969, "that it is in these limited identities that 'Canadianism' is found." Since the 1970s, Canadian historians have followed Careless's lead. The Canadian historiographical canon of the past forty years is replete with examples of that agenda: regional histories of the Maritime Rights movement; the Quiet Revolution and the sovereignty movement in Quebec; the farmers' revolt in western Canada; working-class histories of struggle and revolt in Winnipeg, Hamilton, Cape Breton, among other places; and studies of immigrant groups and ethnic cultural adaptation across Canada, to cite but a few (see Shore 1995). Here again, hockey echoes Canada's historical narrative. Hockey has been a site for the expression of these limited identities and a locus for the articulation of historically Canadian problems.

Regional and racial fissures in Canada have a conspicuous place in hockey history. In the nineteenth and twentieth centuries, Canadians drew regional lines between wealthy Central Canada (Ontario and Quebec) on one hand and the West and Atlantic Canada on the other, where the slimmer returns from resource-extraction economies contrasted with the wealth and political power of the central industrial core. Economic inequalities bred regional resentments that were echoed in sport. When the Western Hockey League's Victoria Cougars easily defeated the NHL's Montreal Canadiens for the Stanley Cup in 1925, as John Herd Thompson and Allen Seager note (1986, 188), "Western editorialists crowed their satisfaction.... 'The Easterners are learning how hockey should be played from Western teams.'" The 1935 national senior champions (Allan Cup winners) were the Halifax Wolverines, who assumed that their victory would earn them the customary right to represent Canada in the 1936 Olympic Games in Germany. When they were denied that chance by the CAHA in favour of a central Canadian team, the Port Arthur Bear Cats, eastern Canadian partisans could interpret the decision in only one way: yet another central Canadian trespass (Savoie 2000).

Hockey's history reflects Canada's racial woes, too. Hockey, despite its Indigenous roots, was raised white, in the house of amateurism; an elite, gentlemanly British ideal that assumed whiteness. Before the 1960s, proportionately few non-whites played the game, and, even then, almost always on teams dominated by white players. In the Maritimes, one all-black hockey league thrived from about 1895 until the onset of the First World War, but its principal historical significance rests in its uniqueness. In the NHL, non-white players "broke in" in the middle decades of the twentieth century—Fred Sasakamoose, from the Ahtahkakoop Cree Nation, in 1954 with the Chicago Black Hawks, and African-Canadian Willie O'Ree in 1958 with the Boston Bruins. Still, it was only in the late twentieth century that First Nations and African- and Asian-Canadian players became conspicuously numerous in hockey's elite levels. "There was a reason why Herb Carnegie did not play in the NHL," Hall of Fame NHL referee Red Storey recalled of the semi-professional Quebec Provincial League scoring star in the mid-1940s. "It's very simple; he's black" (quoted in Pitter 2006, 133). Hockey has never been a "race-less" sport. In fact, the absence of non-whites in the game has been a curious cultural statement about Canada, a country that publicly proclaims itself equitable, inclusive, and multicultural. Here, the experience of non-whites in Canadian hockey parallels a bigger, national challenge to the country: to live up to its bold rhetoric, invented in the 1890s and reinvented in every generation of government discourse since, that Canada is a land of immigrant acceptance and multiracial embrace (Pitter 2006).

Hockey has reflected Canada's divisions even more cogently with respect to language. Canada is riven by its two principal language groups, the majority anglophone and the minority (a little less than 25 per cent) francophone—the latter of which mostly trace their heritage to New France, a colony conquered by the British in 1760. That event created a long memory, and a spirit among French Canadians once called *survivance*, a firm determination to preserve their distinctiveness. Since before Confederation, Canada's cultural existence has largely been one of two solitudes, English and French, and that found expression even on the ice. Hockey got a relatively late start in Quebec, the Canadian province where the vast majority of French speakers live. Clubs were founded among students at classical colleges in and around Montreal, but francophone hockey received its biggest boost in 1909, when the Montreal Canadiens—a professional team—was founded. In the early twentieth century, when English-Canadian and American capitalists held control of Quebec's economy, French Canadians saw themselves as the nation's "hewers of wood, and drawers of water"—second-class citizens in their own country, in their own province. But on the ice, in the uniform of the Montreal Canadiens, French Canadians found a forum where they could win, even if it was only fleeting and symbolic (Harvey 2006). The *porte-étendard* among Canadiens players was Maurice "Rocket" Richard, who dazzled spectators with his scoring abilities and rugged play over eighteen NHL seasons. When he died, in 2000, the Canadiens sponsored a "state funeral" in the team's arena, the Montreal Forum, where his body lay for public viewing, and which 115,000 mourners, many in tears, visited in a parade of nostalgia and ethnic pride (Ramos and Gosine 2002; Melançon 2009). Only in the 1980s, during the heady days of Quebec's sovereignty movement, did the Canadiens' hold on French-Canadian loyalties begin to wane. The decline in French-Canadian players on the roster and the entry of a second Quebec NHL franchise—the Quebec (City) Nordiques (whose colours and rhetoric mirrored the separatist cause)—all served to shake the Canadiens' hold as the *équipe nationale* of French Canada (Gitersos 2009). In French Canada, then, hockey has served as a visible proxy for linguistic difference and mimics the nation's centuries-long political conundrum: how to create a lasting rapprochement between the country's two competing cultures of nationalism, Canada's and Quebec's. Two provincial referenda (1980 and 1995) asked Quebecers if they wished to separate and become a sovereign nation. Both failed (narrowly), but the case for Quebec's sovereignty and the creation of a French-Canadian nation-state remains. So too, it seems, in hockey. In 2006, as Quebec City began its preparations to co-host the International Ice Hockey Federation (IIHF) Men's World Hockey Championship, one prominent Quebec lawyer made a telling popular argument: that Quebec enter its own team in the competition, separate and distinct from Team Canada (*Le Devoir* 2006; Duhatschek 2006).

Finally, gender inequality in the country is also expressed in Canadian hockey. Women have played hockey in Canada since the early 1890s, when formal games were reported to have taken place among women in Barrie, Ontario, and in Ottawa, the latter involving Isobel Stanley, the daughter of the Governor General. Fully equipped teams in league play emerged by the time of the First World War and in special festival tournaments, such as the Banff Winter Carnival (1917–1939) (C. Adams 2014). The first heyday of women's hockey was unquestionably the interwar years, when the sport was host to strong organizations, such as the Ladies Ontario Hockey Association (1922–1940) and the Dominion Women's Amateur Hockey Association (1933), and held a national championship for the Lady Bessborough Trophy. These years saw the rise of powerhouse teams such as the Vancouver Amazons, Calgary Regents, Northern Electric Verdun, and the incomparable Preston Rivulettes (from what is now Cambridge, Ontario), which won ten provincial champion-ships and four national titles in the 1920s and 1930s (C. Adams 2008, 2009). The sport developed its own "stars," moreover, among them the Rivulettes' Hilda Ranscombe, the University of Saskatchewan's Ginger Catherwood, and the Toronto Patterson Pats' Fannie "Bobbie" Rosenfeld (Hall 2002).

Though the Second World War and the early years of the Cold War brought on a three-decade torpor, hockey for women and girls experienced a remarkable revival in the late 1960s and throughout the 1970s. This was made manifest in the return and growth of university women's teams and regional senior club teams and leagues, such as the Winnipeg Women's Hockey League and the Ligue Féminine de Hockey Les Canadiennes, a four-team, French-speaking circuit in East Montreal (Baril 2013). It was visible, too, in the return of a national championship, the Dominion Ladies' Tournament in 1968, and in Ontario (where women's hockey was thickest), in the creation, in 1975, of a separate governing body, the Ontario Women's Hockey Association (OWHA). In the 1980s and 1990s, the numbers of women players and leagues grew at a mercurial pace: between 1990 and 2014, the number of girls and women Hockey Canada registrants grew from about 8,000 to more than 85,600, while registrations for boys and men stagnated. What's more, at the highest levels of competition, increasingly more was at stake. An international tournament for women was first staged by the OWHA in North York in 1987, and its success spawned more competition and encouraged the IIHF to recognize women's hockey and sanction the first ever IIHF Women's World Hockey Championship, in 1990 in Ottawa. Since 1998, Canadian women have sent teams to the quadrennial Winter Olympic Games, in which they have won the gold medal four out of six times. Today, several of Canada's elite women's players ply their trade in a semi-professional league, the Canadian Women's Hockey League, which has four of its franchises—Calgary, Montreal, Markham, and Toronto—based in Canada.

And yet, despite its impressive accomplishments, the growth of women's hockey in Canada has come in an essentially segregated sector, and the question of equality remains. More and more girls and women play the game than ever before, but rancour over access—to desirable ice times, to coaching and managing expertise, to basic funding—persists. And more than four decades of legal and ethical wrangling over the issue of integration—can girls play on boys' teams?—has not been resolved wholly. Though Justine Blainey's 1986 Ontario Court of Appeal victory ruled in favour of girls' rights to play on boys' teams (citing the Canadian Charter of Rights and Freedoms), the question remains, in the minds of feminist organizations such as the Canadian Association for the Advancement of Women and Sport and Physical Activity: *should* they? (Brodsky 1986). Or, does the migration of skilled female players to male teams impoverish those who are left behind? Which road to hockey equality? This, too, is a Canadian problem. And challenging hockey's male privilege is daunting. The remarkable recent success of women's hockey in Canada has been a fraught development, and it places in stark relief the still-dominant and disconcerting feeling among many in Canada that, as Nancy Theberge writes (2000, 325), men's hockey is still "the 'real' game." What scholar Mary Louise Adams wrote (2006, 71) about this more than ten years ago is true today: "If hockey is life in Canada, then life in Canada remains decidedly masculine."

Taking Hockey Seriously

What is there in a mere game, a favoured leisure pursuit among Canadians that could possibly be useful to students of Canada? Can studying sport help us understand this complex nation? This essay argues "yes." Since the 1990s, academic historians have begun to take hockey seriously, to *read* it as a cultural text, and to examine the ways in which it has functioned in the Canadian past. Scholars of hockey must strip away the bluster and jingoism that years of uncritical, popular writing about the sport have attached to it. But when they do, they see hockey history as a rich body of evidence that reveals much about who Canadians have been and who they think they have been. Hockey is a Canadian phenomenon worth studying for reasons deeper than the game's natal origins. Hockey history is Canadian history writ small. It is a site where the influences of colonialism and "continental drift," the project and possibility of national unity and the perennial fissures of division—regional, linguistic, racial, and gendered—are made manifest. In Canada, as poet Beth Goobie writes (1999, 27),

a hockey player's body is intended
as a national anthem, flag of tendons,
bones that undulate down the ice,
heart sung by crowds in the stands
hot dogs and beer in their hands…
history building itself into one man's flesh…

Bibliography

Adams, Carly. 2008. "'Queens of the Ice Lanes': The Preston Rivulettes and Women's Hockey in Canada, 1931–1940." *Sport History Review* 39 (1): 1–29.

———. 2009. Organizing Hockey for Women: The Ladies Ontario Hockey Association and the Fight for Legitimacy, 1922–1940. In *Coast to Coast: Hockey in Canada to the Second World War*, ed. John Chi-kit Wong, 132–59. Toronto: University of Toronto Press.

———. 2014. "Troubling Bodies: 'The Canadian Girl,' the Ice Rink, and the Banff Winter Carnival" *Journal of Canadian Studies* 48 (3): 200–20.

Adams, Mary Louise. 2006. The Game of Whose Lives? Gender, Race, and Entitlement in Canada's 'National' Game. In *Artificial Ice: Hockey, Culture, and Commerce*, ed. David Whitson and Richard Gruneau, 71–84. Peterborough, ON: Broadview Press/Garamond Press.

Avery, Martin. 2008. *Zen Writing*. Raleigh, NC: Lulu.

Baril, Lynda. 2013. *Nos Glorieuses: Plus de Cent Ans de Hockey Féminin au Québec*. Montréal: Les Éditions La Presse.

Berger, Carl. 1970. *A Sense of Power: Studies in the Ideas of Canadian Imperialism, 1867–1914*. Toronto: University of Toronto Press.

Blake, Jason. 2010. *Canadian Hockey Literature: A Thematic Study*. Toronto: University of Toronto Press.

Bossin, Bob. 1970. "What this country needs is a sport it can call its own. We used to have one. Hockey." *Maclean's* 83 (7) (July): 13–14.

Branch, John. 2010. "For Canada's Faithful, a Goal that Means Most." *New York Times*, March 1, A1.

Brodsky, Gwen. 1986. "Justine Blainey and the Ontario Hockey Association: An Overview," *Canadian Association for the Advancement of Women in Sport Newsletter* 17.

Buma, Michael. 2012. *Refereeing Identity: The Cultural Work of Canadian Hockey Novels*. Kingston and Montreal: McGill-Queen's University Press.

Careless, J. M. S. 1969. "'Limited Identities' in Canada." *Canadian Historical Review* 50 (1): 1–10.

Dennis, Robert. 2009. Forever Proud? The Montreal Canadiens' Transition from the Forum to the Molson Centre. In *Canada's Game: Hockey and Identity*, ed. Andrew C. Holman, 161–79. Kingston and Montreal: McGill-Queen's University Press.

Dryden, Ken. [1983] 1999. *The Game*, 3rd ed. Toronto: MacMillan Canada.

Dufresne, Sylvie. 1983. "Le Carnaval d'hiver de Montréal, 1803–1889." *Urban History Review* 11 (3).

Duhatschek, Eric. 2006. "Not this lunatic proposal again." *Globe and Mail*, November 2.

Farrell, Arthur. 1899. *Hockey: Canada's Royal Winter Game*. Montreal: C.R. Corneil.

Field, Russell. 2008. "Constructing the Preferred Spectator: Arena Design and Operation and the Consumption of Hockey in 1930s Toronto." *The International Journal of the History of Sport* 25 (6): 649–77.

Fitsell, J. W. 1987. *Hockey's Captains, Colonels & Kings*. Erin, ON. Boston Mills Press.

Flaherty, David H., and Frank E. Manning, eds. 1993. *The Beaver Bites Back? American Popular Culture in Canada*. Kingston and Montreal: McGill-Queen's University Press.

Francis, Daniel. 1997. *National Dreams: Myth, Memory and Canadian History*. Vancouver: Arsenal Pulp Press.

Gitersos, Terry Vaios. 2009. "'Les "frogs" sont menaces': Media Representations of the Nordiques and Canadiens, 1979–1981." *Sport History Review* 40 (1): 69–81.

Globe and Mail. 1969. "Only Two Junior Hockey Clubs Escape U.S. College Raiding Parties." September 6.

Globe and Mail. 2004. "Saving the Game." March 27, A19.

Goobie, Beth. 1999. A hockey player's body. In *Ice: New Writing on Hockey*, ed. Dale Jacobs. Edmonton, AB: Spotted Cow Press.

Good, Charles H. 1925. "Will U.S. Cash Cripple Hockey?" *Maclean's*, March 1, 13, 55–56.

Granatstein, J. L. 1989. *How Britain's Weakness Forced Canada into the Arms of the United States.* Toronto: University of Toronto Press.

Gruneau, Richard, and David Whitson. 1993. *Hockey Night in Canada: Sport, Identities and Cultural Politics.* Toronto: Garamond Press.

Hall, M. Ann. 2002. *The Girl and the Game: A History of Women's Sport in Canada.* Peterborough, ON: Broadview Press.

Harrison, Richard. [1994] 2004. *Hero of the Play.* Toronto: Wolsak and Wynn.

Harvey, Jean. 2006. Whose Sweater Is This? The Changing Meanings of Hockey in Quebec. In *Artificial Ice: Hockey, Culture, and Commerce*, ed. David Whitson and Richard Gruneau. Peterborough, ON: Broadview Press/Garamond Press. 29–52.

Here's Hockey! 1953. Directed by Leslie McFarlane. Montreal: National Film Board of Canada.

Hockey: More than a Game. 2011. Directed by Alan Aylward. Buffalo: WNED.

Holman, Andrew C. 2007. "The Canadian Hockey Player Problem: Cultural Reckoning and National Identities in American Collegiate Sport, 1947–80." *Canadian Historical Review* 88 (3): 439–68.

Holzman, Morey, and Joseph Nieforth. 2002. *Deceptions and Doublecross: How the NHL Conquered Hockey.* Toronto: Dundurn Press.

Hyatt, Craig, and Julie Stevens. 2009. Are Americans Really Hockey's Villains? In *Canada's Game: Hockey and Identity*, ed. Andrew C. Holman, 26–43. Kingston and Montreal: McGill-Queen's University Press.

Jackson, Steven. 1994. "Gretzky, Crisis, and Canadian Identity in 1988: Rearticulating the Americanization of Culture Debate." *Sociology of Sport Journal* 11 (4): 428–46.

Kennedy, Brian. 2009. Confronting a Compelling Other: The Summit Series and the Nostalgic (Trans)Formation of Canadian Identity. In *Canada's Game: Hockey and Identity*, ed. Andrew C. Holman, 44–62. Kingston and Montreal: McGill-Queen's University Press.

Kidd, Bruce. 1970. Canada's 'National' Sport. In *Close the 49th Parallel etc: The Americanization of Canada*, ed. Ian Lumsden, 257–74. Toronto: University of Toronto Press.

———. 1996a. "Brand-Name Hockey." In *The Struggle for Canadian Sport*, 184–231. Toronto: University of Toronto Press.

———. 1996b. "The Making of a Hockey Artifact: A Review of the Hockey Hall of Fame." *Journal of Sport History* 23 (3): 328–34.

Kidd, Bruce, and John MacFarlane. 1972. *The Death of Hockey.* Toronto: New Press.

Kivinen, Osmo, Jani Mesikämmen, and Timo Metsä-Tokila. 2001. "A Case Study in Cultural Diffusion: British Ice Hockey and American Influences in Europe." *Culture, Sport, Society* 4 (1): 49–62.

Lennox, Patrick. 2009. *At Home and Abroad: The Canada-U.S. Relationship and Canada's Place in the World.* Vancouver: UBC Press.

Le Devoir. 2006. "Une nation, un club de hockey, dit Guy Bertrand." March 28.

Loeffler, T.A., and Natalie Beausoleil. 2004. Crossing the Blue Line: Women's Hockey Experiences at Mid-Life. Paper presented at the conference "Women's Hockey: Gender Issues On and Off the Ice," Saint Mary's University, Halifax, NS, March 26–29.

Lorenz, Stacy L., and Geraint B. Osborne. 2006. "'Talk About Strenuous Hockey':Violence, Manhood, and the 1907 Ottawa Silver Seven-Montreal Wanderer Rivalry." *Journal of Canadian Studies* 40, (1): 125–56.

McKinley, Michael. 2000. *Putting a Roof on Winter: Hockey's Rise from Sport to Spectacle.* Vancouver: Greystone Books.

Melançon, Benoît. 2009. *The Rocket: A Cultural History of Maurice Richard.* Vancouver: Greystone Books.

Mellanby, Ralph. 2008. *Walking with Legends.* Toronto: Key Porter Books.

Metcalfe, Alan. 1987. *Canada Learns to Play: the Emergence of Organized Sport, 1807–1914.* Toronto: McClelland and Stewart.

———. 1992. "Power: A Case Study of the Ontario Hockey Association, 1890–1936." *Journal of Sport History* 19 (1): 5–25.

Montreal Gazette. 1875. "Hockey." *Montreal Gazette,* March 4.

———. 1877. "Hockey on Ice." *Montreal Gazette,* February 1.

Morrow, Don. 1996. "Frozen Festivals: Ceremony and *Carnaval* in the Montreal Winter Carnivals, 1883–1889." *Sport History Review* 27 (2): 173–90.

Morrow, Don, and Kevin B. Wamsley. 2009. *Sport in Canada: A History.* Don Mills, ON: Oxford University Press.

Mott, Morris. 2002. "'An Immense Hold in the Public Estimation': The First Quarter Century of Hockey in Manitoba." *Manitoba History* 43. http://www.mhs.mb.ca/docs/mb_history/43/hockeyhistory.shtml.

Oxley, J. Macdonald. 1895. *My Strange Rescue and Other Stories of Sport and Adventure in Canada.* London: T. Nelson.

Pitter, Robert. 2006. Racialization and Hockey in Canada: From Personal Troubles to a Canadian Challenge. In *Artificial Ice: Hockey, Culture, and Commerce,* ed. David Whitson and Richard Gruneau, 123–39. Peterborough, ON: Broadview Press/Garamond Press.

Podnieks, Andrew. 2006. *A Canadian Saturday Night: Hockey and the Culture of a Country.* Vancouver: Greystone Books.

Poulter, Gillian. 2003. "Snowshoeing and Lacrosse: Canada's Nineteenth-Century 'National Games.'" *Culture, Sport, Society* 6 (2/3): 293–320.

———. 2004. "Montreal and its Environs: Imagining a National Landscape, c.1867–1885." *Journal of Canadian Studies* 38 (3): 69–100.

Purdy, Al. [1965] 2005. Hockey Players. In *Going Top Shelf: An Anthology of Canadian Hockey Poetry,* ed. Michael P.J. Kennedy, 25–26. Victoria: Heritage House.

Ramos, Howard, and Kevin Gosine. 2002. "'The Rocket': Newspaper Coverage of the Death of a Québec Cultural Icon, A Canadian Hockey Player." *Journal of Canadian Studies* 36 (4): 9–31.

Robidoux, Michael. 2002. "Imagining a Canadian Identity through Sport: A Historical Interpretation of Lacrosse and Hockey." *Journal of American Folklore* 115 (456): 209–25.

Ross, J. Andrew. 2015. *Joining the Clubs: The Business of the National Hockey League to 1945.* Syracuse, NY: Syracuse University Press.

Savoie, Marc. 2000. "Broken Time and Broken Hearts: the Maritimes and the Selection of Canada's 1936 Olympic Hockey Team." *Sport History Review* 31 (2): 120–38.

Scanlan, Lawrence. 2002 *Grace Under Fire: The State of Our Sweet and Savage Game.* Toronto: Penguin Canada.

Shinny: The Hockey in All of Us. 2001. Directed by David Battistella. Montreal: National Film Board of Canada.

Shore, Marlene. 1995. "'Remember the Future': The *Canadian Historical Review* and the Discipline of History, 1920–1995." *Canadian Historical Review* 76 (3): 410–63.

SIHR (Society for International Hockey Research). 2017. "The Birthplace or Origin of Hockey." http://www.sihrhockey.org/__a/public/horg.cfm.

Theberge, Nancy. 2000. Gender and Sport. In *Handbook of Sports Studies*, ed. Jay Coakley and Eric Dunning, 322–33. London: Sage Publications.

Thompson, John Herd, and Allen Seager. 1986. *Canada 1922–1939: Decades of Discord*. Toronto: McClelland and Stewart.

Time. 1961. "Imported Canadian Club." January 6.

Van Manen, Max. 2016. *Researching Lived Experience: Human Science for an Action Sensitive Pedagogy*. 2nd ed. London: Routledge.

West, J. Thomas. 1990. "Beers, William George," *Dictionary of Canadian Biography: 1891–1900*. Vol. XII. University of Toronto/Université Laval. *Dictionary of Canadian Biography Online*: http://www.biographi.ca/en/bio/beers_william_george_12E.html.

Whalen, James M. 1994. "Kings of the Ice." *Beaver* 74 (1).

Wong, John Chi-Kit. 2005. *Lords of the Rinks: The Emergence of the National Hockey League, 1875–1936*. Toronto: University of Toronto Press.

Young, Scott. 1989. *100 Years of Dropping the Puck: The History of the O.H.A.* Toronto: McClelland and Stewart.

Chapter 2
Re-Imagining the Creation: Popular Mythology, the Mi'kmaq, and the Origins of Canadian Hockey

PAUL W. BENNETT

Few subjects in Canadian sport arouse as much passion as debating the origins of ice hockey, Canada's mythical national pastime. Hockey fans, hobbyists, and even a few sports scholars have been known to "mix it up" off the ice when the discussion inevitably returns to the hotly contested matter of creationism versus evolution. Seventeen years ago, at the 2001 Saint Mary's University Putting It on Ice Conference, E. Gay Harley likened the search for the "birthplace of hockey" to baseball's creation myth centring on Cooperstown, New York, and made a compelling case for the "evolutionary model," arguing that hockey evolved, from first Amerindian-European contact onward, and that different aspects of the game developed over time in various places (Harley 2002). Today, avid hockey partisans continue to pour over obscure archival records, mine archival newspapers, date Mi'kmaq hockey sticks, and assess decaying wooden pucks for further clues to hockey's origins (Bundale 2011). The popular Anglo-Canadian quest for the genesis of hockey continues unabated as a "family squabble" among defenders of rival geographic claims, all reflecting a Eurocentric perspective on the development of the game (Bennett 2013).

Moving beyond the competing claims to be hockey's "birthplace," this chapter will look at the great debate in the context of what British historian Eric Hobsbawm termed "invented tradition" (Hobsbawm 1983), informed by recent studies of "settler colonial societies" sparked by the work of Australian anthropologist and ethnographer Patrick Wolfe. Applying deep insights from Wolfe's seminal book *Settler Colonialism and the Transformation of Anthropology* (1999), the origin and evolution of ice hockey can be seen as another innovation assumed to be associated with settler colonialism. Like the Australian settlers in Wolfe's work, British North Americans operated according to the perception of *terra nullius*—empty land—despite the presence of Indigenous peoples, with their own complex socio-economic practices, political economies, and games culture. For all the writing and energy devoted to debating hockey's origins, we may be missing a critical piece, the Eurocentric social "structure" that has supported the advance of settler-colonial society by obscuring, submerging, or erasing Indigenous presence on the land. The settler colonizers, in Wolfe's oft-quoted maxim, "come to stay: invasion is structure not an event" (Wolfe 2006, 388). In the case of

hockey's origins, this exploratory chapter attempts to confront the limitations of the dominant settler-colonial perspective and approaches the whole question though a broader
Indigenous lens, namely that of the Mi'kmaw people and their unique tradition.[1] In the
process, the origin and evolution of hockey begins to look more like a dynamic process of
cultural exchange and transformation. It involves stepping back and practicing what the
Mi'kmaq call "two-eyed seeing." It is, according to Mi'kmaw Elder Albert Marshall, when
we "learn to see" from one eye with Indigenous knowledge and the best of "Aboriginal
ways of knowing," and from the other eye with the "best in the Western (mainstream) ways
of knowing"—and "learn to use both eyes together, for the benefit of all" (Marshall 2010).

The Invented Tradition

Staking a popular claim to the origins of hockey is very much a part of the politics of
commemoration, fueled each year by the contemporary CBC Sports *Hockey Night in Canada*
search for "Hockeyville." In his introduction to *The Invention of Tradition*, Hobsbawm argues
that the commemorative impulse was an outgrowth of the transformation of Europe and
North America into mass industrial societies. Confronted with economic and social change,
nations developed traditions and practices as a bulwark of permanence and continuity.
According to Hobsbawm, "invented traditions," like national hockey culture, emerged to
"establish continuity with a suitable historic past," and to serve the state as a way of preserving threatened social cohesion, of legitimizing institutions or status, or inculcating beliefs,
value systems, and conventions of behaviour (Hobsbawm 1983). Established hockey tradition, then, can be viewed as a means through which ideas, social practices, and social relations
are perpetuated that reflect the power and influence of the hegemonic Anglo-Canadian
class and related dominant groups.

Transmitting tradition is, in Hobsbawm's view, a manifestation of the overarching influence of the state. For more recent scholars such as David Lowenthal, Michael Kammen,
and John Bodnar, the process of cultural transmission is much more complex and fraught
with ambiguity. In *The Past Is a Foreign Country*, Lowenthal drew upon British and American
examples to make the case that past tradition is essentially "an artifact of the present,"
continually being made and remade by changing concerns and patterns of perception.
Rather than being expressions of material interests, he saw traditions as being, essentially,
expressions of popular culture and imagination (Lowenthal 1985, xvi). A critical piece of
the puzzle was provided by Kammen in his ground-breaking study *The Mystic Chords of
Memory: The Transformation of Tradition in America*. In stark contrast to Hobsbawm, Kammen
saw traditions reflecting different class, ethnic, race, and sectional groups—and providing a
way of containing and deflecting feelings of anxiety and displacement in societies undergo-
ing unsettling social and economic change (Kammen 1991, 14). A prime example of this
multiplicity of cultures approach is George and Darril Fosty's imaginative and controversial
book *Splendid Is the Sun*, purporting to tell the 5,000-year history of hockey, in all its variety,
from its supposed origins in ancient Mesopotamia to twenty-first-century Canada (Fosty
and Fosty 2003).

---

1. First Nations hockey research in North America is still in its infancy, but the story lies embedded
    in Native oral and material culture. Robidoux (2012) makes the connection between the sport
    and Native survival, and points the way for further research.

Perpetuating tradition through commemoration, according to John Bodnar, was more the result of an interplay of forces and influences. He saw the invention of tradition as a struggle between a nationally oriented "official" past aimed at promoting unity, harmony, and cohesion, and a locally-based vernacular past rooted in immediate memory and personal experience. While Bodnar saw tensions between nationalist formulations and the "multi-vocal" popular outlook, he also spotted the growing tendency of hegemonic groups and interests to appropriate the memories of "ordinary people" and to recast them for the purpose of perpetuating "official culture" (Bodnar 1992). Ken Dryden's popular rumination on hockey, *The Game*, captures well this tradition of rising from Canadian backyard-rink dreams to National Hockey League glory, which he achieved, as do hockey bestsellers like Steven Brunt's *Gretzky's Tears: Hockey, Canada, and the Day Everything Changed* and Paul Hollingsworth's positively gushing *Sidney Crosby*, a picture book for teen readers (Dryden 1983; Brunt 2009; Hollingsworth 2010).

The "Family Squabble" over Hockey's Origins

Canadian "hockeyists"—hockey enthusiasts—have been relentless in pressing the competing claims for Windsor, Deline, Kingston, Montreal, and Halifax-Dartmouth. Since the 200th anniversary of King's-Edgehill School (previously King's Collegiate School), in 1988, Windsor, Nova Scotia, cranked up its campaign, adopting "The Birthplace of Hockey" as the town's motto, publishing Garth Vaughan's 1996 book *The Puck Stops Here* and capital-izing on CBC-TV's 2002 Hockey Day in Canada broadcasts (Vaughan 1996, 2002). In May 2002, the Society for International Hockey Research (SIHR) took the unprecedented step of investigating and discounting the so-called Windsor claim (SIHR 2002). Yet that same year, a Dartmouth lawyer, Martin Jones, entered the fray with a new book, *Hockey's Home*, and civic leaders in Deline, Northwest Territories, have since surfaced with an Aboriginal claim, endorsed by the Government of the North-West Territories (Jones 2002).

The raging controversy over the origins of hockey is more of "a family squabble" than an academic, historical debate. Over the past forty years, a small group of hockey enthusiasts, known as hockeyists, have been engaged in a protracted shinny contest of their own over the origins of the game. It is fed by an incurable psychological condition that might be described as hockey madness. William (Bill) Fitsell of Kingston, Ontario, the Grand Old Man of hockeyists and co-founder of the SIHR, has been the leading propagator of the search for hockey's equivalent of Genesis. "Having spent 25 years trying to shoot down the legend that hockey was 'born' in Kingston, Ontario," he wrote in December 1994," I don't relish the task of trying to discourage the ambitious residents of Windsor, Nova Scotia, from believing that the game was first played there. Legends are more popular and lasting than factual evidence and the facts say neither center can claim to be hockey's nativity center" (Fitsell 1994).

Hockey's most rabid zealots, the Windsor creationists, are deadly serious, and they can put on quite a show. On February 24, 2001, the leading Windsor proponents were featured on CBC-TV News *Saturday Report,* hosted by Suhana Meharchand. Windsor's celebrated pumpkin grower, the late Howard Dill, and his collaborator Garth Vaughan, a retired doctor, were both in fine form. "Howard Dill is hockey mad," said CBC reporter Phonse Jessome, "but it's not the photos, pucks, and pennants that bring skate-toting pilgrims to Dill's

Windsor, Nova Scotia, farm out back. Dill's Long Pond, many believe, is the site where hockey was born two-hundred years ago when students put the Irish game of 'hurley' on ice." While researchers question the veracity of that statement, Dill was adamant: "There's only one Long Pond." Vaughan stood by that claim, presenting the evidence of Windsor's nativity from his 1996 book *The Puck Starts Here* (CBC 2001). That compelling message was repeated, once again, on CBC-TV's 2002 Hockey Day in Canada broadcasts, this time with TV personality Don Cherry of *Coach's Corner* conferring his blessing on Long Pond.

The CBC-TV *Saturday Report* feature on Windsor's Long Pond drove Canadian hockey-ists from elsewhere into near apoplexy. News that the Town of Windsor was twinned with Cooperstown, the so-called birthplace of baseball, only added to the frenzy of debate. The CBC was startled by the response to its coverage of what came the Windsor claim. Debate raged in coffee shops, arenas, and pubs over where hockey actually originated. Old novels, lost letters, paintings, and even wooden pucks have been produced as evidence in the matter. The claim supporting Dill's Long Pond, or another in Windsor, was challenged by the other claims for competing sites across Canada and even in New York state.

Fuelling the controversy was the perplexing question of what actually constitutes the game of hockey. Going as far back as the 1500s, or earlier, ball-and-stick games were played on ice, taking various forms, including those of hurley, cricket, and shinty. The SIHR, spurred on by Fitsell, launched its unprecedented commission to assess the facts of the Windsor claim. In May 2002, the SIHR research team, led by Paul Kitchen of Ottawa, ruled decisively against Windsor and adopted a rather narrow definition of hockey as "a game played on an ice rink in which two opposing teams of skaters, using curved sticks, try to drive a small disc, ball or block into or through the opposite goals" (SIHR 2002).

The SIHR report raised the ire of Windsorites, and did little to settle the matter. The fact-finding mission fixated on a literary passage from Thomas Chandler Haliburton describing King's Collegiate students playing "hurley on ice," dismissing it as fiction. It also did a great disservice to the massive body of research amassed by Vaughan on hockey's Nova Scotian roots far and beyond Windsor. Although Vaughan was closely identified with the Windsor claim, as Harley pointed out, his overall thesis was, and is, much broader than that, recognizing that "hockey evolved from a number of disparate influences" (Harley 2002, 3; see also Poulton 2010, 9–10, 17–25).

Searching for hockey's genesis continues to inspire passions that can be likened to chasing a puck on a sheet of ice. The roots of the game can be traced back not only to field hockey in the ancient world but also to Indigenous history in North America (Fergusson 1965, 36). Games that were precursors to modern ice hockey included the Mi'kmaq game known as *Oochamkunutk*, and more is being rediscovered every year about the origin of the original ice-hockey stick, another Mi'kmaw invention. Sportswriter Bruce Dowbiggin's *The Stick* (2001) provided the missing link. Two cultures, Mi'kmaq and European Irish, contributed to the origins of the game. Played on an open field with a crooked wooden stick and ball, hurley was not unlike the traditional Mi'kmaq game. "In the winter climate of their new home," Dowbiggin wrote (2001, 11), "Europeans adapted their games and equipment for use on ice. Soon the two cultures were playing *Alchamadijk*, as the Mi'kmaq called it. The white men would call the new game hockey. And the best sticks for this new game came from the carvers of the Mi'kmaq." (Figure 2.1)

Figure 2.1 Mi'kmaw Carvers Producing Mic-Mac Hockey Sticks, c. 1890

Origins of the Game—Widening the Lens

The family squabble over hockey's origins has run its course. Colin Howell's *Blood, Sweat and Cheers: Sport and the Making of Modern Canada* showed the way by demonstrating the value of taking a more comprehensive approach, encompassing economic and social forces, rooted in people's social experiences, and explaining the transition of early hockey from play to organized sport (Howell 2001). Distinctions need to be made between elemental (free-form) play and organized games, and between the physical recreational activities of Indigenous and white European societies. Instead of looking for the missing piece of evidence, it is time to begin the process of socially reconstructing the evolution of hockey in a series of different places across Canada. Doing so will allow us to situate the points of origin of critical aspects of the game, first competitive contact, and rules, as well as track the advent of sticks, pucks, and skates, the tools of the game.

While the roots of the Anglo-Canadian game are most likely to be found in Nova Scotia, that is only a part of the full story of the evolution of hockey. "The cultural confluence of the various military outposts and bases, North America's first private school (King's College Windsor), and the cultural influence of the Mi'Kmaq and the Acadians," as Harley noted in 2001, "established the foundation for the playing of the game of ice hockey in Canada" (Harley 2002, 3). More recent claims like that of Deline in the Northwest Territories, dating from Sir John Franklin's 1825 expedition and off the shores of Great Bear Lake, are based upon a November 6, 1825, letter, but appear too circumstantial. That observation was also made some twenty years after similar references in and around Windsor, Nova Scotia (Poulton 2010, 30–31).

The origins of ice hockey, like American baseball, were evolutionary, and so tracing the uncovering roots of the game should not about be about "staking claims." Hockey-mad researchers and hobbyists have played their role in unearthing "the facts" and flagging the surviving evidence, in what historians refer to as "the first draft of history." Much of the ensuing debate over hockey's origins has focused on the detective work of searching out, and mining, the often-fragmentary evidence, a popular pastime for the hockeyists affiliated with the SIHR. Some of the beset fact-finding, exemplified in Carl Giden, Patrick Houda, and Jean-Patrice Martel's 2014 book *On the Origin of Hockey*, actually pushes back the European origins of the game, tracing it back to the ice-covered ponds of England, decades before its appearance in British North America (Giden, Houda, and Martel 2014).

Social historians have approached hockey evolution through a broader, more comprehensive lens. In their work, sports-history scholars like Alan Metcalfe (1987), Bruce Kidd (1969), and Colin D. Howell (2001) have challenged us to assess the origins of the game in the context of larger economic, social, and cultural forces shaping the advent and development of games that formed the basis for organized sport in Canada. Back at a Hockey Conference in 2001, E. Gay Harley put it most diplomatically: "We understand cultural;

growth through our symbols, heroes, and myths, but cultural phenomena (like the game of hockey) grow out of the complex interplay of productive forces, historical circumstances, cultural influences and the exchange of ideas" (Harley 2002, 3).

Garth Vaughan may have been a Windsorite, but he was on the right track. Pursuing creationism need not devolve into ferreting out facts, validating the evidence, and putting it on display in a museum. It begins with Vaughan's most significant observation: "Hockey was not invented. Rather, it grew or evolved gradually from hurley-on-ice.... If putting the game on ice was stage one of the process, then playing it on skates was the second step" (Vaughan 1996, 19).

Thinking about the origins of our most popular sport will always remain connected with our sense of national identity. Popular history, written by hockey hobbyists and folklorists, has a place in creating and sustaining national myths and reinforcing belief systems. Pucklore, as many in the SIHR recognize, is not really history because it reduces the story down to single narratives nicely covering selected facts. History, as Harley reminded us, is not "static, carved in stone, or definitive" but rather an interpretation grounded in research and subject to change (Harley 2002, 4).

The Mi'kmaw Claim—from *Duwarken* to Hurley on Ice

Like North American society itself, the game of hockey most likely began with First Nations people, possibly in the Maritime region by the Mi'kmaq. Instead of chasing down surviving letters, journals, or papers written in English or French, First Nations experts like Michael Robidoux, Nova Scotia Museum curator David Carter, and Mi'kmaw specialists Roger Lewis and Bernie Francis have begun to solve the mystery by piecing the story together from oral and material culture, applying insights gleaned from an intimate knowledge of Mi'kmaw language, culture, and ways.[2] That ground-breaking research focuses on authenticating the Mi'kmaw claim to have pioneered in the development of an early Indigenous form of "hurley-on-ice."

In the Harry Piers Ethnology Papers of the Nova Scotia Museum, Dr. Jerry Lonecloud, a Mi'kmaq of Elmsdale, Nova Scotia, on October 8, 1913, described in vivid detail a traditional Mi'kmaw game called *Duwarken*. *Duwarken*, he recounted, meant "a ball played on ice." In that game, "a round stone" was "hit on the ice" by a stick, most likely "a spruce root," which was called *Duwarkenaught*. The stone ball was hit by a striker, causing the round stone to roll along the ice and be chased down by other players. The other players tried to interfere with the stone carrier and take it from him before it was returned to the striker. The player who returned it safely was permitted to hit the ball next. "The game," Lonecloud told Piers, was "not played now" and had "been very long out of use," but "the tradition" apparently remained. A little lake above Barren Lake, at the head of the Tusket River, near Nine-Mile Ridge, in Yarmouth County, Nova Scotia, was also reported to be known as *Duwarkenich*, or "place where they play [D]uwarken" (Nova Scotia Museum 1913).

Indigenous ice games existed in Mi'kmaw society at or shortly after first contact with white Europeans in what was known as the Land of the Mi'kmaki, extending throughout the entire Maritime region. The Mi'kmaw language contains words referring to field and

---

2. Personal interviews with Michael A Robidoux, University of Ottawa, May 14, 2012, and Roger Lewis, Nova Scotia Museum, May 15, 2012.

ice games called *Oochamkunutk,* which eventually melded with European-influenced ice hurley to become a distinct new game called *Alchamadijik.* Mi'kmaw-language scholar Bernie Francis has confirmed that the Mi'kmaq had various ways of describing the act of playing hockey, varying by their location in the region. The word *alje'ma'tijik,* for example, is believed to have originated with Mi'Kmaq living in what is now New Brunswick. It translates into the phrase "they are playing hockey."[3] Taken together, the presence of such words and phrases testifies to the prevalence of early forms of the sport in Mi'kmaw society and tradition.

Mi'kmaw wood carvers have long been associated with the carving and making of early hockey sticks. Discovering that the Mi'kmaq played *Duwarken* with spruce roots, curator David Carter contends, provides another missing link in the origin of the hockey stick. Studying the development of sticks from the 1830s to the 1930s, the hockey club may have originated with spruce roots and then melded with the stick used in the Irish ground game of hurley. The stick, according to Carter, is "a product of evolution and innovation from multiple sources."[4] With their understanding of wood species and carving skills, the Mi'kmaq fashioned wooden handles and utilized their coopering tools to make the distinctive sticks.

Surviving sticks have been uncovered, one of which is made of darkened yellow birch, and has been carbon-14 dated to the period from 1633 to 1666 (Hopper 2008). By studying the surviving artifacts from material culture, handles and sticks, Carter is confident that the spruce root and the hurley-on-ice stick are early points in the evolution of Mic-Mac sticks, as they were commercially branded, a forerunner of the modern hockey stick (see below).[5] With every new discovery, anthropologists and ethnologists are getting closer to explaining the points of cultural transmission, exploring in more depth the metamorphosis of the Mi'kmaw game into the emerging hybrid known as *Alchamadijk,* the likely precursor to what we call ice hockey (Sable and Francis 2012).

The King's College Hockey Tradition—Real or Imagined?

From a distinctly Britannic perspective, the game known as hurley on ice most likely appeared in a variety of locales over time in early British North America. Of the competing claims, Nova Scotia in the late 1790s and early 1800s remains the most fertile ground for explaining the evolution of Anglo-Canadian hockey. Dismissing Thomas Chandler Haliburton's fictional account in *The Attaché, or Sam Slick in England,* published in London in 1844, would be a missed opportunity. It is clear that Haliburton was reminiscing about his childhood as a student at King's College, Canada's oldest independent school, founded in 1788, long before most other surviving institutions in Nova Scotia or elsewhere. The passage is written in the unique idiom that made Haliburton famous around the English-speaking world. It reads: "boys let out racin', yelpin', hollerin' and whoopin' like mad with pleasure ... hurley on the long pond ice on the ice, or campin' out a-night at the Chester lakes to fish" (Fergusson 1965, 36; Vaughan 1996, 16; Young 1988).

---

3. Email correspondence, Bernie Francis to Roger Lewis, April 30, 2013.
4. Email correspondence, David Carter, curator, Nova Scotia Museum, to Bernie Lewis, April 26, 29, 30, 2013.
5. *Ibidem.*

Games were fundamental to early British Canadian boys' schools like King's. First known as King's Collegiate School, the Church of England academy which Thomas Haliburton attended was founded with a grant of £400 and opened in 1788, under the direction of Archibald Payne Inglis. It was first opened in a house near the Windsor Court House, but when the university preparatory college was built, shortly after 1810, classes moved to the larger schoolhouse. The original wooden box-like college building occupied some seventy-five acres, very close to Long Pond and nearby Devil's Punch Bowl Pond, and one mile from the village centre (DeWolf and Flie 1972, 8, 16; Harris 1996, 13–14, 18–19; Loomer 1996, 154–155). (Figures 2.2 and 2.3)

A clearer picture of Haliburton's Windsor has emerged since the 1996 edition of the Thomas Raddall Symposium, marking the bi-centenary of the renowned writer's birth (Davies 1997). Young Thomas, born at Windsor on December 17, 1796, entered King's College in the early 1800s. In 1804, eight-year-old Haliburton and his friend James C. Cochrane spent much time together, acting as "village escort to the Halifax ladies who came up in the summer to get rosy cheeks, by cantering about our pure Windsor atmosphere." Letters and journals indicate that, like the other Windsor village children, they skated and played "hurley on the long pond on the ice," roamed the banks of the Avon River and the St. Croix along with another mutual friend, Samuel Cunard, the future steamship mogul (Davies 1997, 70–71). At age fourteen in the fall of 1810, Haliburton entered King's Collegiate School and College, and enrolment never exceeded twelve during his time (1810–1815) as an undergraduate (Davies 1997, 85–86, appendix A).

Figure 2.2 Thomas Haliburton
Haliburton House Museum
Thomas Chandler Haliburton of Clifton, Windsor, N.S.
Nova Scotia Archives Photograph Collection, 201701190

Popular images of Windsor as the "Playground of Halifax" emerged after 1816 when the first stagecoach line made the village more accessible to Haligonians. With the opening of that route, the gentry of Halifax began, in increasing numbers, to enrol their sons at King's, where they could come on weekends, enjoy town life, and escape the noise and hustle of city life (Vaughan 1996, 33).

Outdoor games were very much a part of a boy's daily life at the school and college. In the early years, the school's official historian, F. W. Vroom, reported that students lived a relatively isolated existence and were left to organize their own activities. With no "intercollegiate contests" and "few entertainments to lure men away in the evenings," students like Thomas made up their own games and activities. "Games of various kinds in their simple and unscientific character," he wrote, "could afford exercise, if not much excitement. Hockey

Figure 2.3 King's College School
Haliburton House Museum
Collegiate School, Windsor, N.S., 1869
Nova Scotia Archives Photographic Collection
King's College Nova Scotia from Saulsbrook, May 1803
Nova Scotia Archives Photographic Collection, 201104014

(or shinny) and all kinds of skating on the ponds and flooded marshes in winter, and snowshoe tramps and tobogganing were fairly common" (Vroom 1941, 59).

Windsor's frozen ponds were favourite spots for King's Collegiate boys playing a rough-and-tumble brand of hurley on ice. In 1876, the *Windsor Mail* ran a series called "Early Sketches of Windsor." An anonymous writer, described in graphic detail what King's student life was like during his time at the college, from 1816 to 1818. "The Devil's Punch Bowl and Long Pond, back of the College," he recalled, "were favourite resorts, and we used to skate in winter, on moonlight nights, on the ponds." Then he recounted a memorable incident: "I recollect John Cunard (Brother of Sir Samuel of steamship fame) having his teeth knocked out with a hurley by Pete Delancey of Annapolis" (King's–Edgehill School Archives 1988; Orr 1988). That may well be the first reported high-sticking incident in the annals of Canadian hockey.

Whether the first ice-hockey games in British North America were played by King's College boys or not, the game had clearly entered the popular culture of colonial Nova Scotia in the early 1800s. In January 1927, *Acadian Magazine*, based in Halifax, published a poem with lines similar to those found in Halliburton's *The Attaché*. It read: "Now at ricket with hurlies some dozens of boys/chase the ball o'er ice, with a deafening noise" (Nova Scotia Archives and Records Management 1827; West Hants Historical Museum and Long Pond Historical Collection 1829; Poulton 2010, 36). Two years later, the *Colonial Patriot* of February 4, 1829, carried a fascinating open letter to the editor:

> Every idler who felt disposed to profane the Lord's day, may now secure from any consequences turn out with skates on feet, hurly in hand, and play the delectable game of break-shins without any regard to laws which were made solely for the levity of manners which prevailed in the days of Charles 1st and which are declared by our Judges to be of no validity. (West Hants Historical Museum and Long Pond Historical Collection 1829, Poulton 2010, 36)

Hurley on ice was so prevalent by the 1820s that such hurley-burly on the Lord's Day was disrupting the propriety of early Nova Scotian society.

Early forms of hurley on ice evolved into ice hockey and spread throughout Nova Scotia from the 1820s onward. Such games did not develop in isolation from larger economic and social forces affecting colonial society. With the rise of industrialism, small farmers and their sons in pre-industrial Nova Scotia were beginning to leave rural townships, reducing the numbers of young boys, the traditional players of folk games. Just as in Britain, elite boys' schools like King's served as what Bruce Kidd described as a "crucible" for the development of boys through games. Informal, often brawling, outdoor games were the early precursor for "manly sports," aimed at instilling athleticism, masculinity, military bearing, and class solidarity (Kidd 1996, 13–14; Newsome 1961; Mangan 1985; Bennett 1990, 2–5).

Boys attending King's Collegiate were central to the diffusion of the game, since many of the students were from nearby Halifax and Dartmouth. The game spread "naturally," as Vaughan described, from Windsor to Halifax and Dartmouth, aided and supported by Irish Nova Scotians and the men of the British military garrisons (Vaughan 2011, 2; 1996, 15–16).

Competing claims, like those of Martin Jones's in *Hockey's Home*, that Halifax–Dartmouth was the point of origin remain largely speculative, and apply more to the advent of hockey skates pioneered by the Starr Manufacturing Company in Dartmouth (Jones 2002, vi–viii, 8–12; Cuthbertson 2005).

Over a fifty-year period (1800 to 1850) in pre-industrial Nova Scotia the game evolved from hurley on ice, and was called ricket, wicket, and, finally, hockey. The early game drew upon the traditional skills of Nova Scotia's Indigenous artisan culture. During that time, Mi'kmaw carvers began to meet the growing demand for the first hand-crafted hockey sticks. By 1859, the *Boston Evening Gazette* reported that "hockey" was being played on frozen ponds in Nova Scotia and issued a request for a set of brand-name Mic-Mac sticks (Vaughn 2011, 2). In 1863, the Starr Manufacturing Company began to mass-produce Mic-Mac sticks, patented after those produced by Mi'kmaq carvers (Cuthbertson 2005, 61).

Passion for the Game—a Canadian Tradition

Canadians remain passionate about hockey, and that continues to propel the unsettled debate over the origins of the game. The respected national polling firm Environics periodically asks Canadians to rate the importance of national symbols. Eight in ten Canadians surveyed in March 2011 ranked hockey slightly above bilingualism and far ahead of the Queen. Such sentiments run deep among Canadians born in Canada, but hockey's appeal is not limited to "old Canadians." Some 49 per cent of Canadians born outside the country said they watch hockey at least occasionally, compared with 64 per cent of those native born. Seventy-four per cent of immigrants agreed with 77 per cent of the Canadian-born that "hockey is part of what it means to be Canadian" (Adams 2011, A17; 2012, A11).

Social-trends analysts like Michael Adams, president of Environics, read great significance into such public-opinion findings. Hockey, in Adams's view, remains close to our hearts as Canadians, even though fewer experience the exhilaration of playing shinny on a frozen pond. Only 26 per cent of Canadians today report that they played organized hockey at a younger age, but that figure jumps to 42 per cent for men. While only 36 per cent of Canadians have ever stickhandled a puck on a frozen pond, some 49 per cent of Canadians have played road hockey. Why does hockey continue as a national obsession? Adams offers this assessment: "It's these neighborhood games—mythologized in television ads where Dad floods the backyard or Sidney Crosby shows up at the pond—that keep the idea of hockey close to the hearts of Canadians, even as many of us cringe at the excesses of the NHL's titans" (Adams 2011, A17; Martin 2012).

Hockey is Canada's game, and it permeates our popular culture. While academics and writers have been perplexed by the question of what it means to be Canadian, as Andrew Holman has aptly observed, ordinary citizens inhabiting the local library, coffee shop, or Legion lounge are decidedly more certain: "Hockey is Canadian." And, perhaps less adamantly, to be Canadian is to be "not American" (Holman 2009, 4). With the appearance of Richard Gruneau and David Whitson's *Hockey Night in Canada: Sports, Identities, and Cultural Politics* (1993), the contested nature of Canadian hockey culture was laid bare, opening up new dimensions to be explored, including hockey's central place in our national culture, as national icon, as a place of work and entertainment, as a spectator sport, as a business enterprise, and as the source of multiple identities. In spite of these advances, national mythology remains intimately connected with the game, and what is termed "Tim Horton's Nation" breathes new life into familiar hockey tales.

Canada's hockey creationists, a mixed group of rabid fans, zealous hockeyists, and intrepid collectors, are a fascinating collection of purists, staking claims for their hometowns and reliving a childhood and adolescence deeply affected by hockey culture. Most are steeped in the popular hockey culture espoused in popular books like Dryden's *The Game* (1983) and Roy MacGregor's *The Home Team: Fathers, Sons and Hockey* (1996). Since the infamous SIHR hockey-origins inquiry, Bill Fitsell and his band have produced a book of their own, *Pucklore,* implicitly accepting that the society is, in Brian McFarlane's words, a collection of "curious chroniclers of hockey lore and legend" (quoted in Milks 2010). During the fortieth anniversary of the 1972 Canada-Russia Summit Series, a concerted effort was made to rekindle the national mythology and re-invent it for a new generation. Paul Henderson and Jim Prime's *How Hockey Explains Canada*, soared to new heights, with its subtitle of "The Sport that Defines a Country" (Henderson and Prime 2011, esp. xix–xxiii). The celebrations came and went, only reinforcing the irrepressible hold hockey has on the popular consciousness and the mass media.

A recent book looking at Canada's hockey obsession, written by Canadian expatriate Brian Kennedy (2011), is entitled *My Country is Canada*.[6] It again makes a compelling case for hockey as an integral part of the national mythology. "My country is Canada" is one way of looking at the question, but "hockey is my country" fits more comfortably when applied to the hockey creationists in Canada. For hockey zealots seeking its genesis, hockey is essentially their country and, to a large degree, the source of their identity. Based upon the analysis offered in this chapter, it is also a classic example of an "invented tradition" of the nationalist variety, albeit one that still exerts a powerful hold on the national psyche of Canadians. It is also, as usually constructed, the expression of a popular narrative rooted in a colonial outlook, where the cultural symbols and practices of "settler society" not only obscure but essentially erase Indigenous forms of, and contributions to, the game.

The Wisdom of "Two-Eyed Seeing"

The unending Great Debate over the origins of hockey is now on the verge of an epiphany. Today, ever more Canadians recognize that Canada now includes its First Nations and, too, their traditions and ways of knowing. Ground-breaking books like Michael Robidoux's *Stickhandling through the Margins* have the potential to bring First Nations hockey into sharper relief and the Aboriginal contribution into the Canadian popular consciousness (Robidoux 2012, esp. 132–44). We are also discovering that the origins of hockey go back much earlier in time than previously recognized, as different aspects of the game emerged at different points and in various geographic sites. It is also highly probable that Indigenous peoples made their own contribution to the origin and diffusion of the game (Bennett 2013).

Squabbling over the "birthplace of hockey" in early British North America will eventually give way. By embracing "Two-Eyed Seeing," the veil covering the Indigenous contribution to Canada's national game is lifted and we are better able to explore more fully both Indigenous and British North American contributions to the origins and early evolution of

---

6. The subtitle of which reads: "How Hockey Explains Canadian Culture, History, Politics, Heroes, French-English Rivalry and Who We Are as Canadians."

hockey. Playing stick games on ice, the introduction of skating, and the evolution of the ice-hockey stick may end up being the progeny of cultural contact and interchange, melding together Mi'kmaw and British North American practices, rules, and innovations[7] (Vaughan 1996; Dowbiggin 2001). If and when it does, hockey historians and enthusiasts alike will owe much to Elder Albert Marshall and the wisdom of Mi'kmaw ways of seeing and knowing.

Bibliography

Adams, Michael. 2011. "Hockey: Still close to our hearts." *Globe and Mail*, March 16, A17.

———. 2012. "Social Norms: Hockey, fighting and what it means to be a man." *Globe and Mail*, May 28, A11.

Bennett, Paul W. 1990. "Learning to Rule: The World of the Elite Boys' School," in *"Little Worlds": The Forging of Social Identities in Ontario's Protestant School Communities and Institutions, 1850–1930*, Bennet. EdD. thesis, University of Toronto.

———. 2013. "Re-Imagining the Creation: 'Two-Eyed Seeing' and the 'Family Squabble' over the Origins of Canadian Hockey." Paper presented at the North American Society for Sports History Annual Conference, Saint Mary's University, May 25.

Bodnar, John. 1992. *Remaking America: Public Memory, Patriotism, and Commemoration in the Twentieth Century*. Princeton, NJ: Princeton University Press.

Brunt, Steven. 2009. *Gretzky's Tears: Hockey, Canada, and the Day Everything Changed*. Toronto: Random House

Bundale, Brett. 2011. "Antique hockey stick likely to score millions." *Chronicle Herald* [Halifax], October 17.

CBC. 2001. "The Birthplace of Hockey?" CBC-TV *Saturday Report*, February 24, http://www.cbc.ca/player/play/1586100470.

Cuthbertson, Brian. 2005. "Starr Manufacturing Company: Skate Manufacturer to the World," *Journal of the Royal Nova Scotia Historical Society* 8:1–25.

Davies, Richard A., ed. 1997. *The Haliburton Bi-centenary Chaplet: Papers Presented at the 1996 Thomas Raddall Symposium*. Wolfville, NS: Gaspereau Press.

Deline. 2010. "Deline – The Birthplace of Hockey," Website. Destination Deline. http://www.destinationdeline.com/deline-northwest-territories-canada/

DeWolf, Mark, and George Flie. 1972. *1789: All the King's Men: The Story of a Colonial University*. Halifax, NS: Alumni Association of the University of King's College.

Dowbiggin, Bruce. 2001. *The Stick: A History, a Celebration, an Elegy*. Toronto: Macfarlane Walter and Ross.

Dryden, Ken. 1983. *The Game*. Toronto: Macmillan.

Fergusson, C. Bruce. 1965. "Early Hockey at Halifax," *Nova Scotia Journal of Education*, June: 36.

Fitsell, Bill. 1994. "Windsor, Nova Scotia: The 'Birthplace of Hockey?" *The Hockey Research Journal*, December.

Fosty, George, and Darril Fosty. 2003. *Splendid Is the Sun: The 5,000 Year History of Hockey*. New York: Stryker-Indigo Publishing.

Giden, Carl, Patrick Houda, and Jean-Patrice Martel. 2014. *On the Origin of Hockey*. Chambly, QC: Hockey Origin Publishing.

Gruneau, Richard, and David Whitson. 1993. *Hockey Night in Canada: Sport, Identities, and Cultural Politics*. Toronto: Garamond Press.

---

7. See note 2.

Harley, E. Gay. 2002. "Of Cultural Identity and Creation Myths: The Subject of 'Beginnings' and the Writing of Hockey History." In *Putting It on Ice: Volume I: Hockey and Cultural Identities*, ed. Colin D. Howell, 1–5. Halifax, NS: Gorsebrook Research Institute, Saint Mary's University.

Harris, Reginald V. 1996. *The History of King's Collegiate School, Windsor, N.S., 1788–1938*. Middleton, NS: The Outlook.

Henderson, Paul, and Jim Prime. 2011. *How Hockey Explains Canada: The Sport That Defines a Country*. Chicago: Triumph Books.

Hobsbawm, Eric. 1983. "Inventing Traditions," in Hobsbawm and Terence Ranger, eds., *The Invention of Tradition*. Cambridge, UK: Cambridge University Press: 1–14.

Hollingsworth, Paul. 2010. *Sidney Crosby: The Story of a Champion*. Halifax, NS: Nimbus Publishing.

Holman, Andrew C. 2009. "Canada's Game? Hockey and the Problem of Identity," in *Canada's Game: Hockey and Identity*, ed. Andrew C. Holman. Montreal: McGill-Queen's University Press.

Hopper, Tristan. 2008. "Artifact kindles debate on origins of hockey." *Yukon News*, April 12.

Howell, Colin D. 2001. *Blood, Sweat and Cheers: Sport and the Making of Modern Canada*. Toronto: University of Toronto Press.

Jones, Martin. 2002. *Hockey's Home: Halifax-Dartmouth: The Origin of Canada's Game*. Halifax, NS: Nimbus Publishing Ltd.

Kammen, Michael. 1991. *Mystic Chords of Memory: The Transformation of Tradition in America*. New York: Vintage Books.

Kennedy, Brian. 2011. *My Country Is Hockey*. Toronto: Argentia Press.

Kidd, Bruce. 1996. *The Struggle for Canadian Sport*. Toronto: University of Toronto Press.

King's-Edgehill School Archives. 1988. A.J. Sandy Young, press release, "Hockey Evidence Unveiled," October 28, Nova Scotia Sport Heritage Centre, Halifax, and King's-Edgehill School, Windsor, N.S.

Loomer, L. S. 1996. *Windsor, Nova Scotia: A Journey in History*. Windsor, NS: West Hants Historical Society.

Lowenthal, David. 1985. *The Past Is a Foreign Country*. Cambridge: Cambridge University Press.

MacGregor, Roy. 1996. *The Home Team: Fathers, Sons and Hockey*. Toronto: Viking Books.

Mangan, J.A. 1985. *The Games Ethic and Imperialism: Aspects of the Diffusion of an Ideal*. Harmondsworth, UK: Penguin.

Marshall, Albert. 2010. "Ta'ntelo'lti'k: Mi'kmaq Knowledge + Two-Eyed Seeing." Oral presentation to the Time and a Place Conference, University of Prince Edward Island, June 13 18.

Martin, Lawrence. 2012. "The hockey prime minister." *Globe and Mail*, January 3.

Metcalfe, Alan. 1987. *Canada Learns to Play: The Emergence of Organized Sport, 1807–1914*. Toronto: McClelland and Stewart.

Milks, James, ed. 2010. *Pucklore: The Hockey Research Anthology*. Kingston, ON: SIHR and Quarry Press.

Newsome, David. 1961. *Godliness and Good Learning*. London: John Murray.

Nova Scotia Archives and Records Management. 1827. *Acadian Magazine* [Halifax], January.

Nova Scotia Museum. 1913. Dr. Jerry Stonecloud, Micmaq, Elmsdale, NS, to Harry Piers, October 8. Harry Piers Ethnology Papers, vol. 3.

Orr, Bob. 1988. "Windsor said to be birthplace of hockey." *Chronicle Herald* [Halifax], October 28, 8.

———. 1988. "Historians say Windsor is hockey birthplace," *Hants Journal* [Windsor, NS], November 2.

Poulton, J. Alexander. 2010. *A History of Hockey in Canada*. Montreal: Over Time Books.

Robidoux, Michael A. 2012. *Stickhandling through the Margins: First Nations Hockey in Canada*. Toronto: University of Toronto Press.

Sable, Trudy, and Bernie Francis. 2012. *The Language of this Land, Mi'kma'ki*. Sydney, NS: Cape Breton University Press.

SIHR (Society for International Hockey Research). 2002. "The Origins of Hockey. Report of the Sub-Committee Looking into the Claim that Windsor, Nova Scotia, is the Birthplace of Hockey." Toronto: SIHR. http://www.sihrhockey.org/origins_report.cfm.

Vaughan, Garth. 1996. *The Puck Stops Here*. Fredericton, NB: Goose Lane Editions.

———. 2002. *Hockey Day in Canada, January 5, 2002, Long Pond*. Windsor, NS: The Cradle of Hockey, Long Pond.

———. 2011. *Ice Hockey in Nova Scotia: The Early Years*. Windsor, NS: Windsor Hockey Heritage Society and Hants Regional Development Authority.

Vroom, F. W. 1941. *King's College: A Chronicle, 1789–1939: Collections and Recollections*. Halifax, NS: The Imperial Publishing Company.

West Hants Historical Museum and Long Pond Historical Collection. 1829. *Colonial Patriot*. Windsor, Nova Scotia. February 4.

Wolfe, Patrick. 1998. *Settler Colonialism and the Transformation of Anthropology: The Politics and Poetics of an Ethnographic Event*. London: Cassel.

———. 2006. "Settler colonialism and the elimination of the native," *Journal of Genocide Research* 8 (4) (December 2006): 387–409.

Young, A. J. Sandy. 1988. "Nova Scotian Hockey Roots Traced Back to the Time of Napoleon." Unpublished manuscript, King's-Edgehill School, West Hants Historical Museum, Windsor, N.S.

Chapter 3
Imagining a Canadian Identity through Sport: An Historical Interpretation of Lacrosse and Hockey[1]

MICHAEL A. ROBIDOUX

In *Imagined Communities*, Benedict Anderson convincingly reduces the concept of nationalism to an imagining; imagined "because members of even the smallest nation will never know most of their fellow-members, meet them, or even hear of them, yet in the minds of each lives the image of their communion" ([1983] 1991, 6). It is this notion of communion that motivates nations to define and articulate their amorphous existence. If Anderson is correct—which I am purporting to be the case—the task of defining a national identity is a creative process that requires constructing a shared history and mythology(ies) that best suits the identity *imagined* by those few responsible for responding to this task. For a nation as young as Canada (confederated in 1867), this constructive process is somewhat recent and largely incomplete, which is disconcerting for Canadians who have twice witnessed the threat of national fragmentation.[2] As a result, what it means to be Canadian is scrutinized, lamented, and at times even celebrated (perhaps most famously in a Molson Canadian beer advertisement).[3] Yet through all of this there has been one expression of

---

1. This chapter was originally published as Michael Robidoux in *Journal of American Folklore* 115(456):209–225. Copyright © 2002, American Folklore Society. It appears here with permission.
2. The province of Quebec has twice voted on independence from Canada (1980 and 1995). The most recent referendum saw only 51 per cent voting "No" to sovereignty.
3. The commercial gained notoriety because of its uncorked nationalism. It depicts an ordinary "Joe" pronouncing his Canadian identity in contrast to perceived stereotypes of Canadians in what has become known as "Joe's Rant":
    Hey. I'm not a lumberjack, or a fur trader. And I don't live in an igloo, or eat blubber, or own a dogsled. And I don't know Jimmy, Sally or Suzy from Canada, although I'm certain they're really, really nice. I have a Prime Minister, not a President.
    I speak English and French, not American. And I pronounce it "about," not "aboot."
    I can proudly sew my country's flag on my backpack. I believe in peace-keeping, not policing: diversity, not assimilation. And that the beaver is a truly proud and noble animal. A toque is a hat, a chesterfield is a couch, and it is pronounced "zed" not "zee."

nationalism, which has remained constant since confederation, that being the game of hockey.

Since the Second World War Canadians have been internationally perceived more as peacekeepers, and perhaps even as being unreasonably polite—both political constructions in themselves—which makes it difficult to comprehend why a game such as ice hockey,[4] known for its ferocity, speed, and violence, would come to serve as its primary national symbol. The mystery intensifies if we consider that the game of hockey was born out of a period of social reform in Canada, where popular pastimes that involved violence, gambling, and rowdiness were being replaced by more *civilized* leisure pursuits imported from Europe, such as cricket. Cricket, as Richard Gruneau states, was

> especially palatable to Canada's colonial merchants and aristocrats because it combined an excellent and enjoyable forum for learning discipline, civility, and the principles of fair play with a body of traditions and rules offering a ritual dramatization of the traditional power of the colonial metropolis and the class interests associated with it. (1983, 104)

The question becomes, then, how did a sport such as hockey not only take shape in Canada but become "frequently cited as evidence that a Canadian culture exists" (Laba 1992, 333)? Furthermore, to what extent does the game of hockey embody a Canadian collective sensibility, or is this *imagining* of Canadian identity without justification, even at a symbolic level? In order to respond it is necessary to explore early vernacular forms of sport in this nation and consider how these sensibilities have maintained themselves in a contemporary sporting context.

The Process of Modernization

Sport historians and sociologists have documented extensively the development of physical activity from a traditional folk (vernacular) pastime to a modern organized event.[5] Much of this discourse, however, concerns itself with the impact of modernization on traditional physical activities without taking into account the influences of traditional sporting behaviour and its role in shaping (at least from a Canadian perspective) a national sport identity. Colin Howell is critical of these prejudicial tendencies and writes:

> Modernization theory views history as a linear continuum in which any given circumstance or idea can be labeled "pre-modern" or traditional, and thus, can safely be

---

Canada is the second largest landmass, the first nation of hockey, and the best part of North America!
My name is Joe, and I am Canadian!
Thank you.

4. From this point forward, ice hockey will be referred to as hockey.
5. See R. Gruneau (1983, 1988, 1993), E. Dunning (1975), J. Hargreaves (1986), V. Burstyn (1999), A. Metcalfe (1987), Morrow (1989), A. Guttmann (1994), and D. Guay (1981).

ignored as something that the seemingly neutral process of "modernization" has rendered anachronistic. (1995, 184)[6]

What needs to be understood is that the process of modernization was not a linear progression, but rather a series of contested stages that maintained certain aspects of the past, while housing them in an entirely different framework. Before discussing the relationship between traditional and modern sport further, a brief explanation of these terms is necessary.

In sport theory, loosely organized, periodic and self-governed sporting contests fit under the rubric of "traditional" sport (Metcalfe 1987, 11). This form of physical activity is devoid of field or participant specifications, and "was closely interwoven with established conventions of ritual ... as well as the daily and seasonal rhythms of domestic and agrarian production, entertainment and religious festivals" (Gruneau 1988, 12–13). There is a tendency to refer to traditional sport as rural, tribal, and/or in the past tense, but this manner of participation continues to exist in a variety of forms. An example would be road/ball/pond hockey, where people engage in variations of the game of hockey in unspecified locales, with unspecified participants in terms of age, number, gender, and skill, and it is performed around daily routines, whether these routines be dictated by work, school, personal, or familial responsibilities. For this reason, I have substituted the term "traditional" with "vernacular" as it connotes similar meanings but remains viable in a contemporary context.

The significance of the term "modern" sport is twofold, in that it relates not only to the changes that took place in the way people engaged in play, but implies also the political motivations which dictated these changes. To begin, modern sport is not a random pursuit, but rather a highly organized event played within specific boundaries and performed with uniform rules maintained by leagues and organizations. Equipment became standardized and play became recorded and measured. The result was greater uniformity over time and space, reducing the "localized forms of individual and community-based expressions of pleasure, entertainment, physical prowess, and ritual display" (Gruneau 1988, 13). Important to us here is that the consequence of this reductive process was not simply the limiting of specific expressions of sport; instead, behaviour itself was being reduced to satisfy a limited and highly specific social order. Pierre Bourdieu explains that "it would be a mistake to forget that the modern definition of sport is an integral part of a 'moral ideal', i.e. an ethos which is that of the dominant fractions of the dominant class," (1993, 344) which were instilled and maintained by religious and educational institutions (Wheeler 1978, 192). It was through the standardization of sport that undesirable qualities of vernacular pursuits could be eliminated—such as violence, public disorder, and mass rowdiness—thus controlling behaviour to ensure a compliant and non-volatile populace. Again, it must be stressed that while levels of control were successfully manufactured through sport, and that play was indeed standardized, "undesirable" vernacular elements were not entirely eliminated and remain critical features of specific sports, such as lacrosse and hockey.

The political motivations behind the modernization of sport cannot be separated from the actual changes that occurred in expressions of physical activity, and in Canada these

---

6. Gruneau, in "Modernization and Hegemony," similarly recognizes the shortcomings of "overlooking, or misconstruing, the importance of social and cultural continuities in sport" (1988, 19).

motivations stemmed from a British Victorian sensibility. By the turn of the eighteenth century, sport in Britain was being realized as an excellent means of social control and conditioning (Jarvie and Maguire 1994, 109). The successes church and school officials encountered providing the ever-increasing urban working class with productive non-threatening activities, such as cricket and a (refined version of) football, were soon being implemented in the colonies as a means of correcting the rougher, more vulgar, vernacular pastimes. But perhaps even more importantly, there was symbolic value in having newly colonized peoples engaging in these uniquely British activities, and sport quickly became a vehicle for cultural imperialism. Metcalfe speaks to the imperialistic role of cricket by stating that it "illustrated the powerful forces of tradition and the way in which dominant social groups perpetuated their way of life in the face of massive social change" (1987, 17).

In early-nineteenth-century Canada, attempts were well underway to introduce imported European games such as cricket and curling to a nation only beginning to take shape. However, in its earliest stages, organized sport was something suitable only for "gentle-man," and was not intended for the working class or ethnic minorities. Howell points out that while "middle-class reformers advocated a more disciplined and rational approach to leisure, seeking to replace irrational and often turbulent popular or working-class recreations with more genteel and improving leisure activities," these "bourgeois sportsmen" primarily "concentrated their attention on the improvement of middle-class youth" (1995, 14). It was not until later in the century that schools and churches took a more active role in introduc-ing these structured forms of physical activity to Canadians of various class and ethnic backgrounds. The intent was threefold: to acquire levels of control over increased amounts of leisure time made possible by industrialization and a shorter workweek; to reduce class conflict by enabling male participants of various backgrounds to compete on an equal playing field; and to ensure a physically fit yet subordinate workforce to ensure maximum levels of production. In short, institutionalized sport served as an important means of reproducing a Victorian social order in Canada, where young men learned to be honourable and genteel. As with any hegemonic process,[7] however, control was never absolute, and emergent and residual cultures affected the desired outcome.

Resisting an Imported Canadian Identity

The development of sport took an important turn by the middle of the nineteenth century, with a new emergent class, led by Montreal-born dentist, George Beers, responding to impositions of British nationalism in Canada. Beers's role in Canadian sport history is that of romantic nationalist, as his politics were comparable to Johann Gottfried Herder's roman-tic nationalism of eighteenth-century Germany. Like Herder, Beers understood that to construct a national identity, two things needed to occur. First, foreign influence needed to be eliminated—Herder was contending with French influence, Beers contended with English. And second, a national history/mythology needed to be constructed. Instead of turning to Indigenous poetry and language, as Herder had done, Beers turned to Indigenous sport as a means of portraying the soul of a nation. What better place to look, then, than

---

7. Guttmann expresses (1994, 178) his dissatisfaction with the term "cultural imperialism" to describe sport diffusion. Instead, he prefers the term "cultural hegemony," which better com-municates the lively "contestation that has accompanied ludic diffusion."

to Canada's first peoples, whose game of *baggataway*, filled with speed, violence, and skill appeared to best embody the harsh and grueling existence of early Canadian settlers in this new and untamed land.

The game *baggataway*, renamed lacrosse by French settlers,[8] was played by many First Nations across North America prior to European contact, and was a game that both fascinated and repulsed early settlers (Eisen 1994, 2). English Europeans were least sympathetic to First Nations leisurely activities, largely because of puritanical sensibilities that tended to perceive all forms of play as wasteful and unproductive. It is not surprising that English observations of lacrosse disparaged the violence, yet these comments were often countered with admiration for First Nations' players who exuded remarkable sportsmanship and respect for their opponents. One late-eighteenth-century account reads:

> The Chippewas play with so much vehemence that they frequently wound each other, and sometimes a bone is broken; but notwithstanding these accidents there never appears to be any spite or wanton exertions of strength to affect them, nor do any disputes ever happen between the parties. (Carver [1796] 1956, 237)

More detailed accounts of lacrosse come from French missionaries and settlers who, unlike the English, lived with First Nations peoples and made efforts to learn their language, customs, and social practices. One of the earliest accounts comes from Nicolas Perrot, who encountered the game while living as a *coureur des bois*[9] between 1665 and 1684:

> Il y a parmy eux un certain jeu de crosse qui a beaucoup de raport avec celuy de nostre longue paume. Leur coustume en joüant est de se mettre nation contre nation, et, s'il y en a une plus nombreuse que l'autre, ils en tirent des hommes pour rendre égale celle qui ne l'est pas. Vous les voyez tous armez d'une crosse, c'est à dire d'un baston qui a un gros bout au bas, lacé comme une raquette; la boule qui leur sert à joüer est de bois et à peu près de la figure d'un oeuf de dinde.[10] (1973, 43–44)[11]

He continues by describing the violent nature of the sport:

8. It has been argued that the term "la crosse" was applied to the game because the sticks used by the participants resembled a bishop's crozier (Thwaites 1959, 326). Maurice Jetté argues (1975, 14), however, that the name comes from "an old French game called 'la soule' which was played with a 'crosse' very similar to the Indian implement."

9. Literally means "runner of the woods." More specifically, coureurs des bois were French male fur traders and trappers who lived as the Indigenous population did during the seventeenth century. Miller writes (2000, 56) that these young males were "neither French peasants nor Indian braves, they were a bit of both."

10. All translations provided by Robidoux unless otherwise noted.

11. Among them there is a certain game of crosse that compares to our tennis. Their custom is to play nation (tribe) against nation (tribe), and if one side has more players than the other, more players are brought forth to ensure a fair game. Each has a stick, called a crosse, that has a curve at the end that is laced like a racket; the ball that they play with is made of wood and looks a little bit like a turkey's egg.

Vous entendez le bruit qu'ils font en se frapant les uns contre les autres, dans le temps qu'ils veulent parer les coups pour envoyer cette boule du costé favorable. Quand quelqu'un la garde entre les pieds sans la vouloir lascher, c'est à luy d'eviter les coups que ses adversaires luy portent sans discontinuer sur les pieds; et s'il arrive dans cette conjoncture qu'il soit blessé, c'est pour son compte. Il s'en est veü, qui ont eü les jambes cassées, d'autres les bras, et quelques uns ont estez mesme tüez. Il est fort ordinaire d'en voir d'estropiez pour le reste de leurs jours, et qui ne l'ont esté qu'à ces sortes de jeu par un effect de leur opiniâtreté.[12] (ibid., 45)

For many young French males, the rough nature of the sport was appealing, and, as result, these men became enamoured with not only the game of lacrosse but with its participants as well, which bears tremendous significance.

The radical impositions of European colonization on North American Indigenous peoples has been taken to task in academic and popular discourse, but arguments that perceive this relationship to be unidirectional are often overstated. In *Skyscrapers Hide the Heavens*, Miller offers some balance to this historical analysis by revisiting early European-Indigenous relations and discussing them in terms of cultural change, both "non-directed" and "directed" ([1989] 2000, 95). In other words, Miller understands these relations as being far more equitable than is often portrayed. Not only did First Nations peoples often *willingly* take advantage of such things as European technology to benefit their own situations, Miller documents the heavy reliance of European settlers on First Nations knowledge and technologies. In fact, he states that European survival in Canada would not have been possible without First Nations assistance and charity. Further to this, and more importantly for our purposes, are the extensive cultural borrowings of European settlers (in this case, French) from First Nations peoples.

For a certain sector of French-Canadian males—later known as *les Canadiens*—the First Nations male provided an alternative model of masculinity, where physicality, stoicism, and bravado were valued and celebrated, not repressed, as it was in the Christian model of masculinity:

The young voyageurs struggled to copy the Indians' stoicism in the face of adversity and their endurance when confronted with hardship, deprivation, and pain. They also copied, to the extent that their employers and governors could not prevent, the autonomy that Indian society inculcated in its young. French males found the liberated sexual attitudes of young Indian women before matrimony as attractive as the missionaries found them repugnant. (Miller 2000, 54)

These Frenchmen began emulating First Nations males, and in so doing began sharing in their cultural practices. Occupational and survival-related pursuits such as canoeing,

---

12. One can hear the noise they make when they hit one another, while they attempt to avoid receiving blows in order to throw the ball to a favourable location. If one secures the ball in his feet without letting it go, he must fend off blows from his opponents who continually strike his feet; and if in this situation he is injured, it is his own concern. Some are seen with broken legs, or arms, or are even killed as a result. It is common to see players maimed permanently, yet this does not change the way they play the game on account of their obstinacy.

snowshoeing, and hunting were obvious pastimes that were learned and performed. Team sports such as lacrosse also proved to be of tremendous interest to *les Canadiens*, as it gave both First Nations and French males the opportunity to prove their worth to one another as men. According to Joseph Oxendine, these white settlers did not fare very well, however, "because of the Indian's clear superiority of the game. Indians were frequently reported to have used fewer players in an effort to equalize the competition" (1988, 48). First Nations proficiency at lacrosse was highly regarded by early sport enthusiasts, but these skills were also perceived by others to be violent and dangerous, which began generating its own folklore.

Perhaps the most popular lacrosse event was a legendary contest between two First Nations tribes at Fort Michilimackinac in 1763. According to Alexander Henry's ([1809] 1901) account of the contest, the tribes used lacrosse as a means of staging an attack on the British fort during Pontiac's War. Francis Parkman supports this in his account (1962, 254), which states:

> Suddenly, from the midst of the multitude, the ball soared into the air and . . . fell near the pickets of the fort. This was no chance stroke. It was part of a preconcerted stratagem to insure the surprise and destruction of the garrison . . . . The shrill cries of the ball-players were changed to the ferocious war-whoop. The warriors snatched from the squaws the hatchets, which the latter . . . had concealed beneath their blankets. Some of the Indians assailed the spectators without, while others rushed into the fort, and all was carnage and confusion.

It was this legendary status the sport commanded that made it the perfect vehicle for George Beers's nationalist agenda. The game ran counter to British bourgeois sensibilities that understood sport to be refined and gentlemanly, and ultimately a breeding ground for proper British mores and values. Instead, lacrosse was a display of rugged, brutal, and aggressive behaviours that were said to embody what it meant to be a Canadian settler in this unforgiving northern territory. Thus, Beers called to Canadians to refrain from engaging in the imperial pursuit of cricket and take up lacrosse as the new national game, in effect ridding Canada of foreign influences and reacquainting the population to the soul of the nation.

In order to make this fictitious proposal possible, the game of lacrosse had to be claimed and then incorporated into a modern sporting climate. Lacrosse as First Nations peoples played it was not merely sport but spiritual and religious occasions, often having healing or prophetic significance.[13] The game also had regional and tribal idiosyncrasies, which meant that there was no standard form of play, making Euro-Canadian adoption difficult. Thus, lacrosse as a vernacular entity needed to be transformed, which meant eliminating traits that were linked to First Nations culture. To achieve this transformation it was necessary to standardize the rules to create a sense of uniformity. An important step was made by George Beers, who published the first rules of lacrosse, under the name "Goal-keeper," in a series

---

13. Jean De Brebeuf, a Jesuit priest, writes in 1636, "There is a poor sick man, fevered of body and almost dying, and a miserable Sorcerer [Shaman] will order for him, as a cooling remedy, a game of crosse. Or the sick man himself, sometimes, will have dreamed that he must die unless the whole country shall play crosse for his health" (quoted in Thwaites 1959, 185).

of advertisements in the *Montreal Gazette* in 1860 (Cosentino 1998, 15). These rules were later adopted by the Montreal Lacrosse Club to become the "official" rules of lacrosse, and were republished in the *Gazette* in July of 1867 (Morrow 1989, 47). Efforts to standardize the game not only eliminated regional variations but dictated how the game of lacrosse was to be played. All that was left, then, was to attract people to the game, and again, Beers was instrumental.

Through various print forms (magazines and newspapers), Beers was able to promote lacrosse as Canada's national game and deride cricket as foreign and irrelevant to Canadians.[14] In an article suitably entitled "The National Game," Beers (1867) writes:

> As cricket, wherever played by Britons, is a link of loyalty to bind them to their home so may lacrosse be to Canadians. We may yet find it will do as much for our young Dominion as the Olympian games did for Greece or cricket for our Motherland.

Interestingly, Beers makes no apologies for appropriating an Indigenous game and promoting it as the national pastime. Instead, he sees appropriation as an accurate depiction of European presence in Canada, and argues, "just as we [Canadian colonialists] claim as Canadian the rivers and lakes and land once owned exclusively by Indians, so we now claim their field game as the national field game of our dominion" (ibid.). Beer's proselytizing was enormously effective, to the extent that a National Lacrosse Association was formed— the first national sporting body in Canada—and lacrosse was erroneously being touted as Canada's official national game.[15]

These developments, however, which saw a vernacular sporting pastime transformed into a modern sport, were not as complete as scholars have suggested. Don Morrow states (1989, 46): "At first heralded in adoption, then transformed in nature, the Indian origins of the game were finally shunned by nineteenth-century white promoters and players." While ritual/sacred components and regional variations were erased from modern lacrosse competitions, there were elements of the game that remained, largely to the chagrin of elite sporting officials who were governing these developments. To begin, the popularization of lacrosse did not arise merely because of George Beers's ideological ravings. It is incorrect to claim, as Morrow does (ibid., 54), that the new national affinity of lacrosse was achieved through the word of Beers: "if something is claimed to be true enough times, it is often accepted as truth." This simply does not allow for human agency, and while public consciousness can be influenced, it is not something that can be dictated. In other words, there needed to be some pre-existing value in lacrosse that allowed it to be so willingly adopted by Canadian sport enthusiasts. It is here, then, that we can begin examining the cultural value of lacrosse (and later, hockey) and its relationship to Canadian identity.

---

14. Most important of these were "A Rival to Cricket" and "The National Game."
15. Despite claims made in *One Hundred—Not Out: The Story of Nineteenth-Century Canadian Sport* (1966) and in the 1894 edition of the *Dictionnaire canadien-francais* that lacrosse was the national game of Canada, there are no official records that substantiate this claim (Morrow 1989, 52–53).

Sport Sensibilities in Conflict

One of the primary reasons lacrosse served as a viable alternative to imported British sports such as cricket was its emphasis on physical aggression, volatility, and danger. The game appealed to males who identified with a more physically aggressive notion of masculinity, rather than the reserved and civil expressions of masculinity exemplified in cricket. In essence, the attraction to lacrosse was an extension of early French Canadians' infatuation with First Nations masculinity, where the emphasis was on physical superiority, bodily awareness, and perseverance. Lacrosse provided males the opportunity to display these heralded qualities and challenge them through formal competitions. However, in the attempt to modernize lacrosse and market it to a broader audience, the game needed to become less violent and to be played in a manner more suitable for "gentleman"; otherwise, the game would not enter dominant sport culture. Efforts were in place to sanitize the game, but they were not entirely successful. In fact, those who were most successful at the sport were First Nations and working-class players who played the game as it was originally designed—aggressively and intensely. Attempts to turn the game into something else merely put those who engaged in it as "gentlemen" at a clear disadvantage to those who maintained its aggressive style of play. One team renowned for its aggressive play was the Montreal Shamrocks, which also spun off the Montreal Shamrocks hockey club, who "were, without question, the most successful team prior to 1885 . . . . The Shamrocks were out of place both socially and athletically. Social misfits on the middle-class playing fields, the Shamrocks were Irish, Roman Catholic, and working-class" (Metcalfe 1987, 196).

What is critical here is that the ideological value of lacrosse paled in relation to the actual meanings early participants experienced through playing it. Howell correctly observes that lacrosse was "a relatively minor sport" that "was suddenly elevated to prominence because of the symbolic role that was associated with it at the time of Confederation" (1995, 103). However, those elite officials who helped elevate the status of lacrosse understood lacrosse symbolically, not its literal value as a meaningful expression of Canadian consciousness. I do not wish to imply that this is a singular phenomenon, but there is evidence that lacrosse did have value for certain Canadian males as being an identifiable articulation of who they were as men. In essence, lacrosse did signify class, gender, and ethnic values, but these values were generally unacknowledged by elite sporting officials who were suddenly threatened by their own ideological maneuverings. Their recourse was to prohibit the "people" from playing the game it symbolically represented and to make it the game of an exclusive minority:

> The logical conclusion for lacrossists was that the incidence of disputes, violence, and undesirable conduct on the field of play could mean only one thing—some players were not gentlemen. The truth of this observation was given substance by the presence of Indians, who always played for money and, by race alone, could not be gentlemen, and of the working-class Shamrock team. (Metcalfe 1987, 195)

This prohibition of undesirable participants was made possible through the introduction of amateurism.

Amateur athletics in Canada did not merely function as a means of ensuring that athletes engage in sport in a gentlemanly manner,[16] but served as a discriminatory system that prevented undesirable players from playing. Prior to 1909, the year when a national amateur athletic union was formed in Canada, national sporting bodies used the concept of amateurism to best suit their sport's needs. In the case of the National Lacrosse Association, league officials decided to make it an amateur association restricted to those players who fit under the definition of amateur. An amateur was conveniently defined by the Amateur Athletic Union of Canada as someone who had "never competed for a money prize, or staked bet or with or against any professional for any prize," or one who "never taught, pursued, or assisted in the practice of athletic exercises as a means of obtaining a livelihood" (Metcalfe 1987, 105–06). The stipulations were highly restrictive and deliberate in design.

First, it made working-class participation virtually impossible, in that wage earners were no longer able to receive financial compensation for taking time off work to play. Keeping in mind that it was illegal to play sports on Sunday, and that the workweek ran from Monday to Saturday, working-class participation in sport was reduced generally to Saturday afternoons. As a result, players were not only prevented from receiving payment for time lost at work, those players who at one time received compensation for their services were no longer eligible to play. The second aspect of this definition was equally effective because it denied access to individuals who at one time gambled on sport. During this period in Canadian history, gambling and sport were virtually inextricable; gambling made up part of the fabric of vernacular sporting pastimes. For First Nations cultures in particular, gambling in sport (by spectators and participants) was deeply ingrained in their traditions, and at times even played a role in their overall economies (Oxendine 1988, 31). Therefore, by these first two stipulations alone, most ethnic minorities and working-class peoples were considered ineligible players and could no longer play amateur athletics. The final stipulation reinforced economic divisiveness further, making it clear that sport was not the property of the people, but of men who "had the leisure, economic resources and social approval to explore intensive athletic training in a financially disinterested manner" (Burstyn 1999, 224). But once again, however, true to hegemonic relations, the restrictive measures imposed by the National Lacrosse Association did not go unchallenged. Teams tried to circumvent the rules by covertly using "professional" players to become more competitive, and in certain cases even paid players for their services. In response, the National Lacrosse Association was compelled to enforce disciplinary measures to contend with these dissident organizations. Teams who were caught cheating at such were brought before the Canadian Amateur Athletic Union[17] to face arbitration and potential censuring. As these arbitration cases grew in number, tremendous pressures were being placed on the National Lacrosse Association to retract its strictly amateur policy and permit both professionals and amateurs into the league. Despite this, the association remained steadfast in its position to prohibit professional players and was ultimately

16. Varda Burstyn writes (1999, 49), "For many of the founding sport associations of the late nineteenth century, 'amateur' athletics meant 'gentlemen' athletics."

17. The Amateur Athletic Association of Canada changed its name in 1898 to the Canadian Amateur Athletic Union in an attempt to strengthen its position as a national sport-governing body (Metcalfe 1987, 110).

successful in maintaining itself as an amateur association; this success, however, proved to be its inevitable downfall.

By maintaining its exclusive membership, the association forced would-be lacrosse players to pursue alternative sporting options. Other team-sport leagues (baseball, football, hockey) were not as resistive to the influences of professionalism, and thus they provided working-class and ethnic minority players alternatives to play and be financially compensated at the same time. While baseball and football did attract many of the players, these sports did not possess the symbolic and literal value found in lacrosse. Instead, it was hockey that early Canadian sport enthusiasts embraced by the turn of century, for the same reasons they were attracted to lacrosse twenty years earlier. Unlike baseball or football, it was uniquely Canadian in origin and character. Hockey, which was an amalgam of modern and vernacular sporting pastimes, resembled lacrosse in design and in the manner it was played. Play was aggressive and often violent, providing men the opportunity to display this emergent notion of masculinity. At a symbolic level, it was played on a frozen landscape, embodying perfectly what life as a Canadian settler was supposed to be like. Thus, hockey provided all that lacrosse entailed, but without the restrictions of amateurism. By the 1920s, hockey had succeeded where lacrosse had failed, ultimately becoming Canada's national sport pastime.

Violence, Masculinism, and Canadian Identity

Let us here return to the politics of identity and the manner in which hockey, a game notoriously aggressive and violent, serves as a potential symbol for national expression. I, along with other social scientists,[18] have been critical of popular discourse that tends to mythologize hockey and locate it as a unifying force in this nation. Gruneau and Whitson astutely observe:

> The myth of hockey as a "natural" adaptation to ice, snow, and open space is a particularly graphic example of what Barthes is alerting us to—about how history can be confused with nature . . . . This discourse of nature creates a kind of cultural amnesia about the social *struggles* and vested interests—between men and women, social classes, regions, races, and ethnic groups—that have always been part of hockey's history. (1993, 132)

While these sentiments are certainly valid, it would be incorrect to say that hockey is without cultural or historical relevance in Canada. In fact, it is my contention that hockey is more than a mythological construct; it is a legitimate expression of Canadian national history and identity. Hockey *does* speak to issues of gender, race, ethnicity, and region in this nation, albeit not entirely in a positive manner. For this reason, hockey moves beyond symbol and becomes more of a metaphoric representation of Canadian identity.

First, hockey was born out of post-Confederation Canada,[19] in a period of political uncertainty and unrest. It was a disparate nation, divided in terms of language, region, and

18. See Robidoux (2001), Gruneau and Whitson (1993), and Laba (1992).
19. Canada became a confederation in 1867, and the first recorded game of hockey took place in 1875.

ethnicity, lacking in identity and national unity. Thus, using hockey ideologically to express national sentiment certainly did occur, but again, like the game of lacrosse, its value as a vernacular entity was equal to, if not greater than, its symbolic value. From the outset, hockey's violent and aggressive style separated itself from other bourgeois (European) pastimes, but also from the increasingly popular game of baseball that was entering Canada from the United States. Early contests at times appalled certain sport writers and sport officials, who saw the violence on the ice and in the stands as unfit for gentleman. J. W. Fitsell provides two accounts of the first recorded game of hockey, which took place in 1875. The first, from the *Daily British Whig*, states that "Shins and heads were battered, benches smashed and the lady spectators fled in confusion" (quoted in Fitsell 1987, 36). The other report, from the *Montreal Witness*, claimed that:

> Owing to some boys skating about during play an unfortunate disagreement arose: one little boy was struck across the head, and the man who did so was afterwards called to account, a regular fight taking place in which a bench was broken and other damages caused. (ibid.)

These accounts of violence are undoubtedly extreme, yet what is significant is that even in its earliest stages hockey was a sport that was perceived as excessively aggressive and violent within a modern European context.

It was largely because of this excessiveness that hockey was a sport that Canadians could call their own, and they quickly began showcasing it in international contexts. By the mid-1890s, competitions were being staged between Canadian hockey teams and American ice-polo teams. The Canadian teams dominated these early competitions and revelled in the press they received, which applauded their skill but at the same time was critical of their rough play. The *Daily Mining Gazette*, of Houghton, Michigan, described one game as "rush, slash and check continually.... Calumet were knocked off the puck by Portage Lakes 'any old way.' Many a man had to be carried to the dressing room" (quoted in Fitsell 1987, 120). In a game in Sault Ste. Marie, Michigan, an incident occurred where "Stuart [an American player] was laid out by a board check from Jack Laviolette. He recovered and tangled with the same player, fans rushed on the ice and as Stuart bled from the facial cuts, police were called in" (ibid.). These accounts illustrate that within twenty years of organized existence, hockey was internationally known as, first, being Canadian, and second, notoriously violent. Further evidence of this is found in two American cartoons depicting Canadians playing hockey in Pittsburgh in 1904 (Figures 3.1 and 3.2).[20]

The distinction hockey received as being a rough sport was also a means for Canadians to display their proficiency in the clearly demarcated context of a sporting event, making it such a valuable vehicle for expressing national identity. But it was not simply being proficient, it was being proficient physically within the masculinist tradition that was earlier identified in terms of lacrosse. Hockey displayed men that were perceived to be stoic, courageous, and physically dominant: precisely the same images of masculinity that were

---

20. The figures and caption are taken from J. W. Fitsell's *Hockey's Captains, Colonels & Kings* (1987, 119). The cartoons depict games that took place in Pittsburgh in 1904, but there is no information indicating where these cartoons were originally published.

THEY CALL FOOTBALL BRUTAL SPORT!

American cartoonists took to the slash and crash of Canadian players in Pittsburgh.

Figure 3.1 "They call football a brutal sport!"
Within twenty years of organized hockey, the game was identified as Canadian and as violent. These two cartoons from Pittsburgh, in 1904, illustrate the discursive connections between hockey, violence and Canada.
J.W. Fitsell, 1987.

valued in First Nations culture, and later by early Canadian settlers. These historically pertinent attitudes were what attracted Canadians to hockey as it provided Canadian males with an identifiable image that was outside of a British Victorian framework. Moreover, through competition, Canadians could exude superiority over Americans, illustrating for many a "victory for the industrious Canadian beaver over the mighty U.S. eagle" (Fitsell 1987, 106). In essence, hockey became a vehicle of resistance against British and American hegemony, and something that Canadians continue to call on in periods of political or national uncertainty.

One such occasion was the 1972 Summit Series, which saw Canadian professional hockey players engage in an eight-game series against the national team of the Soviet Union. The event was a debacle, yet it is considered by many to be the greatest Canadian story ever told. The series was described as East meets West—communism versus capitalism—and as the players rightfully admitted, it went beyond hockey. Reflecting on the series, Team Canada member Phil Esposito stated: "It wasn't a game anymore; it was society against society . . . it wasn't fun. It was *not* fun" (MacAskill, 1997). The series was filled with incidents of extreme violence: one Canadian player (Bobby Clarke) followed instructions from a coach and broke a Soviet player's ankle with his hockey stick during play. Other incidents involved a Soviet referee nearly being attacked by a Canadian player; throat-slitting gestures; kicking (with skates); fighting; and an in-game melee with tournament promoter, Alan Eagleson, the Soviet Guard, and the Canadian hockey team. The event, which was advertised as an expression of goodwill between nations, turned sour when the favoured Canadians were defeated in the initial games, and were outclassed in terms of skill and sportsmanship. Canadian players were simply unaware of the tremendous hockey abilities of their opponent,

Figure 3.2 American cartoonists took to the slash and crash of Canadian players in Pittsburgh.

ostensibly amateurs, and were initially humiliated by the Soviets on the ice and by a disheartened Canadian public, who lambasted them with jeers at the home games.

In response to their dire predicament, Canadian players resorted to bullying and intimidation tactics, and literally fought their way back into contention. In a miraculous comeback, overcoming real and imagined barriers, the Canadian team proved victorious, winning the final game and the series with a goal in the last minute of play. Their "heroism" became permanently etched into the memory of Canadians, despite actions that have recently been described by two American journalists as "hacking and clubbing the Soviet players like seal pups and bullying their way to a thrilling, remarkable comeback" (Klein and Reif 1998, 31). While there have been critics of the series, it remains in the Canadian collective consciousness as "an orgy of self-congratulation about the triumph of 'Canadian virtues'— individualism, flair, and most of all, character" (Gruneau and Whitson 1993, 263). Historically speaking, these seemingly appalling behaviours are compatible with Canadian hockey in general, and for this reason are embraced, not denounced. The players performed in a manner that was consistent with Canadian play throughout history, illustrating a Canadian character that has yet to be defined in more concrete fashion. Therefore, despite Canadian behaviour that was an assault on international hockey, and on international competition in general, this assault was distinctly Canadian, something which is invaluable for the construction of a national identity.

Conclusion

The connection I have tried to make between hockey and Canadian nationalism is that there is, in fact, a connection. In so doing, I am not making the claim that Canadians are predisposed to violence, or that they even condone violent behaviour. What I am saying, rather, is that hockey enabled Canadians to display qualities that have been valued in patriarchal relations: stoicism, courage, perseverance, and proficiency. The singularity of the game and the manner in which it was played were critical for a young and disparate nation to have as its own in the face of encroaching social, political, and cultural interests from Europe and the United States. At a more pedestrian level, hockey was accessible to men of various ethnic and class backgrounds, and thus, to a greater degree than lacrosse, it became a game of the people. The fact that the term *people* here is specific to males only established hockey as a male preserve, making it a popular site for males to define their worth as men, drawing on notions of masculinity that date back to seventeenth-century Canada. In this sense, understanding hockey beyond its mythological rhetoric does acknowledge the "social *struggles* and vested interests—between men and women, social classes, regions, races, and ethnic groups," and that hockey was, as Gruneau and Whitson state, "all of these" (1993, 132; emphasis added).

Finally, by linking hockey to Canadian nationalism I am not situating either as being positive. In fact, the Canadian penchant to understand itself through hockey repeats masculinist formulas of identification that poorly reflect the lives of Canadians. The physically dominant, heterosexist, and capitalist associations of this specific identity are certainly exclusionary, but, for that matter, all nationalist expressions cannot suitably speak for the polyphony of a nation. But despite the obvious fallibility of nationalistic representation, the legitimacy of nationalistic expression remains. Canada's history is based in patriarchy, heterosexism, and capitalism, and thus the use of hockey to promote national pride and unity was not random, nor is it today. It is a means of constructing an image of a nation in the manner in which dominant forces within wish to be seen. With this, hockey does not merely symbolize the need to define a national identity; it offers insight into the actual imaginings of what this identity entails. Thus, hockey provides Canada a means by which to be distinguished, which, as Anderson astutely observes ([1983] 1991, 6), is not "to be distinguished by "falsity/genuineness, but by the style in which" it is "imagined."

Bibliography

Anderson, Benedict. [1983] 1991. *Imagined Communities: Reflections on the Origin and Spread of Nationalism*. Rev. ed. New York: Verso.

Beers, W. G. 1867. "National Game." *Montreal Gazette*, August 8, sec. Sporting Intelligence.

Bourdieu, Pierre. 1993. "How Can One be a Sports Fan?" In *The Cultural Studies Reader*, ed. Simon During, 339–58. London: Routledge.

Burstyn, Varda. 1999. *The Rites of Men: Manhood, Politics, and the Culture of Sport*. Toronto: U of T Press.

Carver, J. [1796] 1956. *Travels through the Interior Parts of North America*. Minneapolis: Ross and Haines.

Cosentino, Frank. 1998. *Afros, Aboriginals and Amateur Sport in Pre World War One Canada*. Ottawa: Canadian Historical Association.

Dunning, Eric. 1975. "Industrialization and the Incipient Modernization of Football." *Stadion* 1 (1): 103–39.

Eisen, George. 1994. Early European Attitudes toward Native American Sports and Pastimes. In *Ethnicity and Sport in North American History and Culture*, ed. George Eisen and David K. Wiggins. Westport, CT: Greenwood Press. 1–18.

Fitsell, J. W. 1987. *Hockey's Captains, Colonels, and Kings*. Erin, ON: The Boston Mills Press.

Gruneau, Richard. 1983. *Class, Sports, and Social Development*. Amherst: University of Massachusetts Press.

————. 1988. Modernization or Hegemony: Two Views on Sport and Social Development. In *Not Just a Game: Essays in Canadian Sport Sociology*, ed. Jean Harvey and Hart Cantelon, 9–32. Ottawa: University of Ottawa Press.

Gruneau Richard, and David Whitson. 1993. *Hockey Night in Canada: Sport, Identities and Cultural Politics*. Culture and Communication in Canada Series. Toronto: Garamond Press.

Guay, D. 1981. *L'Histoire de l'Éducation Physique au Québec: Conceptions et Événements (1830–1980)*. Chicoutimi, QC: Gaetan Morin.

Guttman, Allen. 1994. *Games and Empires: Modern Sports and Cultural Imperialism*. New York: Columbia University Press.

Hargreaves, John. 1986. *Sport, Power and Culture: A Social and Historical Analysis of Popular Sports in Britain*. New York: St. Martin's Press.

Henry, Alexander. [1809] 1901. *Travels and Adventures in Canada and the Indian Territories Between the Years 1760 and 1776*. Ed. James Bain. Toronto: G.N. Morang.

Howell, Colin D. 1995. *Northern Sandlots: A Social History of Maritime Baseball*. Toronto: University of Toronto Press.

Jarvie, Grant, and Joseph Maguire. 1994. *Sport and Leisure in Social Thought*. London: Routledge.

Jetté, Maurice. 1975. "Primitive Indian Lacrosse: Skill or Slaughter?" *Anthropological Journal of Canada* 13 (1): 14–19.

Klein, Jeff Z., and Karl-Eric Reif. 1998. "Our Tarnished Past." *Saturday Night Magazine* 113 (10): 30–33.

Laba, Martin. 1992. Myths and Markets: Hockey as Popular Culture in Canada. In *Seeing Ourselves: Media Power and Policy in Canada*, ed. Helen Holmes and David Taras, 333–44. Toronto: Harcourt Brace Jovanovich Canada.

Metcalfe, Alan. 1987. *Canada Learns to Play: The Emergence of Organized Sport, 1807–1914*. Toronto: McClelland and Stewart.

Miller, J. R. [1989] 2000. *Skyscrapers Hide the Heavens: A History of Indian-White Relations in Canada*. 3rd ed. Toronto: University of Toronto Press.

Morrow, Don. 1989. Lacrosse as the National Game. In *A Concise History of Sport in Canada*, ed. Don Morrow et al. Toronto: Oxford University Press. 45–68.

Parkman, Francis. 1962. *The Conspiracy of Pontiac*. 10th ed. New York: Collier Books.

Perrot, Nicolas. 1973. *Mémoire sur les Moeurs, Coustumes, er Relligion des Sauvages de l'Amérque Septentrionale*. Edited by J. Tailhan. Montreal: Éditions Élysée.

Oxendine, Joseph B. 1988. *American Indian Sports Heritage*. Champaign, IL: Human Kinetic Books.

Robidoux, Michael A. 2001. *Men at Play: A Working Understanding of Professional Hockey in Canada*. Montreal: McGill-Queen's University Press.

September 1972. 1997. Directed by Robert MacAskill. Toronto: CTV.

Thwaites, Reuben G., ed. 1959. *The Jesuit Relations and Allied Documents: Travels and Explorations of the Jesuit Missionaries in New France, 1610–1791*. Vol. 10. New York: Pageant Book Company.

Wheeler, Robert F. 1978. "Organized Sport and Organized Labour: The Workers' Sports Movement." *Journal of Contemporary History* 13:191–210.

Document 1
Excerpts from *The Survivors Speak:*
A Report of the Truth and Reconciliation
Commission of Canada (2015)

The *Final Report of the Truth and Reconciliation Commission of Canada* was released in 2015, after seven years of consultations. The *Truth and Reconciliation Commission of Canada* (TRC) heard from six thousand witnesses, most of them Indigenous former students of the system of forced-assimilation in Canada. Public awareness of the system of forced assimilation has improved residential schools because of the report of the TRC. At the same time, there is still much to be known about residential schools in Canada and their long-term impact on those who attend. Among the most poignant of the TRC's publications was *The Survivors Speak*, former students' testimonies to the commission. "Survivor" was the term adopted by the commission to describe former students who shared their stories. "Survivor" means more than someone who "made it through" the schools. Survivors were people "who had taken all that could be thrown at them and remained standing at the end."[1] Hockey was a part of the residential-school experience. Survivors shared their experiences of hockey, good and bad, for the public record. Excerpts about hockey from the report appear below in the order and context that they were presented in the original document.

1. Name Redacted, Key First Nation, Saskatchewan
One student, who attended the Gordon's, Saskatchewan, school, recalled the ways in which the churches competed against one another to recruit students:

> But when we look at the residential schools, you know, and the churches we recognize, you know, at least I've seen it, you know, that we've had these two competing religions, the Anglican and the Catholic churches both competing for our souls it seemed. You know, I remember growing up on the reserve here when they were looking for students. They were competing against each other. We were the prizes, you know, that they would gain if they won. I remember they, the Catholic priests coming out with, you know, used hockey equipment and telling us, you know, "Come and come to our school. Come and play hockey for us. Come and play in our band. We got all kinds of bands here; we got trombones and trumpets and drums," and all that kind of stuff. They use all this stuff to encourage us or entice us to come to the Catholic school. And then on the other hand, the Anglicans, they would come out with what they called "bale clothes." They bring out bunch of clothes in a bale, like, a big bale. It was all used

---

1. *The Survivors Speak: A Report of the Truth and Reconciliation Commission of Canada*, 2015, xiii.

clothing and they'd give it to the women on the reserve here, and the women made blankets and stuff like that out of these old clothes. But that's the way they, they competed for us as people.[2]

2. Doug Beardy, Thunder Bay, Ontario
Beardy said that at the Stirland Lake, Ontario, school, the principal punished him with blows administered with

"a hockey stick, a goalie stick . . . that was cut off like. . . a paddle."[3]

3. Mervin Mirasty, Saskatoon, Saskatchewan
Mervin Mirasty said that at the Beauval, Saskatchewan, school, boys caught throwing snowballs were punished with blows to their hands from the blade of a hockey stick:

There was about thirty of us. Every one of us got ten smacks. Every one of us cried except one, one guy, and he refused to cry, but it hurt so much. That was for playing with the snowballs, being a kid, just playing around.[4]

4. Robert Malcolm, Winnipeg, Manitoba
Robert Malcolm, who was sexually abused while attending the Sandy Bay school, said there were positive aspects to the residential school experience:

I guess it, it wasn't all, it wasn't all bad, like, even though I received an education, I actually did fairly well in, in my studies when I was there. Like, I'm thankful that I was able to be involved in sports, when those sports weren't part of my home environment before. I was able to play hockey, and baseball, and stuff like that, basketball.[5]

5. Christina Kimball, Winnipeg, Manitoba
Christina Kimball attended the Roman Catholic school near The Pas, where she experienced physical, sexual, and emotional abuse. She believes that it was only through her involvement with sports that she survived:

2. TRC, AVS, [name redacted], Statement to the Truth and Reconciliation Commission of Canada, Key First Nation, Saskatchewan, 21 January 2012, Statement Number: SP039, *The Survivors Speak*, 16–17.
3. TRC, AVS, Doug Beardy, Statement to the Truth and Reconciliation Commission of Canada, Thunder Bay, Ontario, 14 December 2011, Statement Number: 2011-4197, *The Survivors Speak*, 141.
4. TRC, AVS, Mervin Mirasty, Statement to the Truth and Reconciliation Commission of Canada, Saskatoon, Saskatchewan, 21 June 2012, Statement Number: 2011-4391, *The Survivors Speak*, 141–142.
5. TRC, AVS, Robert Malcolm, Statement to the Truth and Reconciliation Commission of Canada, Winnipeg, Manitoba, 17 June 2010, Statement Number: 02-MB-16JU10-090, *The Survivors Speak*, 187.

I was very sports-oriented. I played baseball. Well, we play baseball, and even hockey. We had a hockey team. That was benefited, benefited me in a way 'cause I loved playing sports. Well, that's one way, too. I don't know how I did it but I was pretty good in sports.[6]

6. Paul Andrew, Inuvik, Northwest Territories

Paul Andrew spent seven years at Grollier Hall in Inuvik. One of his strongest and most positive memories related to school sports. At a Truth and Reconciliation Commission of Canada public dialogue in the school gymnasium in the Inuvik school, he recalled that he:

ran around this gym a lot of times, and this gym was a saviour for a lot of things because we were good at the physical stuff, we were good athletes, we were good at the sports. I don't know about people, I didn't do very good in classrooms because I didn't have the basics, the background in education. And there was times when I was called dumb and stupid and there were times when I felt dumb and stupid. But put me in a gym, there was not too many people better than I am. There were some, but not too many better than I. And so I loved it in the gyms. I loved it all in the cross-country trails, I loved it on the hockey, hockey arenas because they made me feel like I'm part of, they made me feel good. But in the education it wasn't quite the same.[7]

7. John Kistabish, Montreal, Quebec

John Kistabish was another of the students who took refuge in sports:

I really liked to play hockey. I liked a lot because we helped each other, you weren't alone, because I wanted to win. And, we had fun because we helped each other a lot.[8]

8. Albert Fiddler, Saskatoon, Saskatchewan

When [Albert] Fiddler got into trouble at school, the priest who coached the school team spoke up on his behalf:

He didn't want to lose his hockey player, he didn't want to lose his runner, because we get, we'll lose points if we want to compete.

Fiddler said the boys would often use department-store catalogues for shin pads, but a new principal had a greater interest in sports:

6. TRC, AVS, Christina Kimball, Statement to the Truth and Reconciliation Commission of Canada, Winnipeg, Manitoba, 17 January 2011, Statement Number: 03-001-10-020, *The Survivors Speak*, 189.
7. TRC, AVS, Paul Andrew, Statement to the Truth and Reconciliation Commission of Canada, Inuvik, Northwest Territories, 30 June 2011, Statement Number: NNE202, *The Survivors Speak*, 189–190.
8. TRC, AVS, John Kistabish, Statement to the Truth and Reconciliation Commission of Canada, 26 April 2013, Montreal, Quebec, Statement Number: 2011-6135190, *The Survivors Speak*, 190.

We started having new skates, start having good, good socks. We starting having bought, what you call, Toronto Maple Leafs and the Canadiens, those were the two, so we, we had two set of sweaters. And Maple Leafs, we used them at home, and then when we go out and play out we have to be Canadiens, so but none of those things, just toques, that's all, no facemask, nothing, no, no. We had little, finally we got those things, too. So, he bought all that stuff for us. So, we start getting bigger, better hockey players, too. We started competing. We came, we came and compete in town, in Meadow Lake. We had, they, they call us bush hockey players, but we, they couldn't beat us because we were, we were, we had a good coach, so we started winning.[9]

9. Orval Commanda, Spanish, Ontario

Orval Commanda recalled that sports played a positive role in his life at the Spanish, Ontario, boys' school, and that the opportunity to play sports was used as an incentive to get the students to do their school work:

So anyway in, when I came here, in '52, there was a lot of sports going on, and, and I was into sports, you know. I played hockey, and basketball, and at the time they played softball, like, and also played pool, because I started playing pool when I was seven years old. . . And I liked playing sports. You know if you wanted to be on a hockey team, you had to have your work done, you know?[10]

10. William Antoine, Little Current, Ontario

William Antoine was one of the students who credited Jesuit Father Maurice for the extensive sports program at the Spanish school.

The one thing I liked over there was the sports. Oh, there's, there's any sport you wanted to play. You know, there's basketball in the fall of the year, you know. And then hockey, you know, in the winter time. And, summer time there was softball, baseball, lacrosse. Lacrosse was my, my favourite sport; I really loved that sport and I was good at it too. A little ball you threw around to get in the net, yeah. I really liked that sport. And I was good at running; you know I was fast, I was skinny. You know I was pretty agile, that's why I loved that sport.[11]

---

9. TRC, AVS, Albert Fiddler, Statement to the Truth and Reconciliation Commission of Canada, Saskatoon, Saskatchewan, 24 June 2012, Statement Number: 2011-1760, *The Survivors Speak*, 190–191.

10. TRC, AVS, Orval Commanda, Statement to the Truth and Reconciliation Commission of Canada, Spanish, Ontario, 13 September 2009, Statement Number: 2011-5022, *The Survivors Speak*, 191.

11. TRC, AVS, William Antoine, Statement to the Truth and Reconciliation Commission of Canada, Little Current, Ontario, 12 May 2011, Statement Number: 2011-2002, *The Survivors Speak*, 191.

11. Roddy Soosay, Hobbema, Alberta

Not all students were athletic, and not all athletic experiences were positive. Roddy Soosay recalled that one of his physical education teachers at the Hobbema school was particularly sadistic.

> All I remember about him is grabbing the dodge ball and making me run and throwing it and hitting me in the head and thinking it was funny, and sent me flying. I remember him picking me up by the throat and holding me up in the air and I remember him dropping me and I was like—I don't know, thinking back, no more than three feet tall. And dropping me, and he's probably, what, six foot two, six foot three, somewhere around there. And holding me up in the air saying, I'm probably dropping from, you know, four or five feet over, and landing on my head. And all I remember is trying to stand up and getting kicked in the butt there from him. And this hockey stick—his broken hockey stick that everybody knew—he called it Hector. And he'd hit me and made me stand up. And I remember clearly because I wasn't able to straighten out my head. My head was on my shoulder like that and I couldn't straighten out my head. And I couldn't understand why I couldn't straighten out my head. It was a long time before I was able to stand up straight.[12]

12. Fred Sasakamoose

Even for successful students, sports might provide only limited comfort. Fred Sasakamoose, who became the first Treaty Indian to play in the National Hockey League, attended the Duck Lake, Saskatchewan, school in the 1940s. He said that the priests who ran the school were from Québec and loved hockey. During the winters, the boys had the opportunity to skate every day. But the school staff employed the same sort of discipline in sports as they did in every other aspect of school life. According to Sasakamoose:

> The priests never talked twice. The second time, you got the strap. But Father Roussell had a dream. He told me, "Freddie, I'm going to work you hard, but if you work hard, you're going *to be successful.*"[13]

He was correct: Sasakamoose was the star player on a team that won a provincial championship.[14] But he had also been seriously abused at the school. He left it as soon as he could.

> I said, "I'm going home to my mother." I was fifteen years old. "I'm going home." My gosh, I felt good. I felt that the world had changed, had opened a gate for me. There was no more wall on the other side of these girls that I never seen that were there for

12. TRC, AVS, Roddy Soosay, Statement to the Truth and Reconciliation Commission of Canada, Hobbema, Alberta, 25 July 2013, Statement Number: 2011-2379, *The Survivors Speak*, 193.
13. Don Marks, *They Call Me Chief: Warriors on Ice* (Winnipeg: J. Gordon Shillingford, 2008), 34—as cited in *The Survivors Speak*, 193.
14. TRC, NRA, INAC – Departmental Library – Ottawa, "Saskatchewan Midget Hockey Champions," Indian Record, volume 12, number 5, May 1949. [SMD-002829] and Marks, 31.

last ten years. We were segregated from them; you couldn't talk to them, even my own sister.[15]

When a priest brought a hockey scout to his family's home, Sasakamoose hid, convinced he was going to be taken back to school. It was only with coaxing that he agreed to play junior hockey in Moose Jaw.[16] Although he was a good player, he never felt that he fit into the world of professional sports:

> I look at myself sometimes and say, 'How in the hell did I ever get there?' I didn't want to be an athlete, I didn't want to be a hockey player, I didn't want to be anything. All I wanted was my parents."[17]

15. TRC, AVS, Fred Sasakamoose, Statement to the Truth and Reconciliation Commission of Canada, Prince Albert, Saskatchewan, 2 February 2012, Statement Number: SP043, *The Survivors Speak*, 193.
16. Marks, 35.
17. Sasakamoose, *The Survivors Speak*, 193.

PART II
Childhoods

Document 2
In the Beginning Was the Sweater:
L'abominable feuille d'érable of Ste-Justine

John Willis

Hockey is to Canadians what soccer has become for Europe, Latin America, and the rest of the world. It is the focus of intense loyalty, and sometimes bitter partisanship. We dream of the game and live through its ups and downs from one day to the next by following some combination of talented or favorite players, or, more commonly, by selecting a team whose cause we espouse until death do us part. Each NHL team can rely on a loyal fan base. The wearing of the hometown sweater is the symbol of belonging to the tribe. Many more Canadian cities have junior teams, instead of NHL ones, with enthusiasts numbering in the thousands, all more than willing to come out to the game. After all, the tickets cost a third to one-tenth of a ticket for an NHL game.

Each town has its amateur and professional fan traditions that, taken together, affect how the population experiences the game. The culture of hockey is shared, mediated, and passed from one generation to the next. You learn while young what to expect, whom to adulate. Thus it was that when Maurice Richard stood out on the ice at the final game to be played at the Montreal Forum, in 1996, and though it had been thirty-six years since he had retired from the Montreal Canadiens, he received a fifteen-minute standing ovation from the more than 18,000 fans in attendance. The vast majority of those present had never seen him play. No matter: this was the Rocket *en personne*. Richard was succeeded by Jean Béliveau and, later, Guy Lafleur, both of whom would fetch a roar of approval from the crowd when they stepped on the ice. But the engagement with the Rocket went much deeper, nowhere more so than in Quebec and French Canada. This brief piece is one effort to understand his popularity and, through him, that of our national sport, hockey. I will examine the issue simultaneously on two different scales, the one general, the other particular, for each feeds off the other. Certain general trends helped reinforce the popularity of hockey; other manifestations can only be ascertained at a more local, intimate level, for example, in Sainte-Justine, Quebec.[1]

1. My perspective on Sainte-Justine is informed by interviews conducted with Roch Carrier in May 2002: CMH Archives: A2015-0111. Two telephone interviews took place on January 19 and February 6, 2017. Je remercie vivement M. Carrier de sa collaboration. Stéphane Brûlé, président de la Société du Patrmoine de Sainte-Justine-de-Langevin, was also most

Canada's national sport today is broadcast to us on widescreen television on various channels. If worse comes to worse, we can listen to the game on a car radio or stream it online. When you pull into town for a short stay, you can always find out the score in the game from someone in the know: an airport worker or restaurant employee, or someone with a cell or wireless connection. One evening in May of 2010, the dispatcher of a St John's taxi service radioed all his drivers that the Canadiens had just scored a goal in a playoff game against the Pittsburgh Penguins. It was something they and their customers wanted to know. Word gets around fast and, to be honest, Canadians make for a willing audience. How to explain the popularity of the game in our country? Surely the media are important. But there are other agencies at work, not to mention the evolving historical context.

One explanation for the popularity of hockey here lies in the fact that so many of us learned how to skate and shoot the puck in our youth. The rudiments of the game can be learned by playing organized hockey on an artificial surface, indoors. Yet most of us carry an image of playing the game outdoors in sub-zero weather on a rough-edged natural surface. I spent part of my youth playing on outdoor rinks in Montreal and later Québec. To say the least, I was not a good player. I remember most the winter of 1968, when our parents took the family to the country in the lower St. Lawrence River region for a winter holiday. The highlight was an afternoon of pickup hockey on a rink squeezed behind the village school and the parish hall of Notre-Dame-du-Portage, where I could face off against the Saint-Pierres, Bouchers, Dickners, and those most formidable skaters from the Bélanger family of Chemin-du-Lac. My parents patiently watched me for a couple of hours; I was far outclassed by the others, but I didn't give a damn for I was living out a boyhood dream. In this perfect setting, I was surrounded by figurants who fully espoused and personified the hockey culture of Quebec, predicated on the principle of *le tout pour le tout*. When the puck went over the boards, it fell somewhere on or under the frozen ice surface of the St. Lawrence, never to appear again. The stakes were that high (Figure D2.1).

Across Canada, it is still to the outdoor rink that boys and girls turn when they want a quick game of hockey. The rink might be down a city street or beside the school or church in the heart of a village. In my neighbourhood of Aylmer, Quebec, the noise made by pucks hitting the boards of the outdoor rinks can resonate for a distance of meters and meters. With each shot, as we approach the ice to put on our skates, the sense of anticipation and excitement increases. It is like this for me, for my sons, indeed for many Canadians and Quebeckers, boys and girls. This is not just a game. This is a ritual, with historical roots.

Sainte-Justine, Quebec

History records that there were at least four different rinks succeeding one another in the village of Sainte-Justine, beginning in 1928 (Royer 1987). Sainte-Justine is located miles from nowhere, not far from the Canada-U.S. border, in the Appalachian backcountry east of Quebec City and Levis (Figure D2.2).[2] The third of these rinks, dating from 1942 and

---

helpful. Years ago Jacques Saint-Pierre did research on hockey in mail-order catalogues for me: merci!

2. Were one to properly define nowhere, it would have to be located on the American side of the border where, circa 1940, human habitations were few and landmarks bore such enchanting names as Mud Pond, Desolation Pond, etc.

Figure D2.1 Hazy Photograph, Sharp Memory
This hazy image captures the outdoor rink at Notre-Dame-du-Portage in the winter of 1968. The author is in the background.
Personal collection of John Willis

situated near the church, was the work of M. le curé A. Bourque, who, unlike his predecessor, believed that sport in general and hockey in particular was good for his parishioners. (A fourth rink would come in 1947, complete with regulation four-foot-high boards, a changing room, and a new string of electric lights for nighttime play. The old rink had lights as well.) The church-side 1942 rink is the starting point of Roch Carrier's classic tale, *The Hockey Sweater*. Originally published in a collection of short stories in 1979, then under the title "L'abominable feuille d'érable sur la glace," and subsequently broadcast on a network morning show of CBC Radio, Carrier depicts how he first experienced the game as a participant on the outdoor rink at Sainte-Justine.[3] The mother of the protagonist in the

3. Carrier informs me that Sheila Fischman translated the draft in one weekend.

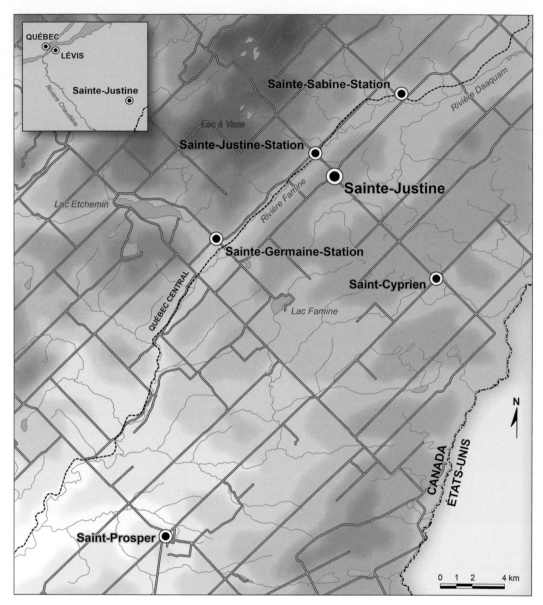

Figure D2.1 Ste-Justine, Quebec
Map showing location of Ste-Justine in eastern Québec and the immediate environs of the village.
Map by Andrée Héroux

story orders a new hockey sweater for her son (Roch) from the Eaton's catalogue. Tragically, she is sent the blue sweater of the Toronto Maple Leafs, not the red, white, and blue one of the Montreal Canadiens. She makes him wear it, this despite that all the skaters on the ice at Sainte-Justine wore the number-nine sweater of Maurice Richard. Out on the ice, it was five skaters impersonating the Rocket facing off against five others, identically attired like the Rocket. The story, fabulously narrated by Carrier in the NFB animated film (1980), shows how the loyalty of the young players to the image of Richard is cultivated by a process of re-enactment, in which all the players imagine they are Richard. Even the parish priest gets into the act, for he refereed the games. These kinds of theatrical re-enactments, village by village, rink after rink, were essential to the star system that underlay the popularity of NHL players like Richard.

The story is set in 1946. The NHL, founded in 1917, was barely thirty years old. The league was not then a venerable institution. Moreover, other sports such as baseball were very, if not equally, popular as of the 1920s.[4] Carrier's elders could easily recall the year when the NHL was first introduced. That would be at roughly the same time that the first telephone lines were brought into the backcountry of Bellechasse and Dorchester counties. These were built by the federal government over 1917–1918, perhaps as a wartime measure? They may have been designed to complement a larger, private network, whose lines extended down toward the lower St. Lawrence.[5] At the conclusion of the First World War, the lines and equipment of the federal system were leased to a small local private company, which in turn was succeeded by other local private concerns over the next two decades. The system was somewhat defective. The poles were not set deep enough in the ground, and according to one inspection dating from 1934, "trees (instead of poles) are much used when handy."[6] It would take some time to integrate these small patches into an interlocking whole.

The Carrier's had a phone in their home. Access to it was governed by Mother; it was not a device for children. She would speak with her husband, a travelling salesman, who was frequently on the road. Meanwhile, grandfather Tanguay would literally shout into the mouthpiece to make sure that his son at the other end of the line, in Saint-Eustache, could hear what he had to say. Grandpapa reasoned that it was necessary to raise his voice, as if shouting at someone at the far end of a field.

The telephone helped keep the people of Sainte-Justine in touch with the rest of the world. So did the railway. Beginning in 1909, the village was serviced by the Quebec Central Railway.[7] The eastern branch of the Quebec Central ran from Saint-Georges de Beauce, by Sainte-Justine Station, then past the neighboring village of Sainte-Sabine and onward to Lac Frontière, the end of the line. This end of the line, true to its name, was astride the border. Canada Customs established a small outport and warehousing facility there in 1930.[8] As a youngster, Roch Carrier and friends would watch the train go by from a hill up by the village. The train ran along a valley formed by the two rivers: the Daaquam and the

---

4. J. Dion, "Le baseball, populaire au fil de générations," *Le Devoir*, January 9, 2017.
5. The larger private network was the Bellechasse Telephone Company. Its lines extended from Bellechasse and Montmagny all the way downriver to Rimouski and Matane. Jonathan Vance, *Building Canada: People and Projects that Shaped the Nation* (Toronto, Penguin, 2006), 177. Vance (184–85) points out that small rural independents made a vital contribution to the spread of the telephone in rural Quebec as elsewhere in Canada.
6. L.A.C.: RG-12 vol. 1696, file 7282-182, Telegraphs Telephones St-Cyprien and Ste-Justine, Qué.; Volume 2. Memo for Dep Min of Public Works from General Sup of Gov Tel Serv, July 28, 1934. See same series volume 1 ; Memorandum, for Deputy Minister of Public Works, Dorchester County: Lines Ste-Justine-St-Cyprien, Jan. 12, 1926.
7. Serge Courville et al., *Histoire de Beauce-Etchemin-Amiante* (Collection Les Régions du Québec 16) (Québec: Presses de l'Université Laval – IQRC, 2003), 372.
8. *National Revenue Review* 3 (7) (April 1930): 13.

Famine; the village was buttressed to the south by a series of four hills, each 1,400 feet in elevation or more. There was always something to see down by the station, or at the sawmill next door. Later in his youth, while travelling back home on the train from boarding school in Saint-Georges, Carrier received his first course on how to swear from a group of helpful and possibly inebriated lumberjacks. The trains carried lumber, freight, and people, all of which or whom had to get off somewhere with their baggage, cultural and physical.

With the railway came the mail, day in, day out. Sainte-Justine-Station had a post office, as did the village proper. Mail contractor Monsieur Brochu carried mail bags on his horse-drawn buggy the short distance, back and forth, between the train station and the village post office. At the village post office, in 1925, Arthur Rancourt took over as postmaster following the death of the previous incumbent, Misrael Tanguay.[9] A veteran of the First World War, with striking tattoos on his forearms, which are depicted in *The Hockey Sweater*, Rancourt ran the post office from an add-on structure adjacent to the family home for the next thirty years. He was, recalls Carrier, on a one-and-one basis an affable man, but he was a strict disciplinarian when his post office was invaded in late afternoon following the arrival of the mail. Rancourt had a son, Zalpha, who was four or five years older than Carrier. Zalpha was blind yet he was respected by one and all. He even served as umpire in local sandlot baseballs games. No matter the ball-game situation, his decisions were accepted, "aucune chicane quand Zalpha a dit ça," recalls Carrier. This sign of respect was perhaps a recognition of his belonging to the family of the postmaster. Postmasters were well-respected village notables in their day.[10]

It was during Rancourt's time behind the wicket that teams in the NHL undertook more aggressive marketing campaigns, reaching out to hockey fans present and prospective. The mail would play an important role in popularizing the game. Readers of *The Hockey Sweater* will recall that it was by mail that the young Roch received his abominable Leafs sweater (Figure D2.3).

Selling the NHL

In the 1930s, popular and or talented NHL hockey players increasingly became ambassadors of the sport. On the ice, players' sweaters were given numbers so that it was easier for spectators to identify them. Off the ice, their names were prominently featured on the sports pages of newspapers. Hockey stars were recruited to help sell hockey equipment with their likeness appearing in mail-order catalogues. The catalogues had been selling hockey equipment for decades, what was new was the enrollment of NHL stars in the campaign. Both Joe Malone and George Hainsworth were endorsing hockey equipment, and therefore their own team, the Canadiens, in the 1931–32 catalogue of the Omer de Serres department store. Two years later, we find this in the Eaton's fall-winter (1933–34) catalogue: "Now use the stick of your favorite player." Fans could chose an autographed hockey stick with the

---

9. Tanguay is a common family name in and around Sainte-Justine, a name synonymous with generations of businessmen, farmers, and hockey players. A list of postmasters at Ste-Justine (Langevin) can be found at https://www.bac-lac.gc.ca/eng/discover/postal-heritage-philately/post-offices-postmasters/Pages/item.aspx?IdNumber=12451&.

10. Chantal Amyot and John Willis, *Country Post. Rural Postal Service in Canada, 1880 to 1945* (CPM Mercury no. 1), Gatineau, Canadian Museum of Civilization, 2003.

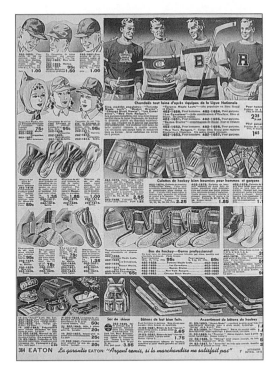

Figure D2.3 Eaton's Fall-Winter Catalogue, 1941–42 Men's NHL hockey sweaters for $2.35; A variety of hockey sticks, socks, and pants were also for sale from Eaton's.
Reproduced from a private collection

name of one or other of three popular players on the Toronto Maple Leafs: Ken Deraty, King Clancy and goal tender Lorne Chabot." Red Horner, a 190-pound hard-hitting defenceman, was a favorite of Leafs fans. Not surprisingly, he was a regular feature of the Eaton's catalogue in the 1930s. Joe Primeau, centreman for the Leafs' well-known Kid Line, endorsed hockey gloves for Eaton's and hockey sticks for Simpson's. Eventually, by the early 1940s, the star Leafs player Syl Apps would make it onto the pages of the Simpson's catalogue as well.[11]

During the 1950s, Rocket Richard started appearing in the French-language editions of Eaton's catalogues, endorsing skates and hockey outfits. A good-looking windbreaker (plus overalls and sweatshirt) sporting his image could be ordered from the mid-winter Dupuis Frères catalogue of 1951–52. Throughout Quebec, the mail-order catalogue helped sustain the Richard brand. But the groundswell of popular support was likely ignited at the outset by extensive coverage of the Rocket's exploits in the written press—these newspapers were likely delivered to Sainte-Justine through the post—and regular broadcast of Habs games over the airwaves of Radio Canada from the Montreal Forum, beginning in 1939.[12]

The advent of radio broadcasting from the Montreal Forum was timely. It came after one of the two Montreal teams in the NHL, the Maroons, was disbanded in 1938.[13] The Canadiens were now the only show in town; they had the Forum ice and the airwaves of Quebec unto themselves. Moreover, they acquired the star player of the Maroons, Hector "Toe" Blake. In a sense, Blake would for a time replace Howie Morenz, the Habs star player who tragically died during the 1936–37 season. Maurice Richard first played for the

11. See John Willis, "Professional Hockey and the Mail-order Catalogue," Canadian Museum of History, http://www.historymuseum.ca/cmc/exhibitions/cpm/catalog/cat2207e.shtml. I wish to acknowledge the work of Jacques Saint-Pierre in this research.

12. Beginning in 1928, the Montreal games were broadcast by CKAC, the private station owned by the daily newspaper *La Presse* (see "L'invention de la radio," Société Radio-Canada, http://ici.radio-canada.ca/emissions/l_invention_de_la_radio/2011-2012/chronologie.asp). Meanwhile, in the rest of Canada, Foster Hewitt was broadcasting Leaf games from Maple Leaf Gardens, in Toronto, to a national English-speaking audience as of 1933 via a network of private stations. He would broadcast the games to Canadian troops stationed overseas during the Second World War.

13. This was a business decision, not a sentimental one. Both teams belonged to the same owner.

Canadiens, in the 1942–43 season, scoring his first goal in the second period of a home game against the Rangers, on November 8. The Habs defeated their rivals that night by a score of ten to four. Richard's goal was the result of an end-to-end rush. He ultimately managed to get around the defenceman and put the puck in the top-right corner of the net. It was, according to the report in *La Patrie*, "le plus bel exploit de la soirée" and earned him an "ovation formidable." The fans liked what they saw, and they wanted more.[14] A few games later he was injured and had to sit out the rest of the season. The following year he rebounded, scoring thirty-two goals in forty-six games. The next season, 1944–45, he set a record by scoring fifty goals in fifty games. He played on a trio nicknamed the Punch Line, together with Elmer Lach and Blake, the former Maroon. The team was successful, winning the Stanley Cup in 1943–44 and again in 1945–46. By the time Carrier begins his memoir of playing hockey in 1946, the Rocket had three years of celebrity status behind him.[15] He had become a star in the media. The people of Sainte-Justine were more than ready for him.

Sainte-Justine in the Late 1940s

In 1946, Roch Carrier was nine years old. He belonged to a generation that was hooked on radio; radio as a source of news on the war in Europe and the Pacific; radio as a means of spending an intense Saturday night listing to the weekly broadcast of the Habs game from the Forum. Entire families assembled to listen to these broadcasts, Carrier recalls. They might gather in a private home, as did the Carrier's—they had their own radio—or at the general store of J. A. Sirois, located next to the rink, where radio-less hockey fans would rub shoulders.[16] A cut above the others, the Sirois household was known for owning the first Edison phonograph in their village, and one of the first Kodak cameras. The next day, the game was the talk of the town, inside church or outside: on the steps, at the barbershop, at the general store, or, of course, out on the rink. Youngsters dreamed of "playing on the radio" just like the professionals. To the children, hockey was more important than the war itself. It is as if they inhabited an adolescent world hived off from the adult one.

> Already night is spreading over the village. Windows glow with a yellowish light. We haven't noticed that the day is over. The match goes on. Shouts of triumph, insults, the clatter of sticks as they meet. The click of the blades of our sticks against the turd. Our mothers shivering in their open doorways, call us to come in and do our homework. It's pointless. When we're playing hockey we don't hear our mothers.[17]

In Carrrier's day, a hockey stick cost all of 69¢. He would pay for it out of his meagre pay as an altar boy, 10¢ per mass. Out on the ice, Carrier recalls strapping Eaton's catalogues to his shins for protection, held in place by pieces of rubber cut out from a tire's inner tube.

---

14. *La Patrie*, November 9, 1942. The game started at 9 p.m.; tickets cost between $1.25 and $2.50, taxes included.
15. This accurately depicted in Sheldon's Cohen's illustration that appears in *The Hockey Sweater*.
16. Royer et al. (1987, 421). The Sirois radio can be viewed at the historic site operated by the Société de patrimoine de Sainte-Justine.
17. Roch Carrier, *Our Life with the Rocket: The Maurice Richard Story* (Toronto: Viking, 2001), 15–16.

For Christmas, he received new, felted shin pads, but they were mostly leather and offered little protection. Carrier went back to using the catalogues. And even these did not always do the job properly. Carrier recalls the time that Pousse Gagné, a young veteran of the Second World War and son of the station master, bore down on him, Carrier was playing defence at the time, and took a shot that hit his leg and hurt an awful lot. So much for catalogue protection.

Of his experience on the ice, Carrier has vivid memories, which include putting skates on at home and skating over to the hockey rink. The village roads were perfect for skating as they hardened under the repeated passage of horse-drawn sleighs. The rink was a school of life. He learned to compete and assert himself, find tricks to go through the defence, all the while improving his overall performance. These social skills—*se faire reconnaître, se faire respecter, comment négocier, comment jouer en équipe, comment jouer individuellement*—prepared him for the boardrooms and council tables he would frequent later in life. The point he makes implicitly is that despite the micro scale of social life, a surprisingly broad brand of human behaviours could be encountered on and off the ice in a village. The experience was of a piece with communities nestled in larger, urban-industrial societies. As historians and urban villagers, we do ourselves no good by underestimating the depth of human experience in past rural societies.

The farmers and villagers of Sainte-Justine, as elsewhere, moved within their respective conclaves but were rarely out of touch with the wider society. News, fashion, gossip from the outside was seized upon with vigour. Back in his day, Carrier recounts, one couldn't watch (or listen to) one or more hockey broadcasts per night. Television was unknown, computers and Internet unimaginable; even books were sparse—likely a disappointment to Carrier, who was a good student. Movies were shown, on occasion, at the parish hall, but they only became a regular feature during the late 1940s.[18] We had few things Carrier says: "C'est pourquoi on donnait tellement d'importance au peu de chose qu'on avait. Le hockey faisait partie de ce peu de chose." Hockey brought an extra dash of colour to daily life in Sainte-Justine. It weaved itself into the interstices of village daily life.

With a population of 1,904 people in 1951, Sainte-Justine was not a big town. Nearby Sainte-Germaine (3,554) and Saint-Prosper (2,865) were larger.[19] The population was overwhelmingly Catholic and French-speaking; there was one person of the Jewish faith and one person of "other" persuasion. Parishioners went to church in a building dating from 1937—the previous church burnt down the year before—and children attended school either at the village convent, where Carrier went, or at one of the schoolhouses in the outlying areas. A few craft shops were located in the village. These made axe handles, iron implements, and school trunks. The main business of economy was out of town and revolved around the cultivation of hay and dairy farming. The 176 farmers shared between them 1,860 cattle, almost as many swine (1,852), and 261 horses. Farmers took care of their

---

18. Royer et al. (1987, 207–08). The Sainte-Justine movie business truly came into own in 1948, when the Chabot brothers established the Cinéma Étoile and began showing 35-mm films at the parish hall specifically leased for this purpose.
19. Data from Canada, Dominion Bureau of Statistics, Census of Canada 1951: volume 1 "Population. General Characteristics"; see Table 6-16, Dorchester County; Volume 6 Agriculture: Canada, Newfoundland, P.E.I., Nova Scotia, New Brunswick, Québec", Table 31. >>

livestock, spraying the stables with DDT to keep out pesky insects; they apparently also sprayed the interior of their homes for the same reason.[20]

Aerial photos show substantial land clearings, but the forest was never far away. The nearby and heavily wooded mountain slopes, with their large stands of sugar maples, were ideal for maple-syrup production. A boiled maple-sap concoction—known as *petit reduit d'eau d'érable*—was used to combat the grippe.[21] The bush provided ample seasonal opportunities for workers and entrepreneurs. Local member of Parliament Tremblay advised the minister of transport in December of 1948 not to commence work on the telephone line between Sainte-Justine and the nearby village of Saint-Cyprien until the following year as local manpower was already engaged in winter logging activities. One enterprising resident of Sainte-Justine, Clothaire Nadeau, ran a cross-border logging operation in New Hampshire in 1948. It is more than likely that some of his workers and his horses were from Sainte-Justine.[22] Above, Carrier refers to the distance between mother and sons: when boys were out on the ice they ignored the call to come home. The space between mothers and sons may have had something to do with the fact that not a few fathers in Sainte-Justine, as elsewhere, were absent for weeks at a time, seasonally employed as *bûcherons* in one forest shanty or another. There were grandparents around. Did they, could they, pick up the slack in terms of paternal authority?

Over the years the economy of Sainte-Justine experienced its ups and downs. The depression of the 1930s devastated rural people here and elsewhere, for there was no viable market for agricultural produce, maple syrup, and lumber. By the 1940s the economy was rebounding.[23] There was more money to spend, more to deposit in the local savings-and-loan institutions. The first caisse populaire, a financial co-operative, in Sainte-Justine dates from 1938. Farmers did there banking here, Carrier recalls, while the villagers would entrust their savings to the local branch of the Banque canadienne nationale. Life was improving for Roch Carrier's peers and parents. The people were not becoming rich, but they were better off. Perhaps the relative increase in wealth helped foster a rising enthusiasm for the game. Victory in the battlefield, victory on the ice, and money in the bank were all part of a more buoyant social and economic scene.

In the Sainte-Justine of 1946, in a manner of speaking, the lights were coming on out on the rink and down on the farm. Whatever it was that people did over and above their daily routine of shovelling manure, chopping wood, and cooking for a large and hungry family was bound to symbolize that part of life that was making things better. No culture can forgo a certain sense of play and leisure over and above the satisfaction of immediate needs. And in Sainte-Justine, what better symbolic lightning rod for the new life than hockey.

---

20. Interview with Roch Carrier, January 19, 2017.
21. Royer et al. (1987, 194).
22. Library and Archives Canada: RG-17 Vol. 3417, File no. 1500-33-10, Claim for subsidy on Export oats made by Cloutaire Nadeau, Sainte-Justine, Quebec, correspondence dated October 26, 1948 (this includes a plea for support from Prime Minister Louis Saint-Laurent). See also LAC RG-12 vol. 1696, file 7282-182, Telegraphs Telephones Saint-Cyprien and Sainte-Justine, Qué.; Vol. 2 . Deputé (L.D. Tremblay) au Min des transports (L. Chevrier), 3 déc 1948. On the petie reduit d'eau d'érable, see Royer et al. (1987, 194). A peppered molasses syrup was used for throat infections.
23. Courville et al. (2003, 605–06).

Dressed in team sweaters, youngsters played in full view of the rest of the village, who attended the games, paid for the rink and equipment, and at times shovelled off the ice. As they skated and scored, the players mimicked what the professionals were doing on radio's *Soirée du hockey*. Here was a concrete re-enactment of the wider imagined community. A dream at once aspired to and played out *in situ* and in plain view. Here is one explanation for the rise of Maurice Richard and our national sport—a tradition invented in the 1930s and 1940s, and cherished, oh so dearly, to this day (Figure D2.4).

Bibliography

Amyot, Chantal and John Willis, *Country Post. Rural Postal Service in Canada, 1880 to 1945* (CPM Mercury no. 1), Gatineau, Canadian Museum of Civilization, 2003.

Carrier, Roch, *Les enfants du bonhomme dans la lune*, Montréal, Libre Expression, 2007 (originally published in 1979 by les éditions Stanké)

Carrier, Roch, *The Hockey Sweater*, Toronto, Tundra Books, 1984.

Courville, Serge et al., *Histoire de Beauce-Etchemin-Amiante* (Collection Les Régions du Québec 16), Québec: Presses de l'Université Laval – IQRC, 2003.

Canada, Dominion Bureau of Statistics, *Census of Canada 1951*: volume 1 "Population. General Characteristics"; see Table 6-16, Dorchester County; Volume 6 Agriculture: Canada, Newfoundland, P.E.I., Nova Scotia, New Brunswick, Québec", Table 31.

Lapointe, Etienne, « Maurice Richard ; l'origine d'une passion partisane, 1942–1945 », in *HistoireEngagé. ca* (4 avril 2017). http://histoireengagee.ca/?p=6907

Melançon, Benoit, *Les yeux de Maurice Richard : Une histoire culturelle*, Montréal, Fides, 2006. (See as well H-Net review of English translation of this book by Jason Blake, H-Net Reviews, August 2009)

Posen, Sheldon, *626 par 9. Une énumération chronologique des buts marqués par Maurice « Rocket » Richard*, Gatineau, Musée canadien des civilisations, 2004.

Figure D2.4 Outdoor Game in Ste-Justine, Quebec, during the 1940s
With a priest officiating, young players take to the ice at Ste-Justine, Québec.
Société du Patrimoine de Ste-Justine-de-Langevin

Royer, G. et al. 1987. *Cent vingt-cinquième Sainte-Justine, 1862–1987*, Sainte-Justine : s.n.

Vance, Jonathan, *Building Canada. People and Projects that Shaped the Nation*, Toronto, Penguin, 2006.

Willis, John, "Professional Hockey and the Mail-order Catalogue," *Before E-Commerce*, Canadian Museum of History : http://www.historymuseum.ca/cmc/exhibitions/cpm/catalog/cat2207e.shtml

Chapter 4
Decolonizing the Hockey Novel: Ambivalence and Apotheosis in Richard Wagamese's *Indian Horse*

SAM McKEGNEY AND TREVOR J. PHILLIPS

> "White ice, white players," I said. "You gonna tell me that isn't the case everywhere? That they don't think it's their game wherever a guy goes?"
> He took his time answering. "It's not a perfect country," he said. "But it is a perfect game."
> Richard Wagamese, *Indian Horse*

Through the story of Saul Indian Horse, an Ojibway hockey prodigy who learns the game in residential school and whose potential rise to hockey stardom is hindered by traumatic legacies of personal abuse and the entrenched racism of Canadian hockey culture, Ojibway novelist Richard Wagamese lays bare, in his 2012 novel *Indian Horse*, heinous transgressions conducted in the name of Canadian nationhood. Yet part of what has made the novel such a commercial success in Canada is its fluency with and seamless incorporation of popular cultural tropes about the game—tropes that tend to glorify white-settler citizenship, thereby normalizing senses of territorial belonging for white players, fans, and coaches, while clouding the history of dispossession of Indigenous lands and the dehumanization of Indigenous peoples through which the Canadian nation state has been forged.[1]

In this chapter, we seek to understand and unpack the ambivalence of Wagamese's portrayal of hockey as both confining and liberating, as both a tool of Canadian nationalism and a means of Indigenous self-expression and resilience. Despite awareness expressed in the

---

1. As Michael Buma and others have argued, these tropes are found throughout most literature about hockey in Canada. There are three book-length investigations of Canadian hockey literature as a genre, or sub-genre: Hughes-Fuller (2002) focuses on hockey as a sub-culture, Blake (2010) offers the first extensive look at hockey books, and Buma (2012) investigates what he refers to as "the Canadian hockey myth" in literary representations of the sport. Other work that looks specifically at the relationship between Canadian nationalism and hockey includes Dryden and MacGregor (1989), Gruneau and Whitson (1993), McKinley (2001), Howell (2001), Dopp and Harrison (2009), and Dowbiggin (2011).

novel that hockey has functioned as a tool of settler colonialism in Canada and that it continues to be implicated in nationalist mythologies that normalize white privilege while effacing colonial transgressions, *Indian Horse* conveys such an abiding affection for hockey's beauty, grace, and artistry that it seems open to the claim articulated in the epigraph above: "But it is a perfect game" (Wagamese 2012, 150). Ultimately, we argue that *Indian Horse* does not tear down popular conceptions of hockey in Canada and offer some radically decolonial alternative in its stead; rather, in order to depict the healing journey at the novel's core, it tears those representations open in order to expose the traumatic colonial foundations upon which hockey narratives are frequently built, and which they often work to conceal.

And herein lies the novel's decolonial potential: written during the Truth and Reconciliation Commission of Canada's (TRC) exploration into the legacy of Indian residential schools, *Indian Horse* adopts the form of both a retrospective retirement narrative, so common to sport literature, and a residential-school survivor's testimony. In the retirement-narrative form, much of the story's overarching pathos emerges from the reader's recognition that, although he is still a relatively young person at age thirty-three, Saul, the narrator, considers his best self forever confined to the past; the narrative arc conscripts remembrance of past glory and past failure in a struggle to grieve the loss of the elite athletic self and to reconcile with an altered life stage in search of a renewed sense of purpose. In the testimony form, residential-school survivors share personal truths about their experiences in order to embolden the public record and disseminate greater knowledge that might form a foundation of understanding upon which various forms of reconciliation—with oneself, one's family, one's community, perhaps even one's oppressors—might become possible. Wagamese weaves these narrative postures together meticulously to speak in a semiotic register that resonates with urgent Indigenous concerns and that is simultaneously capable of leveraging hockey's popular cultural caché to illuminate ongoing colonial oppression in Canada. In this way, Wagamese's novel targets both Indigenous and settler audiences, opening up sovereign spaces for Indigenous reflection while struggling to change the nation by changing how Canadians understand "their" game. Thus, although *Indian Horse* is defiantly not a decolonial novel, we argue in what follows that it performs significant decolonial work by imagining an indigenized apotheosis of hockey that might foster individual healing by elaborating an ethic of community; rather than locating the wounded Indigenous player as the primary site for pursuing positive change, *Indian Horse* concludes with an awareness of the vitality of Indigenous communities as the foundation upon which such individual healing is contingent. The game that readers experience at the novel's conclusion is thus an indigenized form of hockey that reaffirms the game's collaborative energies in the cause of Indigenous communal empowerment.[2]

---

2. As settler scholar Patrick Wolfe argues (2006, 388), "invasion is a structure not an event" because in settler colonial contexts, the colonizers have not left, they often outnumber the Indigenous inhabitants they have displaced, and they continually work to naturalize and re-entrench logics and institutions that reify the legitimacy of their sense of belonging. We consider "decolonization" an expansive collection of activist practices and ideas that works to destabilize the authority of that structure, mute the expressions of its power, and open up possibilities for alternative ways of being in the world that emerge from Indigenous world views. Because hockey literature

Indigenous Ambivalence and Settler Belonging through Hockey

As the Calgary poet Richard Harrison has argued (personal communication), hockey is a vehicle through which Canadians "make meaning out of winter" and thereby establish a sense of belonging in the northern landscape. Popular discourse celebrating hockey as "Canada's game" naturalizes the Canadian nation state while valorizing those who participate in it (players, coaches, and spectators) as authentic inhabitants of the "True North" from which the game has supposedly sprung. According to Michael Buma (2012, 37), the central pillars of what he calls "the Canadian hockey myth" are the resilient beliefs (i) that hockey arises naturally from the Canadian landscape, (ii) that the game fosters social cohesion and civic virtue, and (iii) that the game ultimately offers a synecdoche for Canadian culture. In this way, hockey has functioned as a vehicle for what literary critic Terry Goldie terms "indigenization," a process through which settlers confront "the impossible necessity of becoming indigenous" (1989, 13): responding to the psychological compulsion to legitimize entitlement *to* the land, settlers seek to manufacture senses of belonging *in* the land. As hockey becomes reified as a natural by-product of the Canadian landscape, purveyors of the game promote senses of "Native Canadian" identity among those who play it, in the process erasing—or denying—differential senses of belonging among First Nations, Inuit, and Métis people who may or may not self-identify as "Canadian." Saul's narrative in *Indian Horse* exposes the incongruously exclusionary nature of this process of claiming territory through sport: "The white people thought it was their game. They thought it was their world" (Wagamese 2012, 136).

Ironically, the semiotic capital of indigeneity is often retained in this process of national legitimation via the circulation of language and images that conjure a stereotyped Indigenous-warrior past in team logos, mascots, and names—Warriors, Blackhawks, Braves, Redmen—while ignoring the political persistence of Indigenous nations. It is unsurprising that the first non-Indigenous team against which Saul's Manitouwadge Moose play is the "Chiefs." Goldie frames this form of semiotic accumulation as "indigenization by inclusion for the white who, one might say, 'acquires Indian.' Note that my word is 'acquires,' not 'becomes.' . . . The indigene is acquired, the white is not abandoned" (1989, 215). In this way, the characteristics associated with (imagined) Indigenous hyper-masculinity are absorbed within an almost exclusively white-settler arena, thereby advancing the colonial imperative that the future belongs to white-settler Canadians and that living Indigenous people remain anachronistic. Thus, the imagined relationship between hockey and landscape in Canada has tended to foster a sense of "authentic" belonging for settler and other non-Indigenous Canadians while obfuscating the relationships to land that continue to obtain for Indigenous individuals, communities, and nations. It is hardly surprising, then, that *Hockey Night in Canada* was a cornerstone of nationalist programming on radio and then television for the Canadian Broadcasting Corporation for more than eighty years: the program, now under licence by another network, continues to enable settler populations—including those who have never set a booted blade upon a frozen pond or lake anywhere

---

tends to obfuscate the horrific realities of settler-colonial history and to reify the Canadian nation state, we write from the position that hockey literature is most often a colonial genre.

in lands claimed by Canada—to collectively envision and indeed participate in the "imagined community" of the Canadian nation.[3]

Complicating matters further, hockey was mobilized historically in residential schools as a tool of colonial social engineering designed to encourage Indigenous youth to shed connections with Indigenous cultural values and self-identify as Canadian citizens. Several historical studies have documented (generally male) students playing hockey at residential schools (e.g., Milloy 1999, Miller 1996, Johnston 1988), activities permitted according to the belief that sport fosters civic virtue. As such, the sport is also laden with the historical weight of its use within systemic structures designed to "kill the Indian, and save the man." In *Indian Horse*, upon arrival at the residential school, Saul is told, "At St. Jerome's we work to remove the Indian from our children so that the blessings of the Lord may be evidenced upon them." Father Quinney continues: "Industry, boys. . . . Good, honest work and earnest study. That's what you'll do here. That's what will prepare you for the world" (Wagamese 2012, 47). Hockey and other recreational activities become what Michael Robidoux calls "disciplining device[s]" (2012, 13) within the residential school's pedagogical arsenal designed to inculcate Eurocentric notions of "industry" among the students.

However, despite the game's deployment to enforce prescriptive identity formations in young players like Saul, the experiences of Indigenous residential-school students playing the game did not always—nor perhaps even regularly—align with the motivations of institutional overseers. At the celebrations for the delivery of the TRC's *Final Report*, chairperson Chief Wilton Littlechild, of the Maskwacîs Cree Nation, explained how playing hockey was imperative to his ability to endure the trauma of his residential-school years, an experience corroborated by scores of survivors throughout the TRC's statement-gathering process. The summary of the TRC's report states (TRC 2015b, 112) that sport "helped them [students] make it through residential school," and the *Final Report* itself says (TRC 2015a, 199) that "the opportunity to play sports at residential schools made their lives more bearable and gave them a sense of identity, accomplishment, and pride." Evan Habkirk and Janice Forsyth (2016) write that although these statements are "certainly true," they worry that this

> glosses over the distinct and diverse ways to understand the role and significance of physical activities in these schools. We wonder, for instance, to what extent did school officials, including instructors, missionaries, and government agents, use physical activities to exploit the students for social, political, and economic gain? And how did the students transform the meanings that were attached to these activities to "make it through" these highly oppressive environments, especially since many of the activities were intended to eradicate and replace traditional Aboriginal values and practices?

The False Promise of Inclusion

Wagamese's novel takes as its thematic core the tensions between hockey as a means of achieving momentary emancipation from the carceral space of the residential school and hockey as an activity laden with racist, sexist, and anthropocentric ideological baggage that

---

3. Tellingly, Saul describes *Hockey Night in Canada* as "the personification of magic" (Wagamese 2012, 59) when he encounters it in Father Leboutilier's quarters at the residential school. Here, we rely on Benedict Anderson's (2006) theorization of imagined communities.

has served to mask and make possible the abuse of Indigenous youth. Wagamese thus lays bare two significant contradictions that conspire to marginalize Indigenous peoples in Canada: the first pertains to the insidious false promise of assimilation through residential-school social engineering, and the second involves the pervasive lie (so often treated as truth within Canadian hockey literature) that hockey is inevitably a vehicle for intercultural inclusion and social harmony. We explore each of these contradictions below.

In 1887, Prime Minister John A. Macdonald explained the motivations behind the Indian Act: "The great aim of our legislation has been to do away with the tribal system and assimilate the Indian people in all respects with the inhabitants of the Dominion as speedily as they are fit for the change" (quoted in Ennamorato 1998, 72). In 1920, Minister of Indian Affairs Duncan Campbell Scott famously related this assimilative objective to residential-school policy, arguing, "I want to get rid of the Indian problem. . . . Our objective is to continue until there is not a single Indian in Canada that has not been absorbed into the body politic, and there is no Indian question, and no Indian Department" (quoted in Milloy 1999, 46). Beyond signalling the culturally genocidal motivations behind both the Indian Act and residential schooling, these quotations express strategic goals of absorption and inclusion that residential schools were fundamentally incapable of facilitating because of structural limitations and widespread racism within the broader cultural milieu.

While official rhetoric suggested that residential schooling would place Indigenous students on par with their mainstream Canadian counterparts in order to foster equality, the education they received was so far below that received by mainstream Canadian students as to engender profound disadvantages (even apart from the debilitating traumatic cultural loss, separation from loved ones, and rampant abuse). Most residential-school students received formal education for only a fraction of their nominal school day, with the rest taken up by prayer and the manual labour upon which the institutions relied, and the instruction students did receive was commonly delivered by religious staff with no formal pedagogical training. Furthermore, Indigenous students tended to be taught outmoded skills related to domestic work, manual trades, and farming, while most non-Indigenous students across the country experienced a breadth of instruction designed to prepare them for entry into an industrialized Canadian economy (see Milloy 1999, 157–80). When they finally emerged from residential school, Indigenous students needed to compete for jobs within a labour market characterized by racist hiring practices of employers whose views about Indigenous people were influenced by the very cultural biases that undergirded residential-school policies in the first place. Thus, the supposed goal of integration and assimilation through social engineering was disingenuous from the beginning.

In fact, at the same time that the residential-school system was expanding to its peak, in the 1940s and 1950s, Indian Affairs was embarking on a policy of "centralization" on the East Coast designed to relocate Mi'kmaq people from sundry communities and small reserves to two large reserves at Eskasoni and Shubenacadie as a means of ensuring the *absence* of Indigenous peoples within or around white communities in Nova Scotia. Clearly the goals of assimilation and absorption articulated by Macdonald and Scott ran counter to the segregationist thrust of centralization. Such are the contradictions within the federal government's treatment of Indigenous peoples over time. As one of us has written elsewhere,

Residential school policy has always been . . . perplexed with its 'cultural progressivist' agenda dogged by endemic racism; never has the political goal of assimilating the Native population, and thereby abolishing their distinct rights, truly contained the social corollary of ignoring ethnic difference and abandoning white perceptions regarding the inferiority of Native blood, nor has it striven to ease the divide between white economic superiority and Indigenous poverty. (McKegney 2017, 115)

This is why policies and practices purportedly designed to engender equality have consistently entrenched difference and exacerbated marginalization.

Indian Horse demonstrates how the contradictions embedded within public discourse on residential schooling are mirrored by those relating to the social function of hockey in Canadian culture. As mentioned above, hockey is often conceived as a vehicle for manufacturing settler belonging, and Indigenous iconography is often marshalled as inclusive of "indigenization" (Goldie 1989, 13).[4] While Indigenous-inspired images may adorn the fronts of jerseys and teams may adopt Indigenous-themed names, the game's "proper" player in the popular imaginary remains fundamentally a white-settler Canadian. Indigenous iconography in hockey culture therefore constitutes what Anishinaabe writer Gerald Vizenor calls an "inscribed absence" (2009, 3) that stands in for and serves to replace the lived realities of Indigenous peoples; Indigenous emblems are desired, while Indigenous people are not. This is why the landscape of frozen lakes and rivers that is conceptualized as the "True North," and replicated in NHL advertising and beer commercials, is one that tends to be portrayed as devoid of Indigenous presence. The irony here, of course, is that while hockey is imagined as a force of social cohesion that works to "indigenize" the nation, Indigenous peoples are either ignored or actively excluded from full participation in the game.

Wagamese's novel depicts just how anxiously the limits on Indigenous inclusion in Canadian hockey culture have historically been policed. Despite that Saul is repeatedly shown to be the best player in each level at which he plays, he is actively—and often violently—discouraged from feeling as though he fully belongs by white coaches, players, fans, and the media. In one notable example, Saul arrives at the rink to play with the non-Indigenous competitive midget team for which he has scored a scorching fourteen points in ten games as a thirteen-year-old underage player. There, he finds he has been cut from the team because "The parents of other players want their own kids to play." Seeking clarification, Saul asks, "It's because I'm Indian, isn't it?" which Father Leboutilier confirms, before adding, "They think it's their game" (Wagamese 2012, 91–92). Although Saul had been brought onto the roster to help the team win, such inclusion is tenuous and proves contingent on his not disturbing the game's—not to mention the team's—naturalized culture of white entitlement. Even though Saul proves an asset on the scoresheet, his presence troubles the untouchable "rights" of his white teammates to the ice, and he is cut unceremoniously.

White entitlement is enforced even more vehemently when the all-Indigenous Manitouwadge Moose squad enters the non-Indigenous hockey circuit and begins defeating white teams. Unable to simply eliminate the team (as the midget team had axed Saul),

---

4. Note, however, that in Goldie's use of "indigenization," indigeneity is trapped within the semiotic, as images of indigeneity are mobilized by settlers in the absence of Indigenous people.

fans engage in acts of performative disavowal designed to mark the bodies of the Indigenous players as other, as out of place, as ultimately disposable: they pelt the Moose players with garbage, slash the tires of their van, and urinate and defecate in their dressing room. When the Moose win an otherwise all-white tournament, anxieties about white ownership of the game are heightened and such performative disavowal takes a violent turn. Stopping at a small-town café en route home from the tournament, the Moose team is confronted by a mob of "working men, big and strong-looking with stern faces," one of whom declares: "You boys got kinda big for the britches . . . you win a little hockey tournament and then you think you got the right to come in here and eat like white people" (133). Framing the conversation in a juridical vernacular of "rights" that delineates insider and outsider status, the man elaborates racialized distinctions between those who belong—"white people"—and those whose access to the space is provisional and contingent. Because the men's belief in white superiority has been challenged by the Manitouwadge team's tournament victory, the men prove sadistically eager to reinscribe a colonial hierarchy of white entitlement and Indigenous inferiority onto the bodies of the Moose players, taking each member of the team, with the exception of Saul, out back of the café, where they beat them mercilessly before showering them with spit and urine. The beatings mark the victims with signifiers of supposed racialized inferiority, with spit and urine signalling their dehumanization. The use of bodily excretions to shame the players seems tactically concocted to register their disposability in the service of colonial erasure. Whereas the white men present themselves as entitled to eat at the restaurant, and thereby to be nourished and endure as a community, the Indigenous players are performatively associated with detritus to signal their symbolic elimination in the service of white progress. The Indigenous players become associated with the casualties of modernity as the white future is heralded and the Indians vanish.

Like residential-school technologies of discipline, the violence here constitutes a form of social engineering designed to remind the Indigenous men of their "place." And the brutality of the lesson proves chillingly effective. On the long van ride back to Manitouwadge, one of the victims explains the incident to Saul, stating, "We crossed a line. Their line. They figure they got the right to make us pay for that." When Saul inquires, "Do they?" his teammate responds: "Sometimes I think so" (136). The effects of this incident and ones like it cast a protracted shadow over the novel. Saul notes that, although they never speak about it, "there were moments when you'd catch another boy's eye and know that you were both thinking about it. Everything was contained in that glance. All the hurt. All the shame. All the rage. The white people thought it was their game. They thought it was their world" (136).

Returning to a cadence found throughout the novel—that white Canadians think it is "their game"—Wagamese again demonstrates how the belief that hockey is a space of white authority, power, and privilege comes to be leveraged in the often-violent naturalization of white entitlement in Canada and thereby in the reification of settler colonialism as an unquestioned norm. Wagamese's novel thus forces both Indigenous and settler readers to ask certain questions: Is it indeed "their/our game"? Does hockey belong only to white Canadians? And if not, how might exposure of these claims' falsity be mobilized to trouble the colonial corollary that it is "their world"?[5] In the final section of this essay, we interrogate the resilient affection for the game that is evident in *Indian Horse* and Wagamese's use of apotheosis to examine hockey's capacity to participate in the individual and collective transformations necessary to pursue a more just and balanced world.

From Ambivalence to Apotheosis: Individual Achievement and Communal Resurgence

By the end of the novel, it seems as though Saul's unshakable faith in hockey as something sacred and incorruptible is criminally naïve. For many readers, the novel's eventual disclosure that Father Leboutilier had used his power as a coach—along with the secret practices, the private hockey-viewing sessions in the priest's quarters, and Saul's vulnerability as an orphaned residential-school student desperate for affection—to exploit and sexually abuse the young protagonist would inspire rejection of any romantic vestiges the game might retain. Curiously though, it does not. Rather than turning away from hockey completely while facing the return of his repressed past in the contemporary time frame of the novel's final section, Saul concedes that hockey was and perhaps still is his salvation: "As long as I could escape into it, I could fly away. Fly away and never have to land on the scorched earth of my boyhood" (199). The declaration sounds remarkably similar to those quoted by Habkirk and Forsyth from the TRC's *Final Report*. Hockey, in Saul's opinion, in spite of itself, retains its ability to lift a person up, an apotheosis rather than a metamorphosis. Whether or not hockey has "an alchemy that transforms ordinary men into great ones" (57), as Saul gushes earlier in the novel, the game continues to present definitive opportunities for individual acts of athletic brilliance that are transformative—even at this late point in the novel; the novel expresses skepticism, however, about whether such individual transformations work in the service of decolonization. Saul had come the closest to his own apotheosis earlier in the novel during his otherworldly performance at the Espanola tournament, during which he seemed to rise above both his teammates and opponents, yet even this transformation had proven incapable of fostering the genuine healing toward which the novel is directed and which ultimately led Saul to the New Dawn Centre, where he began to craft his life narrative.

If hockey is a symbolic playing out of white Canadianness, then the Espanola tournament acts as a collision point between white entitlement and Indigenous-embodied sovereignty. The Manitouwadge Moose is the first Indigenous team to participate in the tournament, where all the teams have "a pedigree" and "only the best teams got invited" (137). White teams from cities like North Bay and Owen Sound attempt to subdue Saul's dazzling skill and speed with physicality, racist verbal assaults, and irritating stick infractions designed to goad him into fighting or taking retaliatory penalties. This style of play bends

---

5. To reiterate, the ideological collapse between the game itself and the northern territory from which it is imagined "naturally" to have sprung enables white-settler participants to marshal hockey in the (re)production of beliefs that *they belong* in the land they and their ancestors have colonized, and that both the land and the game, in turn, *belong to them*—a self-perpetuating dynamic that undergirds Saul's repeated lament that white players "think it's their game" (31). *Indian Horse* is actively engaged with the destabilization of these persistent beliefs while making use of the representational inheritance through which they have historically been reified.

the rules of gentlemanly decorum and white civility that pervade white Canada's self-perception as performed through the national winter sport. Saul sits neatly astride both the white teams' hostility and his teammates' insistence that he retaliate. Instead of taking the bait and throwing punches, he "stepped out onto the ice and reclaimed the game" (144) with speed, skill, and imagination.

The connection to the game that Saul displays in Espanola transcends time and space, representing the consummation of the clairvoyance he experienced upon being introduced to the game as a young child—an innate sense of the pace and rhythm of hockey that was passed on to him from his ancestors. Saul tells the story of his family:

> There are teachers among our people who could determine where a particular moose was, a bear, the exact time the fish would make their spawning runs. My great-grand-father Shabogeesick, the original Indian Horse, had that gift. The world spoke to him. It told him where to look. Shabogeesick's gift had been passed on to me. There's no other explanation for how I was able to see this foreign game so completely right away. (58)

Saul's invocation of the term "foreign" here is telling, since it registers both a rejection of residential schooling's assimilative objective of domesticating Indigenous youth within the Canadian nation state *and* an autonomous intervention in Canadian hockey literature by an Anishinaabe world view in which intergenerational knowledge sharing and land-based foresight regarding the world's rhythms are not only possible but are necessary to survival.

For Saul, hockey is a sensory experience—one involving foresight and anticipation in a predatory way, like hunting, but also one attuned harmoniously to the natural spiritual energies of the earth and nature. In this way, Saul seems to be divining his mythical and spiritual aptitude for the game from his heritage, which is antithetical to the typical codifications of the game as inherently settler Canadian. Yet, in doing so, Saul relies upon one of the dominant representations of the Canadian hockey novel: that the game arises naturally from the Canadian landscape and is therefore attuned to the Canadian environment (only, in this case, the landscape need not be coded "Canadian" but could as readily be framed "Anishinaabe" or, more generally, "Indigenous"). Nonetheless, the tournament in Espanola becomes a turning point in the novel, as Saul's initial experience of love for the game, a love that facilitated transcendence, is attacked relentlessly by settler opponents and fans. Their affronts to Saul's spiritual connection, their repeated assaults to his body, and their dehumanizing racist chants are epistemological strikes to Saul's spirit and playing style. In literary terms, hockey played Saul's way is an act of what Anishinaabe intellectual Gerald Vizenor calls "survivance" or the expression of ongoing, creative, evolutionary/revolutionary Indigenous culture through imagination in prose, plays, and poetry: "Natives, by communal stories, memory, and potentiality create a sense of presence not an inscribed absence" (Vizenor 2009, 3). Saul reaches to the spiritual and practical modes of being of his forbears, but rather than ossifying that knowledge as a fixed, romanticized set of stereotypes—like the "inscribed absence" implied by settler imaginings of an Indigenous hyper-masculine past on team logos and in team names—he expresses it anew through what 'ōiwi scholar

Ty Tengan might call "embodied discursive action" within the "foreign" arena of elite hockey (2008, 17).[6]

The irony of Saul's success in Espanola is that he earns an invitation to try out with a major-junior team in Toronto, for which he eventually plays. Wagamese's novel exposes ambivalences within the Canadian culture of the game in which, despite the continual reification and policing of settler entitlement, admiration for exceptional skill occasionally intervenes in the game's general exclusivity. For example, after being named the first star in the Espanola tournament's final game, Saul expected "boos to rain down" during his "turn around centre ice," but instead he was surrounded by "applause and stamping feet . . . like thunder rolling around the arena" (Wagamese 2012, 128); in addition, as noted above, Saul was the only player not to be assaulted at the café after the Espanola victory. Nonetheless, upon his arrival in Toronto, now alone and in the big city, Saul feels the resistance to his presence manifest ever more vociferously. Facing the reality of ongoing Indigenous persistence, white media and audiences prove fanatically invested in returning the living body of Saul Indian Horse to the falsified myths of a colonial past: "The press would not let me be. . . . When I made a dash down the ice and brought the crowd to their feet, I was on a raid. If I inadvertently high-sticked someone during a tussle in the corner, I was taking scalps. When I did not react to getting a penalty, I was the stoic Indian" (163). The reinscription of Saul's hockey actions with stereotypically "Indian" representations is a dual act of erasure—first of Saul's skills, which are above and beyond those of the average player, and then again of Indigenous presence in the Canadian game. What's more, Saul is demoralized by the representations, conceding, "I wanted to rise to new heights, be one of the glittering few. But they wouldn't let me be just a hockey player. I always had to be the Indian" (164).

The individualist myth of apotheosis through hockey, which Saul had learned about "from those books" back at residential school (56), is proven time and again to be inadequate or incomplete for an Indigenous player like Saul. Although he does receive accolades for his transcendent performances on the ice, the dominant, nationalistic culture in which those performances occur actively prevents Saul's internalization of a sense of belonging, of purpose, and of valued personhood. In other words, while Saul's hockey skill allows him to be elevated beyond the quotidian crowd of the average player, the persistent racism of the game's dominant culture ensures that such elevation for the individual Indigenous player does not translate into a resilient apotheosis characterized by healing. Early in the novel, Wagamese prepares readers expertly for this catch-22 by following Saul's discovery that hockey had "an alchemy that could transform ordinary men into great ones" with the resonant sentence fragment, "The white glory of the rink" (57). So long as the hockey rink's "glory" remains forcibly bound to a culture of "white" entitlement steeped in individualism and hyper-masculinity—as the "ordinary men" and "great ones" would suggest—the potential for the game to participate in genuine decolonial change remains hampered. Under such circumstances, Saul's defection from the Toronto Marlboros major-junior team and

---

6. In *Native Men Remade*, Tengan describes (2008, 151) the "embodied discursive practice," in which Indigenous "men come to perform and know themselves and their bodies in a new way." Referring to rituals enacted at an event in Puʻukoholā, Hawaiʻi, in 1991, Tengan explains that "bodily experience, action, and movement played a fundamental role in the creation of new subjectivities of culture and gender" (87).

his subsequent spiral into alcoholism constitutes a rational response to the corrosive effects of Canadian hockey culture. Saul's singularity as a player emerges from the visionary skill set inherited from his Anishinaabe ancestors, enlivened and enacted in the contemporary moment. Yet Saul's living and evolving cultural knowledge is continually denied and over-written by settler stereotypes of bygone and backward indigeneity; his unique gifts are obscured within a racialized, nationalistic discourse that works not only to disempower Saul but to further dispossess the Anishinaabe nation and Indigenous peoples more generally. To confront such unjust conditions, Saul cannot reach simply to his own "greatness" but must, in fact, envisage more community-based solutions.

In rehab for alcoholism at the New Dawn Centre, Saul has a spiritual transformation in the form of a vision of communal regeneration. While out in the bush, he watches the beavers work on their home in unison and is distracted from getting back to the centre before dark; he is forced to camp among "the cedars" on "a flat table of rock" (191). In an interstitial space between "awake or dreaming" (192), Saul is visited by his great-grandfather Shabogeesick, the person from whom he inherited his special hockey skills, and his grand-mother, whom he loved more than anyone. The effect of the vision is immediate: Saul needs to return to Manitouwadge and hand his skills down to the next generation. Ultimately, the novel's depictions of the residential-school survivor's healing journey and the nostalgic elite athlete past his prime fuse together in a triumphant gesture of Anishinaabe survivance expressed through communal agency and solidarity. Returning to skate with his old teammates on the Manitouwadge rink, Saul finds that behind a full line of the "original Moose . . . were some kids of assorted ages and sizes and behind them were young girls and older women. Everyone had a hockey stick." With at least eighteen skaters on the ice—at different life stages, levels of ability, and genders—Saul asks Virgil, his former teammate, confidante, and surrogate brother, "How are we gonna do this?. . . I mean with all these people. How are we gonna play the game?" Virgil responds, "Together. . . . Like we shoulda all along" (221).

Conclusion: To Transform a Game, Not an Individual

Saul Indian Horse was first introduced to the game of hockey through literature within the racist, nationalistic, and assimilative space of the residential school. "From those books," he declares, "I got the idea that hockey had an alchemy that could transform ordinary men into great ones" (57). Saul's journey throughout the novel is structured as a (perhaps doomed) search for such greatness. The novel tracks its protagonist's development as a seer and a gifted athlete, but the apotheosis that Saul imagines as a child proves consistently unachiev-able in the context of ongoing colonial power relations configured to ensure his second-class status. The healing arc of the novel as a residential-school survival narrative offers other transformative possibilities; however, it too cannot point in the direction of the narrator's personal well-being until he has broadened the individualist focus on "ordinary men" and "great ones" to encompass the realities of living Indigenous communities.

This is why the novel concludes with Indigenous players of various ages and genders playing "together." Rather than seeking after his own singular transformation to hockey superstar (or even to healthy and sober individual), Saul needs to recognize that his capacity to become the fullest expression of himself is deeply interdependent with his community's capacity to transform the game—to disentangle it from the threads of individualism, racism, sexism, and capitalism that together form the web of ideological inheritance from colonial heteropatriarchy.

In this way, Wagamese's novel has richly decolonizing properties. These properties, however, persist through a deep and abiding love for the game of hockey rather than in opposition to it. But in order for that love to begin to engender positive social change, the racism of hockey culture must be exposed; its own implication in violent colonial history must be laid bare; and the ongoing capacity of Indigenous players, fans, coaches, and communities to reimagine the game within the frameworks of their own world views must be recognized and affirmed. These are the lessons gifted to both settler and Indigenous audiences within Wagamese's forcefully non-colonial—as opposed to *decolonial*—hockey novel.

Bibliography

Anderson, Benedict. 2006. *Imagined Communities: Reflections on the Origin and Spread of Nationalism.* London: Verso.

Blake, Jason. 2010. *Canadian Hockey Literature: A Thematic Study.* Toronto: University of Toronto Press.

Buma, Michael. 2012. *Refereeing Identity: The Cultural Work of Canadian Hockey Novels.* Montreal: McGill-Queen's University Press.

Dopp, Jamie, and Richard Harrison. 2009. *Now Is the Winter: Thinking About Hockey.* Hamilton, ON: Wolsak and Wynn.

Dowbiggin, Bruce. 2011. *The Meaning of Puck: How Hockey Explains Modern Canada.* Red Deer, AB: Red Deer Press.

Dryden, Ken, and Roy MacGregor. 1989. *Home Game: Hockey and Life in Canada.* Toronto: McClelland and Stewart.

Ennamorato, Judith. 1998. *Sing the Brave Song.* Schomberg, ON: Raven Press.

Goldie, Terry. 1989. *Fear and Temptation: The Image of the Indigene in Canadian, Australian, and New Zealand Literatures.* Montreal: McGill-Queen's University Press.

Gruneau, Richard, and David Whitson. 1993. *Hockey Night in Canada: Sport, Identities and Cultural Politics.* Toronto: Garamond Press.

Habkirk, Evan J., and Janice Forsyth. 2016. "Truth, Reconciliation, and the Politics of the Body in Indian Residential School History." ActiveHistory.ca, January 27. http://activehistory.ca/papers/truth-reconciliation-and-the-politics-of-the-body-in-indian-residential-school-history/.

Howell, Colin D. 2001. *Blood, Sweat, and Cheers: Sport and the Making of Modern Canada.* Toronto: University of Toronto Press.

Hughes-Fuller, Patricia. 2002. "The Good Old Game: Hockey, Nostalgia, Identity." PhD diss., University of Alberta.

Johnston, Basil H. 1988. *Indian School Days.* Norman: University of Oklahoma Press.

McKegney, Sam. 2017. *Magic Weapons: Aboriginal Writers Remaking Community After Residential School.* Winnipeg: University of Manitoba Press.

McKinley, Michael. 2001. *Putting a Roof on Winter: Hockey's Rise from Sport to Spectacle.* Vancouver: Greystone Books.

Miller, J. R. 1996. *Shingwauk's Vision: A History of Native Residential Schools.* Toronto: University of Toronto Press.

Milloy, John S. 1999. *"A National Crime": The Canadian Government and the Residential School System, 1879 to 1986.* Winnipeg: University of Manitoba Press.

Robidoux, Michael. 2012. *Stickhandling through the Margins: First Nations Hockey in Canada.* Toronto: University of Toronto Press.

Tengan, Ty P. Kāwika. 2008. *Native Men Remade: Gender and Nation in Contemporary Hawai'i*. Durham, NC: Duke University Press.

TRC (Truth and Reconciliation Commission of Canada). 2015a. *Canada's Residential Schools: Reconciliation. The Final Report of the Truth and Reconciliation Commission of Canada*. Vol. 6. Montreal: McGill-Queen's University Press.

———. 2015b. *Honouring the Truth, Reconciling for the Future: Summary of the Final Report of the Truth and Reconciliation Commission of Canada*. Winnipeg: Truth and Reconciliation Commission of Canada. http://www.trc.ca/websites/trcinstitution/File/2015/Findings/Exec_Summary_2015_05_31_web_o.pdf.

Vizenor, Gerald. 2009. *Native Liberty: Natural Reason and Cultural Survivance*. Lincoln: University of Nebraska Press.

Wagamese, Richard. 2012. *Indian Horse*. Vancouver: Douglas and McIntyre.

Wolfe, Patrick. 2006. "Settler Colonialism and the Elimination of the Native." *Journal of Genocide Research* 8 (4): 387–409.

Chapter 5
"Here they come! Look them over!": Youth, Citizenship, and the Emergence of Minor Hockey in Canada

CARLY ADAMS AND JASON LAURENDEAU

In Canada, children and youth play hockey in extraordinary numbers. Currently, more than 600,000 Canadian kids under the age of eighteen are registered for minor hockey.[1] This is a striking number considering that there are approximately six million Canadians between five and nineteen years of age.[2] What is more, hockey is part of the fabric of the nation and has been mobilized in the production of (particular) citizens and, indeed, notions of Canadianness (for discussions of how hockey has been mobilized in discourses of Canadian identity and nationhood, see: Robidoux 2002; Gruneau and Whitson 1993, C. Adams 2014; Scherer and Koch 2010; Allain 2011). As such, the game of hockey figures centrally in the experiences of many Canadians (whether as participants, fans, casual spectators, and/or cultural consumers), including children. Meanwhile, critics of organized competitive hockey for children have excoriated the commercialization of the game, parental pressure, the prevalence of a win-at-all-cost attitude, the promotion of violence and aggression, and the escalating costs of playing the game (Gruneau and Whitson 1993, 156).

In this chapter, we respond to recent calls for sport scholars to take "kids' sport," and childhood and youth—not as stages of life, but as sets of ideas—more seriously in our investigations of the histories, discourses, and practices of sport and recreation (Messner and Musto 2014; Laurendeau and Konecny 2015). We aim, on the one hand, to address a gap in sport-history scholarship by considering not professional and/or elite hockey but hockey played by hundreds of thousands of Canadian children annually. While Michael Robidoux's important work on professional hockey in Canada focuses on "how professional hockey players' identities are *shaped* and *defined* through the labour process" (Robidoux 2001, 5), in this chapter we draw on the history of minor hockey to interrogate the production of particular ideas about childhood and adolescence, and about nationhood and citizenship more generally, in the process of co-opting children into the Canadian hockey system.

1. Hockey Canada Annual Report, June 2016–June2017, https://cdn.hockeycanada.ca/hockey-canada/Corporate/About/Downloads/2016-17-annual-report-e.pdf.
2. Statistics Canada, "Population by Sex and Age Group," http://www.statcan.gc.ca/tables-tableaux/sum-som/l01/cst01/demo10a-eng.htm.

Following the work of historical geographer Elizabeth Gagen, we "wish to historicize [children's] bodies—to understand how they were *understood* to constitute identity in a particular epistemic configuration" (Gagen 2004, 423–24). In doing so, we contribute to discussions about the ways children have "been constructed, positioned and experience space and place" (Mills 2013, 5; see also Gagen 2000).

Within the context of the history of minor hockey in Canada, we explore how concerns about childhood and reform discourses were taken up through policies and practices as children became a focus of the provincial and national organizational bodies. We situate the emergence of minor hockey in Canada during the first half of the twentieth century within a broader historical context, interrogating how this important shift in the history of hockey in Canada can be understood in terms of both the process of commercializing hockey and a set of narratives about children and youth ascendant during this historical period. We draw on newspaper reports and Canadian Amateur Hockey Association (CAHA) organizational documents (see Stevens 2006 for more on the CAHA) to explore the cultural politics of (some) young people's sporting experiences in this historical period, highlighting the extent to which these are tied to questions of nationhood, citizenship, and "proper" formations of childhood and family life.

(Minor) Hockey Scholarship

Since the 1990s, hockey, as an academic area of study, has captured the attention of sport scholars. Some argue that the publication, in 1993, of Gruneau and Whitson's *Hockey Night in Canada* broke "open the field of 'Hockey Studies,'" encouraging others in fields as diverse as history, sociology, geography, sport management, and political science to think about the complex ways in which hockey and its place in Canadian folklore offers fodder for examining Canadian society, past and present (Stevens and Holman 2013). Historical research on hockey in Canada focuses on the origins of the game, early professional hockey, media, violence and masculinity, women's hockey and gender, organization of the game, civic boosterism and community building, international hockey, and hockey as both a product and producer of Canadian culture. Despite hockey capturing the scholarly imagination in these varied ways, as Stevens and Holman write, "the dominant perspective of the field is a rarified one" that often fails to consider the ways in which discourses and cultural assumptions shape the game for those playing it. Certainly, in the landscape of hockey research, the history of child and youth participation has received little academic attention (Stevens and Holman 2013, 251).

In their formative work on the cultural politics of hockey in Canada, Gruneau and Whitson offer one of the few assessments of the origins of organized youth hockey. They suggest that minor hockey was central to the CAHA agenda post–Second World War, as it was by the 1940s that the CAHA had committed itself to being a feeder system for professional hockey (Gruneau and Whitson 1993, 170). Gruneau and Whitson also note (1993, 154) that minor hockey organizations often served as "focal point[s] of community spirit" in rural and urban Canadian communities. Groups such as Optimists and Lions Clubs, church groups, and community businesses became involved in the sponsorship and operation of minor hockey in their local communities. Their involvement was fuelled by the "belief that they [were] contributing to making their communities better places for growing up"

(154). As scholars on childhood point out, the idea of "making better communities" is intimately interwoven with the notion of "making better children" (as the citizens and pillars of the community in the years to come) (Gleason et al. 2010, 1, for example).

One of the few lines of inquiry in which we see a focus on minor hockey as embedded within broader narratives about young people is the burgeoning body of work taking up gender in minor hockey (e.g., see Adams and Leavitt 2016; Stevens and Adams 2013). Historically, hockey in Canada developed as a male preserve, though there were and are opportunities for girls and women to play (C. Adams 2009, 2014). Professional players have been, in the words of Gruneau and Whitson (1993, 168), "held up as exemplars of a particularly Canadian kind of masculinity." Hockey was—and remains—a social location for the indoctrination of young boys into the codes of masculine behaviour. It was not until the 1970s that opportunities for girls to play organized hockey became more widely available across the country. This, of course, suggests that minor hockey in Canada is tied to particular ideas about what Canadian boys and girls *should* be doing, what they are capable of, and so on. Adams and Leavitt, in their study of gender inequality in minor hockey in southern Alberta, suggest that girls and women's hockey has been "accommodated into the game in ways that reinforce and perpetuate systems of gender" (Adams and Leavitt 2016, 4; see also Adams and Stevens 2007). They argue that we must continue to question "cultural discourses and persistent historical ideological understandings" of gender and how they are manifest in youth hockey and other social locations (Adams and Leavitt 2016). Hockey, as a "metaphorical representation of Canadian identity," is historically significant (Robidoux 2002). As such, it "creates a kind of cultural amnesia about the social struggles...that have always been a part of hockey's history" (Gruneau and Whitson 1993, 132). The relatively late emergence of institutionalized minor hockey for girls (as well as the continued marginalization of girls' hockey) tells us not only about gender and sexism in sport, but also about (gendered) ways of thinking about young people.

Children, Childhood, and Nation-Building

The turn of the twentieth century marks an important moment in the contemporary history of children's sport in Western nations, as it represents the confluence of three broad and interrelated shifts in the landscape of childhood in Western industrialized nations. First, by the late nineteenth century responsibility for children's health and well-being "became a matter of increasing public importance"; this period represents the emergence of the "public child," who is "constructed through medical discourses of protection, prevention, and statistical attention" (Gleason 2005, 231). This discursive shift in the construction of the child meant that there was a community responsibility for the well-being and proper upbringing of individual children. During this period, medical professionals and social reformers increasingly constructed children and youth as innocent, precious, and in need of constant protection, particularly during their most formative years. Qualities associated with the "public child" in this era guided and "legitimized the work of twentieth-century reformers, defined the essence of children's "nature," and characterized qualities of their physical bodies" (Gleason 2013, 7).

Second, these physical bodies themselves became focal points for moral entrepreneurs. Gagen outlines the profound impact of pioneering psychologist G. Stanley Hall and his colleagues. Hall's most influential text, Gagen says (2004, 426), "outlined a theory of child development and genetic psychology that attempted not simply to describe what happens during childhood and adolescence, but to identify potential moments of intervention through which to secure the most desirable and robust adult." Hall's theories suggested that these moments of intervention were necessarily tied to bodily activity of various kinds, as he understood thought to be essentially a function of muscular activity (Gagen 2004, 428). Hall's influence in terms of childhood development is evident in numerous organizations, including, as Gagen points out (426), "the Progressive education movement, Boys' Clubs, the Camp Fire Girls, the child study movement, and…the playground movement and the campaign for physical education." Moreover, the notion that in training children's bodies one could also train their minds became firmly rooted in both the field of childhood development and in numerous programs, initiatives, and institutions ostensibly developed with children's well-being in mind.

Third, and following from the above, this period was characterized by an expansion of institutionalized leisure opportunities for many young people in Western industrialized nations, as evident in the fact that the national school system in the United Kingdom "not only produced the first literate generations but also at the same time began to encourage team games" (Hopkins 1994, 291). In North America, the early twentieth century bore witness to a number of interrelated industries and institutions fostering sport programs, including, but not limited to, philanthropic organizations, corporate bodies, community and volunteer organizations, and non-governmental and state-sponsored organizations such as athletic associations. As Laurendeau and Konecny note (2015, 338):

> These bodies were not only stakeholders…but actively constituted the form that these institutionalized youth sports took initially, as well as the ways in which they were reshaped in following years. The work of these kinds of organizations both draws on, and serves to (re)produce, particular notions of childhood and youth, not least in order to continue to create new markets.[3]

Our analytic task, then, is to interrogate the development of these kinds of organizations with an eye toward narratives of childhood/adolescence they both draw on and (re)produce.

In Canada, specifically, the emergence of structured (adult-approved) places for children and youth sport was part of a broader social and moral-reform movement that gained momentum by the turn of the twentieth century. The playground movement, for example, that swept the nation in the 1920s and 1930s sought to protect children and youth from the "problems" of society and social delinquency and prepare them for a "proper" life as productive workers and providers (for more on the playground movement, see C. Adams 2011; Retamales and Reichwein 2014). The central goal of supervised playgrounds was to produce "good" citizens by creating a sense of community and loyalty among the participants. For boys, it was hoped this would translate into national loyalty and an understanding of the duties of citizenship.

---

3. Laurendeau and Konecny, "Where is Childhood?," 338. For more on the rise of youth organizations in Canada, see Comacchio 2006, esp. 189–201, and Alexander 2009, 2015.

The Great Depression led to a gradual shift away from young children to concern over youth and young adults and their leisure time. It was thought that increasing recreational services was desperately needed during this period to provide amusement and entertainment during a time of decreasing industrial production and increasing unemployment (C. Adams 2011, 77). This led to the creation of government policy addressing and providing resources for national fitness (Heagerty 1943).

It was at this same moment that sport-governing bodies included youth sport under their umbrella. The move for the CAHA to include youth sport under its organizational mandate coincides roughly with the institutionalization of Little League baseball, founded in 1939, and Pop Warner football, organized in 1929 in Philadelphia for boys aged seven to fifteen and conceived as a solution to the problem of youth vandalism in the city (Overman 2011, 146). As such, the emergence of organized youth sport is situated, historically, within a political economy of risk, characterized by "increasing public concern about, and surveillance of, children and families" (Laurendeau and Konecny 2015, 334; see also Gleason 2005).

The Development and Commercialization of Minor Hockey

Before turning our analytic attention to our central focus on the production of particular ideas about childhood, children, and the nation, we must briefly outline the importance of understanding the emergence of minor hockey in Canada as inextricably intertwined with the commercialization of hockey in North America. Archival evidence suggests that there was a good deal of energy put into growing hockey for young people in the 1930s, in particular. In the early 1930s, the CAHA awarded grants to its active branches, each of which had full control of hockey in its district, subject, of course, to the constitution rules and regulations laid down by the CAHA.[4] For example, the British Columbia Amateur Hockey Association passed a resolution in 1933 to register midget and juvenile divisions (i.e., over the age of fourteen) in their association (Atwell 1989, 18). The first registrations took place for the 1933–34 season, with four juvenile teams registered, resulting in a $500 grant from the CAHA to support this new minor hockey initiative (Atwell 1989, 20). In the minutes of the eighteenth annual meeting of the CAHA, in 1935, first vice-president Cecil Duncan outlined that the purpose of these grants was for the "promotion of juvenile, bantam and, in some instances, intermediate hockey."[5] Provincial associations were required to provide annual reports detailing how the funds were used in support of growing minor hockey in their jurisdictions. The funding of these grants was contingent on the financial health of the CAHA; in 1934, $6,300 was awarded to provincial branches for the promotion of minor hockey, but this funding dried up during later Depression years.[6] In 1935, the Toronto daily the *Globe* reported that the CAHA was experiencing a shortage of funds, with an annual deficit of $10,000, despite an increase in the number of players registering with the governing body. Within a few years, the CAHA coffers were replenished (attributed to then-president Cecil Duncan's stewardship of the organization), and, in 1938, the CAHA

---

4. Minutes of the Eighteenth Annual Meeting, Canadian Amateur Hockey Association, 1935 (consult http://heritage.canadiana.ca/view/oocihm.lac_reel_c4852/17?r=0&s=1).
5. Minutes, CAHA, 1935 (see note [4]).
6. "Marked shrinkage in C.A.H.A Funds," *Globe*, April 11, 1935, 6.

resumed grants to provincial branches, with each province granted $300 toward the promotion of minor hockey.[7]

The focus on institutionalized hockey for young people, described above, takes place amid a number of tensions, particularly with respect to amateurism. The amateur code, which was the stronghold of Canadian organized sport in the early twentieth century, "bound 'the making of men' to the broader project of nation-building" (Kidd 1996, 55; see also Metcalfe 1995). There were also very serious practical implications to the prevalent amateur ideology, as once an athlete turned professional, there was no going back; they were then banned for life from amateur competition. Yet, by the mid-1930s, sport was increasingly being viewed and consumed as a commodity. The development of industrial and consumer capitalism "provided the amateur administrators with their greatest challenge and served to obscure the real nature of amateurism" (Metcalfe 1995, 37). With the explosion of professionalized sports in the 1920s, followed by the Depression in the 1930s, athletes were turning to sports in increasing numbers as a way of making money (Metcalfe 1995, 37). Amateur leaders found this shift troubling, as they felt athletes "would lose sight of the educational and social purposes of participation" (Kidd 1996, 56). They believed that young players enticed by wages and the opportunity to play in the professional leagues were selling their skills without fully understanding the implications of their actions. In 1931, in an article in *Canadian Magazine*, journalist Leslie Roberts encouraged parents to "keep your boy out of professional hockey, baseball and all the money sports, unless you want to see him earn easy money for a few years and find himself, at thirty, jobless and drifting around the fringes of the Big Time, looking for a job driving pegs" (quoted in Kidd 1996, 56).

Similar discussions were taking place within the CAHA. In an exchange captured in the minutes of the 1935 annual meeting, for example, influential member George Dudley noted the importance of "protecting" young players and ensuring they remained amateur athletes for as long as possible. Speaking to a motion to prevent players under age twenty-one from trying out with professional teams, Dudley said:

> The vast majority of players would be trying out at that age [under twenty-one]; that is the age they [professional teams] would like to get a boy. The younger boys are boys who need this protection, because, if a man gets over twenty-one, he is going to get more judgement and he is going to try this thing for himself and therefore, if we debar a boy, he is going to be open to the same temptation; if a professional club offers him a few dollars, he may make this jump to his everlasting regret.[8]

The resolution, put forward by President E. A. Gilroy, read: "No player will be given permission to try out with professional teams after Dec. 1 in the current season, and only players over 21 will be granted such privileges."[9] Ultimately, the resolution did not pass. This was one of a number of discussions within the CAHA related to amateurism and the recruitment

---

7. "C.A.H.A will create trust fund of $35,000," *Globe and Mail*, April 18, 1938, 19.
8. Minutes, CAHA, 1935 (see note [4]) George Dudley was instrumental in the disaffiliation of the CAHA from the AAUC the following year.
9. "Marked shrinkage in C.A.H.A Funds," *Globe*, April 11, 1935, 6.

of younger players by professional leagues that provides a window into discourses of youth both informing and informed by cultural processes such as those under consideration here.[10]

Up until the late 1930s, the National Hockey League (NHL) and CAHA had a formal agreement to govern as separate entities with players allowed to play solely within one or the other (Kidd and Macfarlane 1972, 55). However, this does not mean that the CAHA and the NHL were unaffiliated. As Kidd and Macfarlane suggest (52), the NHL took an interest in youth hockey as early as the 1920s; this changed the nature of the game, especially as "child buying" became a common practice in professional hockey. In the 1920s, NHL teams began identifying talented amateur players, teenage boys, and giving them retainers/ payments in kind to stay in school in exchange for a commitment to sign with the sponsoring team if and when they joined the professional ranks.[11] League names—such as the Peewee National Hockey League that consisted of teams of boys aged nine to fourteen from Winnipeg, Calgary, Vancouver, and Toronto—also suggest the NHL very much had its tentacles in minor hockey from the outset.[12] In 1938, the formal agreement that the NHL would not scout amateur players from the CAHA dissolved.[13] The dissolution of this agreement paved the way for the formal sponsorship agreements between the NHL and CAHA that were put in place in 1947 and 1958 (Kidd and Macfarlane 1972, 55).

By the late 1940s, institutionalized minor hockey in Canada functioned as a formal feeder system for professional hockey, as the NHL and the CAHA developed a mutually beneficial relationship. The NHL needed access to junior players to bolster team numbers as players went off to war (Young 1989, 198). Meanwhile, the CAHA needed NHL money to stay afloat. In 1947, a formal agreement was struck between the NHL and the amateur governing bodies (the International Ice Hockey Federation, the CAHA, and the Amateur Hockey Association of the United States). Through this agreement, the NHL had control over elite levels of hockey in Canada.[14] All amateur players were required to sign a CAHA registration card, and in so doing they signed away their freedom as players and became bound, for life, to the NHL team that sponsored the local junior-league club, if a player advanced to that level.[15] Kidd and MacFarlane argue that this move by the NHL was "genius" in that it made the CAHA "an active partner in the development of a

10. In 1936, the CAHA disaffiliated from the AAUC. Alan Metcalfe suggests (1995, 35) that this was the beginning of the end of the Amateur Athletic Association of Canada (AAUC) and stronghold of the amateur ideology in Canadian sport.

11. For example, from the time he purchased the Toronto St. Pat's in 1926, Conn Smythe brought talented junior players to Toronto. He paid their tuition at St. Michael's College so they could play hockey for St. Mike's or the Marlboros, a junior-league farm team to the Toronto Maple Leafs (Kidd and Macfarlane 1972, 54).

12. "Peewee Baseball League Planned in Calgary," *Globe and Mail*, May 8, 1937, 21.

13. "N.H.L Agreement with C.A.H.A thing of the past." *Globe and Mail*, February 24, 1938, 18.

14. For the provisions of the agreement, see Official Rule Book, Canadian Amateur Hockey Association, 1954, http://heritage.canadiana.ca/view/oocihm.lac_reel_c4852, images 68–69.

15. For example, boys in Fredericton grew up knowing they were "Black Hawk property," boys in Winnipeg were "Boston Bruins property," and so forth. The sponsorship system was replaced with the junior draft in 1966, the year the NHL expanded from six to twelve teams (Kidd and Macfarlane 1972, 56).

country-wide NHL farm system."[16] By 1967, twenty years after a formal sponsorship system was put in place, "27 professional teams in North America, all but five of which were located in the United States, owned 50 Canadian junior teams" (Kidd and Macfarlane 1972, 55).

This development of institutionalized minor hockey and the formal connection to professional hockey was certainly not without its critics. In a 1938 article published as part of a daily series of interviews with members of the Toronto Maple Leafs organization, Leafs coach Dick Irvin opined:

> youngsters are being over-coached. I don't think young fellows who are getting in pro hockey these days are developing their own natural ability as did the players of twenty and twenty-five years ago. Let me illustrate what I mean. During my youth in Winnipeg there was very little organized hockey and no junior hockey at all. We played in the open air on corner lots and on the Assiniboine and Red rivers. Generally there were from fifty to one hundred kids chasing the one puck. If you didn't learn to stickhandle… well, you never got the chance to keep the puck, and you had to learn to be adept at checking in order to get the puck.
>
> It was just dog-eat-dog, and the kids who had skill and stamina became individual stars. They stood out far above the rest.
>
> These days kids are coached, coached, coached from pee-wee and juvenile ranks right up through to pro. Six or seven coaches may handle a youngster before he reaches an N.H.L coach.
>
> Many of the kids these days have never played on a frozen river or pond…where they could play and practice all day. Instead they only have short practice hours in an artificial ice arena, and they've never got the real groundwork or background.[17]

All of the people organizing kids' hockey, write Kidd and MacFarlane (1972, 60), "juggling schedules, driving kids to practice, paying out good money for ice time, gas, insurance, referees, and equipment, were complicit in the NHL apprenticeship system." Moreover, they posited in 1972 that the focus on winning at all cost at the expense of playing for fun signaled "the death of the game" (69). Despite dissenting views from influential figures like Irvin and hockey scholars such as Kidd and MacFarlane, the institutionalization of minor hockey continued to gain steam, bolstered by the growing reach of the NHL.

"Aiding the Youth of Our Nation"

During the first half of the twentieth century, young people were viewed as "citizens-in-the-making" and sport was an "*alternative* arena where youth citizenship was enacted and mobilized" (Mills 2013; emphasis added).[18] In addition to the commercialization issues outlined

---

16. Each NHL team was allowed to sponsor a maximum of three clubs. Clubs were defined as consisting of a senior, junior, intermediate, junior "A," junior "B," or juvenile, midget, and bantam teams, and all of the house-league players associated with those levels as well (Kidd and Macfarlane 1972, 55).

17. Bill Roche, "Dick Irvin Recalls Some Hockey Disappointments, And Explains Why Super Stars are Fading Out," *Globe and Mail*, November 25, 1938, 20.

18. Mills makes this argument in the context of the Scout movement in Britain.

above, our analysis situates the emergence of minor hockey within a framework in which the "physical, mental and moral development of youth," and, indeed, the future of the nation, constitute central concerns (Heagerty 1943, 465).

Discussions among educators, governing bodies, and media reveal a discourse of developing future citizens through sport. For example, on March 29, 1921, five physical-activity advocates addressed the Ontario Educational Association at University College in Toronto, espousing the benefits of various types of athletics. In their speeches, the speakers (H. C. Griffith, Ridley College, St. Catharines; Dr. W. E Gallie, former coach of the University of Toronto hockey team; Mel Brock, physical director at Western University, London; A. L. Cochrane, resident of the Royal Life Saving Society; E. A. Chapman, director of athletics at St. Andrew's College, Aurora) discussed the value of sport and the values children learn and argued that schools should devote more attention to athletics (swimming, track and field, and team sports).[19] By the mid-1920s, the Amateur Athletic Union of Canada, then affiliated with the CAHA, was also promoting the role of sport in teaching "appropriate" Canadian citizenship. In the 1926 secretary's report, Arthur Lamb posited:

> It is my belief that there are tremendous possibilities in the activities under our jurisdiction for aiding the youth of our nation to assume their rightful place as useful citizens of our country. There never was a time as important as the present, with so many debilitating and distracting influences for our young people, against which, concentration upon a vigourous programme of competitive activities is necessary to offset the careless attitude and degrading influences by activities which make and maintain healthy, vigorous and virile manhood.[20]

This language was also reflected in newspaper reports touting the benefits of competitive sport for youth. For example, Bobbie Rosenfeld wrote: "sport exercises a grip on the youthful mind achieved by possibly nothing else… [Sport] is a medium that can be used as a power for cleaner living, cleaner mind, better character."[21]

Also evident in media reports are enthusiastic celebrations of youth physicality. For example, after watching the first Ontario Hockey Association junior teams' tryouts of the season, a reporter for the *Globe* wrote, "Here they come! Look them over! Stout boys, small boys, slim boys and tall boys, all battling for recognition." The tryout spectacle was described as "the annual parade of youngsters."[22] Though the spectacle being described here is one of muscularity, we must recall that at this socio-historical juncture it "was impossible to conceive of moral development without the corresponding development of muscles, because without physical capability, the mind itself became flaccid and incapable" (Gagen 2004, 428). More than mere spectacle, or even *symbol* of national character, these kinds of displays function as evidence of the *development* of national character: "To put bodies on display… proved national character, while at the same time, making it" (Gagen 2004, 438).

---

19. "Men Who Know Laud Athletics," *Globe*, March 30, 1921, 12.
20. Minutes of the Thirty-Ninth Annual Meeting, Amateur Athletic Union of Canada, 1926, http://heritage.canadiana.ca/view/oocihm.lac_reel_c4852, images 8–9.
21. Bobbie Rosenfeld, "Feminine Sports Reel," *Globe and Mail*, April 27, 1940, 14.
22. "Doings in Local Amateur Hockey Circles," *Globe*, November 2, 1932, 13.

Though we argue here that minor hockey should be understood as a space where informal youth-citizenship training took place, it is important to acknowledge that discourses of citizenship always refer to particular *kinds* of citizens (i.e., in terms of gender, race, "ability," etc.). We do not mean to suggest that Canadian youth share a common experience or identity. When hockey is spoken of as a collective identity of Canadians, or as a citizenship project, it ignores and in some cases erases the diverse backgrounds and traditions of youth in Canada.[23] Indeed, discourses of hockey "privilege native-born, white men" and boys (M. L. Adams 2006, 71; see also Robidoux 2002). This was certainly so in the period under consideration here, as organized hockey in Canada was used to develop ("proper") masculinity among boys. While girls were occasionally mentioned in media reports of the time, the clear focus of discussion was on what to do with and about "boys." This is made explicit, for example, in a 1934 article from the *Northern Tribune*. Author J. B. Yule outlines a conversation he had with "R.P. Fitzgerald, who has given so much of his time to the Boy Scout movement and to junior hockey." This article (and others like it) highlight the "problem" of idleness among boys:

> Boys are often blamed for doing things which they should not do when the trouble is they are not kept busy at something else. The boy problem can only be solved through and by organization and the lead must be given by the adult population.[24]

Yule posited that the most promising approach to these questions is co-operation and coordination between "boys' organizations now in existence," and the resultant system of organized competitions "would be most beneficial to the country as a whole."[25] Here, we see the connection between the "boy problem" and the state of the nation. The project was to shape the nation's (white, middle-class) boys in order to shape the future of the nation itself.

The kind of discussion highlighted above raises an important point when considering cultural products ostensibly designed *for* young people; as Galway, Barrett, and Newberry write (2012, 110): "the cultural products produced 'for children' often reflect adult concerns about gender, citizenship, nationhood, and the marketplace." Similarly, Sara Mills, in her study of citizenship and the organizational spaces of the Boy Scout movement in twentieth-century Britain, argues that, like organized hockey, the Scout movement was "designed *by* adults *for* young people" (Mills 2013, 5; italics in the original). She argues that scouting was "originally conceived, emerged and operated as a key social site for the production of knowledge(s) and meaning(s)" (5).

As with the Boy Scout movement, an analysis of organized hockey in Canada sheds light on the practices that have been central to understanding discourses of Canadian children during the first half of the twentieth century. It could be argued that many of the notions of citizenship and children as citizen-subjects embedded in Canadian sport discourse came directly from discussions taking place in Britain (and popularized by books such as Thomas Hughes's *Tom Brown's Schooldays*) about the benefits of muscular Christianity and

---

23. For a discussion of this kind of erasure, see Forsyth 2013; see also Wilson 2006, 58.
24. J. B. Yule, "Along the Trail," *Northern Tribune*, March 29, 1934, 2.
25. Yule, 2.

the positive aspects of learning lessons on the sports field.[26] These ideas were widely diffused in Canadian society by the late 1800s. The *Globe* newspaper, for example, frequently advocated the social benefits of playing sport (Kidd 2006, 704). In late-nineteenth-century Canada, sports garnered meaningful importance and significant resources were devoted to their development (Kidd 2006, 704; see also Morrow and Wamsley 2017). Kidd suggests (2006, 705) that one of the few points of shared perspective among sport clubs, physical educators, sport entrepreneurs, and civic boosters, as well as the athletes, coaches, and spectators, "was the claim that sport could socialize the young in desirable ways." These ideas of socialization and citizenship underpinned the development of youth sport in Canada (Kidd 2006, 701).

By the 1930s, physical educators in Britain were advocating for more state funding for sport facilities and sports programming. In March 1936, Tommy Munns, the *Globe*'s sports editor, reported on discussions about "the ideal of fitness in boys" that took place during an annual conference of boys' clubs held at Queen's College in Oxford, England. The group of 230 international delegates assembled concluded that a boy's ideal level of fitness could best be achieved "through the character-forming attributes of team games."[27] The delegates at the conference advocated for state funding for organizations that were "providing beneficial environment for youth during its more impressionable years." Munn quotes one conference delegate as saying, "the State educates these boys—our future citizens—free of charge, and then it does not raise a hand to help them in the most dangerous period of their lives."[28] Munns suggests that Oxford's example of providing sport facilities such as cricket pitches could be adopted in Toronto and other parts of the province.[29]

Conclusion

Our task in this chapter has been twofold. On one hand, we sought to explore the historical emergence of institutionalized minor hockey in Canada, shedding additional light on an under-studied dimension of sport history. Too often, the focus of sport scholarship is on elite-level competition, whereas the masses of participants—especially younger participants—rarely receive serious scholarly attention (Messner and Musto 2014, 107). Influenced by the work of childhood-development scholars like G. Stanley Hall, moral entrepreneurs used organized sport and leisure as sites of intervention to shape the nation's youth. On the other hand, though, and perhaps more centrally, we set out to theorize this emergence as a phenomenon both shaped by, and productive of, particular ideas about childhood. Like Little League baseball and Pop Warner football in the United States, institutionalized minor hockey in Canada takes root against a backdrop of public concern about the nation's children (particularly the nation's boys) and their physical, mental, and moral development.

In other words, the development of minor hockey was a function of the commercialization of hockey, to be sure. At least as importantly, however, minor hockey came about as part

---

26. For more on muscular Christianity and its origins and influence in North American sports, see Putney 2001.
27. Tommy Munns, "Scanning the Sport Field," *Globe*, March 18, 1936, 6.
28. Munns, 6.
29. Munns, 6.

of a much broader project of physical and moral development in the project of nation-building. Minor hockey, the institutionalization of physical-education curricula, and other adult-organized leisure opportunities all worked in concert as sites of intervention in shaping future citizens. This is not to suggest that all observers agreed as to how best to employ competitive sport as this kind of training ground (e.g., some suggested highly organized sport, while others eschewed such organization, advocating instead that "good sportsmanship" should be the most important guiding principle). It is, however, to highlight that regardless of the particular approach advocated, the various moral entrepreneurs both drew on and produced ideas about the nation's youth that conceptualized young people as in need of the kind of physical and moral development that competitive sport ostensibly provided.

There are a number of current tensions in both the landscape of hockey and thinking about the nation's youth. We still see adult-organized sport for youth marshaled as a form of character development, as evidenced by the prevalence of a "positive youth development" framework. The particular forms that this takes, however, shifted as neoliberal ideologies gained ascendancy. As Coakley points out (2016, 22), more "than building character, youth sports came to be seen by upper-middle-class parents as sites for preserving their privilege into the next generation, and by less advantaged others as pipelines for a child's upward mobility." This is certainly evident in the "revolution taking place in Canadian minor hockey," as large numbers of parents devote extraordinary resources toward their children's (athletic, social, emotional) development in the form of elite hockey programs (Turner 2014). Though the contours of these particular practices continue to change shape, the seemingly natural relationship between sport and youth development remains relatively unquestioned. Our task as hockey scholars is to interrogate the historical roots of these practices, and question and challenge the easy narratives about the place of sport in general, and hockey in particular, in the lives of Canadian children.

We gratefully acknowledge the skilled research assistance provided by Jasmine Saler, without which this chapter could not have been written.

Bibliography

Adams, Carly. 2014. "Troubling Bodies: 'The Canadian Girl,' the Ice Rink, and the Banff Winter Carnival." *Journal of Canadian Studies* 48 (3): 200–20.

———. 2009. "Organizing hockey for women: The Ladies Ontario Hockey Association and the fight for legitimacy, 1922–1940." In *Coast to Coast: Hockey in Canada to the Second World War*, ed. John Chi-Kit Wong. Toronto: University of Toronto Press.

———. 2011. "Supervised Places to Play: Social Reform, Citizenship, and Femininity at Municipal Playgrounds in London, Ontario, 1900–1942." *Ontario History* 103 (1): 60–80.

Adams, Carly, and Julie Stevens. 2007. "Change and Grassroots Movements: Re-conceptualizing Women's Hockey Governance in Canada." *International Journal of Sport Management and Marketing* 2 (4): 344–61.

Adams, Carly, and Stacey Leavitt. 2016. "'It's just girls' hockey': Troubling progress narratives in girls' and women's sport." *International Review for the Sociology of Sport*, 1–17. http://journals.sagepub.com.ezproxy.uleth.ca/doi/pdf/10.1177/1012690216649207.

Adams, Mary Louise. 2006. "The Game of Whose Lives? Gender, Race, and Entitlement in Canada's "National" Game." In *Artificial Ice: Hockey, Culture and Commerce*, ed. David Whitson and Richard Gruneau. Peterborough, ON: Broadview.

Alexander, Kristine. 2009. "The Girl Guide Movement and Imperial Internationalism During the 1920s and 1930s." *The Journal of the History of Childhood and Youth* 2 (1): 37–63.

———. 2015. "Canadian Girls, Imperial Girls, Global Girls: Race, Nation and Transnationalism in the Interwar Girl Guide Movement." In *Within and Without the Nation: Canadian History as Transnational History*, ed. Karen Dubinsky, Adele Perry, and Henry Yu. Toronto: University of Toronto Press.

Allain, Kristi. 2011. "Kid Crosby or Golden Boy: Sidney Crosby, Canadian national identity, and the policing of hockey masculinity." *International Review for the Sociology of Sport* 46 (1): 3–22.

Atwell, Leo G. 1989. *A History of the British Columbia Amateur Hockey Association*. Victoria: British Columbia Amateur Hockey Association.

Coakley, Jay. 2016. "Positive Youth Development Through Sport." In *Positive Youth Development Through Sport*, 2nd ed., ed. Nicholas L. Holt. New York: Routledge.

Comacchio, Cynthia. 2006. *The Dominion of Youth: Adolescence and the Making of Modern Canada, 1920 to 1950*. Waterloo, ON: Wilfrid Laurier University Press.

Forsyth, Janice. 2013. "Bodies of meaning: Sports and games at Canadian residential schools." In *Aboriginal Peoples and Sport in Canada: Historical Foundations and Contemporary Issues*, ed. Janice Forsyth and Audrey R. Giles. Vancouver: University of British Columbia Press.

Gagen, Elizabeth A. 2000. "An Example to Us All: Child Development and Identity Construction in Early 20th-century Playgrounds." *Environment and Planning A* 32 (4): 599–616.

———. 2004. "Making America Flesh: Physicality and Nationhood in Early Twentieth-century Physical Education Reform." *Cultural Geographies* 11 (4): 417–42.

Galway, Elizabeth, Louise Barrett, and Janice Newberry. 2012. "Discovering, Exploring, and Colonizing Childhood: Multidisciplinary Approaches to Childhood Studies." *Jeunesse: Young People, Texts, Cultures* 4 (1): 107–18.

Gleason, Mona. 2005. "From 'Disgraceful Carelessness' to 'Intelligent Precaution': Accidents and the Public Child in English Canada, 1900–1950." *Journal of Family History* 30 (2): 230–41.

———. 2013. *Small Matters: Canadian Children in Sickness and Health, 1900–1940*. Kingston, ON: McGill-Queen's Press.

Gleason, Mona, Tamara Myers, Leslie Paris, and Veronica Strong-Boag, eds. 2010. *Lost kids: Vulnerable children and youth in twentieth-century Canada and the United States*. Vancouver: University of British Columbia Press.

Gruneau, Richard, and David Whitson. 1993. *Hockey Night in Canada: Sport, Identities and Cultural Politics*. Aurora, ON: Garamond Press.

Heagerty, J. J. 1943. "The National Physical Fitness Act." *Canadian Journal of Public Health / Revue Canadienne De Sante'e Publique* 34 (10): 465–69.

Hopkins, Eric. *Childhood transformed: Working-class children in nineteenth-century England*. Manchester: Manchester University Press, 1994.

Kidd, Bruce. *The Struggle for Canadian Sport*. Toronto: University of Toronto Press, 1996.

———. 2006. "Muscular Christianity and Value-Centred Sport: The Legacy of Tom Brown in Canada." *International Journal of the History of Sport* 23 (5): 701–13.

Kidd, Bruce, and John Macfarlane. 1972. *Death of Hockey*. Toronto: New Press.

Laurendeau, Jason, and Dan Konecny. 2015. "Where is Childhood? In Conversation with Messner and Musto." *Sociology of Sport Journal* 32 (3): 332–44.

Messner, Michael A., and Michela Musto. 2014. "Where are the Kids?" *Sociology of Sport Journal* 31 (1): 102–22.

Metcalfe, Alan. 1995. "The Meaning of Amateurism: A Case Study of Canadian Sport, 1884–1970." *Canadian Journal of History of Sport* 26 (2): 33–48.

Mills, Sarah. 2013. "An Instruction in Good Citizenship: Scouting and the Historical Geographies of Citizenship Education." *Transactions of the Institute of British Geographers* 38 (1): 120–34.

Morrow, Don, and Kevin B. Wamsley. 2017. *Sport in Canada,* 4th ed. Toronto: Oxford University Press.

Overman, Steven J. 2011. *The Protestant Ethic and the Spirit of Sport: How Calvanism and Capitalism Shaped America's Games.* Macon, GA: Mercer University Press.

Putney, Clifford. 2001. *Muscular Christianity: Manhood and Sports in Protestant America, 1880–1920.* Cambridge, MA: Harvard University Press.

Retamales, Paulina Cecilia, and PearlAnn Reichwein. 2014. "'A Healthy and Contented Band': The Gyro Club and Playgrounds in Edmonton Urban Reform, 1921–1944." *Sport History Review* 45 (2): 96–122.

Robidoux, Michael A. 2001. *Men at Play: A Working Understanding of Professional Hockey in Canada.* Montreal: McGill-Queen's University Press.

———. 2002. "Imagining a Canadian Identity Through Sport: A Historical Interpretation of Lacrosse and Hockey." *Journal of American Folklore* 115 (456): 209–25.

Scherer, Jay, and Jordan Koch. 2010. "Living with War: Sport, Citizenship, and the Cultural Politics of Post-9/11 Canadian Identity." *Sociology of Sport Journal* 27 (1): 1–29.

Stevens, Julie. 2006. "The Canadian Hockey Association Merger and the Emergence of the Amateur Sport Enterprise." *Journal of Sport Management* 20 (1): 74–100.

Stevens, Julie, and Carly Adams. 2013. "'Together we can make it better': Collective action and governance in a girls' ice hockey association." *International Review for the Sociology of Sport* 48 (6): 658–72.

Stevens, Julie, and Andrew C. Holman. 2013. "Rinkside: New Scholarly Studies on Ice Hockey and Society." *Sport in Society* 16 (3): 251–53.

Turner, Randy. 2014. "Parents Who Can Afford It Scramble to Get Kids into Elite Hockey Programs." *Winnipeg Free Press*, February 2. http://www.winnipegfreepress.com/opinion/fyi/spring-fever-189487451.html

Wilson, Brian. 2006. "Selective Memory in a Global Culture: Reconsidering Links Between, Youth, Hockey and Canadian Culture." In *Artificial Ice: Hockey, Culture and Commerce*, ed. David Whitson and Richard Gruneau. Peterborough, ON: Broadview, 2006.

Young, Scott. 1989. *100 Years of Dropping the Puck: A History of the OHA.* Toronto: McClelland & Stewart.

Chapter 6
A Myth within a Myth: "Outdoor Shinny" as the Nursery for Canada's National Game

ROBERT RUTHERDALE

This chapter offers a reflection on the meaning and power of outdoor ice as a national symbol of the roots of hockey. As a northern country, Canada's climate and abundant water in most regions creates conditions, historically and culturally, for ice hockey to emerge as the dominant sport played by children, youth, and many young adults. Alongside such dominant symbolic imagery as the maple leaf, the beaver, and maple syrup, Canadians playing hockey outdoors on natural ice surfaces and outdoor rinks, especially in unorganized games of shinny, deserves a special place in discussions of Canada's nordicity, its degree of "northerness" at the intersection of the country's geography, social histories, and national emblems.[1]

Two settings can be considered. Beginning in the late 1830s, the frozen surfaces of lakes, ponds, and rivers come to mind, reminiscent of scenes from Thomas Haliburton's Sam Slick stories set in rural Nova Scotia.[2] Then, from the early twentieth century onward, a variety of specially built outdoor surfaces appeared in parks and other public spaces, and, later, especially after the Second World War, in suburban backyards—rinks sprang up, typically built by fathers across Canada. In all cases, the fact that these skating surfaces were outdoors and could be easily taken over, until the mid-1980s, by boys who organized themselves into play with no official rules lent such situations an aura of the ideal and the virtuous, as well

---

1. The concept of "nordicity" was introduced in mid-1960s by geographer Louis-Edmond Hamelin. Hamelin (1979) combined indices of latitude, climate, ice and precipitation, as well as human factors that included populations and economies. While Hamelin introduced the idea to a wider public, historians have increasingly explored its wider implications; see, for instance, Graham 1990 and Grace 2002.
2. Thomas Chandler Haliburton (1796–1865) was a Nova Scotian politician, judge, and author. While his serialized work, *The Clockmaker*, offered tales from the late 1830s for light reading throughout the British Empire, which featured the adventures of his central character, Sam Slick, mention of "hurly on the long pond on the ice" appears in the second volume of *The Attaché* or *Sam Slick in England* (1844). This and related passages, in fiction, are considered the first known reference, in fact, to ice hockey, played by King's College boys in Windsor, Nova Scotia—see Davies 2004.

as the value of spontaneous play over organized sport. Cast as uniquely Canadian, the ideal of outdoor ice is largely romantic, but it serves as a myth within a myth when placed at the heart of ice hockey itself—the notion that, traditionally, boys best learn the skills and fast rhythms of their sport playing with their peers on unsupervised, outdoor ice surfaces.

That the compelling myth of pond hockey resides within the larger myth of ice hockey as Canada's national sport recognizes that both fact and fiction dwell in generalizations about the inclusiveness of such recreation, as popular as play on natural ice has always been. As a national symbol, hockey played in scrimmages on outdoor ice can be approached through what cultural historians inspired by Eric Hobsbawm and Terrence Ranger have called an "invented tradition." "Invented tradition," as these authors put it in their introduction to an immensely influential volume of essays (1983, 1), "is taken to mean a set of practices, normally governed by overtly or tacitly accepted rules and of a ritual and symbolic nature, which seeks to inculcate certain norms of behaviour by repetition, which automatically implies continuity with the past." As constant as the constant return of winter is, this amateur, sporting pastime, unorganized and initiated, until recently, largely by boys, outdoor hockey as a made-in-Canada tradition stands today as one of Canada's most durable symbols (see, e.g.. Holman 2009; Dryden 1983). The symbolic allure of outdoor ice as Canada's most authentic site for unorganized amateur sport ideal also connects to Benedict Anderson's (1983) approach to "imagined communities" that seek a broader sense of belonging through the generating of nation-building symbolism. Although references could be made to "road hockey," played since the early 1960s with a ball on paved streets and suburban driveways, nothing compares to the symbolic charm of outdoor ice hockey, played in its most pristine form with skates, sticks, pucks, and a minimum of protective equipment. If outdoor ice hockey is approached as an immensely popular pastime played in virtually every region of Canada, save for British Columbia's warmer Lower Mainland and Vancouver Island, its mythical attachment to a traditional rite of becoming a "true" Canadian invites further investigation. How has this myth evolved, and why construe the free and *unorganized* play, until the latter 1980s, of boys as a myth within a myth vis-à-vis the league-based and local community sport of *organized*, largely indoor, ice hockey in Canada?

Placing Outdoor Hockey's Symbolic Appeal in Historical Context

Between 2002 and 2013, the Bank of Canada featured on the back of its five-dollar note an illustration of outdoor hockey and figure skating. *Globe and Mail* journalist Roy MacGregor (2015) wrote of "a charming illustration of a backyard hockey rink" with "no picture of the Queen, no reference to God—where four children are playing shinny and another is learning to skate while holding the hand of a proud parent." At this banknote's official release, Canada's Minister of Finance and subsequent Prime Minister Paul Martin reinforced the idea of outdoor ice recreation as a national pastime, part of Canada's "national heritage." Martin stated that the "new $5 note pays homage to children as Canada's future, and to play as a healthy part of their physical, social, and cultural development." He added a reference to tradition, unique to hockey in wintertime Canada: "It is also a celebration of Canada's northern climate where our winter pastimes—in particular the game of hockey—reflect our sporting heritage" (quoted in Bank of Canada 2002).

When journalists and politicians alike frequently refer to hockey, with its roots in the hurley (widely considered the first reference to "hockey") of the 1830s Thomas Haliburton described as a rustic, even "countryside" experience of youth, nature, and sport, they resurrect a *pastoral sense of Canadian* heritage and tradition in which the outdoor game sits at the centre (Bouchier 2003; Metcalf 1987) (Figure 6.1). Symbolically, and at the professional level, North America's National Hockey League now organizes an official league game played on a temporary ice surface constructed on the field of a football or baseball stadium. These annual games, played since 2008 typically on or near New Year's Day, are known as the NHL's Winter Classic, originally known as the Heritage Classic. The "classic" aspects harkens back to the outdoor game itself. Teams typically don original or retro jerseys and warm up with toques, as would a child playing outdoors, with goaltenders often keeping theirs on their helmets for the entire game if desired. Stadia crowds often exceed 70,000 and television ratings reach record levels for hockey broadcasts (Dowbiggin 2010). As one broadcaster, NBC's Bob Costas, put it, "Seeing hockey that way, it just went beyond the importance of one game. It became a tradition in one year" (Dowbiggin 2010).

Invented traditions and imagined community identities intersect with sport both in terms of gender and age when attention is paid to the roots of outdoor play. Boys' participation far outnumbered girls' until the latter 1980s. The outdoor surfaces they played on, typically by themselves without adult supervision, had served by then as the seasonal

Figure 6.1 The Most Canadian photo?
Two Canadian national icons, a uniformed Royal Canadian Mounted Police officer, Cpl. Shaun Begg, and outdoor ice, are captured in this photograph. Set against the remote Purcell Mountains of British Columbia, this image of Begg went viral in 2015.
Copyright Rick Wiltse

playgrounds for Canadian boyhood for nearly a century. Given that girls and women now play ice hockey across Canada on organized teams indicates the significant shift toward more gender-inclusive participation, especially following a 1986 Ontario Court of Appeal decision that granted Justine Blainey the right to play on an organized boys' team (Avery and Stevens 1997; Findlay 2013).

Prior to the arrival of significant numbers of girls into the game, natural ice hockey, or shinny, had long been a realm of boyhood masculinity. As Christopher Grieg (2014) suggests in his study of boyhood in post–1945 Ontario, "teamwork" stood out as a dominant ideal for boys as they grew up. And hockey, both organized and unorganized, was at the centre, drawing the highest participation rate for any team sport across the country in those years. Adult proponents of the virtues of teamwork in the postwar decades were many: coaches, parents, league conveners. But they had varied objectives, from strengthening the male body in its formative years to face the communist threat to building an efficient middle-class male workforce. An appealing set of values came together: "teamwork, togetherness, selflessness, loyalty, hard work, duty, and discipline" were the hallmarks of this ideal," Grieg concludes (27). And he goes on to note that "radio broadcaster and writer Foster Hewitt described the hockey rink as an "outdoor nursery" for Canadian boys" (40). Basic skills, boyhood camaraderie, and healthy exercise came together on skates, chasing, passing, or shooting a puck.

Organized hockey offered a recreational context for boys to grow up playing the game in league-designated teams. Yet within that tradition, the outdoor pond or backyard rink has often been considered, often with some nostalgia, by former players as the best place to perfect skills, to practice without structure in self-motivated or loosely organized team play. A parallel tradition of boys supervising themselves required a fair degree of boyhood masculine teamwork to organize as shinny scrimmages without official teams, referees, timekeepers, and such. Typically, the first job was to join shoulders and clear, *their* ice, with "borrowed" snow shovels, in their impromptu squads. Ordinarily, they did not wear equipment, beyond skates and perhaps a pair of hockey gloves. As well, they were free to practice individual skills on their own, before or after their game. And their rules were flexible. Instead of playing by the clock, for instance, they might agree to play up to a team's, or side's, first ten goals. Without nets, they often played without a goalkeeper and might use stones or boots to mark goalposts. Compared to the organized games of the rink, played with full equipment, the outdoor game was essentially a non-contact contest and depended more on stickhandling ability and passing. The teams themselves varied in number, and positional play was not emphasized, with players often communicating with each other during the play of who should "move up" and who should "stay back." Approaches to such forms of play informally circulated in a popular culture of boyhood that emphasized improvisation, spontaneity, and freedom.

Theoretically, such play took place within what (borrowing from Arnold van Gennep) anthropologist Victor Turner conceived of as a "time out of time." As a boyhood recreation, as well as a set of rituals, the efforts to skate, to pass, to stick-check, to stickhandle, and to score, to succeed altogether on the ice, was a rite of passage (Turner 1969). With respect to time and outdoor play, often only the hours of sunlight, or a parent's appeal to "come inside" at a certain point in real time, placed limits on the game, in addition to, as many accounts describe, the rigours of extreme cold. If organized team play had emerged as an ideal "nursery" for Canadian boys, the less-inhibited, rule-governed, free time of unorganized outdoor play had become its ideal crib.

Don Morrow and Kevin Wamsley, writing in Oxford University Press's *Sport in Canada: A History*, offer a thoughtful discussion of ice hockey and Canada's national identity: "While ice hockey may not presently be important to all or the majority of Canadians," they assert, "one cannot overstate its historical significance in creating a national identity." Recognizing the importance of all forms of ice hockey, both unorganized outdoor play and organized indoor arena play, as a Canadian *winter* sport they add that the "inescapable reach of hockey into the lives of Canadians has been described as almost an organic connection, a 'natural extension of seasonal rhythms'" (Morrow and Wamsley 2013, 315).

Here, they are borrowing from Richard Gruneau and David Whitson, whose work places a winter-sport tradition in the context of local community participation across Canada's regions in a periodically (with the exception of some areas in southern British Columbia) sub-zero winter climate (Gruneau and Whitson 1993, 3). And although lacrosse has been long associated with its Aboriginal roots (see Downey 2012; Robidoux 2014), in most local communities in Canada no sport can contend with hockey as a cultural ideal, underpinning its popular and mythical associations with being Canadian. As Morrow and Walmsley put it (2013, 314; italics in the original), "hockey remains central for individuals who seek to elaborate an ostensibly unified Canadian national identity. In this respect, *hockey invented Canadians as much as Canadians invented hockey*."

Morrow and Walmsley make an important point, however, in emphasizing that sport does not transcend social and cultural differences of language, religion, and ethnicity; and Canadian hockey, including unorganized outdoor hockey, is no exception to this general rule: "In Canadian history," they observe for all sports, both team and individual, "sport has not transcended these cultural differences; rather, it has tended to reinforce or reproduce them." They go on to elaborate on the power of the myth of hockey as a unifying, defining aspect of "Canadianness": "The meanings produced through sport in the construction of national identities seem fragile and temporary. Yet, mythologies have always been important to people" (Morrow and Walmsley 2013, 314).

Perhaps no better place to see the myth of outdoor hockey's essential Canadian character reiterated is in an introductory statement from the Canadian Pond Hockey Association (CPHA), a voluntary association dedicated to promoting outdoor ice hockey. The CPHA also organizes tournaments across Canada each winter. They promote the idea of pond hockey as unique to the Canadian experience. In so doing, the CPHA reiterates the myth within the myth that gives this winter pastime its enduring power. As its homepage link, "In the Land of Maple Syrup," proclaims:

> In the land of maple syrup [another national symbol], the double-double [a particular serving of coffee from an popular coffee-shop chain, founded by hockey great Tim Horton] and Bob & Doug [an early-1980s "Second City TV" comedy duo, known for their use of a distinctly English-Canadian vernacular, deliberately accentuated with a common colloquialism that punctuated their folksy banter—"eh?"] is there anything more Canadian than grabbing a shovel, skates, sticks and nets, and bundling up in all our gear to play a relaxed game of hockey on a frozen pond or backyard rink?

Heck—even our $5 bill once depicted a picture of 4 children playing a game of shinny on a frozen pond. At one time, it was the rite of passage, a tradition held dear for every young Canadian during the cold, winter months. Most of us can think of at least one field, back yard rink, or frozen body of water that we had the chance to skate on at some point in our lives. This is where generations of young people learned to play hockey and where great memories are still being made. This is where we spent hours outdoors playing the game until our fingers and toes were frozen. (Canadian Pond Hockey Association n.d.)

Countless stories, laced with nostalgia, trace back to the 1960s, 1970s, and 1980s. And many, based on memories of growing up in wintertime, can be evaluated as a gendered script rooted in boyhood experiences of sport. The same could be said for basketball, baseball, soccer, football, or any team sport that is fed by pickup play on sequestered city streets or open fields, the spaces around the world that boys appropriate and transform through impromptu team play. In terms of the backyard rink, however, while the focus is on children and youth, adults are not far behind in the background. Some of the cases assessed below involve a high degree of parental supervision, from fathers especially, when it came to preparing backyard rinks—in most cases, in the rear of their suburban family homes. Roy MacGregor has written revealingly about the myth of natural ice in a well-researched report for the *Globe and Mail* on backyard rinks.

Assessments of the Outdoor Rink in Life, Writing and Memory

Born in 1948, MacGregor grew up in Huntsville, Ontario, and has written eloquently about hockey, both professional and amateur, with much of his commentary grounded in his own experience as a young player and, later, a father. He has vivid memories of growing up playing in the winter months on "outdoor" ice. Along with his career as a journalist, MacGregor has authored several bestselling books that incorporate hockey themes, including *The Home Team: Fathers, Sons and Hockey* (1995) and *A Life in the Bush: Lessons from My Father* (1999), both published by Penguin. While much of his work is tinged with an appealing sense of nostalgia, he has produced some useful accounts of play on outdoor ice, with a focus on its domesticated surface—the backyard rink.

In January 2015, the *Globe and Mail* published a special report by MacGregor entitled "Backyard hockey rinks remain a rich winter tradition in Canada." MacGregor drew from a valuable research base—some seventy responses from across the country to a call the *Globe* put out for reader's photos and reflections on their own backyard rinks. MacGregor begins with a wistful look back to the Bank of Canada's decision two years before to replace the outdoor-skating imagery on the five-dollar bill with something new: in November 2013, the outdoor scene was replaced "by an astronaut floating in space," as he put it, in homage to Canada's accomplishments in space science and technology (MacGregor 2015). His lament, however, takes readers back to the *authenticity* of outdoor ice as *intrinsically* Canadian—the myth within the myth, "outer space is not where Canadians live—certainly not in winter." Canadians, symbolized by outdoor winter play, found their "real life" "on the skating rink," echoing Roch Carrier's imagined sense of national identity epitomized in *The Hockey Sweater*.

MacGregor reminds readers of one of Canada's most endearing short stories, one of boys playing hockey on an outdoor rink. This classic tale was later narrated for wide audiences in the National Film Board/Office national du film du Canada's adaptation.[3] "Our real life was on the skating rink," is how Carrier opens his story. Set in rural Quebec, these boys of winter, Catholic francophones, skated with identical sweaters, each with the same number on their backs as their revered champion, Maurice "Rocket" Richard, who wore number nine with the Montreal Canadiens. The Rocket's status as a Quebec folk hero, the subject of recent study by Benoît Melançon (2009), is undisputed. The Rocket became a Quebec icon, idolized and idealized, as did his number-nine Canadiens jersey.

MacGregor (2015) begins by celebrating what is, in fact, a persuasive anachronism: "Carrier was writing about Sainte-Justine, Que., in the 1940s," he states. "But it could have been Lakehurst, Ont., in 2015 where, this week, Garry Hall—with the help of his father and a neighbour—has his backyard rink up and running once again for the local kids to enjoy." As appealing as the image of schoolboys moving up and down the rink in sweaters identical to a sport icon has become through Carrier's story, when MacGregor suggests that that world reappears each winter, like the snow itself, he tends to overlook the changes in gender participation, the actual cost of play for parents and guardians, and the shifts in the ethnicity of players. To this extent his approach is *ahistorical* and glosses over significant changes in both organized and unorganized forms of wintertime hockey play. While his talent for splendid journalism, consumed by large reading audiences across the country, is well established, MacGregor's preconceived (around the myth within the myth) approach is selective, and can overlook the shifts in class, ethnic, and gender boundaries that separate Roch Carrier's romantic sense of the social past with the actual historical past. Myths are often cast as timeless. So, too, with hockey, especially outdoor play, which conforms to the traditions of a simple game of shinny.

Garry Hall's seasonal rink-making operation behind his Lakefield home is indeed typical of many present-day fathers who flood their own properties, usually their backyards to, in a sense, privatize if not domesticate the outdoor pond. A very popular off-the-job pastime for some fathers is now a Canadian tradition: working with a garden hose and fluctuating temperatures to build a rink for their own and neighbourhood kids. Such efforts parallel the expansion of suburban areas, when a comparative severe postwar housing shortage gave way to a housing boom by the mid-1950s. A diminutive patchwork of backyard and local community rinks were maintained across Canada, but their expansion, in concert with the postwar baby boom, was a very real Canadian phenomenon, especially for the middle class. Moreover, the surfacing and resurfacing of outdoor ice surfaces, natural or manufactured, as something essential to family, community, and national identity stands out in story after story: "It's a labour of love," Hall says of his small masterpiece. "I can't imagine a winter without it. It's part of who I am" (MacGregor 2015).

MacGregor continues by extending the myth as far back as the late nineteenth century, back to Thomas C. Haliburton, the first to write about outdoor hockey as part of an appealing, nostalgic world of the past. The outdoor hockey myth, in MacGregor's words, "has been a part of who we are since before we were even Canada. More than two centuries

---

3. *The Hockey Sweater*, directed by Sheldon Cohen, written and narrated by Roch Carrier (National Film Board, 1980).

have passed since Thomas C. Haliburton, the creator of the Sam Slick adventures, heard the boys of King's Collegiate School "racin', yellin', hollerin', and whoopin' like mad with pleasure" as they skated on Long Pond in rural Nova Scotia." MacGregor sees a fundamental Canadian tradition spawning what can be more acutely described as a national symbol, a myth within a myth: "Connect that backyard rink, pond or slough," he writes, "with what would evolve into the national game and that little ice surface takes on iconic status" (MacGregor 2015).

Examples are drawn from the outdoor nurseries of Canadian hockey greats from different eras, beginning with "The Great One's" now famous backyard rink of the 1960s:

> Wayne Gretzky always claimed he became the player he would turn into 'right in my own backyard,' stickhandling pucks around Javex bottles his father, Walter, would set up in the Brantford Ont., an outdoor rink the five Gretzky kids all called 'Wally's Coliseum.' In Victoriaville, Que., it was the 'Béliveau Forum,' where young Jean learned to stickhandle, Arthur Béliveau building the rink and his wife Laurette laying industrial-strength linoleum under the kitchen table so Jean could keep his skates on while eating. (MacGregor 2015)

These tales seem timeless—united in the myth within myth: a seasonal narrative evoking national pride and conjuring many heroes and, more recently, heroines on the ice. Tom Wickenheiser raised two children: Tim, who played in the NHL, and Hayley, who led Canada's women's Olympic team for over a decade, winning four Olympic gold medals. As MacGregor relates, "Tom Wickenheiser, who built his backyard rink in Shaunavon, Sask., once recalled a night in December 1985, when he could not sleep for a mysterious knocking sound from outside. It was after midnight and minus-20 C, and when he went to check he realized seven-year-old Hayley had slipped out of her bed, dressed in full gear and was out working on her shot in the dark" (MacGregor 2015). Such stories, of girls obsessed with perfecting their hockey skills on the backyard rink appeared first in the latter 1980s, now abound.

MacGregor is cognizant of the appeal of the folklore and tradition his report taps into: "These are the tales that take on mythological status, but there are backyard rink stories told every winter across this land, many just as charming even if the children involved do not end up wining Stanley Cups and Olympic gold medals." At this point, he refers to something familiar to anthropologists that this chapter began with: "there can be no doubting that a great many Canadians believe a backyard rink is a rite of passage for their children. Julie Saunders of Telkwa, B.C., wrote to say, 'We only went to look at this house because it advertised an ice rink in the yard.' They liked what they saw, and bought" (MacGregor 2015).

Appropriate to a report stressing the positive, MacGregor concludes his piece with reference to a current global concern of real significance—diminishing ice and snow in circumpolar regions: "Perhaps the Bank of Canada dumped the old fiver because it had come to believe, as many have, that climate change has already doomed the backyard rink. Well, they could at least have waited, for last winter [2014] was as good as it gets for ice, and this winter, despite a Christmas thaw in much of the country, many backyard rinks opened earlier than they had for years. Nestor Kelba wrote from Calgary to say the Kelba neighbourhood rink is now into its 33rd winter, adding: 'This year's ice is looking like the best ever'" (MacGregor 2015). Myths often serve as a distraction from difficult changes that every society faces. Canadian outdoor ice as a timeless icon is no exception.

As we might expect, MacGregor also draws from, indeed inspires, the myth within a myth: of free play on outdoor ice as the ideal nursery for Canada's national sport. He contrasts popular notions of backyard rinks as rustic installations, at best, with attention paid to elaborate projects of planning, building, and maintaining: "Many rinks are simple—pound down the snow, flood with a hose, banks for boards and old boots for goal posts—but some are almost as extravagant as the rinks where top teams play." (MacGregor 2015). For example: "Boards are common but so, too, are rinks with curved corners just like NHL arenas have. There are outdoor rinks with blue lines and red lines painted into the ice, faceoff circles, creases and floodlights. There are even backyard rinks with board advertising, PA systems and pumped-in music for romantic evening skates" (MacGregor 2015). Recreational rinks, supported by Canadian municipalities, rarely include such items, and commercial advertising is, of course, restricted.

Such elaborate backyard rinks may be less common, but they do have a long history when we turn to the creation of postal worker, amateur hockey coach, and father, Michael Zuke, a backyard-rink maker whose annual installation became famous in the east end of Sault Ste. Marie, Ontario, for some forty-four years, up until the end of the 1990s. Zuke's rink helped spawn two NHL players (Ron Francis and Mike Zuke Jr.) and several generations of, for the most part, boys playing pickup hockey. The "Zukedome," as it was affectionately known, became the most noteworthy of its kind anywhere in Canada at that time.

Community Fatherhood and Memories of the "Zukeadome"
The creator of the extraordinary backyard rink, Michael Zuke, grew up playing the game he loved in the east end of "the Soo," near the Algoma Steel plant. As an adolescent in the late 1940s, he recalled stealing away either in town or on the ferry across the border to Michigan to watch senior-level amateur hockey games. Hockey journalist Chris Cuthbert recounts that "he'd hide in the basement 'dungeon' of the old Gouin Street rink to avoid paying admission to senior games." From this period, Zuke's "most cherished memory is opening night of the Sault Memorial Gardens in 1949 when the Sault Indians, featuring [his] brothers Walter and Bill, entertained the Port Arthur Bearcats" (Cuthbert and Russell 1997, 259). As his three sons—one went on to play eight seasons in the NHL—and two daughters grew up, he volunteered as a bantam and Junior A–level coach.

Zuke recalled flooding his first backyard rink even before he first became a father in 1954. "The year after we were married we went to a city skating rink. There were about four hockey games going on and pucks whizzing all over the place. We skated for about twenty minutes and left. As I'm walking back, I looked at all the land I had and said, why can't we have our own rink? I started one the next day." For Zuke, preparing the surface and first flooding became a forty-four-year wintertime labour of love. His rink grew to attract the outdoor play of surrounding neighbourhoods at a time of expanding family formation in the Sault during Canada's baby boom, with plenty of local children who simply had to walk to the Zukeadome.[4] So many children came to skate that Zuke needed

---

4. On Canada's baby boom, see Owram 1996.

to consider how to reserve ice for girls who wanted to figure skate. He remembered posting a schedule of "public skating" (for girls) and "hockey" (mostly shinny sessions for boys) (Cuthbert and Russell 1997, 258). As a community father who both coached boys' teams and maintained his rink, it involved considerable commitment. Zuke recalled sometimes flooding the Zukeadome three times a day, and it was certainly used: "One Saturday," he noted, "we counted sixty-eight different kids who had come over" (Cuthbert and Russell 1997, 258).

By the late 1990s, his wife, June, had grown to love the rink too, especially as a grandmother: "At the end of November, we decided it was too much to do again this winter," Zuke recalled, with some sadness as he approached a final year of being the father of a legendary backyard rink." The boys, the "rink rats" as such youngsters were known across the country, were dedicated to their "free" ice time. "Then my wife goes into the grocery store and meets one of the boys who was a rink rat at our place. Now he has a son who is six or seven. The boy comes to June and says "Mrs. Zuke, I'm going to play on your rink this year." My wife had tears in her eyes, so I said we'll make a small one" (Cuthbert and Russell 1997, 257).

Zuke's respect as a coach of organized hockey—he led his AAA bantam teams to eleven provincial championship rounds—grew throughout the city while the Zukeadome became a magnet for outdoor shinny. As a private, backyard venture, the rink complemented the community rinks maintained by the city's Parks and Recreation Department. There was only "one complaint issued" from a comparatively tranquil neighbourhood regarding Zuke's creation and unofficial role as a communal father: "We had an old couple across the street," he says, pointing to a blue house fifty yards away. "The guy used to get up for work at five in the morning. Late at night in twenty below weather, you could hear the puck hitting the boards for miles. His wife called over and asked us to keep the noise down. So I decided to use a ball. It was the best thing that ever happened. I read a book by the Russian coach [Anatoly] Tarasov twenty-five years later. He said the best way to develop shooting accuracy is with a ball. I thought, Holy geez, we've been doing it all along" (Cuthbert and Russell 1997, 258).

As a father, Mike Zuke's enthusiasm for the game and for his rink's local claim to fame revived the boy within the man, a strong sentimental attachment to the joy of movement, play, and identity with team sporting excellence (Bourdieu 1991). His son Mike Jr. had "superior talent, if not his father's boundless enthusiasm." "When kids would come over to play I'd join in," laughs Zuke, whose hooked nose has been rearranged by at least one high stick. "I'd call my son Michael and say, "Come on, let's play." He'd say, "I can't until I finish my homework." Usually, it's the parent telling the kid to do his homework" (Cuthbert and Russell 1997, 259). "My dad was a great coach," Mike Jr. later recalled: "He built an ice rink in our backyard that was half the size of a regulation NHL rink. It was wonderful, with lights and a screen and everything" (Zuke 2005).

Zuke's leisure time spent as a hockey father was, however, hardly transformed by the consumer revolution associated with the stereotypical backyard father, barbecuing in the summer months and flooding backyard rinks in the winter.[5] During the Zukeadome's early years, Zuke worked with materials close at hand to transform his backyard space into a

---

5. On backyard barbecuing, see Dummitt 1998.

legendary neighbourhood backyard rink. However, after the last of his children had left home, Zuke decided to exchange his leisure-time work for his paid work: "I could have worked for more years for a full pension," he chuckled. "I had three jobs and only one paid. I decided to retire from the job that paid. I gave the post office one month's notice and that was it" (Cuthbert and Russell 1997, 258). A father's leisure time could be consumed as part of his active parenting, but it did not have to be. He might in some pursuits choose how and where he spends it. Whatever off-the-job choices were made, a father's influence as a role model for his children increased in significance as they grew up. It certainly was in the case of Mike Zuke. Each winter, his leisure time was consumed with making his Zukeadome part of what actually had become by the 1960s and 1970s part of a much larger slice of Canadian history, one demonstrating, with fathers at the centre, how outdoor ice could erode the distinction between private property and public space.

The Symbolic Appeal of Outdoor Ice and Canada's National Game

Powerful myths are based, in part, on powerful truths, in this case the experiences reflected in the inspired responses to the *Globe and Mail's* request for stories of backyard rinks and Roy MacGregor's colourful employment of them. But such a useable sense of the past can gloss over significant historical changes. As an origin myth—that the rebirth each winter of Canada's great national game takes place on outdoor ice, not in indoor arenas—there can be a tendency to overlook significant shifts in gender and play and ethnicity and play, and the changing history of childhood itself.

As Morrow and Walmsley assert, sport does not actually transcend social differences, it reflects and reinforces them. Beginning in the mid-1980s a minority of girls first joined boys' teams, until participation rates supported girls' hockey leagues and, ultimately, women's hockey as a world-class competitive sport. Tom Wickenheiser's backyard rink in Shaunavon, Saskatchewan, was fundamental for Hayley, who became a gold-medal team captain in Olympic women's hockey, and her older brother also played at the highest competitive level professionally. This is relatively new. And many of the stories here overlook this fact. The conflation of "childhood" with boyhood in stories of outdoor ice hockey, prior to the rise in girls' and women's participation, indicates how this myth of outdoor hockey as the "true" or "authentic nursery of Canada's national sport obscures historical change. As well, the generations of children, mostly boys, who could play on outdoor ice did not reflect the ethnic diversity of Canada, though recently signs of change are apparent. As gender and ethnic differences renegotiate their boundaries in the twenty-first century, Morrow and Walmsley's dictum does not, in fact, break down; rather, it is reflected in the new participation dynamic in the changing social contexts of children and youth sport participation.

Finally, what about social class? At present, the rising costs of hockey sticks and ice skates, apart from the complicated range of full equipment for organized leagues and ancillary team costs, has intensified the socio-economic barriers to play that a growing proportion of children face (Cantelon and Hollands 1988). Children's friendship networks and the more active participation of parents, as economic providers, in organizing children's recreation also suggest some closed pathways, as well as opportunities, to simply learn to skate for poorer children.

Nonetheless, the myth within a myth remains a useful, indeed positive force as an ideal aspiration. Loosely organized play, open to all, on outdoor ice is unquestionably an important national symbol. The emblematic appeal of the free play of hockey as played outside has passed through many manifestations, from Haliburton's hurley on a frozen pond to the NHL Winter Classic. Along the way, it has served to absorb changes in who plays, though there is still room for increased participation despite the challenge posed by warmer winters. Although the popular narratives and imagery outdoor hockey has spawned obscure long-standing historical impediments to sport participation—from social and cultural boundaries to the physical challenges accommodated in the comparatively recent emergence of sled hockey—Canada's myth within a myth appears destined to continue to serve as a timeless model for a better future in the face of the formidable barriers, for some children, to the freedom to play on natural ice in a northern climate.

Bibliography

Avery, Joanna, and Julie Stevens. 1997. *Too Many Men on the Ice: Women's Hockey in North America*. Victoria, BC: Polestar Books.

Anderson, Benedict. 1983. *Imagined Communities: Reflections on the Origin and Spread of Nationalism*. London: Verso.

Bank of Canada. 2002. "The Bank of Canada Launches a New $5 Bank Note." Press release, March 27. http://www.bankofcanada.ca/2002/03/bank-canada-launches-new-5-bank-note.

Bouchier, Nancy B. 2003. *For the Love of the Game: Amateur Sport in Small-Town Ontario, 1838–1895*. Montreal: McGill-Queen's University Press.

Bourdieu, Pierre. 1991. "Sport and Social Class." In *Re: Rethinking Popular Culture: Contemporary Perspectives in Popular Culture*, ed. Chandra Mukerji and Michael Schudson, 357–73. Berkeley: University of California Press.

Canadian Pond Hockey Association. n.d. "In the Land of Maple Syrup." Canadian National Pond Hockey Championships. http://canadapondhockey.ca/in-the-land-of-maple-syrup.

Cantelon, Hart, and Robert Hollands, eds. 1988. *Leisure, Sport and Working Class Cultures: Theory and History*. Toronto: Garamond Press.

Cuthbert, Chris, and Scott Russell. 1997. *The Rink: Stories from Hockey's Home Towns*. Toronto: Viking.

Davies, Richard A. 2004. *Inventing Sam Slick: A Biography of Thomas Chandler Haliburton*. Toronto: University of Toronto Press.

Dowbiggin, Bruce. 2010. "How hockey found its signature moment." *Globe and Mail*, December 30. https://www.theglobeandmail.com/sports/how-hockey-found-its-signature-moment/article1321803.

Downey, Allan. 2012. "Engendering Nationality: Haudenosaunee Tradition, Sport, and the Lines of Gender." *Journal of the Canadian Historical Association / La Société historique du Canada* 23:319–54.

Dryden, Ken. 1983. *The Game: A Thoughtful and Provocative Look at Life in Hockey*. Toronto: Macmillan Canada.

Dummitt, Chris. 1998. "Finding a Place for Father: Selling the Barbecue in Postwar Canada." *Journal of the Canadian Historical Association / Revue de la Société historique du Canada* 9: 209–23.

Findlay, Hilary A. 2013 "Blainey, Pasternak and Sagen: Courts and Public Opinion." In *Playing it Forward: 50 Years of Women and Sport in Canada*, ed. Guylaine Demers et. al. Toronto: Second Story Press and Feminist History Society.

Grace, Sherrill E. 2002. *Canada and the Idea of the North*. Montreal: McGill University Press.

Graham, Amanda. 1990. "Indexing the Canadian North: Broadening the Definition." *Northern Review* 6 (Winter): 21–37.

Grieg, Christopher J. 2014. *Ontario Boys: Masculinity and the Idea of Boyhood in Postwar Ontario, 1945–1960.* Waterloo, ON: Wilfrid Laurier University Press.

Gruneau, Richard, and David Whitson. 1993. *Hockey Night in Canada: Sport, Identities, and Cultural Politics.* Toronto: Garamond Press.

Hamelin, Louis-Edmond. 1979. *Canada's Nordicity: It's Your North Too.* Translated by William Barr. Montreal: Harvest House.

Hobsbawm, Eric, and Terrance Ranger, eds. 1983. *The Invention of Tradition.* Cambridge: Cambridge University Press.

Holman, Andrew C., ed. 2009. *Canada's Game: Hockey and Identity.* Montreal: McGill-Queen's University Press.

MacGregor, Roy. 2015. "Backyard hockey rinks remain a rich winter tradition in Canada," *Globe and Mail* Digitized Edition, January 2. https://www.theglobeandmail.com/sports/hockey/why-backyard-hockey-rinks-remain-a-rich-winter-tradition-in-canada/article22282662/.

Melançon, Benoît. 2009. *The Rocket: A Cultural History of Maurice Richard.* Translated by Fred A. Reed. Vancouver: Greystone Books.

Metcalf, Alan. 1987. *Canada Learns to Play: The Emergence of Organized Sport, 1807–1914.* Toronto: McClelland and Stewart.

Morrow, Don, and Kevin Wamsley. 2013. *Sport in Canada: A History.* Toronto: Oxford University Press.

Owram, Doug. 1996. *Born at the Right Time: A History of the Baby Boom Generation.* Toronto: University of Toronto Press.

Robidoux, Michael A. 2014. *Stickhandling Through the Margins: Hockey in Canada.* Toronto: University of Toronto Press.

Turner, Victor W. 1969. *The Ritual Process.* London: Penguin.

Zuke, Mike Jr. 2005. "Between the Pipes." *MSU Blue Line Club.* Newsletter published by the MSU Blue Line Club, Hancock, Michigan.

PART III
Whose Game?

Document 3
Skating in the Drainage Ditches[1]

HAYLEY WICKENHEISER

I have had many defining moments in my career; certainly, history would point to glory at the Olympics or some other shining moment. But I have also had equally defining experiences that are unlikely to be recorded in reviews of my career. In fact, some of them continue to be driving factors in my daily life, on and off the ice. They continue to push me to do what I can to further the female game beyond what it did for me, to what it could do for other young girls and women who share my love of the sport (Figure D3.1).

When I began playing hockey as a little girl in Shaunavon, Saskatchewan, the sport was dominated by boys. While that is still the case today, there are so many more options for girls who want to play hockey, and they are the fastest growing demographic in the sport. But, back when I started (which wasn't all that long ago), there was no such thing as girls' skates and pink sticks, and there were very few, if any, girls' leagues. The choice came down to playing on boys' teams or not at all. I was just a kid who wanted to play hockey, so I opted to join a boys' team, without any forethought to the discrimination I would face.

I grew up playing with my family on a rink in our backyard, and I used to skate in the drainage ditches to school during the winter. So I was a strong skater and loved the game, which made me better than many of the boys my age. Great for my future career. Not so great for my daily existence at the rink.

Not just the boys I played against (and sometimes with), but their parents, too, would sometimes chide, taunt, and say horrible things to me as I entered the rink to dress in a bathroom (there were no dressing rooms for girls) or hit the ice. My parents were extremely supportive and sheltered me as best they could from the politics of hockey, especially when it concerned being a female in the game, but many times it still came through.

I remember thinking that it was wrong that anyone would make a little girl feel so discouraged and frustrated just because she played a sport that closed-minded people believed belonged to boys. I became defiant and driven to deliver. Back then, I chose this behaviour so it would show on the scoreboard that I could compete. Nowadays, I'm determined to play a small role in creating an atmosphere that nurtures girls' desire to play and ensures they are provided the same opportunities as boys. One way I have done this is by developing a program for female hockey players that not only allows them to participate in high-quality tournament competition, but also gives them access to world-class experts

---

1. This chapter was originally published as "Skating in the Drainage Ditches" in *Playing It Forward: 50 Years of Women in Sport in Canada*. Toronto: Second Story Press, 2013.

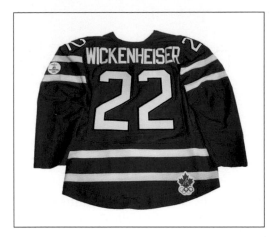

Figure D3.1 Women's Hockey at the Olympics
A Team Canada veteran and five-time Olympic medallist, Hayley Wickenheiser plays leadership roles on and off the ice, inspiring young players to make a difference in the world. Wickenheiser wore this jersey as captain of the Canadian women's national team. The team won gold at the 2010 Olympic Winter Games.
Wickenheiser Jersey
Worn in Vancouver, B.C.
2010
Canadian Museum of History, 2015.24.4, IMG2016-0253-0004-Dm

and trainers from my own network through workshops and clinics addressing everything from nutrition to being involved in community. In addition, all the proceeds from the annual World Female Hockey Festival, in Calgary, which is a celebration of hockey and the young women who play it, are donated to KidSport and Right To Play—two humanitarian sports organizations that promote the concept that EVERYONE has the right to access sport, no matter their gender, socio-economic class, geographic or political environment.

To this day, when I see a little girl walking up to an arena toting a hockey bag, stick in hand, smile on her face, I can't help but smile, knowing that she is entering an ever-evening playing field—or should I say *rink*?

Chapter 7
Thirty Years of "Going Global": Women's International Hockey, Cultural Diplomacy, and the Pursuit of Excellence

JULIE STEVENS

Introduction

After twenty years of international expansion, women's hockey hit a bump in the road at the 2010 Winter Olympic Games, in Vancouver, British Columbia. For Canada, success was sweet as the women claimed their third consecutive Olympic gold. However, Canada's golden result was met with staunch criticism about the lack of parity in international women's hockey. Canada, along with its rival the United States, who won silver in Vancouver, have dominated every international competition since the 1990 world championship (Waldie 2014). Even the International Olympic Committee president, Jacques Rogge, noted that the imbalanced competition raised concerns about the status of the women's hockey Olympic program (Proteau 2014).

At the time, such comments were widespread within the media and triggered a debate about the status of women's hockey on the world stage (Proteau 2014). Those who denounced the female game and questioned its inclusion in the Winter Olympic Games based their position upon observations at two events—the International Ice Hockey Federation (IIHF) Women's World Championships and the Olympics. Women's hockey receives limited media attention, and a majority of the coverage afforded to the female game occurs during very short, punctuated moments of time that are one and four years apart, respectively. As a result, claims of the seemingly imbalanced international women's hockey landscape present an incomplete view. The media, and the popular audience they communicate to, are unaware of what is done to build international women's hockey in the months and years between these marquee events. Hence, the criticism about the lack of parity among national women's teams is based upon a partial understanding. In truth, Canadian women's hockey leaders have served an important role in building women's hockey around the world. The discussion in this chapter offers insight about the global growth of women's hockey and ways in which cultural diplomacy involving Canadian female hockey leaders is utilized as a strategy for international expansion while, at the same time, the Canadian women's national team strives for global superiority.

147

As a nation that celebrates the game in various forms and forums, Canada has stood at the forefront of women's international hockey (Stevens 2006; Vincent and Crossman 2012). Given this, it is valuable to reflect upon what Canadian women's hockey leaders have done to advance the game around the globe. To that end, secondary research was conducted to gather information about specific Canadian women and their roles within, and impact upon, female hockey in other parts of the world. While women's hockey scholarship continues to expand, the majority of information about the workings of international women's hockey is found within popular print and online media, and within documents and accounts of various initiatives and programs by national and international hockey federations. In this chapter, the examples generated from secondary sources identify the role of nine Canadian women's hockey builders, coaches, and players in advancing female hockey in various countries. Each profile is placed in a particular section of the chapter in order to best highlight the individual's impact in relation to different stages of growth in a transnational women's game (Figure 7.1).

Cultural Relations, Cultural Diplomacy, and Hockey

Cultural diplomacy is a part of public diplomacy that emphasizes relationship building (Mark 2008). According to American political scientist Milton C. Cummings, cultural diplomacy involves the "exchange of ideas, information, art, and other aspects of culture among nations and their peoples in order to foster mutual understanding" (Cummings 2003, 1). Cultural diplomacy is much broader than simply policy goals associated with culture (Cummings 2003). Thus, when it comes to women's international hockey from a cultural-diplomacy view, the sport can become, and even has become, the tie that binds.

Central to the view of cultural diplomacy as an "all in it together" notion is the belief that cultural diplomacy is a strategic diplomacy tool utilized by governments for political positioning. Dutch professor of diplomacy Jan Melissen (2006) responds to this claim by suggesting cultural diplomacy "involves engagement, dialogue and mutuality." Yes, it may be used as a means to an end, but political scientist Joseph Nye (2003) argues it is an element of soft power, where persuasion leads to others adopting your goals. Having said this, the women's hockey examples shared in this chapter reflect a more informal, idea-driven exchange carried out by non-state actors, who, the cultural analyst Dragan Klaic (2007) argues, must work through complex processes to pool resources, finances, and technical assistance.

Figure 7.1 Portrait of a Player
As captain of Team Canada, Cassie Campbell-Pascall won two Olympic gold medals. She is now a commentator with CBC Sports. *Hockey: More than Just a Game* featured this powerful image of Campbell.
Bryan Adams (1959–)
1999
Silver gelatin print on aluminum
Library and Archives Canada, e010752920

Cultural diplomacy promotes a national image, or, in contemporary terms, a national brand. It enables a nation to describe its broad story and particular point of view to the rest of the world (Klaic 2007). Previous scholars examined the relation between sport and Canadian diplomacy, including hockey diplomacy (Macintosh and Hawes 1994; Macintosh, Bedecki, and Franks 1987). These accounts demonstrate that in the realm of Canadian men's international hockey, the stakes were extremely high, and politics frequently trumped culture in the global hockey arena. Macintosh and Hawes critiqued the federal government's politicization of sport from the moment Joe Clark, then secretary of state for external affairs, and Otto Jelinek, minister of state for fitness and amateur sport, announced the federal government "intended to make greater use of sport in promoting Canada's image abroad" in 1987 (Macintosh and Hawes 1994, 3).

Hockey projects an international image of Canada (Potter 2009). The importance of the sport as a global expression of Canadianism was initially leveraged by the federal government in 1966, when the Department of External Affairs became involved in hockey diplomacy (Macintosh and Hawes 1994). The major hockey accomplishment in this regard was the 1972 Summit Series, between Canadian NHL stars and the Russian national team, and to a lesser extent the 1974 Summit Series, between Russia and Canadian players from the short-lived World Hockey Association (Scherer and Cantelon 2013). Canada's decline in men's international hockey during the 1940s and 1950s was a significant precursor to these events, and the federal government took the 1972 series against the Russians so seriously that it formed a new unit with the Department of External Affairs, called International Sports Relations, in the Public Affairs Bureau (Potter 2009). The unit was responsible for preparations for the two Canada-Russia series as well as negotiations and issues regarding protocol (Macintosh and Hawes 1994). As Allison and Houlihan claim, sport has always been, and will remain, a part of political life (Allison 1993). When it comes to men's hockey, success on the ice became undeniably tied to how Canadians—political leaders and citizens—believed the country was viewed by other countries (Kobierecki 2016). According to Macintosh and Hawes, when it came to men's hockey on the world stage, "Canada's prestige was at stake" (Macintosh and Hawes 1994; Allison 1993, 31).

But in women's international hockey the context is different. The need to continuously maintain legitimacy of the sport on the world stage means that, although national prestige is on the line during these competitions, it is the women's game itself that is primarily at stake. The literature recognizes the distinction between women's and men's hockey at local and national levels (Adams and Stevens 2007; Stevens 2000). Although the elevation of men's hockey to international heights was initially driven by a performance goal, its purpose has transformed to commercial and political purposes over time. Change was far more rapid in women's hockey, and while debates over international contests, formats, and rules were held, the discussions rarely strayed from one key hockey purpose: creating the opportunity for women to compete within the global sport forum. There is no doubt that nation-to-nation competition is important, but there is also a recognition that it will take a collective effort among women's hockey leaders from all countries to create change within male-dominated hockey.

The remainder of this chapter makes the case for Canada's role in developing global women's hockey and, in so doing, counters the claims that, because the international performance results have changed little since the first women's world championship, in 1990, women's hockey should no longer be an Olympic sport. Canadian women's hockey leaders do not intend to relinquish Canada's standing atop the podium, but their effort to build the game globally reflects a type of cultural diplomacy that "advance[s] the national interest by presenting the nation in the best possible light to the rest of the world" (Ang, Isar, and Mar 2015, 370). Given this, the dialogue within this chapter depicts a dualism, where cultural relationships "grow naturally and organically, without government intervention," and where cultural diplomacy "takes place when formal diplomats, serving national governments, try to shape and channel this natural flow to advance national interest" (Ang, Isar, and Mar 2015, 366). Further inquiry into global women's hockey is needed, and this chapter also presents a counterpoint to claims that women's hockey does not have an adequate number of countries with female hockey programs, nor enough players, to warrant recognition as an international sport.

How Did We Get Here (2018) From There (1987)?

Past accounts identify two key catalysts that launched women's hockey to the international level (Avery and Stevens 1997; Etue and Williams 1996). The first was the international division at the 1985 Brampton Canadettes Dominion Ladies Hockey Tournament. The Canadettes, an all-girls minor hockey association, was formed in 1967 and, over time, the profile of its marquee tournament reached well beyond Canadian borders. Tournament organizers parlayed their success into the six-team international division, which included two teams from Canada, two from the United States, and one team from each of the Netherlands and Germany.

Two years later, women's hockey leaders staged a larger, exclusively international event. The 1987 tournament included seven teams—two from the host country (representing Canada and the province of Ontario), the United States, Sweden, Switzerland, Japan, and the Netherlands. This tournament is generally recognized as the precursor to the first women's world hockey championship, in 1990, and the subsequent expansion of women's international hockey. Although the event was an invitational tournament as opposed to a sanctioned IIHF championship, it challenged the status quo, where men held hockey's world stage, and moved the male-dominated hockey federations who controlled the international forum a few steps further along the gender-equity path. In a mere ten years, the international women's game went from an invitational tournament to a world championship and an Olympic sport.

Fran Rider

In 2015, Fran Rider, a founder of the Ontario Women's Hockey Association (OWHA), was inducted into the IIHF Hall of Fame. Rider is recognized in the builder category, and noted as the person "most responsible for the very creation of women's hockey at the international level." It is difficult to capture the true extent of Rider's contribution under the gamut of builder. It could be said that women's hockey in Canada and around the globe is the "house that Fran built" as she had a hand in every aspect thereof. She was instrumental in the formation of the Brampton Canadettes, the creation of the Ontario Women's Hockey Association, the reinstatement of the women's national hockey championship, the first international division at the Canadettes Dominion tournament, and the 1987 international tournament. These accomplishments span from 1967 to 1987 (IIHF n.d. 1).

It was Rider's outreach to the United States, Netherlands, and West Germany in the 1980s that started the international opportunities for women in hockey (IIHF n.d. 1.) Further connections with national hockey federations in Europe, namely Sweden, Switzerland, and Czechoslovakia, led to the 1987 tournament. Without Rider's determination "women's hockey would not be a medal event at the Olympics. There would not have been IIHF support for a fully-sanctioned Women's World Championships starting in 1990. There would not have been an [international] tournament in 1987, and there wouldn't have been enormous growth and development of the women's game in Canada and around the world that led to the historic 1987 event."
Fran was recognized by her community and country, having been inducted in the local Mississauga Sports Hall of Fame and appointed to the Order of Ontario and the Order of Canada (IIHF n.d. 1).

As noted on the account of her IIHF Hall of Fame induction, Rider's true contribution was her "fight for the greater good" that transformed women's hockey from a grassroots to a global game (IIHF n.d. 1).

Performing on the World Stage

Sport has evolved into a massive, complex intercontinental bureaucracy that is adept at creating new sport structures. Women's hockey benefitted from this capacity to grow as more and more international activity was added over time. The issue though, is will there be enough teams to fill the spots and be competitive at these international showcases? The annual world championship now includes six categories and thirty-six countries. There is the quadrennial Olympic Winter Games and various competitive forums held in the four-year cycle between the Games, such as the Four Nations Cup, the Asian Women's Hockey Championship, the European Championship, and the Winter Universiade (World University Games). But in order to meet the demand of these competitions, there must be a supply of national teams that are built upon a broad-based female hockey system.

Carla MacLeod

To date, Carla MacLeod is the only female to serve on the Japanese women's national team coaching staff. Macleod, who played and won multiple titles with the Canadian national team, cut her teeth in high-performance coaching in Canada's under-eighteen (U18) women's and the Mount Royal University Cougars programs. The Japanese Ice Hockey Federation approached Hockey Canada's general manager of national women's team programs, Melody Davidson, and fellow Canadian Mark Mahon, who served as the Japanese men's national team head coach from 2004 to 2015, and both recommended MacLeod.
The initial goal of MacLeod's tenure with the Japanese women's team was to qualify for the 2014 Winter Olympics. The team earned its first competitive qualification (Japan

competed at the 1998 Winter Olympic Games, in Nagano, through automatic entry as the host country) and MacLeod went to Sochi, albeit to help behind the bench rather than on the ice.

When she first joined the Japanese national team, MacLeod saw immediate differences between the Japanese women and the women she had coached in Canada. For one, the build of the athletes in Japan are smaller, which gives them an advantage in terms of speed, but they lacked strength and aggressiveness in their play, as well as confidence. MacLeod was an aggressive defenceman in her time with the Canadian women's program, and she was eager to help her athletes implement a more assertive and physical style into their already fast-paced game (Billones 2013).

MacLeod cultivated a unique relationship with her players, being viewed as a big sister to the younger athletes, and was "successful in eliminating the passive attitude that losing to more superior teams was acceptable" (Women's Hockey Life 2014). "I really believe in what's going on within Japanese women's hockey. Those 20 girls in that room are as dedicated to hockey as the women on Canada's roster. We have such negative media attention on the discrepancy between the nations, but many countries are really trying to improve. It's going to take time, but with the right people involved, that gap can be closed" (Brady 2013).

"I was arrogant as a player and I never gave these countries the credit they deserved as far as the effort these players are putting in. Their dreams are the same as ours. They're working just as hard. They just don't have the same level of game that we do here" (Spencer 2013).

Sarah Murray

Hosting an Olympic Games is a major undertaking, but in the case of Pyeongchang, South Korea, it also meant a hosting spot in the women's hockey competition. What did the Korean Ice Hockey Association do to prepare? They hired a Canadian.

Sarah Murray, daughter of former NHL coach Andy Murray, signed a two-year coaching contract with the South Korean women's national team in 2014. After winning two NCAA titles with the University of Minnesota Duluth, playing under Coach Shannon Miller, Sarah played for the top Swiss National League women's team, the ZSC Lions, of Zurich. She gave up her playing career in order to accept the coaching position in South Korea. According to Murray, "coaching is a lot different than playing, but I am very fortunate to have the opportunity to continue to be involved in a sport that I love as well as being a part of a national level program that will be playing in the Olympics" (Merk 2016).

The pressure to do well in Pyeongchang was high but various results moved the program in the right direction. In 2016 the team, which included players between the ages of fifteen and twenty-two, finished second in the IIHF Division II Group A Women's World Hockey Championships. Sojung Shin, the team's starting goalie, played at St. Francis Xavier University in Nova Scotia from 2014 to 2016, and the

2016–17 Metropolitan Riveters in the National Women's Hockey League (NWHL n.d.).

It's been challenging for Murray, who the South Korean broadcaster KBS introduced as the "coach with the blue eyes" (Merk 2016). She is not fluent in South Korean and only one player on the team can translate for her. Though she took lessons to learn, she notes "it is hard as a coach not to be able to talk with every player…one of my dad's coaching mentalities is he wants to talk to each of his players at least once every day. I often try to put this theory into practice but the girls who don't speak English tend to panic or think they are in trouble" (Women's Hockey Life. 2016). She explains that the players "don't want to question the authority of the coach, so at the beginning it was a bit complicated but we've gone to a point now when they're asking questions and we manage to find ways to communicate" (Merk 2016).

The 2018 Winter Olympics lead up was a big challenge for the national team who, according to Murray, "will be centralized and hopefully we get the funding to do multiple North American training camps where we can play exhibition games against D1 and D3 [NCAA] universities" (Women's Hockey Life 2016).

In the summer of 2015, Murray attended a Hockey Canada development camp that supported players from eight countries, including high-scoring South Korean forward Jiyeon Cho. "I'm absorbing everything I'm seeing here. I want us to maintain a good relationship with Hockey Canada, where we can continue to send even managers and strength coaches because it would be amazing for us to learn from this" (Graves 2015).

The South Korean women's hockey team was founded in 1999 and it won its first international match in 2005 (Lee 2015). The program's evolution, including the help of Murray, was documented in a 2016 movie called *Take Off 2*. Their vision of the future is captured by South Korean national-team player Kyousun Lee: "I'm the type that doesn't cry even when we win in international tournaments. But just imagining alone that we will hear the South Korean anthem play after a victory might actually make me cry. I'm not going to retire after hearing only the anthems of other countries" (Lee 2015).

A few weeks before the 2018 Winter Olympics Games began, Murray dealt with an unprecedented scenario in international hockey—coaching a joint South Korea-North Korea women's hockey team. The politics were intense and Murray had to manage not only the individual team dynamics, but also the media coverage on the world stage (Stevens 2018). While the united team did not fare well in the competition, its accomplishment off the ice will influence women's hockey within each of the Korean countries, Asia, and the world as a whole.

Welcoming the World

In the early years of my doctoral studies, at the University of Alberta, globalization and sport was an emerging topic. It had always been explored by scholars, but with a slightly different perspective, such as the sport and diplomacy work by Macintosh and Hawes that I mentioned earlier. One early piece of research by sport sociologist Joe Maguire caught my eye. It was about globalization and the migration of sport labour (Maguire 1994). He conducted a study about hockey that explained the pipeline of hockey talent that wrapped around the world (Maguire 1996). Maguire's work on talent migration in an interdependent world may not have related to women's hockey when he started to publish his work in the early 1990s, but is clearly evident now. Such a change makes sense—as more high-performance women's hockey emerges, athletes will seek the best forums to train and compete in order to reach those forums. The result has been a steady increase in national diversity within the highest levels of women's North American hockey—the Canadian Women's Hockey League, the U Sports (formerly Canadian Interuniversity Sport) league, and the NCAA in the United States.

Shannon Miller

Shannon Miller was the head coach for the Canadian women's team at the 1998 Winter Olympic Games and is a former head coach of the women's hockey program at the University of Minnesota Duluth (UMD).

Miller, a member of the IIHF's ambassador and mentor program, was approached in 2011 to help develop the Russian women's national program. Miller and the Russian women's national team's general manager, former NHLer Alexei Yashin, worked closely together on the 2013 IIHF Women's World Championships in Ottawa (*Duluth News Tribune* 2013).

According to Yashin, women's hockey in Russia needs more support to reach the same level as the men. "The people I talk to want to help with attention, money, experience, so I can be the link to connect women's hockey with the people who are very powerful and want to support Russian sport. Not only financial support, but support for the image," he said. "We want the same attention as the men's team. Hockey is very popular in Russia, but girls' hockey not as much." (*Duluth News Tribune* 2013)

It was during her tenure as head coach at UMD that Miller made a significant contribution to the global development of women's hockey. She was among the first to recruit players from other countries to the NCAA and has developed twenty-eight current and former Olympians (Wellens 2014). Two former UMD players, Iya Gavrilova and Aleksandra Vafina, represented Russia at the 2014 Winter Olympics (IIHF 2014). Gavrilova played for UMD during the 2007–08 season, while Vafina played during the 2012–13 season (*Duluth News Tribune* 2013).

When asked why she participated as an IIHF ambassador, Shannon replied, "I believe in the vision of the mentorship program as it is consistent with what we have been doing at the University of Minnesota Duluth since the fall of 1998. Our approach is the global development of the women's game using a Holistic approach. We have recruited and coached 22 Olympians from many different countries hoping to help grow the international game and win NCAA championships" (IIHF n.d. 2).

Danielle Goyette

Though she has never played or coached for a team outside Canada, Danielle Goyette, of Saint-Nazaire, Quebec, was known internationally for her offensive talents and consistency as a player, raising comparisons to Gordie Howe. Goyette competed for Canada at three Olympic Winter Games, and nine IIHF Women's World Championships, having won gold all but twice (1998 Olympics, 2005 World Championships). Known for her excellent scoring and passing, Goyette averaged a point and a half per game at the end of her international career in 2007, at age forty-one (IIHF n.d. 3). Upon retirement from the Canadian national women's team, in 2008, Goyette joined the University of Calgary women's team as head coach—a position she currently holds (University of Calgary Dinos n.d.).

In 2013, Goyette's international hockey success was recognized when she became the fifth female inducted into the IIHF Hall of Fame (Canadian Press 2013) and the first female player from Quebec inducted into the Hockey Hall of Fame, in Toronto (Ahmad 2017. For Goyette, it was not the records or goal totals she hoped to leave as a legacy when she retired from playing hockey, it was that the next generation would want to continue growing the game. "When you think about what you want to leave behind, it's a chance for girls to be able to play hockey and [for] it to be normal to play hockey," she said. "When the girls start to play hockey at five years old and on a girls' team, I think we did a pretty good job and not just talking about me, but all my teammates who have been through it" (Canadian Press 2013).

Like her former national women's team coach, Shannon Miller, who placed UMD women's hockey on the map, Goyette has built a strong varsity program as head coach of the University of Calgary Dinos. Her vision? To recruit "the best players in the world and to dominant the [league] in Canada" (Lamoureaux 2017). The result? A pipeline of international women's hockey talent that includes European players coming to Canada as well as Canadian players playing abroad after university. For example, Dino veterans Jenna Smith and Chelsea Peterson played professional women's hockey in Jönköping, Sweden, after graduating (Bekkevold 2015). On the opposite side, Ilya Gavrilova, who Goyette recruited from Russia, dominated the Canadian university league and received the top player honour in 2015. She parlayed her playing success into a roster spot for the Russian women's national team at the 2014 Winter Olympic Games in Sochi. Said Gavrilova, "Danielle taught me to play both sides of the game, in the offensive zone and defensive side. She worked with me a lot on my skills and my skating, saying that I have to get stronger working off the ice" (Spencer 2015).

From National Team to Hockey Programs

In response to the criticism leveled against women's hockey at the 2010 Winter Olympic Games, the IIHF designed an ambassador and mentor program (AMP) in order to "create partnerships between some of the world's best women's hockey coaches and players, and countries that are striving to join the sport's global elite" (IIHF n.d. 4). Former international hockey players and coaches who accomplished IIHF success through multiple world-championship medals serve as mentors to countries in the process of building their national women's team programs. AMP, which supported nine countries across various teams, included a coach mentor for both the senior and U18 national teams and two athlete ambassadors (with the exception of Kazakhstan, who had one athlete ambassador). Of the thirty-seven individuals involved in AMP, sixteen were Canadians, and fourteen of the Canadians were women. The program, which was originally called "Women's Hockey to Sochi 2014 and Beyond" ran from July 2011 until December 2013, and included international camps, tournaments, and seminars (Hockey Canada n.d.). The focus was to help women's hockey leaders learn from other women's hockey leaders what it takes to win a major international event, such as the Olympics (Canadian Press 2010).

Margot Page

Margot Page is currently the head coach of Brock University's women's hockey team. She also assists with Switzerland's senior and U18 national teams, working in this capacity with the Swiss Ice Hockey Association since 2011 (IIHF n.d. 5).

Page was an active member of Canada's national women's team from 1990 to 1994, before beginning a professional career as a coach in 1997. Page has coached internationally with Canada's U22 team in 2003–2004 and 2009–2010, as well as with Canada's national women's team from 2004 to 2006. She has coached at the university level at Niagara University (NCAA Division 1) from 1997 to 2009, and at Brock University from 2013 to the present. She is also a certified theory coach and consultant.[1] (IIHF n.d. 5)

When asked why she wanted to serve as a coach mentor in the IIHF program, Page replied "I want to give back as much as possible to make the game and opportunities better for others. It is a critical moment in the women's game and I want to make sure I do what I can to help grow it at home and in other nations" (IIHF n.d. 5).

Laura Rollins

Laura Rollins, a former women's hockey goaltender in Lac Saint-Louis, Quebec, and a student/athlete at Dawson College in Westmount, Quebec, and Carleton University in Ottawa, (*Lac St. Louis Girls Hockey Newsletter* n.d.) was born in and lived in Canada until she moved to Finland in 2007 to coach (Planet Hockey).

---

1. See "Margot Page," LinkedIn profile page, https://www.linkedin.com/in/margot-page-5a182499?authType=NAME_SEARCH&authToken=ccxD&locale=en_US&trk=tyah&trkInf o=clickedVertical%3Amynetwork%2CclickedEntityId%3A351400009%2CauthType%3AN AME_SEARCH%2Cidx%3A1-1-1%2CtarId%3A1482526812848%2Ctas%3Amargot%20page.

Rollins was named an assistant coach of men's youth hockey team called Heinolan Kiekko, and instructed at hockey camps in Hungary and Finland (Planet Hockey). In 2009, Rollins's talent earned her a coaching position in a Finnish women's professional hockey league, where she specialized as a goaltending coach until 2011.

From 2008 to 2010, Rollins participated as a mentor coach at the IIHF international development camp held annually in Vierumäki, Finland. The purpose of the women's high-performance camp was to educate athletes on how to train to compete at the elite level of the game (IIHF n.d. 6). The participants of this camp are athletes at the U18 level who are considered to be the best of their age group from their respective countries of origin. While the intensive, high-performance camp provides personal growth and leadership development to participants, the broader goal of the camp is to develop networks within women's hockey to promote international relations, as well as provide personal growth and leadership development within its participants (IIHF n.d. 6).

Currently, Rollins is a sports director with Stavanger IHK, a women's hockey team within the Kvinner Elite league (European Ice Hockey Online n.d.; Formánek et al.). She was responsible for the Norwegian girl's hockey team at the 2016 Winter Youth Olympic Games, in Lillehammer, Norway, and was the coach for Norway's U18 national women's team from 2011 until 2015 (IIHF 2015). The women who chose to play professionally in the Kvinner Elite are just as serious about playing hockey professionally as the men who chose to play in the GET-ligaen, the premier Norwegian hockey league, however there is a need for both better coaching and conditioning in the women's league, which Laura Rollins endeavours to address (Munkvik 2016).

Lindsay McAlpine

Lindsay McAlpine is currently the head coach for the MacEwan University women's hockey team in Edmonton, Alberta (MacEwan University 2016). While she is not involved in AMP, McAlpine makes an important contribution to women's hockey abroad as the coach of the Australian national women's hockey team (Ice Hockey Australia 2016). Ice Hockey Australia (IHA) felt McAlpine's background—she is the founder of an all-female hockey school, High Tempo Hockey, and a former player with the University of Alberta Pandas and the professional Edmonton Chimos—made her a perfect fit for their burgeoning program (Ice Hockey Australia 2016).

McAlpine was hired by the IHA to help its women's program move up in the world rankings. In just her first year with the team, the Australian national women's team advanced in the IIHF rankings. When McAlpine first started working with the program, the IHA competed in the IIHF Women's Division II Group B. Following their performance in the 2016 IIHF Women's World Championship Division II Group B in Spain, Australia was promoted to Division II Group A (IIHF n.d. 7).

McAlpine is certainly motivated to help Australia develop a non-traditional sport, especially one for women. "I am excited about working in an elite team environment where I can bring energy, a strong work ethic, and tactics from my lengthy playing and coaching background," she said. "My experience with elite women's ice hockey programs will serve Australia well around planning, implementation, and competitiveness" (IIHF n.d. 7).

Community and Competition within Women's International Hockey

A sense of community has always been strong within women's hockey. The cohesion has, at times, waned as high-performance growth brings more individualistic attitudes, but overall women's hockey leaders understand the importance of working together. My past research has identified the value of this approach at the grassroots and national levels—and through my discussion here I highlight how cooperation also occurs at the international level. As Margot Page said,

> We look at women's hockey globally as one big team.... If we do want to get better, you have to help your teammates. Just as you would if you were coming to a team.... If you're a really good teammate, you're trying to make your teammates better so that, in the end, you're not wishing to be better than them. You want them to be just as good as you so you can grow as a team. That's what we want to do with women's hockey (Jurewicz 2015).

So, where do we now stand on the cultural-diplomacy-of-women's-hockey claim? Ang and colleagues state "cultural diplomacy is the linchpin of public diplomacy; for it is in cultural activities that a nation's idea of itself is best represented" (Ang, Isar, and Mar 2015). Women's hockey has reached the peak of the international pyramid. At the same time, its community continues to battle gender bias and push a social-justice and access agenda from the international to grassroots levels. Canadian women included in the profiles represent Canada within the upper echelons of women's high-performance hockey, but they also represent women well within the upper echelons of high-performance hockey.

> In August 2016, I was fortunate to be selected as one of eight head coaches for the under-sixteen high-performance program which is overseen by the Ontario Women's Hockey Association as part of the Ontario Summer Games. The coaching staff I worked with was a fun bunch—my roomie was Lindsey West, from Ajax, Ontario, who had just graduated from Quinnipiac University with Eastern College Athletic Conference athlete-academic honours. Lindsay planned to play women's professional hockey in Sweden come that fall. Knowing she had been playing abroad for a while by the time I wrote this chapter, I asked her to share some thoughts about her role as a Canadian playing in a European league that had players from around the world. She replied, "I...do not believe that there are any expectations from our teammates about who we are as hockey players. We all come together to play the same game, on the same ice, with the same goal in mind and that is to win. Hockey is a language spoken all over the world!"[2]

---

2. Email correspondence with Lindsey West.

Hayley Wickenheiser

Shortly before I started to write this chapter, Hayley Wickenheiser announced her retirement from hockey. I used to coach midget girls' hockey in Edmonton during the late 1990s and remember Hayley playing for Calgary in the Western Shield, a regional Hockey Canada event that includes girls' and women's divisions. She played with a distinct intensity, which she carried throughout her twenty-three-year career with the women's national team (Spencer 2017). The "stompgate" incident at the 2002 Winter Olympic Games in Salt Lake City is a case in point. Wickenheiser elevated the energy for the victorious Canadian team when she claimed that the American team had tramped on the Canadian flag. "I hear they had our flag on their dressing room floor," Wickenheiser said after the final, "I wonder if they'd like us to sign it" (De Remer 2002). It turned out to have been a rumour, and Hockey Canada and USA Hockey later issued a joint statement that a Canadian flag had not been desecrated (IIHF n.d. 8).

At the time, Hayley's words resonated with me as I am a fierce nationalist. Now, as I reflect on the commentary, I see both the on- and off-ice dualism at play. On ice, elite players will go to extremes to compete and win. Off the ice, they, along with other women's hockey leaders, will collaborate in order to build additional opportunities. Wickenheiser was fiercely competitive, yet also generated cultural ties that supported women's hockey in other countries. Her trailblazing helped women's hockey leaders in other countries address the gender barriers inherent within their hockey system (IIHF n.d. 8).

When asked why she was involved in the IIHF's mentorship program, Hayley explained, "It's exciting to be a part of [AMP] because I feel it will make a direct and immediate impact in helping players from countries 5–14 [in IIHF world rankings] gain more information and resources to improve their game. Having direct and immediate access to World and Olympic Champions is invaluable information and will be an important step in continuing to improve and grow women's hockey around the world" (IIHF n.d. 8).

Keep in mind, Wickenheiser did this—helped countries prepare for the 2014 Winter Olympic Games—while she was herself training to compete at the Games.

The chapter explores the actions of Canadian women whose careers, whether as player, coach, or builder, typify the trajectory of international women's hockey development. Each of the women benefited from the great explosion of hope the late 1980s and early 1990s ushered to the women's game. So what has resulted from the Canadian contribution to women's international hockey? These leaders broke through the barriers and established a global women's hockey presence, but are the gains permanent? In some ways, the women highlighted in the profiles reached success and realized their vision, whether it related to their personal goals, the overall advancement of the female game, or both. In other ways, blind alleys and unexpected problems meant failure as the global pathway lead, in part, to new and unexpected problems.

Looking ahead, future research into women's international hockey, and on the Canadian role in the advancement of the international game, must address gender in an age of globalization. Diplomatic historian Thomas Zeiler claims research on sport and international relations includes little on gender and international politics (Zeiler 2014). A specific question that emerges from this critique is, "Do women's issues have a bearing on [sport and] international relations?" (Zeiler 2014). By exploring the expansion of women's hockey as a form of cultural diplomacy the discussion within this chapter expands the literature on hockey and diplomacy. Further, the account presents an alternative to the typical representation of Canada's hockey-diplomat role as action within an "entanglement of competing political-economic, cultural and diplomatic interests" (Scherer and Cantelon 2013, 3).

The progression of female hockey from the local to the national and to the international has been facilitated by a community of practice comprised of women's hockey leaders and advocates from around the world. Their collaboration led to the IIHF annual world championship and to Olympic recognition, while subsequent efforts, such as the IIHF's To Sochi and Beyond, an initiative to improve women's hockey worldwide, have furthered the game's development. However, during the same period, the expansion of a high-performance women's hockey recreated and maintained the ideologies consistent with an ultra-elite sport infrastructure and global entertainment spectacle. The result is a pronounced tension between the pursuit of excellence, which exemplifies the dominant competition model in sports, and cultural diplomacy, which exemplifies an alternative cooperation model. Future research should continue to examine this dynamic and explore how women's hockey leaders try to balance the need to build a global women's hockey forum through collaboration while, at the same time, addressing the values and practices of a high-performance international sport system that celebrates superiority.

Acknowledgements

I would like to thank Ms. Jordyn Moussa, whose work as a research assistant was very helpful.

Bibliography

Ahmad, S. 2017. "Trailblazing Danielle Goyette becomes first Quebec woman to enter Hockey Hall of Fame." *Montreal Gazette*, November 11. http://montrealgazette.com/sports/hockey/trail-blazing-danielle-goyette-first-quebec-woman-to-enter-hockey-hall.

Adams C., and Stevens, J. 2007. "Change and grassroots movements: Re-conceptualizing women's hockey governance in Canada." *International Journal of Sport Management and Marketing* 2 (4): 344–61.

Allison, L. 1993. *The Changing Politics of Sport.* Manchester, UK: Manchester University Press.

Ang, I., Y. R. Isar, and P. Mar. 2015. "Cultural diplomacy: beyond the national interest?" *International Journal of Cultural Policy* 21 (4), 365–81. https://doi.org/10.1080/10286632.2015.1042474.

Avery, J., and J. Stevens. 1997. *Too Many Men on the Ice: Women's Hockey in North America.* Victoria, BC: Polestar.

Bekkevold, M. 2015. "Swedish league Growing into World's Best League Outside of North America." Women's Hockey Life, September 26. https://www.womenshockeylife.com/blogs_view_dsp.cfm?BlogId=1756&CatId=6.

Billones, C. 2013. "Japan women's hockey team gets help with Canada's Carla MacLeod as coach." *Japan Daily Press*, March 12. http://japandailypress.com/japan-womens-hockey-team-gets-help-with-canadas-carla-macleod-as-coach-1225025/.

Brady, R. 2013. "With a former Canadian star helping out, Japan dreams big." *Globe and Mail*, March 11. http://www.theglobeandmail.com/sports/hockey/with-a-former-canadian-star-helping-out-japan-dreams-big/article9652592/.

Canadian Press. 2010. "IIHF to give coaching boost to women's hockey." TSN.ca, November 14. http://www2.tsn.ca/canadian_hockey/story/?id=341210.

———. 2013. "Canada's Paul Henderson, Danielle Goyette enter IIHF Hall of Fame." *Hockey News*, May 19. http://www.thehockeynews.com/news/article/canadas-paul-henderson-danielle-goyette-enter-iihf-hall-of-fame.

Cummings, M. 2003. *Cultural Diplomacy and the United States Government: A Survey*. Washington, DC: Center for Arts and Culture.

De Remer, D. 2002. "U.S., Canada Deny Flag-Stomping Rumors." *Harvard Crimson*, February 27. http://www.thecrimson.com/article/2002/2/27/us-canada-deny-flag-stomping-rumors-salt/.

Duluth News Tribune. 2013. "UMD's Miller gives Russia some hockey help." April 6. http://www.duluthnewstribune.com/content/umds-miller-gives-russia-some-hockey-help.

Etue, E., and M. Williams. 1996. *On the Edge: Women Making Hockey History*. Toronto: Second Story Press.

European Ice Hockey Online. n.d. "Stavanger Hockey." http://www.eurohockey.com/club/7196-stavanger-hockey.html?season=2015&%3Bleague=1053.

Formánek, P. M., G., Formánek, C. M., & Formánek, P. M. (n.d.). Stavanger Hockey. http://www.eurohockey.com/club/7196-stavanger-hockey.html?season=2015&%3Bleague=1053

Graves, W. 2015. "A whole new hockey world." Hockey Canada, August 15. https://www.hockeycanada.ca/en-ca/news/Sarah-Murray-in-whole-new-hockey-world.

Hockey Canada. n.d. "International Ice Hockey Federation brings countries together to boost growth of women's hockey." https://www.hockeycanada.ca/en-ca/Team-Canada/Women/National/2010-11/program-description.

Ice Hockey Australia. 2016. "Overseas coach recruited to lead national team." January 14. http://www.iha.org.au/overseas-coach-recruited-to-lead-national-team/.

IIHF (International Ice Hockey Federation). 2014. Russian Federation Team Roster. IIHF.com, February 7. http://stats.iihf.com/Hydra/389/IHW400000_33_5_3_RUS.pdf.

———. 2015. "Rollins moves: New coach for Norway's women's national team." August 14. http://www.iihf.com/home-of-hockey/news/news-singleview/?tx_ttnews%5Btt_news%5D=9969&%3BcHash=24e179616f859e8c3671acc1d0500.

———. n.d. 1. "IIHF Hall of Fame Inductees." http://www.iihf.com/home-of-hockey/news/iihf-hof-2015/.

———. n.d. 2. "Shannon Miller." http://www.iihf.com/iihf-home/sport/women/ambassadors/shannon-miller/.

———. n.d. 3. "Danielle Goyette." http://www.iihf.com/competition/352/home/hall-of-fame/danielle-goyette/

———. n.d. 4. "IIHF Ambassadors & Mentors Program." http://www.iihf.com/iihf-home/sport/women/ambassadors.html.

———. n.d. 5. "Margot Page." http://www.iihf.com/iihf-home/sport/women/ambassadors/margot-page/.

———. n.d. 6. "2016 IIHF Women's High-Performance Camp." http://www.iihf.com/channels1516/hpc/programs/.

———. n.d. 7. "Tournament Reports." http://www.iihf.com/competition/556/statistics.html.

———. n.d. 8. "Hayley Wickenheiser: Athlete Ambassador Coordinator." http://www.iihf.com/iihf-home/sport/women/ambassadors/hayley-wickenheiser/.

Jurewicz, C. 2015. "Multicultural load of talent: Athletes from eight countries make up 'Team IIHF.'" IIFH.com, August 12. http://www.iihf.com/home-of-hockey/news/news-singleview/?tx_ttnews%5Btt_news%5D=9964&cHash=3380fd7b38742eb6804ff1032f73ec97.

Klaic, D., 2007. *Mobility of imagination*. Budapest: Center for Arts and Culture, Central European University.

Kobierecki, M. M. 2016. "Canada-USSR Hockey Exchanges. Between Positive and Negative Sports Diplomacy." *Historia i Polityka* 25 (18), 19–32. https://www.researchgate.net/publication/314201418_Canada_-_USSR_Hockey_Exchanges_Between_Positive_and_Negative_Sports_Diplomacy.

Lac St. Louis Girls Hockey Newsletter. n.d. Vol. 4, no. 1 (Christmas edition), 2. http://www.hockeylacst-louis.qc.ca/uploads/christmas%20newsletter%20lsl%20girls%20hockey.pdf.

Lamoureaux, P. 2017. "University of Calgary Women's Hockey Presentation." Calgary Hockey Fire, January 13. http://calgaryfirehockey.ca/events.php?news_id=1421431.

Lee, S. 2015. Korean Women's National Ice Hockey Team to be subject of a Movie. Teen 10 Mag, August 9. http://www.teen10mag.com/korean-womens-national-ice-hockey-team-to-be-subject-of-a-movie/.

MacEwan University. 2016. "Coaching women's hockey on opposite ends of the Earth."

MacEwan News, February 24. http://www.macewan.ca/wcm/MacEwanNews/STORY_LINDSAY_MCALPINE.

Macintosh, D., and M. Hawes. 1994. *Sport and Canadian Diplomacy*. Montreal: McGill-Queen's University Press.

Macintosh, D., T. Bedecki, and C. E. S. Franks. 1987. *Sport and Politics in Canada: Federal Government Involvement since 1961*. Kingston, ON: McGill-Queen's University Press.

Maguire, J. 1994. "Preliminary Observations on Globalization and the Migration of Sport Labour." *Sociological Review* 42 (3), 452–80.

———. 1996. "Blade Runners: Canadian Migrants, Ice Hockey, and the Global Sports Process. *Journal of Sport and Social Issues* 20 (3), 335–60.

Mark, S. 2008. "A Comparative Study of the Cultural Diplomacy of Canada, New Zealand and India." PhD diss., University of Auckland.

Melissen, Jan. 2006. "Reflections on Public Diplomacy Today." Speech delivered at the Public Diplomacy Conference, Ministry of Foreign Affairs of the Republic of Turkey, Ankara, February 6.

Merk, M. 2014. "New Era for Korean Women: Sarah Murray to coach PyeongChang 2018 candidates." IIHF.com, October 30. http://www.iihf.com/home-of-hockey/news/news-singleview/?tx_ttnews%5Btt_news%5D=9182&cHash=9f024abeab1e887de0e2d92aa7d447db.

———. 2016. "Taste of Olympics for Korea: Coach, two players at Women's High-Performance Camp." IIHF.com, July 13. http://www.iihf.com/home-of-hockey/news/news-singleview/?tx_ttnews%5Btt_news%5D=10944&cHash=8cb59bf827840828f367d28abbaaf342.

Munkvik, C. 2016. "Rollins overtar Kvinnelandslaget." Norges Ishockeyforbund, March 6. https://www.hockey.no/nyheter/arkiv/2015/laura-rollins-overtar-kvinnelandslaget.

NWHL (National Women's Hockey League). n.d. "Metropolitan Riveters." http://www.nwhl.zone/roster/show/2758659?subseason=327125

Nye, Joseph S. 2003. "Propoganda Isn't the Way: Soft Power." *International Herald Tribune*, January 10.

Planet Hockey. n.d. "Meet the Staff." Planet Hockey. http://www.planethockey.com/page/show/254777-meet-the-staff.

Potter, E. H. 2009. *Branding Canada: Projecting Canada's Soft Power through Public Diplomacy*. Montreal: McGill-Queen's University Press.

Proteau, A. 2014. "IIHF President Fasel's defense of Olympic women's hockey a welcome sight." *Hockey News*, February 18. http://www.thehockeynews.com/news/article/iihf-president-fasels-defense-of-womens-olympic-hockey-a-welcome-sight.

Scherer, J., and H. Cantelon. 2013. "1974 WHA All-Stars vs. the Soviet National Team: Franchise Recognition and Foreign Diplomacy in the 'Forgotten Series.'" *Journal of Canadian Studies* 47 (2), 1–31.

Spencer, D. 2013. "Canada's MacLeod lends hockey expertise to Japanese women for Sochi 2014." *Globe and Mail*, February 16. http://www.theglobeandmail.com/sports/hockey/canadas-macleod-lends-hockey-expertise-to-japanese-women-for-sochi-2014/article8773348/.

———. 2015. "Canadian university hockey star Gavrilova leads Russia into women's worlds." *Globe and Mail*, March 26. http://www.theglobeandmail.com/sports/hockey/canadian-university-hockey-star-gavrilova-leads-russia-into-womens-worlds/article23635080/.

———. 2017. "Canadian hockey star Hayley Wickenheiser announces retirement." *Globe and Mail*, January 13. http://www.theglobeandmail.com/sports/hockey/womens-hockey-star-hayley-wickenheiser-announces-retirement/article33624688/.

Stevens, J. 2000. The declining sense of community in Canadian women's hockey. *Women in Sport and Physical Activity Journal* 9 (2), 123–40.

———. 2006. "Women's Hockey in Canada: After the Gold Rush." In *Artificial Ice: Hockey, Culture and Commerce*, ed. D. Whitson and R. Gruneau, 85–100. Peterborough, ON: Broadview Press.

———. 2018. "Player or pawn: Women's hockey, the Olympics, and the Korean dynamic." The Conversation, February 6. https://theconversation.com/player-or-pawn-womens-hockey-the-olympics-and-the-korean-dynamic-90815.

University of Calgary Dinos. n.d. "Danielle Goyette." University of Calgary. http://www.godinos.com/coaches.aspx?rc=1076.

Vincent, J., and J. Crossman. 2012. "'Patriots at Play': Analysis of Newspaper Coverage of the Gold Medal Contenders in Men's and Women's Ice Hockey at the 2010 Winter Olympic Games." *International Journal of Sport Communication* 5 (1), 87–108.

Waldie, P. 2014. "Women's hockey must go beyond Canada US dominance, Wickenheiser says." *Globe and Mail*, February 5. http://www.theglobeandmail.com/sports/olympics/womens-hockey-future-in-doubt-if-canada-us-dominance-isnt-challenged-says-canadas-flag-bearer/article16705194/.

Wellens, M. 2014. "Women's coach Shannon Miller coaching final season at UMD." Bulldog Hockey Blog, December 15. https://bulldoghockeyblog.areavoices.com/womens-coach-shannon-miller-coaching-final-season-at-umd/.

Women's Hockey Life. 2014. "Carla MacLeod Extends Legendary Career by Contributing to Hockey Abroad with Japan." February 17. http://www.womenshockeylife.com/blogs_view_dsp.cfm?BlogId=1235&CatId=9.

———. 2016. "South Korea Makes History at 2016 Division IIA Women's World Championships." May 17. https://womenshockeylife.com/blogs_view_dsp.cfm?BlogId=1974&CatId=9.

Zeiler, T. 2014. "Conclusion: Fields of dreams and diplomacy." In *Diplomatic Games: Sport, Statecraft and International Relations Since 1945*, ed. H. Dichter and A. Johns, 431–46. Lexington: University Press of Kentucky.

Chapter 8
Women's Recreational Hockey:
A New Player Profile

Denyse Lafrance Horning

Hockey is Canada. Canada is hockey. Regardless of the ordering of the words, this sentiment is proudly expressed by many Canadians when referring to the game of hockey. What differs among individuals, however, is their consideration of and engagement with the sport. Clearly, not all Canadians are actively involved in hockey or even fans of the game. Yet for individuals who do enjoy this sport, hockey can play a special role in their lives. For some, hockey is a fun game of pickup on the outdoor rink or a childhood sport that bonds families and creates lifelong friendships; for others, hockey may be a dream profession that has commanded years of devotion to play at the most elite levels, or it may offer a sense of national pride as fans and supporters of the game. This chapter focuses on a minority segment of players that are often overlooked: women recreational hockey players. While not the subject of media headlines or ever atop Olympic podiums, women recreational players are growing in number and influence, and are increasingly part of the discussion of hockey in Canada. What's particularly interesting with this group is the diversity and generational differences among players.

In this chapter, active female recreational players are profiled in terms of their hockey experience, key influencers, and feelings about the benefits and challenges of play. I will also discuss increasing tension among player cohorts in the recreational hockey ranks. Many older women have overcome years of exclusion in their quest to play a game that they have long loved from the sidelines. In contrast, younger players have enjoyed extensive opportunities to engage in the sport and to advance to the highest levels of collegiate, national, or professional play. While their individual hockey journeys may differ, these women are ultimately united at the recreational level through a common passion for the game. As the growth of women's hockey persists, opportunities and dynamics of play continue to evolve. In an effort to develop positive-participation options for all levels of players, and to preserve the love of the game, specific recommendations are presented in this chapter.

Women's hockey is not a new phenomenon. Canadian women have been enjoying the game for well over a century. The first written account of a women's game was published on February 11, 1891, in the *Ottawa Citizen* newspaper (McFarlane 1994). Once ignited, female enthusiasm and participation in this male-dominated sport spread rapidly as a surge of teams emerged across Canada and parts of the United States throughout the early 1900s. Brian McFarlane's (1994) survey of Canadian women's hockey reveals a rich history, rooted in early interest and casual participation, that has steadily evolved in terms of sophistication, support, and playing opportunities. The Preston Rivulettes sparked early interest in women's hockey as this all-star team from a small Ontario town dominated female hockey throughout the 1930s, attracting unprecedented media attention and fan support (Adams 2008). The demands of the Depression and the Second World War pulled women away from hockey during the 1940s with lagging effects impeding any significant development through the 1950s (Adams 2008, McFarlane 1994). Momentum returned, however, over the following two decades as many Canadian provinces established their own associations to formally govern the development of female hockey. Participation growth at both the amateur and elite levels continued throughout the 1980s. In 1987, women's hockey reached the world stage as Canada hosted the first women's world invitational tournament, with teams representing Canada, the United States, Sweden, Switzerland, Holland, and Japan.

In 1990, the International Ice Hockey Federation (IIHF) sanctioned the first women's world championship, held in Ottawa, effectively extending credibility and worldwide visibility to female hockey players (Reid and Mason 2015). Arguably, the greatest triumph in the history of women's hockey was the International Olympic Committee's recognition of women's hockey as an official medal sport at the 1998 Winter Olympic Games, in Nagano, Japan (IOC 1998). Six teams (Canada, the United States, Finland, China, Sweden, Japan) participated, showcasing the quality of women's hockey in front of a worldwide audience (IOC 2011). Female hockey players have continued to push boundaries by breaking into the professional ranks. The Canadian Women's Hockey League, founded in 2007, presently has seven professional teams, in Toronto, Markham, Montreal, Calgary, Boston, and two teams based in Shenzhen, China. In 2015 another professional league, the National Women's Hockey League, was introduced, with teams based in the hockey-strong states of Massachusetts, Connecticut, New York, and New Jersey. Players in this league were the first to receive an annual salary (averaging $15,000, plus a percentage of jersey sales) in women's hockey (Suddath 2015).

The opportunities available to female players in contemporary Canada reflect the effort, sacrifice, and devotion of earlier women whose passion for the game fueled their quest for acceptance and inclusion in the hockey world. Today, there are 87,500 registered female players in Canada (Hockey Canada 2015) and 196,318 worldwide (IIHF 2016), encouraging numbers in the continued growth of women's hockey.

Review of Women's Hockey Literature

Research into women's hockey has been growing since 2000. The majority of investigations to date has focused on competitive and high-performance players. Theberge (2000) delved into the unique culture and sociology of elite Canadian female players, while, during this same period, Stevens (2000) was critical of the declining sense of community in women's hockey and the growing commercialization and segregation between grassroots and high-performance programs. Collegiate-level play is often the highest rank accessible to female players in North America, therefore several studies have targeted this particular population. Player interviews assisted Pelak (2002) in chronicling the progressive journey of one U.S. university from complete female hockey exclusion to a well-respected women's varsity program. However, Pelak's study also noted the expanding distance between competitive and novice-level players. Auster (2008) also studied female varsity players, and discovered a cohort effect that has benefitted younger generations with enriched opportunities and greater acceptance and support. In comparing the features of men's and women's hockey, a sample of female adolescent players (Theberge 2003, 509) shared their desire for broader recognition as "real hockey players" while also noting a sense of empowerment derived through their involvement in competitive hockey. Weir et al. (2010) examined the relative age effect of Canadian female players and concluded that, similar to men's hockey, elite-level opportunities are greatest for players born earlier in the calendar year. Ransdell and Murray (2011) also studied high-performance female players as they assessed the physiological and performance demands on contenders for the 2010 U.S. women's national team. More recently, Locke and Karlis (2015) expressed concern with the exodus of Canadian collegiate talent toward more lucrative U.S. schools, while Reid and Mason (2015) shared a historical account of the first women's world hockey championships, in 1990, that served as an important catalyst in the development of the game. DiCarlo (2016) further advanced the understanding of women's relationship with hockey by considering a new segment of female hockey players. Through in-depth interviews with women participating on men's teams, this study of seven young-adult players (aged eighteen to twenty-five) confirmed that rigid gender barriers and tensions still exist in such mixed hockey settings.

Another stream of research considers women as fans and spectators of the sport of hockey. The studies reviewed involved men's hockey and identified differentiated strategies to connect with female fans (Armstrong 2001; Crawford and Gosling 2004; Sears and Cipolla 2007). In their study, Crawford and Gosling reported (2004, 478) that female spectators generally remain marginalized as legitimate fans, often dismissed as "puck bunnies" that are uninterested in the sport and mainly intent on pursuing players. However, findings from the research debunked this myth and revealed women to be as knowledge-able and committed as male hockey fans. In addition to game spectatorship, media play a crucial role in the mass distribution of sport. The growth of women's hockey has recently generated increased media attention and studies devoted to the analysis of such coverage. While some progress is recognized, the women's game remains significantly underrepresented in media, and conventional commentary continues to undermine female players' athletic abilities and achievements (Poniatowski and Hardin 2012; Vincent and Crossman 2012).

Only one reviewed study examined recreational players. Wiley, Shaw, and Havitz (2000) measured three involvement factors to better understand the motivations of male and female athletes: attraction, self-expression, and centrality. This study showed that, although male players had higher centrality scores than did the women (i.e., hockey was a greater priority in their lives), women players expressed stronger attraction to the sport of hockey. These authors argued that men's centrality scores are driven by a more supportive social environment (such as available leagues, access to ice, and adequate leisure time), while conflicting demands for women's time and limited playing opportunities may restrict women's practical involvement in hockey. Women's high attraction results were attributed to the value that women place on the pleasure and enjoyment of sport (versus competition) as well as to the novelty of their new-found passion for the game of hockey. It was suggested by these authors that, with time, women's attraction scores may level off. This study considered the perspective of seventy-six female players who were active in recreational leagues in the Greater Toronto Area of Ontario.

The reviewed literature attests to the substantial gains realized in women's hockey and the growing opportunities available to current players. The female hockey community is strong and progressive, however, there is documented concern with the widening gap and division between grassroots and elite, high-performance programs. Several studies have focused on the intensifying characteristics of female hockey players and their continued quest to remove persistent gender barriers and earn respect and recognition as "real" hockey players. Women enjoy hockey and feel empowered by the opportunity to participate in this once male-dominated sport. The features of women's hockey are, however, different, and, as such, warrant these unique research efforts.

Women's Recreational Hockey

While much of the attention in women's hockey is devoted to competitive and high-performance play, recreational women players are steadily growing in the shadow of mainstream Canadian hockey. There are currently 10,461 women registered in Canadian recreational leagues (Hockey Canada 2015). This figure represents a dramatic 40 per cent increase from the previous 2013–14 season, when player registration was reported to be 7,468 (Hockey Canada 2014). The actual number of participants is likely even greater than these reported figures, as many variations of women's recreational leagues continue to operate outside of the governance of Hockey Canada. Continued and accelerated growth is also expected as girls who first adopted the sport of hockey during the peak development period (1990–2000) join adult recreational leagues. As more diverse players enter the

Figure 8.1 Hockey Sticks (detail)
Hockey: More Than Just a Game featured sticks from many contemporary players, including Marie-Philip Poulin, star of the Canadian women's hockey team.
Canadian Museum of History, IMG2016-0253-0025-Dm.tif

recreational ranks, the dynamics of play are evolving, as is the need to better understand this growing segment of hockey enthusiasts.

In order to broaden the understanding of the growing group of women's recreational hockey participants, in 2012 Norm O'Reilly and I conducted a study to explore the motivations of women participating in recreational hockey. Hockey experience, key influencers, and the perceived benefits and challenges of participation were measured in our study. An English-language online survey of a convenient sample of recreational leagues was undertaken, with a goal of securing responses from a hundred players. These research efforts were well received by the women's recreational hockey community, resulting in a significant snowball effect and a final sample size of 782 respondents from across Canada (86.5 per cent of respondents) and the United States (13.5 per cent). The strong response suggests an attentive segment of players that have generally been overlooked and who are eager to be acknowledged and accepted as legitimate hockey players. This work is among the first to solely focus on women's recreational players. While they may not be destined for elite-level competition, this is a growing group of influential and enthusiastic players that are worthy of recognition and better understanding. Findings from this study are detailed below.

Player Profiles

Descriptive statistics were calculated for all the measured variables of this study (data on ethnicity was not collected). All respondents were currently active in women's recreational leagues. The mean age of respondents was 39.2 years old. The youngest respondent was seventeen and the oldest player was sixty-eight. Hockey experience varied significantly as some were novice players participating in their very first season of play, and others reportedly had played for as long as forty-five years. The average tenure of play from this sample of players was 10.1 seasons. Respondents were also asked the age at which they first adopted the sport of hockey. Again, the range of responses varied, from as young as two years old to the mature first timer of fifty-eight, with the average women's recreational player adopting the sport of hockey at 27.3 years of age. This is a late-start age for the game of hockey as most players begin during childhood. By comparison, almost 74 per cent of registered hockey players in Canada are at the minor hockey level (i.e., under the age of eighteen) (Hockey Canada 2015).

In order to assess possible differences across age groups, our data was split into two cohorts: players aged thirty-five and younger ($n=281$) and players older than thirty-five years old ($n=500$). As expected, this analysis revealed that the younger cohort adopted the sport of hockey at a significantly younger age (mean age=16.5 years) than their older counterparts (mean age=33.3 years). This earlier exposure to the game also translates into greater hockey experience (mean experience=10.4 years) among younger players than the older beginners (mean experience=9.9 years). This variation of age and experience creates a unique sport setting, where significantly diverse women interact in the game of hockey. In an effort to further portray these players, the study also considered key influencers in women's decision to participate in hockey.

Key Influencers

The main influencer in women's decision to play hockey is other women. Female friends were credited by 37.4 per cent of respondents as the inspiration to play. The importance of sharing the sport experience with female peers was also a dominant theme in a recent report on the status of female sport participation in Canada (CAAWS 2016). To a much lesser extent (17.9 per cent), male family members were also recognized as influential in committing to this traditionally male-dominated sport choice. While it is normally parents that influence their children's recreational behaviour (Canadian Heritage 2013), 5.1 per cent of women who participated in this study noted that such roles were reversed as their children encouraged them to adopt the sport of hockey. Mass media had the least influence (0.3 per cent) and is likely reflective of the minimal media exposure afforded to women's hockey (CAAWS 2016; Larkin 2015; Suddath 2015).

Among the most impactful findings of this study was the selection of "other" (by 21 per cent of respondents) to the question of who most influenced them to first join hockey. In this case, the overwhelming sentiment involved self-motivation and the expressed lifetime craving to play a sport that was long denied to them. The player comments below effectively convey these passionate views of empowerment and sheer determination.

"I had to convince others to let me play." (aged 31)

"No one could stop me once I figured out that I was allowed to play." (47)

"I always wanted to play but it wasn't available for girls when I was young. My daughter plays and now it's time for me!" (50)

"Myself and another friend pushed the issue to start a women's league. If the guys could do it, why couldn't we?" (35)

Several women also noted that they switched from playing ringette (which is "marketed for girls") to hockey once such opportunities were created. Another respondent (aged 49) referred to playing hockey as being part of her "bucket list" and the realization of a lifetime goal.

Comparing age cohorts once again revealed interesting differences. For the younger group of players, male family members (28.9 per cent) were most influential in their decision to participate in hockey, followed closely by female friends (25.4 per cent). Conversely, older players indicated a much greater reliance on their female peers (44.6 per cent) than on male family members (11.8 per cent) in this same decision making. Also interesting to note is the minimal influence of female family members across both the younger (5.4 per cent) and older (4.8 per cent) cohorts. It is reasonable to expect this gap in influence to narrow as a result of the accelerated development of women's hockey. Younger players have benefitted from greater equality and access to the game of hockey, and will thus serve as important role models for upcoming generations of female players.

Benefits and Challenges of Play

All players recognized that hockey offers great benefits but also several challenges. When considering all respondents, noted benefits of hockey participation included exercise (96.4 per cent), fun (91.6 per cent), social interaction (90.7 per cent), and, to a lesser extent, competition (69 per cent). When asked to select the most important benefit, fun (36.1 per cent) was the primary driver for involvement, followed by social interaction (26.4 per cent), and equally motivating was the health benefit (26.1 per cent) related to participation. Respondents also offered additional considerations by expanding on the selection of "other benefits." In this case, the common themes that emerged included participating in hockey as a stress reliever and for "me time," a passion for the sport of hockey, a sense of accomplishment by learning something new, and the opportunity to better connect with hockey-devoted family members and to serve as positive role models for children, in particular daughters. Here are samples of player statements that articulate this strong attraction to the sport of hockey.

"It's the only night out for myself. The rest of the time, my family comes first." (aged 46)

"It gives me an extraordinary feeling of accomplishment and competence, it makes me feel powerful and really happy." (45)

"I didn't belong to any team organized sports when I was a child, so having the social interaction by being a part of a (hockey) team is inspiring and motivating." (39)

"Showing my daughter that women can be strong, skate fast and have fun, just like the boys." (30)

"I love the physical contact involved in hockey, and the little tiffs that occur between opposing players. It's a great way to burn off some negative energy." (29)

"Hockey is my life. I love all parts of it." (25)

When comparing perceived benefits of play between age groups, fun was consistently the top draw to this sport. The younger segment, however, indicated a more pronounced sense of fun (43.8 per cent) than did the older players (33.5 per cent), while the mature squad placed greater emphasis on social interaction (30.8 per cent versus 20.6 per cent for the younger cohort) and health-related benefits (28 per cent versus 23.9 per cent for the younger cohort). Another discovered difference involved the competitive nature of hockey. Younger players were more likely to select competition (8.8 per cent) as a key benefit of play than were older players (5.9 per cent). Open-ended comments also supported this view, as older players shared a fear of injury given the increasingly physical and fast-paced play of recreational leagues. Further comments pertaining to frustration with self-proclaimed inferior hockey skills may have also contributed to lower fun scores among older players.

This study also considered the perceived challenges of participating in women's recreational hockey leagues. Hockey skills (31 per cent), finding a suitable league (14.8 per cent), high costs (13 per cent), and conflicting time demands (12.8 per cent) were the most commonly cited challenges. Also noted by 9.1 per cent of respondents was the inaccessibility of ice time. Sentiments in this regard alluded to women's low priority in the allocation of scarce ice time, which often results in late-evening games that are inconvenient and taxing on working women. Respondents also commented on poor officiating, suggesting that women's recreational games are not taken seriously and granted the same respect and diligence as other leagues (such as men's, competitive, and minor hockey leagues). This concerning view is captured in the statement below:

> "Things aren't very supportive to women and we get the leftover ice slots. We often get treated horribly and aren't taken seriously as athletes." (aged 42)

Similar to benefits, a relationship between the variables of age and perceived participation challenges was confirmed, revealing further cohort differences. For younger players, hockey skills (21.8 per cent) and high costs (21.4 per cent) were the two main expressed challenges. Additional concerns among this younger group included playing in a suitable league (19.1 per cent) and time constraints (13.6 per cent). Among the most significant differences to surface through this investigation was the prevailing concern among older players regarding their lack of hockey skills. In comparison to 21.8 per cent of the younger participants, 41.4 per cent of the older cohort specified hockey skills as the most challenging aspect of participation. They noted the absence of focused skill-development opportunities, as participation is most often limited to league games with minimal (or no) practice time.

> "Playing one game per week (so less than 15 mins on the ice in total), without any practice time does not allow me to improve as much as I would like." (aged 48)

Finding a suitable league (14.9 per cent) and time constraints (14.5 per cent) were comparable worries for older players, while high costs were less of a barrier (10.5 per cent) than they were for the younger, more price-sensitive segment. Finding a suitable league is a construct worthy of elaboration. This measure captures several views concerning player fit in recreational settings. This includes beginner-level players who find the pace of play to be too advanced, skilled players who express frustration with play that is too slow, and a range of concerns related to competitive and attitudinal differences among a growing diversity of players. The following section offers further insight on the relationships between the age cohorts in women's recreational hockey settings.

Interaction among Player Cohorts

The interaction between different player types was not a construct that was originally included in the design of this study. Many submitted comments, however, voiced an increasing presence and concern for the disparity in skill and competitiveness between different player groups intermixed at the recreational level. From this information, four general player types were revealed. These include older novice-level players, older advanced-skilled players, younger novice-level players, and younger advanced-skilled players. The Table 8.1 portrays each segment of player, with ages and quotations.

Table 8.1: Player Cohorts

Older Player Cohort (over 35)	
Novice Skill Level	**Advanced Skill Level**
"I wish there was a division for over 40 or even over 50. I am worried that no league will take on an old gal like me." (62, seven years of hockey) "As younger, much more skilled players join the league, the game is faster and at times rough. Young players can be aggressive and forget that they are playing rec hockey. I enjoy playing with the better skilled players because it raises my game but I am concerned about injury." (56, seven years of hockey) "I'm a new player with an old body. I like playing but am not very competitive. I fear that leagues are full of hockey skilled players that will knock me down." (51, first season of hockey) "I started playing when I was 35. I think I am at a big disadvantage compared to those who grew up playing the sport. My league only has one division and all ages (18 and up) play together. I foresee a time when I will quit because I can't keep up, not because I don't love the game." (44, nine years of hockey)	"As we older players age, we are finding it harder to play with/against the younger players. It becomes a risk management issue and we are there for a different reason than the younger players. We need leagues similar to 'old timers' for ladies." (52, twenty-six years of hockey) "I find the pace of hockey is faster in the league I play in because of the young girls joining but the Masters league is way below my skill level." (51, twenty-five years of hockey) "Sometimes the lower skill level players can create havoc for the middle skill players. We have to watch twice as hard not to hurt them or get hurt trying to keep out of their way." (40, ten years of hockey). "There needs to be a better way to organize players. Each team in these leagues has 2-3 good players per team and 2-3 weak players. Unless you have strong players that want to play and help teach the newer players, the new players are usually left just skating around and not touching the puck. Oftentimes younger players, after reaching midget age, have nowhere else to play but in house leagues. These players have played competitively and aggressively for many years but this type of league does not suit them. New players need to be part of the team, not just play on the periphery." (15, thirty-eight years of hockey)
Younger Player Cohort (35 and under)	
Novice Skill Level	**Advanced Skill Level**
"I've progressed well over the last three years and will likely progress more. I'm obviously well below the skill level of players who have played since they were children. I look up to them and strive to their skill level one day." (29, three years of hockey)	"A lot of women in our league are intimidated by my higher level of play and would rather I didn't play." (21, twelve years of hockey) "The league I currently play in has players of a variety of different skill levels, making it difficult for myself to play a game of hockey with a basic foundation of skill as many new players do not have these skills or understand basic hockey sense. I feel that I am more skilled than new players which makes it seem as though I am losing my skills." (24, fourteen years of hockey) "My skills are suffering and I'm picking up bad habits because I don't have the competition to push me." (32, seventeen years of hockey)

Based on these player comments, a number of insights are drawn. Across all identified segments there is concern regarding fit and acceptance. Novice-level players (mainly older but also some younger beginners) worry that that they are not adequately skilled, while advanced players fear that they intimidate others and are generally not welcome in recreational leagues. At the same time, there is some indication of admiration toward skilled players that were fortunate enough to have the opportunity to learn and develop their hockey skills at a younger age. The risk of injury stresses older players, while younger players are concerned with diluting their hockey skills. There appears to be a lack of options for women seeking to play hockey into adulthood. Regardless of the paths taken, a wide range of players are drawn to recreational leagues. Several respondents suggested the need to further tier leagues or divisions (based on skill or age) in order to better meet the needs of an increasingly diverse group of players.

The classifications above were simplified based on the initial data gathered in our research. In reality, it is more difficult to categorize such varied players. In addition to age and hockey experience, competitive mindset and recreational motives are significant differentiators among recreational players. More research is needed to further profile such players and to better understand the increasing gap and possible tension rising between multiple player types.

Recommendations

At the recreational level, the objective of the federal Canadian Sport Policy is for Canadians to have the opportunity to participate in sport for fun, health, social interaction, and relaxation (Canadian Heritage 2012). A recent report on the status of female sport participation in Canada revealed a decline in female sport involvement across all demographic groups and declared a state of crisis in need of action. In a quest to fuel lifelong participation in sport, the report recommended (CAAWS 2016, 32) that women be consulted in order to "understand local realities that may hinder participation and to develop programming that meets their needs, interests and experiences." It also advised that sport programs be based on the age and ability of participants in order to offer fun, pleasurable, and challenging sport options. Given the generational diversity and expanding skill gap revealed through this study, special consideration is warranted for women participating in hockey. Based on the findings of this study, a number of recommendations are presented to encourage women of all ages and abilities to enjoy lifelong engagement with the great game of hockey.

Promote Women's Hockey

In order to bring added visibility to women's hockey, all levels of play should seek further promotion. In addition to greater media coverage, this can be accomplished through partnerships with hockey, sport, and women's groups at the national, provincial, and regional levels. Coverage of elite women's hockey is increasing and has proven to positively impact player registration at the grassroots level. Following the broadcast of the first-ever IIHF Women's World Championship, in 1990, female hockey registration increased by 39 per cent (CAAWS 2016, 25). Similar results (+30 per cent) were observed following media coverage of the first Olympic inclusion of women's hockey, in 1998 (ibid.). While recreational leagues may not draw such prestigious coverage, there remains ample opportunities to create awareness at the local level through advertising, press releases, arena postings, community involvement, sponsorship programs, and social media. Several respondents of this study indicated a lack of awareness concerning playing opportunities. To effectively recruit and maintain players, women's recreational leagues should endeavor to adequately promote their leagues and generate word of mouth within their targeted markets.

Focus on Skill Development

This chapter revealed that developing competent hockey skills is the greatest perceived challenge of participation. This is true for both age cohorts but was found to be significantly more pronounced for older players. Given this challenge, it is recommended that league organizers prioritize skill development in the delivery of their programs. In most cases, women's recreational leagues consist of games only, with no dedicated practice time. By offering incremental skill sessions, players (including goalies) can focus on improving their abilities and alleviating some of their frustrations of play. A further recommendation is to partner with local high-performance female players and coaches (such as collegiate/university or midget AA) to deliver these skill sessions. Such interaction offers mutual gains as recreational players would benefit from the expertise of these elite players, who in turn may build a strong network of support and extended fan base for their competitive programs. Women recreational players have diverse backgrounds and professions, which could also encourage further community support for high-level teams through sponsorships and fundraising opportunities.

Women's expressed time constraints may be a hurdle in attending supplementary skill sessions. Many women highlighted that significant accommodations must be coordinated (such as child care, household tasks, taxiing of children) in order for them to be able to escape to the rink. Such efforts are often limited to once-a-week outings. An alternative, therefore, is to extend their precious hockey moments by integrating further practice time into scheduled games. As an example, most games are one hour in length. By extending ice time to ninety minutes, players could devote thirty minutes to skill development and the balance could be preserved for game play. This suggestion is, however, dependent on being able to secure incremental ice time.

Improve Ice-Time Accessibility

Inaccessible ice was also identified as a struggle for many women recreational players. This includes limited time options, late-evening start times, distant commutes, and the rising cost of facility rentals. Several respondents expressed a sense of inequity in terms of the allocation of available ice. While the distribution of ice times is normally beyond the direct control of league administrators, it is recommended that facility managers attempt to improve ice-time options for these time-sensitive players. Another means of alleviating stress among hockey-playing moms is for arenas to offer child-care services during peak hours. This could be resourced through mandatory high-school-student volunteer hours or offered as a paid service.

Restructure Leagues to Expand Participation Options

In order to address the growing disparity and potential conflict between player cohorts, it is recommended that leagues consider separating players through appropriate skill- or age-based divisions. This proposition is dependent on having a sufficient membership base to effectively roster multiple divisional teams. Established men's recreational leagues often distinguish players by age groups (30+, 50+, etc.) or by ascending skill level (division 1, 2, or A, B, etc.) As women's leagues continue to evolve, similar tiered systems should be considered. For instance, these may include groupings based on skill (beginners or advanced), age (18+, 35+, etc.), or desired competitiveness (fun or challenging). Given the accelerated development of women's hockey, such categorizations should be fluid and adapt to changing player compositions. Further research should focus on extending this understanding of evolving player cohorts.

Cultivate a Supportive Female Hockey Community

The chapter confirmed that women influence their female peers and serve as a valued support system throughout recreational hockey. It is therefore essential for all levels of female hockey to unite, assist, and grow together as a strong community within the larger hockey world. Despite past exclusions, women should now have the opportunity to enjoy positive, lifelong hockey involvement. As recommended by the Canadian Sport for Life Society, effective off-ramps should be developed to facilitate player transition through the various forms of participation (CAAWS 2012). Among other roles, this may include player (beginner, competitive, recreational, etc.), coach, official, volunteer, or administrator. The findings of this study suggest that the transition from competitive to recreational play is particularly challenging and threatens the ongoing enjoyment of hockey for many players. Recreational systems should be adapted to extend transitional participation options and to preserve positive playing environments.

Furthermore, women need to proudly demonstrate their support for higher-level play by attending games, watching broadcast events, advocating for the advancement of women's hockey, and generating favourable word of mouth through any possible means. Building critical mass support will ultimately fuel further media coverage, sponsorship interest, and overall participation in and encouragement of women's hockey. As the profile of women's hockey is raised, so is the abundance of quality role models for future generations of female hockey players.

Conclusions

This chapter brings needed visibility and new understanding to a growing group of Canadian hockey players. Women recreational leagues are unique from other established hockey structures as they combine a broad range of polarizing player types. With a common passion for the game, women must team up to overcome significant differences in skill, experience, competitiveness, and motivations of play. Women's hockey has long been and remains an important part of the Canadian hockey fabric. Female players have triumphed through a long history of exclusion and inequity to legitimize their status as "real" hockey players. Several recommendations are presented here in an effort to initiate discussion and cultivate support for this level of play. Women of all ages and abilities are encouraged to enjoy positive, lifelong engagement in hockey. This survey respondent's quote captures the essence of hockey for this passionate group of participants and the spirit of play that should be preserved for all levels of players: "When I step on the ice, the rest of the world seems to disappear. Nothing else matters. My mind clears. It's an amazing feeling."

Bibliography

Adams, Carly. 2008. "'Queens of the Ice Lanes': The Preston Rivulettes and Women's Hockey in Canada, 1931–1940." *Sport History Review*, 1–29. http://www.carhahockey.ca/Userfiles/Files/Women/News/queens-of-the-ice-lanes.pdf.

Armstrong, K. L. 2001. "Self and Product Image Congruency among Male and Female Minor League Ice Hockey Spectators: Implications for Women's Consumption of Professional Men's Sports." *Women in Sport & Physical Activity Journal* 10 (2): 27.

Auster, Carol J. 2008. "The Effect of Cohort on Women's Sport Participation: An Intergenerational Study of Collegiate Women Ice Hockey Players." *Journal of Leisure Research* 40 (2): 312–37.

CAAWS (Canadian Association for the Advancement of Women and Sport and Physical Activity). 2012. "Actively Engaging Women and Girls. Addressing the Psycho-Social Factors." http://caaws.ca/ActivelyEngaging/documents/CAAWS_CS4L_Engaging_Women.pdf

———. 2016. "Women in Sport: Fueling a Lifetime of Participation. A Report on the Status of Female Sport Participation in Canada." http://www.caaws.ca/e/wp-content/uploads/2016/03/FWC_ResearchPublication_EN_7March2016.pdf.

Canadian Heritage. 2012. "Canadian Sport Policy 2012." http://sirc.ca/CSPRenewal/documents/CSP2012_EN_LR.pdf.

———. 2013. "Sport Participation 2010. Research Paper." February. http://publications.gc.ca/collections/collection_2013/pc-ch/CH24-1-2012-eng.pdf.

Crawford, Garry, and Victoria K Gosling. 2004. "The Myth of the 'Puck Bunny': Female Fans and Men's Ice Hockey." *Sociology* 38 (3): 477–93. doi:10.1177/0038038504043214.

DiCarlo, D. 2016. "Playing like a Girl? The Negotiation of Gender and Sexual Identity among Female Ice Hockey Athletes on Male Teams." *Sport in Society* 19 (8–9): 1363–73. doi:10.1080/1743043 7.2015.1096260.

Hockey Canada. 2014. 2014 Annual Report. http://cdn.agilitycms.com/hockey-canada/Corporate/About/Downloads/2014_annual_report_e.pdf.

———. 2015. 2014–15 Annual Report. http://cdn.agilitycms.com/hockey-canada/Corporate/About/Downloads/2014-15_annual_report_e.pdf.

IIHF (International Ice Hockey Federation). 2016. Survey of Players 2016 http://www.iihf.com/iihf-home/the-iihf/survey-of-players.

IOC (International Olympic Committee). 1998. "US Women Strike Maiden Ice Hockey Gold." Olympic News. https://www.olympic.org/news/us-women-strike-maiden-ice-hockey-gold.

———. 2011. Olympic Studies Centre. "Ice Hockey. Participation during the History of the Olympic Winter Games." https://stillmed.olympic.org/AssetsDocs/OSC Section/pdf/QR_sports_winter/Sports_Olympiques_hockey_sur_glace_eng.pdf.

Larkin, Matt. 2015. "The Fight to Sell Women's Hockey." *Hockey News*. http://www.thehockeynews.com/news/article/the-fight-to-sell-womens-hockey-can-the-cwhl-become-the-wnba.

Locke, Marianna Catherine, and George Karlis. 2015. "Canadian Women's Hockey: Concerns and Concerns." *The Sport Journal* 18.

McFarlane, Brian. 1994. *Proud Past, Bright Future: One Hundred Years of Canadian Women's Hockey*. Toronto: Stoddart.

Pelak, C. F. 2002. "Women's Collective Identity Formation in Sports: A Case Study from Women's Ice Hockey." *Gender & Society* 16 (1): 93–114. doi:10.1177/0891243202016001006.

Poniatowski, Kelly, and Marie Hardin. 2012. "'The More Things Change, the More They …': Commentary During Women's Ice Hockey at the 2010 Olympic Games." *Mass Communication & Society* 15:622–41. doi:10.1080/15205436.2012.677094.

Ransdell, Lynda B, and Teena Murray. 2011. "A Physical Profile of Elite Female Ice Hockey Players from the USA." *Journal of Strength & Conditioning Research* 25 (9): 2358–63. doi:10.1519/JSC.0b013e31822a5440.

Reid, Patrick A, and Daniel S Mason. 2015. "'Women Can't Skate That Fast and Shoot That Hard!'" *International Journal of the History of Sport* 32 (14): 1678–96. doi:10.1080/09523367.2015.1121867.

Sears, Donna, and Cal Cipolla. 2007. "GO Team GO: The Pleasure of Being a Sports Fan !" Summary brief. *Society for Marketing Advances Proceedings*.

Stevens, Julie. 2000. "The Declining Sense of Community in Canadian Women's Hockey." *Women in Sport & Physical Activity Journal* 9 (2): 123–40.

Suddath, Claire. 2015. "Women's Hockey Wants to Break Into the Big Leagues." *Bloomberg Businessweek*. https://www.bloomberg.com/news/articles/2015-11-12/women-s-hockey-wants-to-break-into-the-big-leagues.

Theberge, Nancy. 2000. *Higher Goals: Women Ice Hockey and the Politics of Gender*. Albany: State University of New York Press.

———. 2003. "'No Fear Comes' Adolescent Girls, Ice Hockey, and the Embodiment of Gender." *Youth & Society* 34 (4): 497. doi:10.1177/0044118X03252592.

Vincent, John, and Jane Crossman. 2012. "'Patriots at Play': Analysis of Newspaper Coverage of the Gold Medal Contenders in Men's and Women's Ice Hockey at the 2010 Winter Olympic Games." *International Journal of Sport Communication* 5 (1): 87–108.

http://search.ebscohost.com/login.aspx?direct=true&db=sph&AN=74265814&site=ehost-live&scope=site.

Weir, Patricia L., Kristy L. Smith, Chelsea Paterson, and Sean Horton. 2010. "Canadian Women's Ice Hockey: Evidence of a Relative Age Effect." *Talent Development and Excellence* 2 (2): 209–17.

Wiley, Caroline, Susan Shaw, and Mark Havitz. 2000. "Men's and Women's Involvement in Sports: An Examination of the Gendered Aspects of Leisure Involvement." *Leisure Sciences* 22 (1): 19–31. doi:10.1080/014904000272939.

PART IV
Reporting Hockey

Document 5
Hockey in New Media

JOE PELLETIER

My journey to becoming a hockey researcher and new-media journalist began at the local landfill in 1979.

When I was five years old, my father took me to the dump to drop off some tree branches and grass clippings. While he unloaded the debris, I was awestruck with a small piece of cardboard I found in the dirt.

It was a Barry Gibbs hockey card. O-Pee-Chee card number 304 of the 1979–80 hockey card set.

Before that, I do not recall having any earlier hockey memories. But from that moment on, I was enthralled by the game and the players who made it great. I picked up the card and read the teasing of information about the little-known Los Angeles Kings defenseman on the back. I had to know more.

Realizing that this was card no. 304, I concluded there must have been at least 303 other cards out there. I was somehow able to gather a bunch of them, though not all. I got sick on the bubble-gum trying, too! But I was hooked on hockey—and learning about the players that captured my imagination on these small pieces of cardboard.

Ever since, I have been trying to learn as much as I can about hockey players, most of whom I have never seen play. I have read books, collected newspaper clippings and issues of *The Hockey News*, and listened to interviews and television shows. I digested everything I could. And it all started with that fateful trip to the dump!

Of course, all of this was before the Internet. By the time I got online (does anyone remember life before the Internet?), when I was twenty years old, I had amassed a pretty impressive physical library of print materials and a vast database of hockey information in my head.

My love of hockey is my way of sharing what I learn with the world. It is not just a hobby, but a passion—a labour of love. But I needed a way to share it. All of this information accumulation was fine and dandy, but unless I was able to do something with it, it was really rather pointless.

The Internet ultimately facilitated the ability to share it all by creating a community of readers and like-minded people. First, it was creating a stand-alone website. Then, it was blogging. Then social media like Facebook and Twitter changed everything. And who knows, over the next few years it will all likely be revolutionized a time or two again.

But it all comes down to the same common denominators that existed before the Internet—the quest for knowledge, the opportunity to express yourself, and a community to share it with.

Blogging and new media allows you to explore a passion and voice your thoughts, ideas, and feelings, all while giving you the opportunity to connect and network with like-minded individuals who share that same passion.

If the passion is for the subject and not for hopes of fame or fortune, it is amazing how far that can take you. I went from a nobody with a few readers a month twenty years ago to becoming an expert in my field because I built my exposure and network. In addition to my own projects, I have now worked for major publishers and media companies, as well as entities such as Hockey Canada, the National Hockey League, and the Canadian Museum of History. In most cases, they headhunted me.

Who reads my work? According to the statistics, North Americans still dominate my readership, but hockey-playing nations in Europe are also well represented. The average reader tends to be older, likely because my content is largely historical and nostalgic, and male. Based on interactions with readers, a fair number of readers are family members or acquaintances of long-forgotten players.

The feedback is almost always positive, or at the very least, fair. Family members are almost always appreciative. Any criticism tends to be constructive, filling in holes or adding to the story.

In the early days there was some resistance from traditional media people, particularly writers. Nowadays, everything is merged. Traditional newspaper and magazine writers have their content online, including features that never make it to the printed page. Broadcast media all do Internet-based projects.

The lines between traditional media and new media are now not just blurred, they are almost non-existent. Information consumers want the best content. They are savvy, too. It does not matter if it comes in the form of a traditional newspaper article or a blog written in someone's basement. What matters is good content.

Content is king. Passion is the kingmaker.

Chapter 9
O Canada, We Stand On Guard For Thee: Representations of Canadian Hockey Players in the Swedish Press, 1920–2016

TOBIAS STARK

In their 2005 survey of Canadian sport, researchers Don Morrow and Kevin Wamsley state that "hockey has invented Canadians as much as Canadians invented hockey" (2005, 203). Morrow and Wamsley build on numerous academic treatises published at the turn of the twenty-first century on hockey as a cultural practice in Canada. However, while there is a comparatively rich and rapidly growing academic literature on hockey as an integral part of Canadian culture (Kidd and Macfarlane 1972; Gruneau and Whitson 1993; Whitson and Gruneau 2006; Dopp and Harrison 2009; Holman 2009), scholarly interest in how the game has shaped the image of Canada abroad has been limited.

Apart from a number of considerations of the political, cultural, and diplomatic interests at stake in international hockey during the Cold War from a Canadian point of view (Macintosh and Greenhorn 1993; Earle 1995; Jokisipilä 2006; Soares 2011, Scherer and Cantelon 2013; Jesenský 2014; Kennedy 2014), as well as a few studies on the reception of the transnational sport migration of male Canadian hockey players to the United States and parts of Europe (Maguire 1996; Robidoux 2002; Holman 2007), it appears as if the researchers that have touched on the issue have done so mainly in regard to discussions on the influence of the North American brand of the game on its European counterpart, or the construction of particular social identities overseas (Stark 2001, 2012; Backman 2012; Leeworthy 2014; Stark 2014).

But to this point, as far as I have been able to make out, there has been no attempt to present a far-reaching academic investigation of the impact of "Canada's game," as hockey habitually has been labelled, on the perception of Canada and its inhabitants per se in other parts of the world. Needless to say, given that few intellectuals nowadays would contest the relational character of social identity construction—that class, gender, national identities, and such are formed in binary opposition to one or more identifiable groups in a process where "I/we" become what "the other/they" are not—this dearth of research makes for a rather lopsided understanding of hockey as a national phenomenon in Canada (Said 1979;

Robidoux 2002; Allain 2016). To counteract this deficit, systematic examinations of foreign conceptions and experiences of Canadian hockey is needed. Hence, researchers must address questions such as—How has Canadian hockey, and its representatives, been conceived abroad? What has this meant for the notion of being Canadian in Canada?

In this chapter, I will ponder these issues through an analysis of representations of Canadian hockey players in the Swedish press, from the introduction of the sport to Swedes at the Antwerp Olympics in 1920 to the 2016 World Cup in Toronto, on the purported home soil of the game. In doing this, I aim to shed light on the ability of "the Canadian specific"—to use a catchphrase on hockey, coined by the Canadian poet Al Purdy—to build international relations and national unity in Canada over time (Gruneau and Whitson 1993, 3). Ultimately, the purpose is to further the understanding of the perception of hockey as an integral part of Canadian culture.

An analysis of the portrayal of Canadian hockey players in Swedish media accounts makes for an interesting case study on the place of the game in Canadian everyday life for at least two reasons. First, as far as explorations on Canadian national identity in international hockey are concerned, most researchers have focused on Canada's interaction with the United States or the Soviet Union/Russia, i.e. with the superpowers of the world. Subsequently, the information on the effect of Canada's contacts with the rest of the hockey world—not least small-power countries such as Sweden, with its tradition of political and military neutrality—on Canadian material culture and the notion of Canadinaness is in short supply (Earle 1995; Robidoux 2002; Kennedy 2014; Ogden and Edwards 2016).

Second, over the years, Sweden has been one of the foremost producers of NHL players outside of North America, if not the greatest provider, numerically speaking. As late as during the 2015–16 season, eighty-seven Swedes played in the NHL, amounting to 8.8 per cent of NHL players, a high for a non–North American country (Stark 2012; Greder Duncan 2016).

The confluence of these two factors, which relate to broader socio-cultural issues within and outside the game, makes the representations of Canadian hockey players in the Swedish press a particularly enthralling focal point for an investigation of how the game relates to material culture and political history in Canada.

Analytical Considerations

The application of the term "representation" denotes that it is the textual account of Canadian hockey players in Swedish press narratives that is the focal point of exploration. Thus, I am not trying to establish whether the depictions of Canadian athletes are accurate or not. Neither am I interested in mapping out Swedish hockey reportage as a literary genre, nor scrutinizing the opinions of particular writers. Rather, I am concerned with examining how the renderings of the subject matter operates to produce meaning by imposing certain perspectives while disregarding others. Subsequently, the representations in question are not seen as expressions of perpetual conceptions or static ideals, but as active formulations and on-going cultural negotiations of collective and individual identities (Whannel 2002; Tolvhed 2008).

The theoretical framework I use for the analysis draws on media-culture researcher Garry Whannel's work on media sport stars. Whannel argues (2002, 49) that "stardom is a form of social production in which the professional ideologies and production practices of the media aim to win and hold our attention by linking sporting achievement and personality in ways which have resonances in popular common sense." Furthermore, Whannel stresses that star images are not static but are constantly being rewritten in the "continuously present" as the lives of athletes are interpreted in accordance with the dominant discourse at the given moment in time. This incessant construction of star biographies—or the "rein-scription," to use Whannels' own vocabulary—involves three related processes: (i) the mobilization of popular memory, (ii) selective memory, and (iii) the practice of writing history in the present. Hence, the public image of sporting heroes, such as Muhammed Ali and David Beckham, is the accumulated result of all their previous depictions, where some earlier aspects have been gradually obscured or erased while others are more profoundly carved out (ibid., 56).

Thus, rather than perceiving celebrity as intrinsically shallow and meaningless, as many commentators tend to do, Whannel stresses that the athletes who achieve "celebrity status provides important and revealing evidence about the cultural formation they exist within"; consequently, "it is…important to pay close attention to the ways in which they are celebrated, examining the themes, values and discourses that are in play" (ibid., 56).

Though few—if anyone—of the Canadian players cited in the source material could be considered celebrities in the same vein as the global superstars Whannel examines—male luminaries "whose fame spread well beyond the world of sport and its followers" (ibid., 1)—I would argue that the general logic of the re-inscription process at hand applies for the Swedish press accounts of the Canadians in question as well. To be more precise, I contend that the representations of Canadian hockey players in Swedish press narratives are historically grounded and socially produced cultural formations that provide important means for examining the key interface between popular sporting culture and organized political discourse in the construction of the notion of Canada abroad.

Empirically, the chapter builds on a wide selection of Swedish press reports, ranging from an extensive number of daily broadsheets to a plethora of popular magazine and sports journals.[1] The guiding methodological principle of the study has been crosschecking data from multiple sources in search of patterns in the research material. Also, in examining the press narratives I have paid particular attention to issues regarding national identity and considerations of preferred styles of play, as I agree with sociologist Kristi Allain's contestation (2008, 346) that, as there is no universally favoured brand of hockey, it is important to study how the "ideas of difference are taken up within the" game.

The Pioneering Years, 1920–1939

In examining the representations of Canadian hockey players in the Swedish press it is important to note that ever since its "discovery" the American continent has served as a blank canvas for the Old World, upon which Europeans have projected their innermost dreams and fears. Consequently, America and Americanization were frequent topics of

---

1. Most of the source material used in this study was collected for another and much larger project, on the development of hockey as a national phenomenon in Sweden, 1920–1972. In total, more than 5,000 editions were sampled, focusing on the main dailies and on sports and popular journals of the time.

conversation in Sweden at the turn of the twentieth century. For countless Swedes, the notion of America—which primarily appear to have concerned the United States but regularly also involved Canada, as the two nations were largely considered as quite similar, if not the same—meant the promise of a better way of life, as openness, rationality, and personal freedom were cherished features of the social fabric of the New World. Many others dreaded Americanization, equating North American customs with immorality, sensationalism, and alienation. Unsurprisingly, many Swedes migrated to the United States and Canada in search for a better life, or strove to reap the benefits of "the American way of life" in Sweden. Meanwhile, a lot of Swedish conservatives castigated the migrants as misled renegades and/ or tried to protect alleged national traditions and ideals in the face of lures from overseas (Stark 2010; Rönnqvist 2004; Lindkvist 2007).

However, as the First World War was widely regarded as a collapse of European civilization, and with the United States looming as the world's leading political and economic power, modernization and Americanization increasingly tended to be seen as interchangeable concepts. Indeed, before long, Americanization came to be conceived as an almost irreversible force in Sweden, which one could either embrace or risk getting run over by. Correspondingly, the notion of America became more positive among the Swedes in the first few decades of the twentieth century, although it took a turn for the worse during the 1930s in the wake of the Great Depression and amid the burgeoning Swedish welfare state. However, generally speaking, American material and social achievements were held in higher regard than cultural and spiritual welfare in Sweden (Stark 2010).

Thus, when hockey was introduced in Sweden, in the interwar era, there were those who welcomed the game with open arms, depicting it as an international sport perfectly suited for life in a modern society. Still, others strove to thwart the new game since they regarded it as a corrupting force, undermining endemic values and cultural practices. Step by step, however, most of the suspicion in Sweden toward hockey gave way to a widespread appreciation of the game, prompted by, *inter alia*, a growing predilection for American commodities, as well as Swedish triumphs in international championships and the deep admiration of the Swedes for the skillful North Americans—particularly the Canadian players—they came to face on the ice rinks of the world. Accordingly, the Swedish interaction with Canadian hockey players during the decades following the First World War can be said to have played a small but important part in the construction of the general notion of modernity in Sweden during the interwar era (Stark 2010).

However, at first, few Swedes appear to have associated the sport of hockey with North American customs or with Canadian culture or players per se. When it was announced that hockey would be added to the Olympic Games in Antwerp in the summer of 1920 (the first Winter Olympic Games were held in 1924 and included ice hockey), there were a lot of confusing reports in the Swedish press, where commentators intermixed the Canadian game with the similar but different European sport of bandy, a field game, as the former was then regularly referred to as "hockey on ice" (*hockey på is*). The Swedish Olympic Committee realized soon enough that it was not bandy but "Canadian" hockey, ice hockey, that was about to be played in Antwerp, as they had received a set of rules outlining the game. But the general public interested in the Olympics appear to have had a hard time separating hockey from bandy until the first puck dropped at centre ice. Also, most of the

Swedes who could tell hockey and bandy apart seem to have considered the difference to be quite small; given that the general consensus among the top brass of the Swedish sports movement was that the proficient Swedish bandy players were so adept at stickhandling and skating that they would be able to compete for a medal in Antwerp, if only they got to practice hockey before the tournament. When, it was later confirmed that Team Sweden could count on the service of a few countrymen that had played hockey during trips abroad, it was decided that Sweden would participate in the Olympic hockey tournament, with a team primarily made out of bandy players, in an attempt to strengthen the Swedish odds for placing high in the overall standings at the Antwerp Olympics (Stark 2010).

Hence, at the start of the 1920 Olympics, most Swedes had at best only a vague idea of the skills and the mindset of Canadian hockey players. However, it did not take long for the Swedish contingent to get familiarized with the Canadian players. The Swedes were dumbfounded by the athletic ability of the Canadians. The following excerpt taken from Sweden's biggest morning paper at the time, the liberal *Stockholms-Tidningen*, is testimony of that:

> When the boys saw the Canadians…play for the first time, they first looked silently on the play, then on one another, and then they said with one voice "I'll be darned!" You see, these chaps really could play in a way that you never had known. The swiftness, the quick turns and stick-handling, the recklessness and mastery with which they shot the puck…, made one's head spin, it captivated and thrilled the spectators so that they could not keep quiet, but had to shout and applaud ("X", 1920).

The sudden realization of the great aptitude of the Canadian hockey players among the Swedes meant that all hope for the gold medal was lost for Team Sweden. Yet this does not seem to have bothered the Swedes in Antwerp all too much, as they seemed to be captivated by the Canadians spectacular display on the ice. Torsten Tegnér (1920a) of the biggest Swedish sports journal of the time, *Idrottsbladet*, captured the mood well:

> The [winter-sport program of the Antwerp Olympics] have many highlights . . . albeit just one event of the outermost excitement and grandeur . . . , Team USA's game versus Canada. With all due respect to the beautiful art of the figure skaters, but it does not set the world on fire—hardly even an ice rink. The hockey battle [in question] does! From a sport point of view one may hope that this affair is reserved for the final, but for us outsiders it would be more favourable if one of the two star-acts were eliminated from competition as soon as possible…. One scarcely sees an American break the speed on the skates; as it is considered too exhausting, as well as counterproductive as the player loses momentum . . . And their speed is truly marvellous. The Swedes arrived here believing they were tiptop at skating, but we have had to revise that understanding. Thereby, we compare to the Americans (especially so the Canadians) like [a beginner to an expert].

The quotation is a telling example of the instant success of hockey in the eyes of the Swedes in Antwerp, and later their countrymen back home, thanks in large part to the impressive athleticism showcased by the Canadians. Additionally, the account is interesting in that the closing sentence—"we compare to the Americans (especially so the Canadians)"—is a perfect reminder of the notoriously slippery conceptualization of "American," and different derivations of the term, as it every so often was, and still is, used to refer not only U.S. citizens and phenomena but to Canadians and Canadian as well (Lex 1920; Tegnér 1920b, 1927).

Thus, awe-inspiring athleticism and the notion of Canadians as being "the same but different" from Americans must be underlined as two main features in the Swedish press reports on hockey players from Canada from the beginning of the interwar era to 1945 (Lex 1920; Tegnér 1920b, 1927). Another leading motif in the Swedish papers at the time was Canadians as great sportspersons and even greater people. This theme was established already during the Antwerp Olympics—in regard to the Winnipeg Falcons, who represented Canada in the Olympics hockey tournament—but appears to have come in full swing a few years later, with the first visit of a Canadian team, Montreal's legendary Victoria Hockey Club, to Sweden in February 1927 (Stark 2010).

Before the arrival of the Montrealers, the Swedish press was hard at work building up the expectations for their visit among readers, publishing detailed stories on the club's history and its members. The Victorias, readers were told, were nothing short of a sensational, world-class talent, both on and off the ice. When the Victorias finally arrived in Sweden, the interest in the still rather new sport of hockey had reached fever pitch, and the Canadians were treated as royalty. The major Swedish newspapers followed the Canadians every move, and reported favourably on all their exploits. In fact, the Swedes were so taken with the Canadians that even their whooping beating of the Swedish national team (17–1) in the first game in Sweden stirred their popularity and the blooming interest in the game further ("En världsmästare" 1927; Sten 1927a; "Kanadamatchen" 1927). The conservative *Svenska Dagbladet*, which also happened to be the main sponsor of the event, tellingly concluded the following day: "the one who neglects to go and see one or more of the Canadians following games while in Sweden has only [him/herself] to blame" ("Kanadensarna slogo" 1927).

Accordingly, a great many Swedes followed suit: all of the six exhibition games the Victoria Hockey Club played in Sweden attracted extraordinarily big crowds, attendance records at ice rinks were shattered, while several hundreds "gathered outside of [the club's] hotel just to get a glimpse of the celebrities" (Sten 1920b).[2]

Altogether, the 1927 visit of the team from Montreal stands out as a watershed in Swedish hockey history, as well as in the portrayal of the Canadian hockey players in the Swedish press. The matches got the new sport truly got off the ground after a rocky start, whereas the notion of the Canadian athletes took on a life of its own. Before the Victoria Hockey Clubs well-cherished visit only the few Swedes who had seen Canadian hockey players first-hand abroad knew how good they were. Afterward, every published account was filtered through the prism of the golden memories of numerous of Swedish fans shared of the Montrealers, as well as the many affectionate reports published in the Swedish press in the following years. Hence, a distinct discourse on how Canadian hockey players truly

---

2. The Victoria Hockey Club won all six games, while scoring a total of sixty-three goals and surrendering only seven (Stark 2010).

"were" had been established. Consequently, all the media narratives on the subject matter distributed in the next couple of decades tended to be little more than variations of the established themes, working to confirm what the Swedes already "knew" and thus rearticulated what Canadianness "was" to the Swedes (Stark 2010).

The Cold War Era, 1945–1989

In the first half of the twentieth century, Canada ruled more or less supreme in international ice hockey. The superiority of their game was actually so great that student and men's amateur teams from Canada would outplay the best European national squads on a regular basis. Hence, the deep-felt adoration of the great athleticism of the members of the Victoria Hockey Club, and their countrymen, in the pioneering years of the sport in Sweden. However, the successful entrance of the Soviet Union on the international hockey scene in 1954 marked the beginning of a new era in the sport. The Soviet national team went on to dominate international competition the following four decades, winning eighteen world championships and five Olympic Games between 1954 and 1989. The Soviets' prowess, together with the steady improvement of the Czechs and the Swedes, meant that the college and amateur teams Canada used to send to international tournaments could no longer count on winning, let alone placing high in the standings (Stark 2014).

A number of academics have detailed the great concern the shifting power balance in international hockey during the 1950s and 1960s caused in Canada. For example, sport-policy researchers Donald Macintosh and Donna Greenhorn (1993, 96) contended that "the decline of Canada's fortunes in international hockey in the 1950s and 1960s…forced the federal government to intervene" and establish the International Sports Relations unit in the Department of External Affairs, as the lack of success contrasted sharply with the rising ambitions of having Canada playing a leading role in international politics at the time. Besides, sociologist Hart Cantelon has underlined that Canadian hockey representatives soon came to accuse the Soviets of cheating; the state-sponsored Soviet players were not amateurs but cloaked professionals, they maintained. Also, Canadian officials set out to persuade the International Ice Hockey Federation (IIHF) to allow professionals in the world championships, subsequently withdrawing from international hockey in protest of IIHF President John Francis "Bunny" Ahearne's opposition to the proposal. On the ice, the frustration manifested itself among the Canadian players in a growing reliance on force and intimidation tactics (rough play, fighting, verbal aggression) against opponents in international tournaments. Altogether, these measures seem to have made matters worse, as Canadian hockey players came to be increasingly associated with bullying and bad sportsmanship in Europe (Cantelon 2006; Stark 2014).

In Sweden, although there were various accounts of the toughness of Canadian hockey players in circulation in the decades leading up to 1945, most were based on hearsay or referred to the sturdiness of the athletes in terms of their ability to play through pain ("Ishockey" 1920; Tegnér 1920a, 1920b). The first time the Swedes appear to have come to witness an open display of so-called American hockey violence first-hand was in connection with the world championships in Stockholm, in 1949, where both the United States and the Canadian national teams where castigated as troublemakers, especially the Canadians (Stark 2001).

Actually, the problems started before the world championships began, when the Sudbury Wolves—who represented Canada in the tournament—raised more than a few Swedish eyebrows with their purported fierce brand of hockey during a spell of friendly games against local club teams. When the championship tournament began, the agitated Swedish press were on their toes, and commented with increasing disapproval on Team Canada's alleged harsh methods on the ice ("Utvisningar och 'domarmål'" 1949; "Spela spelet!" 1949; "10 000 i panik vid Stadion" 1949). According to the Swedish press, the Canadians were particularly vicious when facing Czechoslovakia, on February 15, a contest that lead to the police having to escort the "unsportsmanlike Americans" (Allison 1949) out of the arena after the game as an angry mob of locals threatened their safety ("Polisvakt som skydd åt kanadensiska ruffgubbar" 1949; "Domarna i rampljuset" 1949).

As it happened, the following day Team Canada was scheduled to meet Team Sweden. Rather than trying to calm the angry mood among their countrymen from the day before, on February 16 the Swedish papers added fuel to the fire in portraying the Canadian players as gangsters and irredeemable perpetrators of violence, while remarking on the expected carnage of the Swedish team at the hands of the Canadians later that day. As a result, at the start of the game, an incensed crowd of at least 10,000 Swedes (some estimations had it close to 50,000) had gathered outside of the stadium, in large part attracted by the antici-pated bloodshed. In all the turmoil, the massive iron gates at the stadium where overthrown and about sixty people were injured as the animated crowd flooded the arena. The next day, the Swedish press was full of alarming reports on the "battle at the Stadium." As far as the game was concerned, the Canadians were made out to have done their outmost to play according to the rules, but their "habitual affection for violence" (Luck 1949) was said to have shown from time to time (Stark 2010).

Thus, for all the hyperbole during the pioneering years, it would seem that the notion of the Canadian hockey player in the Swedish press was transformed from a noble sportsman to a violent recidivist in little more than over the course of a single tournament. In the next few decades, the previously extremely positive image of Canadian hockey players deteriorated even further. For the Swedes, the beginning of the 1960s seems to have been a particularly critical period, as the amateur senior men's team the Trail Smoke Eaters, from Trail, British Columbia, toured Sweden in 1961 and 1963, and literary crushed their oppo-nents. The result was a public outcry on the supposed brutality and unsportsmanlike conduct of the Canadians (Figure 9.1. Allegedly, some Swedish parents even began referring to the Canadians in order to "scare" their children straight: "If you don't behave yourself, the Trail Smoke Eaters will come and get you!" (Stark 2014).

Bobby Bystrom's concluding remark in *Dagens Nyheter* on the Trail Smoke Eaters Swedish tour in 1961 is illustrative on the general notion of Canadian hockey players at the time:

> Mr. Darryl Sly and his Canadian hockey brothers flew to Helsinki yesterday [after the conclusion of their Swedish tour]. Missed by no one, hated by most. Before Sly, whose name translates to "cunning' and "dodgy" in Swedish, entered the plane he said: "Goodbye, Swedes. We'll meet again". He did not say how. While injuring someone's ligament, or face? . . . The whole problem of bridging Canadian and European hockey

Figure 9.1 Unsportsmanlike Conduct

In the post-war era, the general notion of Canadian hockey players was transformed from a noble sportsman to a violent recidivist in Sweden. For the Swedes, the beginning of the 1960s seems to have been a particularly critical period, as the amateur senior men's team Trail Smoke Eaters toured Sweden in 1961 and 1963, and literary crushed their opponents. The illustration is a detailed presentation of alleged typical dirty plays of the Canadians, published in the popular Swedish journal Se, prior to the world Championships in Stockholm, in 1963.
Se, No10, 1963.

is made clear by the roster of the Trail Smoke Eaters. According to the roster, Darryl Sly . . . is a teacher. This must come as a slap in the face for all who tries to figure out the difference between Canadian and Swedish hockey. The worst brute is an educator of the young. Thus, the result can be only one [i.e., mayhem]. (Byström, 1961)

Fittingly, two new recurring features emerged in the representation of Canadian hockey players during the decades following the end of the Second World War. First, close-up accounts of their claimed strategies for playing dirty, such as, using hockey sticks, spearing, butt-ending, and cross-checking (Bood 1963a; "Åter från Kanada" 1963). Second, condescending annotations on the stated ugliness of their often-battered faces (toothlessness, broken noses, etc.) (Byström 1959; Bood 1963b; Eklöw 1964).

Still, it would be incorrect to say that all love for the Canadian hockey players was lost in Sweden. Rather, the unreserved admiration for the Canadian athletes of the pioneering years turned into a love-hate relationship with the North American for the Swedes. If anything, the deep-felt fascination for the Canadian hockey players seems to have grown even stronger in Sweden. For one thing, Canadian teams continued to attract large audiences in the stands—and later on television—in postwar Sweden, perhaps even more than before because of the Canadians' growing reputation as villainous and violent, as an increasing number of Swedes wanted to witness the presupposed eruption of "American hockey violence" first-hand (Stark 2001, 2010).

Besides, while the Swedes became increasingly disillusioned by the Canadian amateur teams that came to Europe after 1945, the skills of the Canadian hockey players were still greatly admired, especially of NHL players, as the NHL was heralded as the best hockey league in the world. As it would seem, with the slowly but steadily increasing NHL coverage in the Swedish press in the postwar era—exceedingly so in the wake of the Swedish player migration to North America in the late 1960s—the NHL received ever more appraisal in Sweden. Needless to say, the superstars—Gordie Howe, Maurice Richard, Wayne Gretzky, Mario Lemieux—received most of the attention, but also tough guys and junior players (i.e., under twenty) got plenty of media exposure. Hence, the Swedish press coverage of the NHL tended to focus on the proclaimed marvelousness of their speed and stickhandling proficiency, together with tall stories of their taken-for-granted fierceness. Interestingly, this would suggest that the Swedes did not frown upon hockey violence in general, as it generated a lot of interest, but rather when Swedish players were being victimized. Also, in contemplating this discrepancy, it is important to note that the harshest criticism of the alleged brutality of the Canadian hockey players in the Swedish press coincided with the climax of the Swedish government's adamant neutrality and pacifistic foreign policy, to the point of Sweden getting the nickname "the world's conscience" (Lundström 1950; Player 1966; Thelenius 1986; Norborg 1999).

Reaction to the 1972 Summit Series, between the USSR and Team Canada, is an example of the Swedish love-hate relationship with Canadian hockey during the Cold War. However, a complicating matter at the time was that the general notion of "America" had just taken a turn for the worse in Sweden, by way of the Vietnam War and the flourishing environmental movement, which saw the United States being criticised for its perceived bullish foreign policy and egotistical and superficial consumer society (Stark 2010, 2014).

Still, though labelled "the fight of the century," the real treat of the Summit Series for the Swedes was not the Canadian and Soviet battle for world hockey supremacy but Team Canada's visit to Stockholm on its way to Moscow en route to the Russian leg of the series. The Swedish Ice Hockey Association was celebrating its fiftieth anniversary and the two exhibition games between the Swedish national team and the NHL-composed Team Canada, on September 16 and 17, were meant as the icing on the birthday cake. In fact, as in the case of the Victoria Hockey Club before, the fuss about the Canadian NHL players being in Stockholm was so great that Swedish reporters followed their every move. Upon arrival, all major Swedish media outlets were brimming with material on the "famous professionals" and the "super phenomenons," as the Canadians were dubbed (Larsson 1972; Norén 1972).

Among the players, the superstars Bobby Orr and Phil Esposito grabbed most of the attention, followed by the solid defender Gary Bergman. In the case of the former, it was the illustrious athletic abilities as well as the luxurious celebrity lifestyle of the idolized players that occupied the Swedes. In the latter case, it was rather Bergman's Swedish heritage that fascinated fans. Swedish pundits also commented on Bergman's "old" age (thirty-two), his baldness, and the fact he had most of his own teeth despite being a seasoned NHL veteran. While these remarks might strike a present-day reader as odd and even offending, they must be understood as expressions of the contemporary conception of sport in Sweden as a youthful undertaking, as well as a recurrent theme amid the criticism of North American professional hockey in Sweden during the Cold War: the spectre of disfiguring facial injuries (Kvärre 1972; Stark 2012).

Before the first faceoff, all agreed that Team Sweden was the underdog. Swedish national-team member and later NHLer Börje Salming has stated that the Swedish players were actually in awe of the Canadians just by reading their names in the paper. On the ice, the Canadians' abrasive and hard-hitting playing style startled the Swedes, who lost 4–1 in the first exhibition game, on September 16. The following day, all major Swedish media outlets ran stories on the contended upsetting actions of the Canadians. Headlines such as "Thrash, Canada" and "Team Ugly" appeared. Overnight, the initial veneration of the prominent visitors was replaced by a belligerent criticism of Team Canada, in some cases bordering on xenophobia. In fact, the disgust at the Canadians was so great that their hotel received a bomb threat that evening, which then had to be searched by police before the players could go to bed. Yet the worst was to come (Byström 1972a; Jansson 1972; Åslund 1972a).

Before the second game, Team Sweden talked about standing up to the Canadians. The result was a brawl-filled bout pigeonholed as the worst tussle the Swedish spectators had ever seen. The game ended in a 4–4 draw, but the score must be characterized as a pyrrhic victory for the involved parties as the ice surface was literary covered in blood when the players left after the final buzzer (Åslund 1972b; Ericson 1972a).

The next day, the Swedish press had a field day, with front-page photographs of the blood-spattered nose of the captain of Team Sweden, later Winnipeg Jet Lars-Erik Sjöberg, while calling the Canadian players "animals," "gangsters," and "perpetrators of violence." Some reporters even suggested the Canadians better leave early for Moscow, as they were no longer welcome in Sweden. In fact, the aggravated situation had the Canadian ambassador, Margaret Meagher, going public to lament the excessive violence in the supposedly friendly games, something most Swedish onlookers must have taken as an apology and proof that Canada as a nation was officially disgraced (Byström 1972b; Åslund 1972b, Sterner 1972). The notion of the Canadian hockey player was at an all-time low in Sweden.

Interestingly enough, most contemporary Swedish analysts agreed that the best team ultimately won the 1972 Summit Series. Sure, the Canadians were still considered to be brutish players, but their ability to rise to the occasion and prevail after a poor start greatly impressed the Swedes. The Canadians may be criminals on the ice, but they are proper gentlemen outside the rink; they only act like villains in order to win, so competitive they do whatever it takes to triumph, it was argued (Ericson 1972b; "Trots allt bråk" 1972). Apparently, the Swedes had an easier time digesting the Canadian's aggressive playing style when they thumped the Soviets than when facing Sweden a week earlier.

Curtain Fall, 1989–2016

Undeniably, Team Canada's ill-fated stay in Stockholm in 1972 put a strain on the Swedish-Canadian relationship. However, although there is a dearth of research on the Swedish notion of "America" at the turn of the twenty-first century, it would seem that hockey in general, and the influx of Swedish talent to the NHL and the World Hockey Association (WHA) in particular, has helped spearhead a growing appreciation of Canada and the United States overall ever since. Actually, the migration of Swedish hockey players really started to take off in the early 1970s, at a time when, as stated, the common perception of "America" had taken a turn for the worse. Hence, it is safe to say that the Swedish NHL and WHA trailblazers have been part of the vanguard when it comes to rekindling the enthusiasm for "America" in Sweden (Stark 2010, 2012; Backman 2012).

Unsurprisingly, the first wave of Swedes to play professionally in North America was met with mixed emotions on the home front. On the one hand, having Swedes playing in the NHL and the WHA was perceived as evidence of the merit of the national hockey program, as its top talent were good enough to play with the best in the world. On the other hand, the representatives of the Swedish elite clubs and the Swedish Ice Hockey Association appears to have felt duped and abandoned by players going abroad, saying it drained the national program of talent (Stark 2012).

However, prompted by a growing number of Swedes starring in the NHL and the WHA, as well as the mounting media coverage of the North American game at large with the advent of the new media technologies, there has been an increasing veneration of the game in Sweden (Backman 2012). Correspondingly, since 1972, the general notion of Canadian hockey players has gradually shifted in a positive direction among Swedes.

A clear sign of this is that aggressive role players—such as Sean Avery and Paul Bissonnette before they retired—were fan favourites in Sweden, alongside more traditional ice-hockey heroes, like the skilled superstars Sidney Crosby and Steve Stamkos. For example, the youth magazine *Pro Hockey* contains a regular section on "bad boys" and "ice fighters," where their trade in violence or plain "outrageous" behaviour on and off the ice is portrayed in not-uncomplimentary fashion. Following this, the scorning of Canadian players with broken noses and missing teeth so common in the postwar era has given way to a newfound romanticism of playing through pain and having the scars to show for it. This transformation is perhaps best illustrated by the eroticization of Börje Salming's scarred face and body, as the former Toronto Maple Leafs great has been repeatedly characterized as one of Sweden's most masculine and sexy men the past couple of decades (Stark 2012; *Pro Hockey* 2012).

However, this does not mean that the Swedes' love-hate relationship with Canadian hockey players is wholly of the past. First, there appear to be a generation gap as far as the general appeal of North American hockey is concerned in Sweden in that young fans seem more smitten by the NHL than the older generation. Second, the Swedish press still publishes aggravated tirades on "American hockey violence" on occasion, especially if a Swedish player has been victimized, although journalists seem less inclined to stir up moral panic therein. Third, a number of notorious incidents from the late 1940s to the present involving venerated Canadian foes—be it a celebrated NHLer like Phil Esposito or the Sudbury, Ontario, native Desmond "Des" Moroney, who spent most of his career playing and coaching in Sweden—have lives of their own, having been recapped with zeal by the press time and again. Hence, this form of re-inscription might be characterized as a new major feature in the Swedish discourse of the Canadian hockey player (Whannel 2002; Stark 2012; Foussianis 2013; Janlind 2016).

Another novel element in the representations of Canadian hockey players in the Swedish press at the turn of the twenty-first century is the reference to gender. While there has always been the odd allusion to women's hockey in Canada in the Swedish papers, closer reporting on female hockey players of any nationality is a recent phenomenon. In fact, women's hockey appears to have once been such a nonentity in the Swedish press that it did not even arouse the derogatory remarks that the otherwise comparable women's soccer underwent. Contemporary media coverage of women's hockey—not least of Canadian stars like Hayley Wickenheiser and Jennifer Wakefield—in Sweden has gone hand in hand with the development of the domestic women's game too. Still, as the sport in general continues to be conceived as a primarily masculine domain, the lack of women's hockey coverage in Sweden can actually be read as testimony of the profoundly gendered media narrative of Canadian hockey (Stark 2001, Hansson 2015).

Also, the preferred masculinity of Canadian hockey players seems to have been quite Victorian among Swedish reporters, as noble amateur players—such as that of the Victoria Hockey Club, from Montreal's socially exclusive English-speaking-community—were held in high regard, while the rather hard-nosed playing style of the more layman-based senior men's teams like the Sudbury Wolves or the Trail Smoke Eaters was disagreeable.

Ultimately, it can then be argued that the perception of hockey as an integral part of Canadian culture and material life in the Swedish press has always had profound social biases, along unambiguous gender, class, ethnic, and linguistic lines.

Bibliography

Allain, Kristi. 2008. "'Real Fast and Tough': The Construction of Canadian Hockey Masculinity." *Sociology of Sport Journal* 25 (4): 462–81.

Allain, Kristi. 2016. "'The Mad Russian': Representations of Alexander Ovechkin and the Creation of Canadian National Identity." *Sociology of Sport Journal* 33 (2): 156–68.

Allison [pseud.]. 1949. "Domarna i rampljuset – slagskämpar i Kanada – osportslig amris." *Dagens Nyheter*, February 16.

Åslund, Nic. 1972a. "Kanada, varför gjorde ni oss detta?" *Aftonbladet*, September 17.

———. 1972b. "Blodet som bevisar Kanadas svaghet." *Aftonbladet*, September 18.

"Åter från Kanada." 1963. *Dagens Nyheter*, September 4.

Backman, Jyri. 2012. *I skuggan av NHL: En organisationsstudie av svensk och finsk elitishockey*. Gothenburg, Sweden: Institutionen för konst- och idrottsvetenskap, Gothenburg University.

Bood, Charlie. 1963a. "Fullträffen." *Se*, No. 10.

———. 1963b. "Det här är kanadensarnas tjuvtricks!" *Se*. No 10.

Byström, Bobby. 1959. "Guld och lärpengar." *Ishockeyboken 1959–1960*, p. 10–16.

———. 1961. "Även vi har skador." *Dagens Nyheter*, February 8.

———. 1972a. "Team Canada en besvikelse." *Dagens Nyheter*, September 17.

———. 1972b. "Kanadaglansen bara beklgnar." *Dagens Nyheter*, September 18.

Cantelon, Hart (2006). "Have Skates, Will Travel: Canada, International Hockey, and the Changing Hockey Labour Market", Artificial Ice: Hockey, Culture, and Commerce, David Whitson & Richard Gruneau (red.), Peterborough, ON: Broadview Press, s. 215–236.

"Domarna i rampljuset." 1949. *Dagens Nyheter*, February 16.

Dopp, Jamie, and Richard Harrison, eds. 2009. *Now Is the Winter: Thinking About Hockey*. Hamilton, ON: Wolsak & Wynn.

Earle, Neil. 1995. "Hockey as Canadian Popular Culture: Team Canada 1972, Television and the Canadian Identity." *Journal of Canadian Studies* 30 (2): 107–23.

Eklöw, Rudolf. 1964. "Skall vi slå på käft eller spela på puck." *Ishockeyboken 1964–65*, Stockholm, 89–94.

"En världsmästare med i Svenska Dagbladets kanadensiska turné." 1927. *Svenska Dagbladet*, January 1.

Ericson, Singel. 1972a. "Slagsmålen fortsatte I pauserna." *Expressen*, September 18.

———. 1972b. "Dödstrött – men överlycklig." *Expressen*, September 29.

Foussianis, Konstantin. 2013. "Han är ishockeyns hårda buse." *Expressen*, January 2.

Greder Dunacan, Annika. 2016. "Nytt rekord för NHL-svenskar." January 14. www.sveriegsradio.se.

Gruneau, Richard S., and David Whitson. 1993. *Hockey Night in Canada: Sport, Identities and Cultural Politics*. Toronto: Garamond Press.

Hansson, Joel. 2015. "Jennifer Wakefield ska spela herrhockey." *Aftonbladet*. August 12.

Holman, Andrew C. 2007. "The Canadian Hockey Player Problem: Cultural Reckoning and National Identities in American Collegiate Sport, 1947–80." *The Canadian Historical Review* 88 (3): 440–68.

———. 2009. *Canada's Game: Hockey and Identity*. Montreal: McGill-Queen's University Press.

"Ishockey." 1920. *Idrottsbladet*, March 12.

Janlind, Fredrik. 2016. "Foppa om fula tacklingen." *Göteborgs–Posten*, March 17.

Jansson, Bertil. 1972. "Skräp, Kanada." *Expressen*, September 17.

Jesenský, Marcel. 2014. "Win Friends or Make Enemies: Team Canada's 1978 Diplomatic Mission to Czechoslovakia." *Canadian Journal of History* 49 (3): 225–46.

Jokisipilä, Markku. 2006. "Maple Leaf, Hammer, and Sickle: International Ice Hockey During the Cold War." *Sport History Review* 37 (1): 36–53.

"Kanadamatchen går oavsett väderleken." 1927. *Dagens Nyheter*, February 4.

"Kanadensarna slogo Stadionpubliken med häpnad." 1927. *Svenska Dagbladet*, February 7.

Kennedy, Brian, ed. 2014. *Coming Down the Mountain: Rethinking the Summit Series*. Hamilton, ON: Wolsak & Wynn.

Kidd, Bruce, and John Macfarlane. 1972. *The Death of Hockey*. Toronto: New Press, 1972.

Kvärre, Stellan. 1972. "Svenske Gunnar gläds att få möta 'svarta ögat" Sterner." *Dagens Nyheter*. September 16.

Larsson, Per-Gunnar. 1972. "Idag kommer NHL–hockeyns fenomen." *Aftonbladet*. September 13.

Leeworthy, Daryl. 2014. Lions in Winter: The Summit Series, Professionalism and the Renewal of Hockey in 1970s Britain. In *Coming Down the Mountain: Rethinking the Summit Series,* ed. Brian Kennedy, 126–42. Hamilton, ON: Wolsak & Wynn.

Lex, Rex. 1920. "Hopp och modlöshet." *Dagens Nyheter,* April 27.

Lindkvist, Anna. 2007. *Jorden åt folket: Nationalföreningen mot emigration 1907–1925.* Umeå University Press.

Luck [pseud.]. 1949. "Gammal kärlek till våldet spräckte Kanadas vinstchans." *Expressen,* February 18.

Lundström, Åke. 1950. "Kanadensisk proffsishockey – sport eller yrkesmässig benknäckning?" *Ishockeyboken 1950–1951.*

Macintoish, Donald, and Donna Greenhorn. 1993. "Hockey Diplomacy and Canadian Foreign Policy." *Journal of Canadian Studies* 28 (2): 96–112.

Maguire, Joseph. 1996. "Blade Runners: Canadian Migrants, Ice Hockey, and the Global Sports Process." *Journal of Sport & Social Issues* 20 (3): 335–61.

Morrow, Don, and Kevin B. Wamsley. 2005. *Sport in Canada: A History.* Don Mills, ON: Oxford University Press.

Norborg, Lars–Arne. 1999. *Sveriges historia under 1800- och 1900-talen: Svensk samhällsutveckling 1809–1998.* Stockholm: Almkvist & Wiksell.

Norén, Helge. 1972. "Här är TV–stjärnorna i proffsens Europa-debut." *Expressen.* September 16.

Ogden, Josh, and Jonathon R. Edwards (2016). "Are Canadian Stakeholders Resting on Their Laurels? A Comparative Study of the Athlete Pathway Through the Swedish and Canadian Male Ice Hockey Systems". Journal of Sport Management, 2016, 30, p. 312–328.

Player [pseud.]. 1966. "274 stygn i huvudet och brutet Nyckelben." *Rekord med sportrevyn.* no 52:44.

"Polisvakt som skydd åt kanadensiska ruffgubbar." 1949. *Expressen,* February 16.

Pro Hockey. 2012. No. 9.

Robidoux, Michael A. 2002. "Imagining a Canadian Identity through Sport: A Historical Interpretation of Lacrosse and Hockey." *Journal of American Folklore* 115:209–25.

Rönnqvist, Carina. 2004. *Svea folk i Babels land: Svensk identitet i Kanda under 1900–talets forsta hälft.* Umeå, Sweden: Umeå University Press.

Said, Edward W. 1979. *Orientalism.* New York: Vintage Books.

Scherer, Jay, and Hart Cantelon. 2013. "1974 WHA All-Stars vs. the Soviet National Team: Franchise Recognition and Foreign Diplomacy in the 'Forgotten Series.'" *Journal of Canadian Studies* 42 (2): 29–59.

Soares, John. 2011. East beats West. In *Sport and the transformation of modern Europe: States, media and markets 1950–2010,* ed. Alan Tomlinson, Christopher Young, and Richard Holt, 35–49. London: Routledge.

"Spela spelet!" 1949. *Expressen,* February 16.

Stark, Tobias. 2001. The Pioneer, the Pal, and the Poet: Masculinities and National Identities in Canadian, Swedish and Soviet–Russian Ice Hockey during the Cold War. In *Putting It On Ice. Volume II: Internationalizing "Canada's Game,"* ed. Colin D. Howell, 39–43. Halifax, NS: Saint Mary's University.

———. 2010. *Folkhemmet på is: Ishockey, modernisering och nationell identitet I Sverige 1920–1972.* Malmö, Sweden: Idrottsforum.

———. 2012. "How Swede It Is": Börje Salming and the Migration of Swedish Ice Hockey Players to the NHL, 1957–2012. In *Constructing the Hockey Family: Home, Community, Bureaucracy and Marketplace,* ed. Lori Dithurbide and Colin Howell, 364–93. Halifax, NS: Saint Mary's University.

———. 2014. From Sweden With Love: The Summit Series and the Notion of the Contemporary Canadian Ice Hockey Player in Sweden. In *Coming Down the Mountain: Rethinking the Summit Series,* ed. Brian Kennedy, 161–78. Hamilton, ON: Wolsak & Wynn.

Sten. 1927a. "Canada vinner med 30–0!" *Idrottsbladet*, February 4.

———. 1927b. "En stad i Canadafeber." *Idrottsbladet*, February 16.

Sterner, Ulf. 1972. "Rena rama gangserttakterna!" *Expressen*, September 18.

Tegnér, Torsten. 1920a. "Matchen." *Idrottsbladet*, April 26.

———. 1920b. "Bandy eller ishockey?" *Idrottsbladet*. May 14.

———. 1927. "Canada." *Idrottsbladet*. February 2.

Thelenius, Conny. 1986. "'The Great' eller 'the Best'…Vem är Nr 1?" *Dagens Nyheter*. February 4.

Tolvhed, Helena. 2008. *Nationen på spel: Kropp, kön och svenskhet I populärpressens representationer av olympiska spel 1948–1972*. Umeå, Sweden: Bokförlaget h:ström.

"Trots allt bråk – Kanada är bäst." 1972. *Aftonbladet*, September 29.

"Utvisningar och 'domarmål." 1949. *Dagens Nyheter*, February 16.

Whannel, Garry. 2002. *Media Sport Stars: Masculinities and Moralities*. London and New York: Routledge.

Whitson, David, and Richard S. Gruneau, eds. 2006. *Artificial Ice: Hockey, Culture, and Commerce*. Peterborough, ON: Broadview Press.

"X" (1920), *Stockholms-Tidningen*, April 27.

"10 000 i panik vid Stadion." 1949. *Stockholms-Tidningen*, February 17/2.

Chapter 10
The *Hockey Night in Canada* Punjabi Broadcast: A Case Study in Ethnic Sports Media

Courtney Szto and Richard Gruneau

During the 2008 Stanley Cup Finals, between the Detroit Red Wings and the Pittsburgh Penguins, the Canadian Broadcasting Corporation (CBC) tried an experiment in multiculturalism with its flagship sports production, *Hockey Night in Canada* (*HNIC*). It offered commentary of the finals in Mandarin, Punjabi, Hindi, Italian, and Inuktitut (an Inuit language). From that experiment, only the Punjabi-language edition has survived. Ten seasons later, *Hockey Night in Canada Punjabi* has become a Saturday-night staple in many Punjabi-Canadian homes, as well as an Internet sensation. The purpose of this chapter is to situate *Hockey Night Punjabi* as part of the evolution and reconceptualization of *HNIC* to better understand what role the Punjabi edition may play in expanding and changing hockey culture and Canadian multiculturalism more generally. Pitter (2006) and Joseph, Nakamura, and Darnell (2012) have pointed out that Canadian sports scholarship has been eerily silent regarding the experiences of racialized Canadians. Yet, as Rinaldo Walcott argues (2012, xi–xii) in the preface to Joseph, Nakamura, and Darnell's 2012 anthology *Race and Sport in Canada: Intersecting Inequalities*, "sport is deeply implicated, not just in the national story, but also in producing the nation itself." This chapter seeks to add to the national story by outlining how *HNIC* has negotiated multiple narratives and contributions, particularly from Canada's South Asian community.

Canada is a self-proclaimed multicultural nation. As such, in 1991, the Canadian Radio-television and Telecommunications Commission mandated "that all licensed broadcasting stations should reflect the racial and multicultural diversity of Canada in their programming and employment" (Ojo 2006, 345; Yu 2016). Still, in spite of this official multicultural rhetoric, Canadian media continues to have a questionable relationship with racialized Canadians either through misrepresentation or simple omission (Ojo 2006). These issues of representation are exemplified by the *HNIC* broadcast, which has employed few people of colour or women to work in front of the camera, and has endured numerous controversies regarding the use of racist and xenophobic language on air. Some of these controversies are addressed later in this chapter.

Even though there has been a considerable amount of literature about how race and ethnicity play out in sports commentary in other places (e.g., Bruce 2004; Juffer 2002; King 2006; van Sterkenburg, Knoppers, and de Leeuw 2012), and in transnational analyses of sports media (e.g., Kim, forthcoming; Nakamura 2005), there continues to be a dearth of literature about ethnic sports media (Regalado 1995; Szto 2016). Moreover, where ethnic sports media do exist, their origins have often been prompted by players of that particular ethnicity breaking into the sport. Spanish-language baseball commentary in the United States is a notable example. In contrast, hockey has fostered a vibrant South Asian,[1] and specifically Punjabi, following in Canada, despite very little South Asian presence at the National Hockey League level.[2]

In their book *Hockey Night in Canada: Sport, Identities, and Cultural Politics*, Gruneau and Whitson (1993) pointed out that cultural commentaries about hockey in Canada have largely fallen victim to four tendencies: (a) a general devaluation of sport as an influential cultural industry, (b) a romanticization of the game, (c) a failure to articulate the socially constructed nature of hockey as well as (d) the complex and often contradictory political economy of the sport. More than two decades later, similar conversations continue, including discussions of stadium debates (Scherer 2016), climate change (Johnson and Ali 2016), concussions (Cusimano et al. 2009), and multiple masculinities (Allain 2010). Over the past twenty-five years, the breadth and sophistication of topics covered in hockey scholarship has grown significantly.

With that said, race remains a difficult subject to broach, both in the game and within Canadian society more broadly. For example, in the 2015 Canadian federal election, a Conservative Party discourse constructed an imagined category of "old-stock Canadians" juxtaposed against so-called new-stock Canadians, clearly challenging the place of racialized Canadians regardless of their birth place (Gollom 2015). Moreover, part of the Canadian Conservative Party's re-election platform was built on the promise of creating a "tip line for reporting 'barbaric cultural practices' to the RCMP" (Powers 2015). In this way, Canadian's self-understanding that theirs is a welcoming and inclusive nation was countered by new attempts to solidify racial hierarchies through legislation and political manoeuvring. The fragile and recently contested state of Canadian multiculturalism puts a production like *Hockey Night Punjabi* in the awkward liminal position of promoting mainstream (white) culture on the one hand while staying true to its own cultural identity on the other. Proponents of equality through opportunity argue that grassroots hockey is more diverse than it has ever been and suggest that equality will trickle up as time passes (Kennedy 2015; Thompson 2013). There is little precedent to suggest that this is likely. For example, Leonard (2016) notes that in the American National Football League, where African-American players outnumber white players, "proximity to [people of colour] doesn't guarantee under-standing, empathy, or even respectful deference." Racial equality is, therefore, not a game

---

1. "South Asian" is a pragmatic catch-all term that references people from India, Bangladesh, Nepal, Sri Lanka, and Pakistan. It speaks to a geographical region without much consideration to the heterogeneity of the area or its people. We use it when acknowledging numerous groups from the region.
2. To date only three players of South Asian heritage have skated in the NHL: Robin Bawa, Manny Malhotra, and Jujhar Khaira.

of numbers, it is one of power, and it is a conversation that media such as *Hockey Night Punjabi* promise to promote in discussions around Canada's national winter pastime.

Our discussion in this chapter of *Hockey Night Punjabi* combines media analysis with in-depth, semi-structured interviews conducted with the five main members of the broadcast team. Access was gained via social media, email, and personal interaction, with interviews lasting between forty and sixty minutes. Our chapter begins with a brief history of the *HNIC* broadcast, from its early days on CBC Radio to a digital age rife with privatization. We then transition into a discussion of ethnic sports media and explain how *Hockey Night Punjabi* went from humble beginnings to an Internet sensation during the 2016 Stanley Cup Playoffs. The chapter concludes with lessons learned from the *Hockey Night Punjabi* case study.

Hockey Night(s) in Canada

HNIC radio broadcasts began in 1931 and soon became a staple of Saturday-night entertainment across the country. They were one of the earliest electronic contributors to the making of a national popular Canadian culture. *HNIC* moved to television in 1952, with a French-language broadcast of the Montreal Canadiens versus the Detroit Red Wings. The following month, Foster Hewitt (legendary for the radio broadcasts) called the first English-language CBC-TV broadcast, on November 1, between the Toronto Maple Leafs and the Boston Bruins. In the early days, NHL President Clarence Campbell was fearful that televising hockey would encourage people to stay at home instead of attending games. In order to temper Campbell's fears, games would begin broadcasting one hour after the opening faceoff (Patskou 2014). "By the mid-1950s, watching NHL hockey on CBC had become a quintessential Canadian pastime, one of the rhythms of the Canadian year for men and boys, especially" (Scherer and Whitson 2009, 216). During the 1960s, the broadcast consistently drew five million viewers each Saturday night. In 1980, former NHL coach Don Cherry was hired to provide commentary between periods, which soon became *Coach's Corner*, a segment known to draw larger audiences than the game itself (Young 1990). Dave Hodge co-hosted with Cherry for seven years on Coach's Corner and was later replaced by Ron MacLean, who hosts to this day on the program. Cherry's impact on hockey in Canada is so significant that when the CBC ran a two-month-long contest to determine "The Greatest Canadian" in 2004, he finished seventh, ahead of Sir John A. Macdonald, Alexander Graham Bell, and hockey great Wayne Gretzky, for example (Dixon 2004). Today, *HNIC* remains Canada's longest-running broadcast and regularly draws audiences of over one million per episode (Scherer and Whitson 2009), a high rating in the Canadian market.

The proliferation of new media marks a significant adjustment for the sports industry by fostering the privatization of broadcasting rights and shifting power away from traditional media outlets toward sports teams and fans. The French sister broadcast to *HNIC*, *La Soireé du Hockey*, aired on Radio-Canada, encountered this problem a few years before the English broadcast when, in 2002, a private French-Canadian broadcaster, Réseau des sports (RDS), bought the French-language rights to televise Montreal Canadiens games. As Scherer and Whitson explain (2009, 214), "this meant that fans of the Canadiens in Quebec would have to either subscribe to cable television or watch *HNIC* in English." The issue was taken to hearings before the House of Commons Standing Joint Committee on Official Languages, and it was agreed that RDS and Radio-Canada would share the French-language television rights for Canadiens games. This agreement lasted until 2004, after which RDS again bought, and kept, the exclusive rights.

Similarly, private interests successfully challenged CBC in 2008, when the public broadcaster lost the rights to the *HNIC* theme song to the privately owned cable sports network TSN (CBC 2008). Five years later, Rogers Communications bought the national broadcasting rights for all NHL games in Canada, at a price of $5.2 billion for twelve years (Rush 2013). A few months later, in an attempt to draw a younger demographic, Rogers announced that Canadian television personality George Stroumboulopoulos would become the host of *HNIC* (Shoalts 2016). Fans expressed their resistance to this decision online, and eventually through lowered ratings. In the summer of 2016, Rogers announced that it was bringing Ron MacLean back to host the show (Traikos 2016). In turn, Stroumboulopoulos, Leah Hextall, and former NHL players P. J. Stock and Corey Hirsch lost their on-air positions, along with a number of behind-the-scenes employees (Shoalts 2016). With these changes in mind, Scherer and Whitson encourage us to question the ability of media conglomerates to purchase broadcasting rights that have traditionally been "part of national cultural life" and the implications of this purchasing power (2009, 214). Sports broadcasts have become integral for subscription television all over the world; unfortunately, this creates a tiered citizenry between those who are able to buy their way into a shared culture and those who are relegated to the category of undesirable consumers. Yet, interestingly, at a time when *HNIC* has been scrambling to find its place in an increasingly privatized and digitized world, *Hockey Night Punjabi* seems to be hitting its stride.

Hockey Night Punjabi is a convergence point for Punjabi culture and communication. It offers loud, energetic, and humorous commentary; described as part international soccer, part Bollywood musical, with "a pinch of [World Wrestling Entertainment] and a generous dose of infectious enthusiasm" (McIntyre 2016). In many ways, the Punjabi edition opposes traditional sports commentary, and journalism more broadly, in North America. *Hockey Night Punjabi* is based on inviting the viewer into the studio instead of keeping them at arm's length. It converses *with* its viewers as opposed to talking *at* them because it is understood that many of the viewers did not grow up watching hockey. It attempts to speak to various generations knowing that families often view the broadcast. The most popular contribution that circulates about the broadcast is how Punjabi grandparents often thank the broadcasters for providing a connection point with their Canadian-born (English-speaking) grandchildren (Deziel 2016). Moreover, because no one on the broadcast team played competitive ice hockey, the show helps challenge the notion that only former athletes can provide sport analysis, a guiding principle that disproportionately affects women (see Hill 2015) and people of colour in Canadian sports media. For example, in 2013, when Nabil Karim and Gurdeep Ahluwalia together hosted TSN's *SportsCentre* for the first time, many viewers shared their ignorant assumptions about South Asian sportscasters via social media (Sager 2013), and, unfortunately, the *Hockey Night Punjabi* team has also received challenges to their legitimacy over the years (Szto 2016). In this way, the existence of *Hockey Night Punjabi* offers a space to experiment with the boundaries of hockey conservatism in the safety of a privately funded, niche-market program. If *HNIC* serves as a reminder of what has been, *Hockey Night Punjabi* symbolizes what is achievable when tradition dares venture beyond the familiar and predictable.

Traditional sportscasting tends to follow and reproduce a rigid set of values that stem from the Protestant notion that sports can imbue certain characteristics, such as determination, humility, and self-denial (Kidd 2013). The accompanying interpretation of "professionalism" in sports-media coverage manifests as detached, elitist, and sometimes condescending. For example, in response to the retirement announcement of Canadian news anchor and national icon Peter Mansbridge from CBC-TV's *The National*, John Doyle (2016) of the *Globe and Mail* wrote:

> The essence of the traditional anchor position now reeks of pomposity.... Pomposity is part of TV stardom. CBC, in particular, is its own bubble of self-regard and remoteness. Its stars often lose perspective, become immune from self-questioning inside that bubble.

Doyle describes the patronizing/paternal TV news anchor as an outdated figure that was needed when television was the main communication medium, when "news events demanded an authority figure to calm the nation. Always male, always urbane, always a dad-like figure. That such anchor types are still presented to us is insulting" (ibid.). This is arguably a philosophy under which the English language *HNIC* continues to operate.

Ron MacLean may be the closest sports equivalent to Peter Mansbridge. And while Don Cherry is far from the urbane and calm presence that Doyle references, the descriptors "pompous and patronizing" certainly fit the bill, and play well against MacLean's measured approach. For decades, Cherry has been the populist voice and face of *HNIC*, yet his words have done anything but create unity within the hockey community or welcome new viewers. Cherry's conservative politics often bleed into his hockey talk, with comments such as "Put that in your pipe, you left-wing kooks," or, in reference to French-Canadians, "They don't like the Canadian flag. You know it's funny, they don't want the Canadian flag but they want our money" (Gates 2012). On more than one occasion, Cherry has referred to NHL players who fail to dress "appropriately" (as defined by Cherry) on game days as "thugs" (Stevenson 2008), a racially charged term that drew some chastising from the CBC and serves to reproduce racialized bodies as "other" in hockey culture (Lorenz and Murray 2014). Beyond *Coach's Corner*, legendary play-by-play commentators such as Jim Hughson and Bob Cole also arguably reproduce a very narrow conception of Canadian masculinity, not to mention what a sports commentator looks like in Canada: an older, cisgendered, heterosexual, white male.

HNIC has always served as a standard for hockey broadcasting in Canada; it also represents the past—a Canada anchored by "old-stock Canadians." *Hockey Night Punjabi* offers an alternative way of talking about, experiencing, and understanding hockey. This is why it has become a powerful symbol for non-white hockey fans, but also for many Canadians who rarely, if ever, see themselves represented in a positive light by mainstream media. *Hockey Night Punjabi* also gets to control the narrative, important for historically marginalized communities.

Ethnic (Sports) Media

Ethnic media is broadly defined as any media created for or by immigrants, minoritized groups (whether ethnic, racial, or linguistic), and/or Indigenous populations (Matsaganis, Katz, and Ball-Rokeach 2011).[3] The growth of ethnic media coincides with increases in human movement across national borders; thus, ethnic media can be read as one metric of globalization. Matsaganis, Katz, and Ball-Rokeach noted that, in 2007 in Canada, "there were more than 250 ethnic newspapers…[representing] over 40 ethnic communities and 40 television channels that provide programming to a variety of ethnic groups" (ibid., 4). There are also more than sixty radio stations that provide broadcasts targeted at minoritized communities.

We use the term "ethnic media" here instead of immigrant media or minority media because the example of *Hockey Night Punjabi* speaks to a specific ethnic segment of the Canadian populace that consists of a mixture of Canadians, both new and old. Indeed, while the broadcast team may come from immigrant families, they are all Canadian-born, as are many of their viewers. Matsaganis, Katz, and Ball-Rokeach (2011, 9) observe that immigrant media tends to introduce "new arrivals to the host country and a new way of life," whereas ethnic media leans toward younger demographics, and therefore have different objectives and programming. Moreover, the term "minority" often invokes a differential in numbers as opposed to a relation of power—the term does a disservice to racialized Canadians by giving the illusion that their lack of social, political, and economic power is associated with smaller population size (Marable 1995).

As mentioned earlier, there is little scholarship on ethnic sports media, particularly regarding the broadcasting of mainstream sports to a local minority-language community. The most notable example focuses on the incorporation of Spanish commentary by the Los Angeles Dodgers in the late 1950s, and the significance of one man, Jaime Jarrín, who some have dubbed the "Latino Vin Scully," a reference to the legendary broadcaster who spent sixty-seven seasons covering the Dodgers (Carpenter 2016):

> Lost behind the year-long farewell to Scully is a remarkable story. It's a story many baseball fans don't know because when they think of the Dodgers they think only of Scully, the team's narrator for nearly 70 seasons and a man who calls games in such vivid detail he was voted into the Hall of Fame more than 30 years ago. Even as they mourn Scully's October retirement, they have barely heard of the regal 80-year-old legend in Scully's shadow. Nor do they realize that for 58 years, millions of southern California Latinos have had a Vin Scully of their own. And that without him the Dodgers might not be the $2 [billion] franchise they've become.

After the Dodgers moved from Brooklyn to Los Angeles, they became the first team to offer all of their games in both English and Spanish on radio. Today, "nearly half of the Dodger Stadium crowd is Latino, and a little less then [*sic*] half of that group speak Spanish as their first language" (ibid., 2016).

---

3. We use the term "minoritized" instead of visible minorities because it speaks to the effects of a socially constructed difference that results from power imbalances, rather than of a demographic.

Both the Dodgers' Spanish commentary and *Hockey Night Punjabi* started out in make-shift broadcast booths and worked from studio recreations for game calls; still, there are some important differences. Where Jarrín was translating Scully's commentary into Spanish, the *Hockey Night Punjabi* broadcasters are not translating hockey for the Punjabi community, they are creating a new linguistic dialect that speaks to both younger and older generations. *Hockey Night Punjabi* host Randip Janda explains when the show started:

> We had a group of people that used to work on OMNI's newscast and they helped us with the vocab, that way we could have a cross-generational kind of Punjabi. There's some people who may watch it of an older generation and they might not get some of the references we give, so we mixed up our vocabulary. There's different levels of Punjabi. What I've learned is different from people who are learning it today and who learned in India so we did have a bit of a language committee, as we called it.

Hockey Night Punjabi commentators do not rely on the English commentary and instead call games from telecasts shown in studio. Additionally, the success of Jarrín's broadcast was fundamentally influenced by the arrival of Mexican pitcher Fernando Valenzuela and the ensuing "Fernandomania" (Regalado 1995). Jarrín explained that the Latino community was rather indifferent to the sport of baseball until Valenzuela came along; the Latino fan base has grown from 8 per cent upon the Dodgers arrival in Los Angeles to the 50 per cent it is today (Carpenter 2016). Jarrín claims that when Valenzuela was pitching the broadcast drew up to fifty million listeners (covering southern California, Mexico, and into the Caribbean) (Regalado 1995). Conversely, with only three players of Indian descent having played in the NHL, hockey has yet to have a breakthrough South Asian player. Still, Punjabi fans are anything but indifferent about hockey, which may help explain why a South Asian star has not been necessary for the continued success of the broadcast. Spanish broadcasting added complexity to baseball in the United States and, arguably, "reflected the impact made by Latino players and the development of Hispanic society at large" (Regalado 1995, 289). Jarrín was inducted into the Baseball Hall of Fame under the broadcasters category; hence, his public memory serves as an additional narrative in the history of baseball. If, as the saying goes, it is as "American as baseball and apple pie," then, one would think, the Canadian equivalent would be: as Canadian as hockey and multiculturalism.

    Hockey Night Punjabi remains the main model for multicultural broadcasting in hockey. The Florida Panthers recently brought back its Spanish-language commentary, after a two-decade hiatus, as a way to reach the large local Cuban community (Johnston 2016). The Panthers estimate that 35 per cent of its fan base is Hispanic. More recently, the Chicago Blackhawks announced a fourteen-game Spanish radio partnership with Univision Chicago (NHL 2016). The trend toward ethnic hockey media is crucial for growing the game, but we should also recognize that minoritized communities are able to contribute to mainstream broadcasting rather than simply mimic tradition.

Hockey Night Canada in Punjabi: From the Sidelines to Centre Stage

Once it was picked up for regular-season shows, the Punjabi broadcast was shot on a hand-held camcorder in a small room for its first four years. Harnarayan Singh, the only member of the broadcast to be involved from its inception, has described not being able to fit more than four people in the original studio. There was no travel budget in the beginning, and Singh had to travel from Calgary to Toronto every weekend to do the show. In a 2016 *Maclean's* article, Singh recounted the sacrifices he made in order to ensure that the broadcast could continue. He paid for his own travel and was sleeping in the airport to save money because he "didn't want anyone to know that [he] was coming out on [his] own dime" (Deziel 2016). This speaks to Singh's dedication to making the Punjabi broadcast a success, but also to the precarious (financial) nature of ethnic sports media and the constant struggle for space and legitimacy. Along with Singh, Bhola Chauhan, Parminder Singh, and Inderpreet Cumo helped anchor the Punjabi broadcast desk during its time in Toronto, and then in Calgary. CBC executive Joel Darling and former NHL goalie and *HNIC* analyst Kelly Hrudey were identified as key actors in making the show possible. Due to lack of sponsorship, *Hockey Night Punjabi* was cancelled by CBC more than once (Allick 2011), but Darling has been instrumental in reviving the show. Furthermore, Hrudey pushed for Singh as the lead play-by-play commentator and brought attention to the fact that Singh had been travelling at his own expense. These are just two of the allies who have contributed to the success and longevity of the program.

In 2014, when Rogers announced it would be taking over *HNIC*, the multicultural channel and Rogers subsidiary OMNI Television made a pitch to continue the show, to be based in Vancouver. The show thus adopted the old Sportsnet set and added Bhupinder Hundal, Randip Janda, and Harpreet Pandher to join Singh as the main broadcasting team (Taqdeer Thindal, Gurpreet Sian, and Mantar Bhandal fill in occasionally). Only Hundal had previous broadcasting experience, as a former producer, reporter, and OMNI news executive. He also provided Punjabi commentary on OMNI during the 2010 Vancouver Olympics for both the men's and women's hockey tournaments. Hundal was central in bringing *Hockey Night Punjabi* over to OMNI, explaining that when the show was on CBC, it did not offer a "different perspective from the Punjabi community. There wasn't a manager working on it looking at it from a business perspective. There [weren't] the tools or the resources that could really lift the show." The show is now broadcast in high definition with its own pre- and post-game shows, enabling the team to provide original programming, such as interviewing pioneer player Robin Bawa, the first NHL player of Indian descent. Additionally, the show has responded to other issues relevant to the Punjabi community, such as the Government of Canada's *Komagata Maru* apology.[4] Hence, while *Hockey Night Punjabi* may not provide substantial coverage of South Asian athletes, it does find ways to

---

4. In 1914, a steamship arrived in the port of Vancouver, via Hong Kong, carrying almost 400 immigrants, British subjects, from the Punjab region of India. It was not allowed to dock based on the Continuous Passage Act of 1908, which required that immigrants travel from their point of origin without any stops. Anchored in Vancouver Harbour for two months, the Canadian military forced the ship to return to India. Nineteen passengers were shot and killed upon returning to India and many others were imprisoned. On May 18, 2016, Prime Minister Justin Trudeau issued a formal apology in the House of Commons, stating "Canada's government was, without question, responsible for the laws that prevented these passengers from immigrating peacefully and securely" (Trudeau 2016).

differentiate itself from mainstream Canadian sports media and contribute to community-specific needs and interests.

The move from CBC to OMNI not only provided the show with a more legitimate physical space, it also gave a platform to, in Hundal's words,

> look like a regular hockey broadcast as opposed to a side project. And I think that was kind of important for the evolution of, not only [the] broadcast, but the connection the community is going to have with it. This is not just a novelty. This is a real, live, robust hockey broadcast for us that's at the same level as what you would get elsewhere, and that was kind of a goal.

An additional tool that has helped elevate the show and make it a legitimate player in sports broadcasting is having a Punjabi social-media host in the production room. Amrit Gill is a diehard hockey fan and broadcasting graduate who managed to create a position for herself following an internship. Gill oversees social media and provides supplementary education for off-ice storylines. Social media has enabled the broadcast to create a substantial online presence beyond Canadian borders, as evidenced in the 2016 playoffs, where social media helped move the Punjabi edition of *HNIC* from the fringes of sports media to a championship parade in downtown Pittsburgh, invited by the Penguins to mark their Stanley Cup victory.

"Bonino Bonino Bonino!"

On May 10, 2016, during the fifth game of the second round of the 2016 Stanley Cup playoffs, Nick Bonino of the Pittsburgh Penguins scored the overtime winner against the rival Washington Capitals. Singh's exuberant call of "Bonino! Bonino! Bonino!" became an instant social-media hit, with thousands of retweets and likes on Twitter. The memorable call was later explained as a typo on the game sheet that had "Bonino" written as all three forward positions: Bonino at left wing, Bonino at centre, and Bonino at right wing. Then, on May 30, 2016, the Pittsburgh Penguins defeated the San Jose Sharks in the first game of the Stanley Cup Finals, with Bonino again scoring the winning goal late in the game. This time, the clip of the goal call—again, "Bonino! Bonino! Bonino!"—received many thousand retweets and likes on Twitter. That evening, #HockeyNightPunjabi was trending on Twitter in Pittsburgh, and the next morning the call had been featured by mainstream media outlets such as Sportsnet, NHL.com, The Score, Deadspin, CBS Sports, Yahoo Sports, and had been turned into a cell-phone ringtone. Fox News even wrote a highlight piece, stating "Hockey Night Punjabi in Canada has the most exciting play-by-play you'll ever hear" (Bathe 2016). (Figure 10.1)

Due to the response that *Hockey Night Punjabi* received from Penguins fans, and given that the broadcast covered three of the team's four playoff rounds, the Penguins organization invited the broadcast team to Pittsburgh to take part in the Stanley Cup parade. Singh, Hundal, Janda, and Pandher were invited to meet the team in private. They were greeted by adoring fans all over the city, and Singh did his iconic "Bonino!" call on stage at the parade. This type of reception is a positive example of how sport can bring people together regardless of differences in language, race, nationality, and religion. It is also an interesting

Figure 10.1 *Hockey Night in Canada Punjabi*
As a hockey commentator, Harnarayan Singh "calls" games in English and in Punjabi. After his "Bonino, Bonino, Bonino . . ." call went viral, the show became even more popular with fans. Singh (right) is pictured here with co-host Bhola Chauhan. CHRIS BOLIN/The New York Times/Redux

example given that this "embrace" of "otherness" occurred in a city with a predominantly white population, during one of the most racially divisive American election years in recent history.

In its 2015 racial demographics report, the University of Pittsburgh School of Social Work reported that Pittsburgh had one of the whitest metropolitan areas in the United States, with approximately 64 per cent of the city self-identifying as "white, non-Hispanic" (Center on Race and Social Problems 2015; United States Census Bureau n.d.). The category of "Asian" was measured as 4.4 per cent of the population, which included those who identified as South, East, and South East Asian (Center on Race and Social Problems 2015); in other words, the Punjabi Sikh population does not have accurate statistical representation in Pittsburgh. Nationwide, there are only approximately one million Sikhs living in the United States, with most residing in California, though there has been a sharp increase in Indic languages in the last twenty years (Ryan 2013). Singh, Hundal, Janda, and Pandher reported seeing few people of colour during their visit, and yet were met with nothing but hospitality and kindness during their time in Pittsburgh. Upon returning to Canada, the broadcast team released a public thank-you letter, which included:

> The truth is, members of our community living in the United States have faced very difficult challenges due to their identity. Our visit was the polar opposite of the

experience many have had, and this has filled much of the community with hope and optimism. This is why our visit to Pittsburgh is so emotional for us, and why all of you deserve our sincerest thanks. (Goffenberg 2016)

Post-9/11, Sikh men have been disproportionately misidentified as Muslims in North America, and have therefore been victims of hate speech and hate crimes (Ahmad 2011; Ahluwalia and Pellettiere 2010; Bahdi 2003). Yet, the experience of *Hockey Night Punjabi* through the 2016 playoffs offers a tempered, but hopeful, example of how sport can sometimes contribute to a more inclusive and understanding society.

Ethnic Sports Media: Lessons Learned

There are four important lessons and/or considerations that can be drawn from the success of the *Hockey Night Punjabi* edition. The first is the importance of alternative narratives and media representations. The second raises questions about enhanced metrics for ethnic media. The third focuses on the need for community-specific media initiatives, and the last brings public memory into question.

On the surface, ethnic sports media simply offer another market in an increasingly privatized society; arguably, they provide multiculturalism in its least offensive (although not uncontroversial) state: equal but separate. The broadcast team of *Hockey Night Punjabi* has expressed that the ultimate achievement, both individually and as a show, would be to have a Punjabi broadcaster on the main *HNIC* broadcast team; in other words, not separate but equal. In an interview with the *New York Times*, Singh mentioned that his ultimate goal would be to call games in English, "nothing would spell multiculturalism in Canada better than having a visible minority on the [*HNIC*] broadcast" (Sax 2013). However, the broadcast team is well aware that such a move would not necessarily be welcomed by everyone. For example, Hundal stated that breaking this particular barrier would likely come with a lot of racist vitriol:

> It's one of those things that the South Asian community in its history has overcome, especially in this country. And I think it would be one of those things, you know the person who's in that chair has to be able to deal with and overcome because I think that would probably be the harder struggle than the hockey part or anything else.

In a way, with *Hockey Night Punjabi* broadcast on a separate channel and sustained through private funding, the flagship *HNIC* broadcast remains insulated from the changing face of Canadian society.[5] Therefore, it seems fair to argue that *Hockey Night Punjabi* is more assimilationist than it is multicultural; it represents a Canadian institution—*Hockey Night in Canada*—spreading its tentacles, ensuring that Canadian nationalism remains robust through the culture of hockey. Yet, while there is truth to this observation, what this debate may miss is what the Punjabi edition contributes to both Canadian and hockey culture: an additional narrative.

---

5. On November 30, 2016, Singh made his English-language debut on Sportsnet's *Wednesday Night Hockey* broadcast (Dormer 2016). And, on February 3, 2018, Singh made his debut on *Hockey Night in Canada* on location from the Saddledome in Calgary, Alberta.

Cultural citizenship acknowledges that participating in and contributing to one's culture represents a valuable entry point for belonging. More specifically, drawing from the work of Boele van Hensbroek (2012), cultural citizenship consists of one's ability to write onto the national narrative. The Punjabi broadcast offers an alternative hockey experience, one that is culturally specific and breaks from the traditional notion of what a hockey fan looks like and how the game should be experienced.

Hockey Night Punjabi sees its role as an instigator of growth for hockey. Recent growth in hockey participation has primarily been driven by female hockey (CBC 2013) and racialized Canadians (Bascaramurty 2013). In order to draw new players and viewers, hockey must appear welcoming, inclusive, and fun. Yet racialized Canadians have rarely seen themselves represented in the NHL or on *HNIC*. When asked if it ever resonated with Singh that none of the commentators he idolized looked like him, he reflected that it did, because as a young boy growing up in Brooks, Alberta, his family doctor once asked him what he wanted to be when he grew up. When he replied that he wanted to be a broadcaster his doctor cautioned, "You have to be realistic! The chances of that happening are so slim. Have you looked at what people look like on TV? They don't look like you." Singh continued,

> I had this postcard of every announcer; every commentator at the time that was working for *Hockey Night in Canada* and it was on our fridge. So you know, whenever I'm going to get a carton of milk for my cereal I would look at it and yeah, it wasn't the most diverse group to say the least. And so all the heads were put together on this postcard and I would wonder, "Do I fit in there?"

Hockey Night Punjabi changes this dynamic, enabling more Canadians to see themselves involved in the game. It has opened a door that many never knew existed, and is perhaps best exemplified by this tweet from the 2016 Stanley Cup playoffs, "@HkyNightPunjabi may have altered my dream to become a sports journalist to becoming a Punjabi sports journalist" (Singh 2016). *Hockey Night Punjabi* arguably empowers more Canadians to write onto the national narrative by expanding what is possible and challenging any singular interpretation of what hockey is and who should be included.

The second lesson to be learned from *Hockey Night Punjabi* is the importance of accurately measuring ethnic media viewership. Ratings data for ethnic media are limited across the board because most operations are small, geographically scattered ventures (Matsaganis, Katz, and Ball-Rokeach 2011). Historically, in the United States, ethnic media ratings, such as those for Spanish-language programming, were separated from English-language ratings, resulting in advertisers often overlooking the fact that more data existed. This segregation of data served as "an excuse for some general market advertisers to focus only on the general market networks" (quoted in Matsaganis, Katz, and Ball-Rokeach 2011). In 2005, Nielsen announced that it would combine all ratings into one national data set; however, the transition was not smooth. The social construction of race makes it difficult to measure ethnic media when, for example, only the "head of the household self-identified as Hispanic and not if anyone else in the household did" (Matsaganis, Katz, and Ball-Rokeach 2011). Furthermore, if the sample sizes of ethnic communities are not representative of the larger population, ratings can often underrepresent actual viewership. For these reasons, without accurate data, ethnic media are faced with structural hurdles when trying to secure advertising revenue.

During *Hockey Night Punjabi*'s days based in Toronto, it could only be viewed on digital television or streamed on CBC.ca, which made its rating hard to tabulate. This is partly due to an antiquated ratings system that fails to accurately account for digital convergence, but also points to a ratings system that is not set up for diverse viewing. Moreover, there is the paradox of needing money to make money; therefore, there must be desire to invest in the longevity of shows that speak to the increasing diversity, fragmentation, and hybridity of Canada. By not investing in ethnic media metrics we are essentially saying that this type of media does not matter, economically, socially, or politically, and, by extension, that viewers of ethnic media do not matter. In a country that prides itself on inclusion and multiculturalism, these actions are telling. Only recently has the broadcast received ratings data with estimates averaging 209,000 viewers per game.

The third lesson to take from *Hockey Night Punjabi* is the importance of tailoring media for a specific audience. As mentioned, *HNIC* editions were attempted in other languages but only the Punjabi one has been able to sustain itself. The Chinese community in Canada is another prevalent group that has shown an interest in hockey, and has the population to support such an endeavour, but Chinese commentary has not been able to establish itself. When Hundal was asked about his thoughts on why the Punjabi broadcast has been so successful, he attributed much of it to creating a broadcast that speaks to the Punjabi community.

> I think what it is, and I've had this conversation a lot with my Chinese friends, the Punjabi or South Asian community is much more outgoing and aggressive in terms of pushing for what they want. The Chinese community, the dynamic, the way [of the] Chinese community is a little bit more reserved, less demonstrative. So you've got this cultural dynamic between these two that is very different and I think that makes a huge difference…you can't apply the same model from the Punjabi community that you can apply to the Mandarin broadcast. I think it's time we see a Mandarin broadcast. It requires delicate management and a long-term plan, but I think tapping into the large Chinese audience across North America is important for the game.

The Punjabi edition is a perfect example of how cookie-cutter models often fail to take cultural differences or styles, generational dynamics, and community needs into consideration.

The last lesson draws on the exclusive nature of public memory. During our interview, Singh commented that he would like to see some of the *Hockey Night Punjabi* artifacts make it into the Hockey Hall of Fame. That would prove to be a significant evolution of hockey in Canada, since, as Bruce Kidd has asserted, halls of fame "play a strategic role in the public remembering and interpretation of sports" (1996, 328), but that the Hockey Hall of Fame "is a disappointing example of effective 'public history'" (331). Kidd contends that the selection process for the hall is notoriously vague, honours very few players outside of the NHL, and has a glaring absence of women.

Moreover, Fosty and Fosty point out (2008, 221) that there is no mention of black Canadian contributions to the game or the Coloured Hockey League of the Maritimes in the hall, "it is as if [that] league had never existed." Notable players of colour, such as Herb Carnegie and Willie O'Ree, remain absent from hockey's hallowed museum. This sanitized version of history provides hockey fans, and Canadians, "not only a history without structure and power, but history without passion" (Kidd 1996, 331–32). And, as Jackson and Ponic (2001) have pointed out, the media play an integral part in interpreting and representing social memory. For these reasons, it is important for us to question *which* people are included in the public's memory and acknowledge that representation is not only an issue for current concern but also that erasing alternative representations/narratives that have existed denies history, legitimacy, and citizenship to certain Canadians. Ignoring our ethnic media also means we ignore our champions of racial equality.

Conclusion

Hockey Night Punjabi offers an important case study in ethnic sports media, and its success encourages Canadian society to grapple with the intersection of multiculturalism and hockey in an ever more race-aware, yet all too often silent, nation. If we continue to exclude certain Canadians from hockey culture, whether as fans, players, or media, we also exclude them from a large portion of Canadian culture, in turn challenging the notion that hockey brings the nation together. There are multiple paths to adoration. Will there be a continued need for Punjabi commentary as Canadian citizens embrace increasingly hybrid identities? Or will an intensification of the need to celebrate difference expand support for such commentary? Some ethnic media scholars such as April Lindgren contend "as the current generation ages and dies, there will be less need for ethnic media as the new generations integrate more with the Canadian economy" (quoted in Fleras 2015). Time will tell; still, the contributions made by the *Hockey Night in Canada Punjabi* edition can be measured in the provision of new voices and new narratives in constructing Canada's national story.

Bibliography

Ahluwalia, Muninder K., and Laura Pellettiere. 2010. "Sikh Men Post-9/11: Misidentification, Discrimination and Coping." *Asian American Journal of Psychology* 1 (4): 303–14. doi: 10.1037/a0022156.

Ahmad, Muneer. 2011. "Homeland Insecurities: Racial Violence the Day after September 11." *Race/Ethnicity: Multidisciplinary Global Contexts* 4 (3): 337–50.

Allain, Kristi. 2010. "Kid Crosby or Golden Boy: Sidney Crosby, Canadian National Identity, and the Policing of Hockey Masculinity." *International Review for the Sociology of Sport* 46 (1): 3–22. doi: 10.1177/1012690210376294.

Allick, Chantaie. 2011. "Fans Fight for Hockey Night in Punjabi." *Toronto Star*, October 27. https://www.thestar.com/news/canada/2011/10/27/fans_fight_for_hockey_night_in_punjabi.html.

Bahdi, Reem. 2003. "No Exit: Racial Profiling and Canada's War Against Terrorism." *Osgoode Hall Law Journal* 41 (2/3): 293–317.

Bascaramurty, Dakshana. 2013. "How Brampton Demonstrates the New Vision of Canada." *Globe and Mail*, June 15. http://www.theglobeandmail.com/news/national/how-brampton-demonstrates-the-new-vision-of-canada/article12581170/?page=all.

Bathe, Carrlyn. 2016. "The Most Exciting Goal Calls of the Stanley Cup Playoffs Aren't in English or French." Fox News, May 26. http://www.foxsports.com/nhl/story/hockey-night-punjabi-stanley-cup-final-penguins-sharks-san-jose-nhl-tampa-bay-canada-052616.

Boele van Hensbroek, Pieter. 2012. Cultural Citizenship as a Normative Notion for Activist Practices. In *Cultural Citizenship in Political Theory*, ed. Judith A. Vega and Pieter Boele van Hensbroek, 73–86. London: Routledge.

Bruce, Toni. 2004. "Marking the Boundaries of 'Normal' in Televised Sports: The Play-By-Play of Race. *Media, Culture & Society* 26 (6): 861–79.

Carpenter, Les. 2016. "Jaime Jarrín: The Remarkable Story of the Latino Vin Scully." *Guardian*, September 15. https://www.theguardian.com/sport/2016/sep/15/jaime-jarrin-los-angeles-dodgers-announcer-vin-scully?CMP=share_btn_tw.

CBC (Canadian Broadcasting Corporation). 2008. "Deal to Keep Hockey Night Theme Song Falls Through." CBC Sports, June 6. http://www.cbc.ca/sports/hockey/deal-to-keep-hockey-night-theme-song-falls-through-1.696643.

———. 2013. "Hockey, Canada's Game, Not Its Most Popular." CBC News, September 30. http://www.cbc.ca/news2/interactives/sports-junior.

Center on Race and Social Problems. 2015. "Pittsburgh's Racial Demographics 2015: Differences and Disparities." University of Pittsburgh School of Social Work. http://www.crsp.pitt.edu/sites/default/files/REPORT.pdf.

Cusimano, Michael D., Mary L. Chipman, Richard Volpe, and Peter Donnelly. 2009. "Canadian Minor Hockey Participants' Knowledge about Concussion." *Canadian Journal of Neurological Sciences* 36 (3): 315–20. doi: https://doi.org/10.1017/S0317167100007046.

Deziel, Shanda. 2016. "BONINO! BONINO! BONINO! How a Hockey Man Found His Calling." *Maclean's*, April 9. http://www.macleans.ca/culture/television/how-harnarayan-singh-found-his-calling/.

Dixon, Guy. 2004. "The Greatest Canadian." *Globe and Mail*, November 30. http://www.theglobeandmail.com/arts/the-greatest-canadian/article1144309/.

Dormer, Dave. 2016. "Harnarayan Singh Makes English Debut in NHL Broadcast from Calgary." CBC News, November 30. http://www.cbc.ca/news/canada/calgary/harnarayan-singh-english-punjabi-nhl-commentator-1.3875319.

Doyle, John. 2016. "It's about time: We've put up with Mansbridge and his pompous ilk for too long." *Globe and Mail*, September 6. http://www.theglobeandmail.com/arts/television/its-about-time-weve-put-up-with-mansbridge-and-his-pompous-ilk-for-too-long/article31720560/?click=sf_globefb.

Fleras, Augie. 2015. "Multicultural Media in a Post-Multicultural Canada? Rethinking Integration. *Global Media Journal* 8 (2), 25–47.

Fosty, George, and Darril Fosty. 2008. *Black Ice: The Lost History of the Coloured Hockey League of the Maritimes, 1895–1925*. New York: Stryker-Indigo.

Gates, Vanessa. 2012. "Top 10 Most Controversial Don Cherry Quotes." *Toronto Sun*, March 11. http://www.torontosun.com/2012/03/09/top-10-most-controversial-don-cherry-quotes.

Goffenberg, Daniel. 2016. "HNIC Punjabi Team Writes Thank-You Letter to Pittsburgh." Sportsnet, June 23. http://www.sportsnet.ca/hockey/nhl/hnic-punjabi-team-writes-thank-letter-pittsburgh.

Gollom, Mark. 2015. "Stephen Harper's "Old-Stock Canadians": Politics of Division or Simple Slip?" *CBC*, September 19. http://www.cbc.ca/news/politics/old-stock-canadians-stephen-harper-identity-politics-1.3234386.

Gruneau, Richard, and David Whitson. 1993. *Hockey Night in Canada: Sport, Identities and Cultural Politics*. Toronto: Garamond Press.

Hill, Tim. 2015. "Jessica Mendoza receives sexist backlash after calling MLB playoff game. *Guardian*, October 7. https://www.theguardian.com/sport/2015/oct/07/jessica-mendoza-espn-mlb-yankees-astros.

Jackson, Steven J., and Pam Ponic. 2001. "Pride and Prejudice: Reflecting on Sport Heroes, National Identity, and Crisis in Canada." *Culture, Sport, Society* 4 (2): 43–62. doi: 10.1080/713999819.

Johnson, Jay, and Adam E. Ali. 2016. "Skating on Thin Ice? An Interrogation of Canada's Melting Pastime." *World Leisure Journal*. doi: 10.1080/16078055.2016.1216889.

Johnston, Chris. 2016. "Tomalo! Meet the Florida Panthers' Spanish Broadcast Team." Sportsnet, April 25. http://www.sportsnet.ca/hockey/nhl/tomalo-meet-florida-panthers-spanish-broadcast-team.

Joseph, Janelle, Simon Darnell, and Yuka Nakamura, eds. 2012. *Race and Sport in Canada: Intersecting Inequalities*. Toronto: Canadian Scholars' Press.

Juffer, Jane. 2002. "Who's the man? Sammy Sosa, Latinos, and Televisual redefinitions of the "American" pastime." *Journal of Sport and Social Issues* 26 (4): 337–59. doi: 10.1177/0193732502238253.

Kennedy, Ryan. 2015. "How Hockey is Becoming More Diverse Than Ever." *Hockey News*, October 18. http://www.thehockeynews.com/news/article/how-hockey-is-becoming-more-diverse-than-ever.

Kidd, Bruce. 1996. "The Making of a Hockey Artifact: A Review of the Hockey Hall of Fame." *Journal of Sport History* 23 (3): 328–34.

———. 2013. "Muscular Christianity and Value-Centred Sport: The Legacy of Tom Brown in Canada." *Sport in Society* 16 (4): 405–15. http://dx.doi.org/10.1080/09523360600673096.

Kim, Kyoung Yim. Forthcoming. "Working Women in a Transnational Space: Korean Media Representations of Women Golfers on the LPGA tour." *International Review for the Sociology of Sport*.

King, C. Richard. 2006. "Defacements/Effacements: Anti-Asian (American) Sentiment in Sport." *Journal of Sport & Social Issues* 30 (4): 340–52. doi: 10.1177/193723506292965.

Leonard, David. 2016. "The NFL is 67% black. Diversity Hasn't Helped White Players and Coaches Understand Racism." *Vox,* September 2. http://www.vox.com/2016/9/2/12751694/colin-kaepernick-nfl-protest-racism-national-anthem

Lorenz, Stacy K., and Rod Murray. 2014. "'Goodbye to the Gangstas': The NBA Dress Code, Ray Emery, and the Policing of Blackness in Basketball and Hockey." *Journal of Sport and Social Issues* 38 (1): 23–50.

Marable, Manning. 1995. *Beyond Black and White*. London: Verso.

Matsaganis, Matthew D., Vikki S. Katz, and Sandra J. Ball-Rokeach, eds. 2011. *Understanding Ethnic Media: Producers, Consumers, and Societies*. Los Angeles: Sage.

McIntyre, Gordon. 2016. "Hockey Night goes viral – in Punjabi." *Vancouver Sun*, May 31. http://vancouversun.com/news/local-news/hockey-night-goes-viral-in-punjabi.

Nakamura, Yuka. 2005. "The Samurai Sword Cuts Both Ways: A Transnational Analysis of Japanese and US Media Representations of Ichiro." *International Review for the Sociology of Sport* 40 (4): 467–80. doi: 10.1177/1012690205065749.

NHL (National Hockey League). 2016. "Blackhawks to Broadcast 14 games on Univision Chicago." https://www.nhl.com/blackhawks/news/univision-to-broadcast-14-games/c-282009998.

Ojo, Tokumbo. 2006. "Ethnic Print Media in the Multicultural Nation of Canada: A Case Study of the Black Newspaper in Montreal." *Journalism* 7 (3): 343–61. doi: 10.1177/1464884906065517.

Patskou, Paul. 2014. "Hockey Night in Canada – The Television Years." *Canadian Communications Foundation*. Last modified March 2014. http://www.broadcasting-history.ca/index3.html?url=http%3A//www.broadcasting-history.ca/sportsonradioandtv/HNIC_TV.html.

Pitter, Robert. 2006. Racialization and Hockey in Canada: From Personal Troubles to a Canadian Challenge. In *Artificial Ice: Hockey, Culture, and Commerce*, ed. Dave Whitson and Richard Gruneau, 123–39. Toronto: University of Toronto Press.

Powers, Lucas. 2015. "Conservatives Pledge Funds, Tip Line to Combat 'Barbaric Cultural Practices.'" CBC News, October 2. http://www.cbc.ca/news/politics/canada-election-2015-barbaric-cultural-practices-law-1.3254118.

Regalado, Samuel O. 1995. "'Dodgers Beisbol is on the Air': The Development and Impact of the Dodgers Spanish-Language Broadcasts, 1958-1994." *California History* 74 (3): 280–89. doi: 10.2307/25177511.

Rush, Curtis. 2013. "NHL Signs 12-year TV, Internet Deal with Rogers; CBC keeps 'Hockey Night in Canada.'" *Toronto Star*, November 26. https://www.thestar.com/sports/hockey/2013/11/26/nhl_signs_12year_broadcast_deal_with_rogers_cbc_keeps_hockey_night_in_canada.html.

Ryan, Camille. 2013. "Language Use in the United States: 2011." United States Census Bureau. https://www.census.gov/prod/2013pubs/acs-22.pdf.

Sager, Neate. 2013. "Gurdeep Ahluwalia and Nabil Karim hosted Sportscentre – and the backlash was appalling." Yahoo Sports, February 20. https://ca.sports.yahoo.com/blogs/eh-game/gurdeep-ahluwalia-nabil-karim-hosted-sportscentre-backlash-appalling-134034332.html.

Sax, David. 2013. "A Punjabi Broadcast Drew in New Hockey Fans." *New York Times*, April 26. http://www.nytimes.com/2013/04/28/sports/hockey/chak-de-goal-a-punjabi-show-draws-new-hockey-fans.html.

Scherer, Jay. 2016. "Resisting the World-Class City: Community Opposition and the Politics of a Local Arena Development." *Sociology of Sport Journal* 33:39–53. http://dx.doi.org/10.1123/ssj.2015-0054.

Scherer, Jay, and David Whitson. 2009. "Public Broadcasting, Sport, and Cultural Citizenship: The Future of Sport on the Canadian Broadcasting Corporation?" *International Review for the Sociology of Sport* 44 (2 3): 213–29. doi: 10.1177/1012690209104798.

Shoalts, David. 2016. "For Hockey Night in Canada Employees, the Party is Over." *Globe and Mail*, June 27. http://www.theglobeandmail.com/sports/hockey/sportsnet-confirms-ron-maclean-to-replace-stroumboulopoulos-on-hnic/article30628596/.

Singh, Satbir. 2016. Twitter (@SatbirSingh_), May 10, 8:27 p.m. https://twitter.com/SatbirSingh_/status/730207592933298177.

Stevenson, Chris. 2008. "A Bunch of 'Thugs?'" Canoe, December 15. http://slam.canoe.com/Slam/Hockey/NHL/Ottawa/2008/12/15/7753301-sun.html.

Szto, Courtney. 2016. "#LOL at Multiculturalism: Reactions to the Hockey Night in Canada Punjabi Broadcast from the Twitterverse." *Sociology of Sport Journal* 33:208–18. http://dx.doi.org/10/1123/ssj.2015-0160.

Thompson, Harry. 2013. "Equal Ice: Diversity in Hockey." *USA Hockey Magazine*, November. http://www.usahockeymagazine.com/article/2013-11/equal-ice-diversity-hockey.

Traikos, Michael. 2016. "Reported Hockey Night in Canada Personnel Shake-Up Not Surprising." *Toronto Sun*, June 20. http://www.torontosun.com/2016/06/20/reported-hockey-night-in-canada-personnel-shake-up-not-surprising.

Trudeau, Justin. 2016. "Komagata Maru Apology in the House of Commons." Prime Minster of Canada (website), May 18. http://pm.gc.ca/eng/news/2016/05/18/komagata-maru-apology-house-commons.

United States Census Bureau. n.d. "Pittsburgh city, Pennsylvania." http://www.census.gov/quickfacts/table/PST045215/4261000#headnote-js-a.

van Sterkenburg, Jacco, Annelies Knoppers, and Sonja de Leeuw. 2012. "Constructing Racial/Ethnic Difference in and Through Dutch Televised Soccer Commentary." *Journal of Sport and Social Issues* 36 (4): 422–42. doi: 10.1177/0193723512448664.

Walcott, Rinaldo. 2012. Preface. Thinking Race in Canada: What the Critique of Race and Racism in Sports Brings to Anti-Racism Studies. In *Race and Sport in Canada: Intersecting Inequalities*, ed. Janelle Joseph, Simon Darnell, and Yuka Nakamura, ix–xiii. Toronto: Canadian Scholars' Press.

Young, Scott. 1990. *The Boys of Saturday Night*. Toronto: Macmillan.

Yu, Sherry. 2016. "Instrumentalization of Ethnic Media." *Canadian Journal of Communications* 41 (2): 343–51.

Chapter 11
Taking Slap Shots at the House: When the Canadian Media Turn Curlers into Hockey Players[1]

Kristi A. Allain

In the spring of 2014, I tasked students in my course on men and masculinities with finding a social problem related to dominant and celebrated expressions of masculinity. In the resulting presentations, one of the students showed our class a video of a broadcast from the recently completed Sochi Winter Olympics. In the video, which aired on CBC TV, prominent Canadian television personality George Stroumboulopoulos interviewed the recently crowned gold-medal-winning men's curling team, Team Brad Jacobs. Curling, a sport Scottish immigrants introduced to Canada in the late eighteenth century (Reid 2010; Tate 2011), requires participants to slide large stones down long narrow sheets of ice. Both women and men curl, sometimes on the same teams, and popular conceptions of the sport link it to small-town Canadian life, rural communities, and the working class (Cosh 2014). Although the sport's origins are Scottish, its popularity in Canada is unmatched, making the Team Jacobs interview with Stroumboulopoulos especially important within the context of popular understandings of Canadian sports.

Team Jacobs, from Sault Ste. Marie, Ontario, is an elite men's curling team. The team has experienced curling success throughout their professional careers, winning several regional titles, a Brier (Canadian men's champions), and an Olympic gold medal. In spite of their success on the ice, they have experienced some criticism off it for their competitive, expressive, boisterous style of play (Montague 2011), with the coach of the British national curling team commenting: "The aggressive style we have seen from [Team Jacobs] here, that's something I don't like about the [changes to the] sport" (*Toronto Sun* 2014). The team's members are not only unique in drawing some consternation from the press and others in the curling community, but they also do not resemble male curlers past, or even of the 1990s and early 2000s, men like Randy Ferbey, Kevin Martin (aka "Old Bear"), and Russ Howard, who were respectively revered for their good nature, calmness, and maturity (Lopresti 2006; Bishop 2010; Pavia 2015). Instead, this team is muscled and young (for

1. Acknowledgement: Thanks to Stephanie Dotto for her editorial assistance. This work was supported by the Social Sciences and Humanities Research Council.

217

curlers), the oldest player thirty-five-years old, with two in their twenties.[2] Stroumboulopoulos called the team "four of the biggest dudes from Sochi" (CBC 2014). During the short segment, he lauded them for changing the popular understanding of curling as a sport where "someone's dad could win a gold medal" to something more akin to professional men's collision sports,[3] with the team expressing their desire to have children emulate their muscular, fit, and aggressive style of masculinity. Team Jacobs lead Ryan Harnden commented, "hopefully the kids growing up will follow in our footsteps." When Stroumboulopoulos asked about the response the curlers received in the Olympic Village, the team exclaimed that they had "changed the perception" of curling, presumably from a sport for older players to one that emulated the style and bodily comportment of other, more youthful Olympic and professional sports, such as hockey. Laughing, the team said that people in the Olympic Village often mistook them for Canadian hockey players.

Until recently, Canadian popular culture held curling, Canada's "other" quintessential winter pastime, as a sport utterly distinct from hockey. The Canadian public and press did not associate the aging bodies of the parents and grandparents who curled with the brawny and aggressive pursuits of young people, as they did and continue to do with hockey players. Curling, with its focus on hospitality and affability, stood well apart from the game of hockey, a sport many Canadians connect to the experiences of boys and men, praised for its pugilistic tendencies and requisite celebration of a particular kind of masculinity. This phenomenon has even expanded into the United States. The *New York Times* published a story during the Vancouver Olympics about the emerging phenomenon of amateur curling in America, quoting a grandmother who compared it favourably to hockey, saying, "There's no contact, the kids don't beat each other up. It's a sport you can keep for a lifetime" (McGrath 2010, SP5).

Jokes made in the popular press and other venues about curling centre on its accessibility, hospitality, and its associated drinking culture (teams and fans often mix after matches in reception areas). Canadians widely view curling as a leisure pursuit, sometimes overlooking its position as an elite-level sport that is both rationalized and highly professionalized (Wieting and Lamoureux 2001). A website cataloguing notable curling quotes describes a popular curling T-shirt that reads "My drinking team has a curling problem." The American media reinforce this view. During the 2002 Winter Olympics in Salt Lake City, *Tonight Show* host Jay Leno told his audience that "the gold medal [in curling] ended up going to a Brazilian cleaning team" (MacQueen 2002). Retired National Basketball Association star Charles Barkley kidded, "Curling is not a sport. I called my grandmother and told her she could win a gold medal because they have dusting in the Olympics now." Hockey jokes, on the other hand, tend to take a different form. Rodney Dangerfield famously joked about the ubiquity of hockey's celebration of violent masculinity, stating, "I went to a fight the other night, and a hockey game broke out." A popular Canadian bumper sticker reads, "Be nice to animals. Hug a hockey player." The disparate jokes circulating in popular culture

---

2. Skip Brad Jacobs was born in 1985, third Ryan Fry in 1978, second E. J. Harnden in 1983, and lead Ryan Harnden in 1986.
3. Collision sports are sports where the purpose is to intentionally make contact with other athletes (and sometimes inanimate objects). This includes team sports such as hockey, rugby, and football.

about curling and hockey demonstrate the differing popular understandings of the two winter sports, with curling linked to a lack of physical exertion and an abundance of hospitality, and hockey (at least in its most celebrated form, male competitive hockey) linked to aggression and violence. In Canada, *Hockey Night in Canada* analyst Don Cherry and numerous others, such as Calgary Flames executive Brian Burke and former NHL player and coach Darryl Sutter, often trumpet this link between hockey and aggressive masculinity, celebrating those boys and men who put their bodies at risk through fighting and rough play, calling them "good Canadian boys" (Allain 2016). Although public celebrations of both hockey and curling link the sports' associations with winter, cold temperatures, and ice to notions of Canadian national identity, the understandings of what this identity might look like were distinct—at least until early 2014.

This chapter explores the potentially problematic ways the Canadian media have reproduced curlers as hockey players. Men's curling is one of the few nationally celebrated sports that focuses on the experiences of old(er) men (i.e., men in mid-life and beyond) and a unique form of bodily comportment not frequently found in other professional men's sports. Yet in recent years the media have drawn on the language of hockey and emphasized the associated qualities of youth, aggression, and muscularity to frame Team Jacobs as ushering into curling an exciting new masculine identity. I argue that the results of this are the potentially problematic erasure of curling's once-unique form of Canadian professional sports masculinity. Examining the relationship between this shifting curling masculinity and a hegemonic Canadian national identity linked to a dominant style of masculinity in men's and boys' ice hockey, I investigate what is at stake when the media reproduce curlers as hockey players.

National Identity and the Reproduction of Canadian Hockey Masculinity

Thinkers such as Michael Billig, Benedict Anderson, Ernest Gellner, and Eric Hobsbawm have outlined the amorphous nature of nations and national identities. Born of the modern era, nations and, more importantly, expressions of nationalism—arise not as natural manifestations of physical boundaries nor geographical terrain; instead, Hobsbawm (2012) says, they are social spaces which depend on public understandings and a shared sense of belonging. Gellner (2009) proposes that while communal religious beliefs were once an important vehicle for constructing and maintaining social communities, today it is the nation that provides this social function. Theorists of nationalism identify various social structures as buttressing the creation of national communities. Gellner, for example, spotlights a collective language and education system as significant in creating shared national meanings. Billig (1995) highlights the importance of banal nationalism, or acts of nationalism like witnessing the national flag on coins, stamps, and uniforms, as reinforcing national belonging. Alternatively, Anderson (2006) describes the significance of capitalism in acting as a conduit to national belonging, in particular the capitalist enterprise of the printing press and the subsequent development of mass media.

What is significant about each of these theories of nationalism is their focus on the "imagined" or "invented" state of the nation (Hobsbawm and Ranger 1983; Anderson 2006). As Anderson points out, nations are "imagined communities," where people do not know one another but nevertheless believe that they share a strong connection. Hobsbawm and Ranger illuminate the idea that although the public understands nations as natural, nations are in fact inventions or mythologies imbued with dynamics of power. The dimension of power is significant, as dominant national discourse does not honour, reproduce, or imagine as legitimate all national identities, a fact hard to ignore for many living in Canada. More directly, "not all nationalisms can be satisfied" (Gellner 2009, 2). Ironically, "regardless of the actual inequalities and exploitation that may prevail in each, the nation is always conceived as a deep, horizontal comradeship" (Anderson 2006, 7). It is therefore important that scholars interrogate just how popular narratives work to produce national imaginings in order to discover the various ways that power operates within national frameworks.

Hobsbawm and Billig each explain that sport is an important entity in the creation of national solidarity and the construction of various national mythologies. Hobsbawm (2012, 142–43) cites the interwar years in particular as a significant time for the growth of sporting nationalism. During this period, national team sports aided in the development of the nation as an imagined community. George Orwell (1945) asserts that national teams have become the embodiment of national identity, competing with other national teams in acts he calls "war minus the shooting." This was the case in the well-watched and widely celebrated 1972 Summit Series, a hockey tournament played between Canadian NHL players and the Soviet Union's national men's team.[4] In the series, both the maple leaf (a symbol of the Canadian nation) emblazoned on the Canadian team's jerseys and their name—Team Canada—helped to solidify the notion that they represented the national populace (including both anglophone and francophone Canadians), its ideologies, and, most importantly, its (capitalist) character (Earle 1995, 114). As Hobsbawm asserts: "the imagined community of millions seems more real as a team of eleven people. The individual, even the one who only cheers, becomes a symbol of *his* nation himself" (2012, 143, emphasis added). Hobsbawm's use of the masculine pronoun here unintentionally flags for its reader an important and often-overlooked feature of nations and their national mythologies: they are gendered and most often privilege the experiences of particular men (Yuval-Davis 1993). As I will interrogate further below, when culture makers construct sport as important to the creation of imagined communities, and elite-level men's hockey as important to the imagined creation of the Canadian nation, the position of men in general—and young, fit, white, straight, able-bodied men in particular—comes to hold a more valued place within the nation (Adams 2006, 71). Therefore, when scholars interrogate the ways that the state, sports media, and other culture makers construct Canadian sporting nationalisms, it is important that they be attentive to the ways these constructions (re)produce privilege and common-sense understandings about the importance of these men.

A critical analysis of Canadian hockey provides an instructive example of intersections of gender, sport, and nationalism, highlighting the dynamics of power that operate when Canadians understand themselves as a nation of hockey players. The media, politicians, athletes, and others both comprehend and portray the link between the nation and hockey as commonsensical and essentialized. After all, hockey is widely known as "Canada's game." One does not have to look far to find various Canadian culture makers asserting that hockey is a

---

4. The final game of the 1972 Summit Series was one of the most-viewed television events in Canadian history, with almost 83 percent of the Canadian population estimated to have watched at least part of the game (Zelkovich 2010).

natural outgrowth of the Canadian environment, particularly given Canada's geographical position in the seemingly cold, hard north. Cherished Canadian humourist and writer Stephen Leacock eloquently described this relationship: "Hockey captures the essence of Canadian experience in the New World. In a land so inescapably and inhospitably cold, hockey is the chance of life, and an affirmation that despite the deathly chill of winter we are alive" (as cited in "Forbes Quotes"). Similarly, in 2014, the year of the Sochi Winter Olympics, then Canadian Minister of State (Sports) Bal Gosal remarked, "Hockey is our national winter game; it is a sport we hold dear in [our] hearts; it is what makes us Canadian" (Department of Canadian Heritage 2014). Even the Canadian financial institution Scotiabank, in an ongoing marketing campaign, celebrates hockey as something quintessential to the nature of Canada and Canadians, declaring hockey season Canada's "5th season" (Scotiabank 2017).

As many inside the nation, and even some from outside, mythologically produce Canada as a northern nation with a natural propensity for developing ice-hockey players, they are also prioritizing certain gendered behaviours. The popular link between Canada and the North is one that helps to privilege particular masculine expressions, perpetuating the idea that Canadian citizens (often white and male) used and continue to use their courageous spirit and brute strength to overcome the harsh physical realities of the land (Allain 2011). Or as Sherrill Grace (1997, 167) states in her examination of gender and representations of the North,

> The north is figured as the place of male adventure, the space for testing and proving masculine identities, where sissies and wimps will be turned into real men or be destroyed, or be sent home/south to the women or the bottle.

This type of masculinity works to devalue the gender expressions of those (e.g., women and "less masculine" men) who do not embrace a style of masculinity linked to hard, rough, tough, and sometimes violent expressions. Further, it works to erase from stories of Canadian settlement the essential role of Indigenous people(s) in aiding settlers. Therefore, as the nation celebrates hockey as its preeminent symbol, expressions of hockey associated with young, aggressive, and often white men become the revered standard for appropriate masculinity. It is this expression of what I call Canadian hockey-style masculinity that is one of the most highly publicized and celebrated versions of masculinity within the nation (Allain 2008). For this reason, numerous academics have called for an interrogation of this overly sentimentalized representation of Canadian identity (e.g., Gruneau and Whitson 1993; Robidoux 2002; Adams 2006; Pitter 2006). In this regard, Rick Gruneau and David Whitson emphatically argue that "at the very least, hockey's enduring link to the idea of 'Canadianness' is something to be analysed rather than romanticized" (1993, 7).

Scholars also point out the various ways that the national celebration of hockey works to erase some "other" Canadians from national mythmaking. Pitter (2006) shows that this kind of national mythmaking (i.e., Canada as a land of hockey players) privileges whiteness and works to erase Indigenous and Black Canadians from the national imagination. Examining the hockey website that Roch Carrier, author of the iconic children's book *The Hockey Sweater*, developed for the National Library of Canada, Pitter finds that it does not feature nor discuss black and Indigenous hockey players. This is surprising given the fame and importance of such players as Willie O'Ree and George Armstrong, and the significance of Indigenous peoples to the early development of the game (Robidoux 2002). Concerned about wholesale erasure of racialized minorities from this dominant national narrative, Pitter (2006, 128) questions, "Do these people not play hockey? Or are they not truly Canadian?" Similarly, Adams (2006, 71) asserts, "If hockey is life in Canada, then life in Canada remains decidedly masculine and white." She continues, "hockey produces a very ordinary but pernicious sense of male entitlement: to space, to status, to national belonging." The celebration of hockey in Canada does work to construct the nation as white and male, but it also works to produce it as young, able-bodied, and linked to a hegemonically masculine style of aggression and the physical domination of some men over other men.

In some ways, curling and its relationship to Canadian national identity pose an important challenge to the dominance of Canadian hockey-style masculinity and the supremacy of a sporting nationalism linked to hockey. The press represents curling, like hockey, as a quintessentially Canadian sport (e.g., see Fitz-Gerald 2015). New Brunswick author David Adams Richards (2001, 155) catalogues the similarities between the two games and their significance to dominant national identity, stating, "As with hockey, curling was our game, and we *hated* when we were beaten at it. . . . It was part of our national consciousness and we couldn't separate ourselves from it." An editorial in the *Calgary Sun* (2016) proclaims, "Canadian winter sports and curling arguably fall just behind hockey for overall and grassroots popularity." Making explicit the link between curling and national identity, the author continues, "while result on the ice is always key, the friendships forged off of it . . . ha[ve] always been about these national celebrations [*sic*] real meaning." An editorial in *Maclean's*, published shortly after the Sochi Olympics, makes similar claims, stating that "we have a triad of distinctively Canadian sports: Canadian football, hockey and curling" (Cosh 2014).

Although curling originated with Scottish settlers, its link to winter, ice, and snow has many writers, reporters, and members of the Canadian public connecting it to Canadian identity, but in ways that are mostly distinct from hockey. Like professional hockey players, the majority of curlers are white, and therefore both hockey and curling privilege whiteness and the significance of white citizens within national storytelling. However, unlike Canadian hockey nationalism, which the press and public understand as focusing on punishing physicality, elite-level play, and professionalization (Stark 2001; Cantelon 2006), curling is linked to small-town and rural life. For example, Cosh (2014) argues that while hockey is the sport of the middle class, curling is "a farmer's game, a peasant tradition. . . . There are still many villages in the West that cannot afford hockey rinks, but that faithfully lay down two curling sheets in a long, narrow shack every fall." Commentators also link curling to various non-athletic factors—factors Stephen Wieting and Danny Lamoureux (2001, 146) call "extra-kinesthetic aspects of bodily style, comportment, and training." Historian Krista McCracken (2013) outlines some of these extra-kinesthetic qualities, including community-mindedness, volunteerism, socialness, good moral conduct, and an attitude that ordinary people can be successful through hard work and dedication. Connecting these to Canadian national identity, she states, "The politeness and sportsmanship [of curling culture] has also been called by some as quintessentially Canadian in attitude" (ibid.). The emphasis on these "every-person" qualities is evident in *Globe and Mail* coverage of the 2016 Brier in Ottawa:

> There was a beer-store manager, a firefighter, a couple of golf pros, a chiropractor, an air-traffic controller, a real estate agent, a heavy-equipment operator, a pilot, an accountant or two, a number of people in sales and small business—and even a couple of curlers. Each day through the week, these Ordinary Canadians will gather for autograph sessions at the nearby Brier Patch [hospitality hall]. (MacGregor 2016c)

Indeed, one of the most controversial moments of the 2015 curling season came when a curler gently tapped a competitor with his broom to remind him not to "puddle" the ice.[5] In a statement countering dominant ideology about Canadian men's hockey, Sean Fitz-Gerald (2015), a sports reporter with the *National Post*, commented: "There are ways to show your frustration in curling. . . . Rarely—if ever—is there an exception for physical contact."

Canadian Hockey Masculinity and the Transformation of Curling

Because curling occupies national mythmaking in ways similar to hockey, it is important to note just how different the two sports are in terms of the cultures they celebrate and the paradoxical ways some members of the press look to represent them as similar. Examining curling coverage in the Canadian press demonstrates a shift in dominant understandings of curling masculinity and a resulting narrowing of celebrated masculinity linked to Canadian national identity.

Team Brad Jacobs, their eponymous champion, broadcaster George Stroumboulopoulos, and others in the Canadian media celebrated their challenge to previous understandings of appropriate gender expression in the sport of curling. First and foremost, the team opposed a curling identity associated with being "fat" and preferred one that was "ripped" (Costa 2014; Hutchins 2014; Gatehouse 2014). The press also drew attention to the team's sex appeal, suggesting a shift from sexy older curlers who appealed to "much, much older women" (Bishop 2010) to younger men who enticed younger women. *Maclean's* cited one young enthusiastic female fan commenting on the team's lead: "I could watch Ryan Harnden curl alllll damn day. You keep on sweeping sir, #hurryhard" (as cited in Hutchins 2014). Like other hyper-masculine Canadian sports (including men's elite-level hockey), heteronormativity abounds in curling coverage today. Finally, even the press's representation of curling fans has changed. In 2012, for example, Curling Canada (2012) reported on a group of fans travelling to various Brier tournaments dressed in entertaining costumes and holding letters spelling "SOCIABLE." The fans had once even donned skull caps as they celebrated balding, middle-aged curler Kevin Martin (ibid.). More recently, prominent Canadian columnist and writer Roy MacGregor (2016a), once called the "Wayne Gretzky of hockey writing" (Allemang 2012), described Brier fans using tin cans, a little spit, and string to produce "homemade 'moose calls'" in support of Jacobs and his Northern Ontario teammates. After describing Jacob's "bushy beard" and suggesting a relationship between the beard and the team's "aggressive" play, MacGregor used the moose call as a metaphor for the team, at one point referring to them as "bull moose," a symbol of hyper-masculine aggression.

---

5. Puddling occurs when a curler keeps his body, usually his knee, on the ice too long after delivering a shot. This causes the ice to melt, changing the playing conditions for both teams (Fitz-Gerald 2015).

Although it is hard to know for sure why this shift is happening at this particular moment in time, there are important factors to consider. First, as Wieting and Lamoureux (2001) document, since curling's inclusion as a full Olympic sport in 1998, professional curling associations have increasingly rationalized and commercialized the game, resulting in it resembling other mainstream men's sports. Second, popular Canadian media representations of national identity have continued to emphasize connections between dominant national identity constructions and a seemingly natural link to rough, tough men in heavily muscled bodies in general, and hockey players in particular. While this is not a recent development, current moral panics about men and "real masculinity" in crisis have reinvigorated and re-entrenched the hegemony of Canadian hockey-style masculinity (Allain 2016). Finally, Canadian sports reporters, athletes, and athletic officials have a tendency to co-opt various men's sports into the field of the hyper-masculine. Adams (2011, 29–31) notes a shift in the kinds of masculinity celebrated within Canadian figure skating culture in the 1980s and 1990s, and critiques skating's "macho turn," arguing that this represents a loss because men's skating (not unlike curling) held an important place within sports culture as "one of only a few competitive athletic activities that do little to validate the masculinities of their male competitors." As with the coverage of curling, the Canadian media widely celebrated this change in skating culture and its alignment with dominant sporting masculinities. In fact, Adams (2006, 77) finds that some reporters use hockey language to describe male figure skaters and their skating, asserting, "Hockey analogies are ways through which Canadians can talk to each other about men and masculinity."

As Team Jacobs became the placeholder for a new, masculine curling identity, the press regularly drew on hockey and other aggressive sports, both in metaphor and language, to describe the game and, more importantly, the team's aggressive, hyper-masculine posturing. For example, an article in the *Globe and Mail* explained that "Canadians are as demanding of their curlers as they are of their hockey players at the Winter Olympics" (Spencer 2014). Continuing, the author utilized hockey language, suggesting the team should "elbow aside" its opponent and beat them with "finesse shots and hits." Indeed, many in the hockey community and beyond understand elite-level Canadian hockey as more physically aggressive and violent than the game developed and played in Europe (Allain 2008). Colby Cosh (2014) from *Maclean's* pulled from an understanding of Canadian hockey as aggressive when he asserted, "Wicked Canadians have confiscated the charming Scots pastime of curling, turning it into an unseemly, crude combat." Similarly, MacGregor (2016b) used hockey discourse when he referred to curling's "surgically precise" play as the "neutral-zone trap," a term referencing a (sometimes boring) style of defensive hockey play. He went further in developing the link between curling and hyper-aggressive sports when he described the "intimidat[ing]" look of the Team Jacobs as "more in keeping with ultimate fighting than curling" (MacGregor 2016a).

The linguistic slippage that sees curling and curlers referenced using hockey terminology is only one piece of a complex social reordering of popular understandings of men who curl. My examples above demonstrate how the Canadian press celebrates a new curling masculinity linked to a certain set of attitudes and types of bodily comportment. Journalists and sports commentators widely praise Team Jacobs and their brawny expressions of masculine style as important for the sport, building sponsorship opportunities and signaling a new era of appropriate masculine expression (CBC 2014). Described by the Canadian Press as "young" and "powerful" (Strong 2013), Jacobs and his teammates are celebrated for shifting curling's identity from fat to fit and from affable to aggressive (Cosh 2014; Fitz-Gerald 2015; Pavia 2015). Writer Jonathan Gatehouse (2014) claims, "They're more like college football players than the folks down at the community bonspiel." MacGregor (2016a) similarly describes the team:

> the bulging biceps, the fist-pumps and fist-taps, the high fives, the grim-faced intensity and the loud, raw emotion are all there, just as they were in Sochi two years ago when Brad Jacobs and his rink from Sault Ste. Marie, Ont., won the gold medal for Canada and were dismissed as a bunch of uncouth bullies by the coach of the team that took silver.

Although some reporters and even the team itself cite this shift in men's curling identity as a move from curlers to "athletes" (Gatehouse 2014; CBC 2014), the examples listed above demonstrate what I argue is a shift in masculine identity that sees curlers reproduced as hockey players in the imaginations of those in the Canadian (sports) media. For example, *Calgary Herald* writer Jeff MacKinnon (2015) remarks that Team Jacobs "spent their free time at the 2014 Games…telling folks they were not hockey players." More recent coverage of the team in the *National Post* uses hockey terms to describe their style of play, stating, "If curling was hockey, they look like they could handle themselves in the corners, too" (Scanlan 2016).[6] Given the seeming importance of hockey to Canada and popular representations of Canadian national identity (Gruneau and Whitson 1993; Robidoux 2002; Adams 2006), it is important to consider what happens when the media, curlers, and others turn curlers into hockey players.

The Problem of Narrowing Canadian Sports Masculinities

Sport sociologists and historians have noted that popular representations of sport in the West have associated it with the pursuits of men and their particular expressions of masculinity (Whitson 1990; Messner 1992; Kidd 2013). Often called "a male institution" (Whitson 1990, 20), men's and boys' sports work to secure particular dominant expressions of masculinity and locate them within the bodies of particular men. Theorists have frequently described the various ways that the sports practiced by men and boys work to distance them from girls and women (ibid.), creating what Michael Messner calls "the fiction of gender" (2002, 1). In North America, it is the professional sports played by young, strong, oftentimes aggressive men—sports like hockey, football, and basketball—that garner the most media and public attention. Even as women gain access to elite-level sports in growing numbers, the American media increasingly ignore these accomplishments, focusing instead

---

6. In men's elite-level hockey, fans, commentators, players, and coaches often consider the corners of a hockey arena the most dangerous places on the ice. Within popular understandings of hockey, it is only the toughest players who can go into the corners, withstand the intense physical contact, and come out unscathed. A player who cannot handle himself in these situations or who refuses to go into the corners is considered as lacking the requisite masculinity to play the North American game.

on men's professional and college sports like baseball, football, and basketball (Cooky, Messner, and Musto 2015). In Canada, sports like hockey, and the requisite expressions of dominant masculinity found therein, are most often associated with the nation and its particularly gendered character.

R.W. Connell and James Messerschmidt (2005) direct our attention to the various ways that dominant expressions of masculinity work through cultural exemplars, such as those found in media representations of professional sports. They argue that sports stars aid in shaping culturally dominant understandings of what appropriate masculine expression should look like. At the same time, many scholars and journalists examining expressions of masculinity in elite-level Canadian (and North American) men's hockey have cited the shockingly narrow versions of masculinity celebrated therein, and their link to masculine expressions damaging to the lives of young men, young women, and others (Robinson 1998; Burstyn 1999; Robidoux 2001; Branch 2014). Sociologist Kevin Young (2012) describes how the culture of (young) men's sports celebrates enduring pain and injury as part of what it means to be an appropriately masculine man. The results of this kind of celebrated masculinity are a legacy of long-term injuries to men's bodies (including their brains). Nick Pappas, Patrick McKenry, and Beth Catlett (2004) argue that the culture of men's hockey and its popular celebration not only leads to the damage and destruction of the bodies of young men and boys, it further promotes a level of violence both against the bodies of other young men (both hockey and non-hockey players) and violence against women. They assert that there is a deep and enduring relationship between the public and institutional celebrations of violence on the ice and related violence off the ice. The celebration of the sport of men's and boys' elite-level hockey not only denigrates the experiences of women and girls, it also demands a level of conformity from its participants that marginalizes those who cannot or will not achieve its revered gender expression and play hockey in ways that the Canadian media and public define as both quintessentially Canadian and ideally masculine (Allain 2008). This is especially problematic given the rapid demographic changes in Canada today.

In Canada, where the baby boomers are beginning to retire, leading to an increasingly old(er) Canadian population, it is surprisingly rare to see the bodies of these old(er) men and women on Canadian sports channels, related websites, and in the sports sections of Canadian newspapers. Aside from occasional NHL old-timers games, which are not widely publicized and are produced only because of their relation to more popular hockey events like the NHL's Winter Classic, Heritage Classic, or all-star weekend, Canadians are generally unable to turn on their TVs and see the bodies of mid- and later-life sports competitors revered and celebrated as athletes, Olympians, and national and world champions. In this regard, men's curling and its celebration of the achievements of men in mid and later life provides an important contrast to common-sense understandings of professional sports and national champions—and perhaps even more importantly, to common-sense understandings of the nation, its mythology, and who matters.

Given the narrow and oftentimes problematic definitions of appropriate masculinity, especially those linked to exalted expressions of Canadian national identity, and the importance of cultural exemplars of appropriate masculine expression (Connell and Messerschmidt 2005), there is something profoundly important about public celebrations of diverse expressions of masculinity. Specifically, they create space for those who cannot or will not express dominant (and sometimes problematic) expressions of masculine style. It is even more important to widely celebrate cultural exemplars of masculinity that are not linked to machismo and youth. Furthermore, Canada is a nation that is growing old. Today there are ever-increasing numbers of Canadians reaching later life; the Canadian public and media need to celebrate aging curling masculinities and frame them as significant in national mythmaking. Moving dominant Canadian masculine identity away from celebrations of using "the body as a weapon" (Messner 1992, 63), and including sports that revere community life, friendliness, and a lack of physical violence is important. The culture of curling also challenges the essentialization of gender-segregated sport, with men and women regularly playing in mixed leagues, and mixed doubles curling premiering in Olympic competition in 2018. Furthermore, in curling clubs, curlers with mobility issues are able to compete both in their own leagues and with able-bodied curlers through modified curling equipment that allows participants to release the curling stone both from a wheelchair and from a standing position. Curling may also allow those who successfully embody hockey-style masculinity the freedom to step away from the performance of aggression, dominance, and violence, and provide them with the freedom to attempt different, less fraught forms of masculinity.

Given the potential of curling to challenge and expand Canadian identity, its requisite link to dominant masculinity, and the way it opens a space to celebrate different forms of bodily comportment, aging, and styles of masculine expressions, we should be concerned about the slippage that now sees media representing and lauding curlers as hockey players. Whereas once the press celebrated curling as a sport joined to the national imaginary in ways *different* from hockey, today they praise men's curling as a sport with the potential to express a similar style of dominant masculinity. As a result, the Canadian media, supported by some curlers and even Curling Canada,[7] are at risk of writing out of the national script these old(er) men and their unique approach to national sport, national identity, and gender. This trend is deeply concerning.

Acknowledgement: Thanks to Stephanie Dotto for her editorial assistance. This work was supported by the Social Sciences and Humanities Research Council.

Bibliography

Adams, Mary Louise. 2006. The Game of Whose Lives? Gender, Race, and Entitlement in Canada's National Game. In *Artificial Ice: Hockey, Culture, and Commerce*, ed. David Whitson and Richard Gruneau, 71–84. Peterborough, ON: Broadview Press.

———. 2011. *Artistic Impressions: Figure Skating, Masculinity, and the Limits of Sport*. Toronto: University of Toronto Press.

Allain, Kristi A. 2008. "'Real Fast and Tough': The Creation of Canadian Hockey Masculinity." *Sociology of Sport Journal* 25:462–81.

———. 2011. "Kid Crosby or Golden Boy: Sidney Crosby, Canadian National Identity, and the Policing of Hockey Masculinity." *International Review for the Sociology of Sport* 46 (1): 3–22. https://doi.org/10.1177/1012690210376294.

7. During Stroumboulopoulos's interview with Team Brad Jacobs in 2014, Ryan Harnden commented that the team had "changed the perception" of curling. Curling Canada, the national curling association, celebrated this claim on their Twitter account, echoing Harnden's statement (Curling Canada 2014).

———. 2016. "'A Good Canadian Boy': Crisis Masculinity, Canadian National Identity and Nostalgic Longings in Don Cherry's *Coach's Corner*." *International Journal of Canadian Studies* 52:107–32. https://doi.org/10.3138/ijcs.52.107.

Allemang, John. 2012. "Roy MacGregor: The Wayne Gretzky of Hockey Writing." *Globe and Mail*, November 7. http://www.theglobeandmail.com/sports/hockey/roy-macgregor-the-wayne-gretzky-of-hockey-writing/article5026381/.

Anderson, Benedict. 2006. *Imagined Communities*. Rev. ed. New York: Verso.

Billig, Michael. 1995. *Banal Nationalism*. Thousand Oaks, CA: Sage Publications.

Bishop, Greg. 2010. "Pride of Canada and Grandmas." *New York Times*, February 24.

Branch, John. 2014. *Boy on Ice: The Life and Death of Derek Boogaard*. Toronto: Harper Collins.

Burstyn, Varda. 1999. *The Rites of Men: Manhood, Politics, and the Culture of Sport*. Toronto: University of Toronto Press.

Calgary Sun. 2016. "Time for Canada to Rock On!" February 16. http://www.calgarysun.com/2016/02/17/time-for-canada-to-rock-on.

CBC (Canadian Broadcasting Corporation). 2014. *George Stroumboulopoulos Tonight*. CBC TV, March 7. https://www.youtube.com/watch?v=4E00Q3iDHM4.

Cantelon, Hart. 2006. Have Skates Will Travel: Canada, International Hockey, and the Changing Labour Market. In *Artificial Ice: Hockey, Culture, and Commerce*, ed. David Whitson and Richard Gruneau, 215–35. Peterborough, ON: Broadview Press.

Connell, R. W., and James W. Messerschmidt. 2005. "Hegemonic Masculinity: Rethinking the Concept." *Gender & Society* 19 (6): 829–59.

Cooky, Cheryl, Michael A. Messner, and Michela Musto. 2015. "'It's Dude Time': A Quarter Century of Excluding Women's Sports in Televised News and Highlight Shows." *Communication and Society* 3 (3): 261–87.

Cosh, Colby. 2014. "Curling Will Never Be Ruined." *Maclean's*, February 28. http://www.macleans.ca/uncategorized/a-game-that-will-never-be-ruined.

Costa, Brian. 2014. "Curlers: They're Not So Fat Anymore." *Wall Street Journal*, January 15.

Curling Canada. 2012. "Meet Canada's Most Sociable Curling Fans!" November 30. http://www.curling.ca/blog/2012/11/30/meet-canadas-most-sociable-curling-fans.

———. 2014. "George Stroumboulopoulos Tonight | Team Brad Jacobs 'We Changed The Perception A Little Bit.'" Twitter (@CurlingCanada), March 13, 1:00 p.m. https://twitter.com/CCACurling/status/444156007841685504.

Department of Canadian Heritage. 2014. "Hockey Canada Marks 100 Years of the 'Good Old Hockey Game.'" Government of Canada press release, June 26. https://www.canada.ca/en/news/archive/2014/06/hockey-canada-marks-100-years-good-old-hockey-game-.html.

Earle, Neil. 1995. "Hockey as Canadian Popular Culture: Team Canada 1972, Television and the Canadian Identity." *Journal of Canadian Studies* 30 (2): 107–23.

Fitz-Gerald, Sean. 2015. "Scotties Tournament of Hearts: Why Canadians Can't Seem to Get Enough of Curling." *National Post*, February 20. http://news.nationalpost.com/sports/why-canadians-cant-seem-to-get-enough-of-curling.

Gatehouse, Jonathon. 2014. "A No Doubt Gold: Brad Jacobs' Rink Thrashes Great Britain in Curling, Their Way." *Maclean's*, February 21. http://www.macleans.ca/society/a-no-doubt-gold.

Gellner, Ernest. 2009. *Nations and Nationalism*. Ithaca, NY: Cornell University Press.

Grace, Sherrill E. 1997. Gendering Northern Narrative. In *Echoing Silence: Essays on Arctic Narrative*, ed. John Moss, 163–82. Ottawa: University of Ottawa Press.

Gruneau, Richard, and David Whitson. 1993. *Hockey Night in Canada: Sport, Identities and Cultural Politics*. Toronto: Garamond Press.

Hobsbawm, Eric. 2012. *Nations and Nationalism Since 1780.* 2nd ed. Cambridge: Cambridge University Press.

Hobsbawm, Eric, and Terence Ranger, eds. 1983. *The Invention of Tradition.* New York: Cambridge University Press.

Hutchins, Aaron. 2014. "'Buff Boys' of Canadian Curling are #Jacked." *Maclean's*, February 11. http://www.macleans.ca/society/buff-boys-of-canadian-curling-are-jacked.

Kidd, Bruce. 2013. "Sports and Masculinity." *Sport in Society* 16 (4): 553–64.

Leacock, Stephen, "Forbe Quotes: Thoughts On The Business Of Life", *Forbes.com.* https://www.forbes.com/quotes/10753/.

Lopresti, Mike. 2006. "No Rockin' Chair for Russ; Forget the Viagra and Depends, Howard's Going for Gold at Age 50." *Ottawa Sun*, February 11, OL8.

MacGregor, Roy. 2016a. "Northern Ontario Doing It Their Way at Brier After Emotional Olympic Gold. *Globe and Mail*, March 8. http://www.theglobeandmail.com/sports/more-sports/northern-ontario-doing-it-their-way-at-brier-after-emotional-olympic-gold/article29095998/.

———. 2016b. "Battle of the Brads Unfolds Between Curlers Jacobs, Gushue at 2017 Brier." *Globe and Mail*, March 11. http://www.theglobeandmail.com/sports/more-sports/battle-of-the-brads-unfolds-between-curlers-jacobs-gushue-at-2017-brier/article29198429.

———. 2016c. "House of Commoners in Session at the Brier Curling Championships." *Globe and Mail*, March 16. http://www.theglobeandmail.com/sports/more-sports/house-of-commoners-in-session-at-the-brier-curling-championships/article29043645/.

MacKinnon, Jeff. 2015. "Curlers Focus on Their Fitness." *Calgary Herald*, February 4, 2015. http://calgaryherald.com/sports/curling/curlers-focus-on-their-fitness.

MacQueen, Ken. 2002. "Curling Comes Out." *Maclean's*, March 4, 48–49.

McCracken, Krista. 2013. "'Hurry Hard!': Community Connections to Curling in Canada." *Active History*, October 28. http://activehistory.ca/2013/10/hurry-hard-community-connections-to-curling-in-canada.

McGrath, Charles. 2010. "Curlers Form Close-Knit Community of Camaraderie and Competition." *New York Times*, February 28, SP5. http://www.nytimes.com/2010/02/28/sports/olympics/28chilliwack.html.

McKinnon, Jeff. 2015 "Curlers Focus on Their Fitness." *Calgary Herald*, February 4. http://calgaryherald.com/sports/curling/curlers-focus-on their-fitness.

Messner, Michael. 1992. *Power at Play: Sport and the Problem of Masculinity.* Boston: Beacon Press.

———. 2002. *Taking the Field: Women, Men, and Sports.* Minneapolis: University of Minnesota Press.

Montague, Bill. 2011. "Reporter's Criticism of Jacobs Rink Completely Ridiculous." *Sault Star*, February 22. http://www.saultstar.com/2011/02/21/reporters-criticism-of-jacobs-rink-completely-ludicrous-montague-column.

Orwell, George. 1945. "The Sporting Spirit." *Tribune* [London], December. http://orwell.ru/library/articles/spirit/english/e_spirit.

Pappas, Nick T., Patrick C. McKenry, and Beth Skilken Catlett. 2004. "Athlete Aggression On the Rink and Off the Ice." *Men and Masculinities* 6 (3): 291–12. https://doi.org/10.1177/1097184X03257433.

Pavia, Joe. 2015. "Ferbey the Last of the Beer-Drinking Curlers." *Ottawa Sun*, November 17. http://www.ottawasun.com/2015/11/17/ferbey-the-last-of-the-beer-drinking-curlersoneplan.

Pitter, Robert. 2006. Racialization and Hockey in Canada: From Personal Troubles to a Canadian Challenge. In *Artificial Ice: Hockey, Culture, and Commerce*, ed. David Whitson and Richard Gruneau, 123–39. Peterborough, ON: Broadview Press.

Reid, Fiona. 2010. "A Geographical Study of Scottish Sport." PhD diss., University of Stirling, United Kingdom.

Richards, David Adams. 2001. *Hockey Dreams: Memories of a Man Who Couldn't Play.* Toronto: Anchor Canada.

Robidoux, Michael A. 2001. *Men at Play: A Working Understanding of Professional Hockey.* Kingston, ON: McGill-Queen's University Press.

———. 2002. "Imagining a Canadian Identity Through Sport: A Historical Interpretation of Lacrosse and Hockey." *Journal of American Folklore* 115 (456): 209–25.

Robinson, Laura. 1998. *Crossing the Line: Violence and Sexual Assault in Canada's National Sport.* Toronto: McClelland & Stewart.

Scanlan, Wayne. 2016. "Where Sweep Takes Muscle." *National Post*, March 9.

Scotiabank. 2017. "The 5th Season." http://www.scotiabank.com/ca/en/0,,8565,00.html.

Spencer, Donna. 2014. "Canada's Brad Jacobs follows Jennifer Jones into Olympic curling finals." *Globe and Mail*, February 19. http://www.theglobeandmail.com/sports/olympics/mens-curling/article16969949.

Stark, Tobias. 2001. The Pioneer, the Poet, and the Pal: Masculinities and National Identities in Canadian, Swedish, and Soviet-Russian Ice Hockey During the Cold War. In *Putting it on Ice Volume II: Internationalizing "Canada's Game,"* ed. Colin Howell, 39–43. Halifax, NS: Gorsebrook Research Institute.

Strong, Gregory. 2013. "2013 in Sport: Brad Jacobs Emerges as the Toast of Men's Curling." *National Post*, December 13. http://news.nationalpost.com/sports/2013-in-sport-brad-jacobs-emerges-as-the-toast-of-mens-curling.

Tate, Marsha Ann. 2011. "The Urban Brethren of the Broom: Curling in Nineteenth-Century America." *Journal of Sport History* 38 (1), 53–73.

Toronto Sun. 2014. "Uptight Curling Coach Rips Brad Jacobs." February 20. http://www.torontosun.com/2014/02/20/uptight-british-curling-coach-rips-brad-jacobs.

Whitson, David. 1990. Sport in the Social Construction of Masculinity. In *Sport, Men, and the Gender Order: Critical Feminist Perspectives*, ed. Michael A. Messner and Donald F. Sabo, 19–29. Champaign, IL: Human Kinetics Books.

Wieting, Stephen G., and Danny Lamoureux. 2001. Curling in Canada. In *Sport and Memory in North America*, ed. Wieting, 140–53. London: Frank Cass.

Young, Kevin. 2012. *Sport, Violence and Society.* New York: Routledge.

Yuval-Davis, Nira. 1993. "Gender and Nation." *Ethnic and Racial Studies* 16 (4): 621–32. https://doi.org/10.1080/01419870.1993.9993800.

Zelkovich, Chris. 2010. "Gold-Medal Hockey Game Watched by Record 16.6 million." *Toronto Star*, March 1. https://www.thestar.com/sports/Olympics/2010/03/01/goldmedal_hockey_game_watched_by_record_166_million.html.

Chapter 12
Tweeting Sexism and Homophobia: Gender and Sexuality in the Digital Lives of Male Major Midget AAA Hockey Players in Canada

CHERYL A. MACDONALD

Since approximately 2009, the landscape of the big four professional men's sporting organizations in North America has begun to shift as concerns openly gay athletes. Three of the four leagues—the National Basketball Association (NBA), National Football League (NFL), and Major League Baseball (MLB)—or affiliates now house or have housed an openly gay player. This is despite a wealth of scholarship that contends that homosexuality is unwelcome in men's sports (Messner and Sabo 1990; Messner 2002, 2007; Burstyn 2000; Adams 2011; Anderson, Magrath, and Bullingham 2016). Things changed in North America when NBA player Jason Collins came out, in 2013, before retiring eighteen months later (Collins 2014). In 2014, Michael Sam became the first openly gay player drafted into the NFL. He, too, has since stepped away from the game, after having become the first openly gay player in the Canadian Football League (Stone 2015). Last, David Denson, a professional baseball player drafted by the Milwaukee Brewers in 2013, announced in 2015 that he is gay, playing in MLB-affiliated minor leagues until retiring in 2017 (Haudricourt 2015). It is also worth mentioning that, outside of these four leagues, Major League Soccer also houses an openly gay player, Robbie Rogers of the LA Galaxy (Gleeson, 2015).

The only league of the big four that does not house an openly gay player—and never has—is the National Hockey League (Lebrun 2015). That said, 2009 marked the NHL's first public brush with open homosexuality. Having informed his family in 2007, Brendan Burke, son of veteran NHL executive Brian Burke, announced to his Miami University hockey team and the world at the age of twenty-one that he was gay (Buccigross 2009). This news left the public waiting intently for the reaction of Burke's father—former general manager of the Toronto Maple Leafs, Vancouver Canucks, Anaheim Ducks, and the 2010 Olympic U.S. men's team—known for his tough, relentless, and unapologetic personality, who is referred to by some as "Mr. Testosterone" (Buccigross 2009). In other words, the public waited to see how one of the icons of hockey masculinity was going to react to having a gay son. Brendan's father, Brian, who is now an executive with the Calgary Flames, was accepting, and is now an advocate of gay rights; Brendan was killed in an automobile accident in 2010. Later, the senior Burke reflected on the 2007 experience, saying that he told Brendan, "You've given me a million reasons to love you—this doesn't change any of that." He added, "I was very proud of my son. I never had a clue, but when my son told me he was gay, it was an event of no significance in my household. But I see the terrible toll it takes on some" (Francis 2015, 1–2). The evident question, then, is what is it about hockey that makes boys and men feel that homosexuality is still proscribed for them? Is it only at the professional ranks, or do players at other levels feel this way? And how do scholarly accounts of the subject compare to the present climate in boys' and men's hockey where homosexuality is concerned?

This chapter provides an account of a content analysis of male major midget AAA hockey players' Twitter accounts that was conducted as part of a broader three-year analysis of the players' understandings of gender and sexuality; their attitudes toward masculinity and homosexuality; and the ways that their self-presentations, where gender and sexuality are concerned, are informed by their interactions with the individuals closest to them, such as teammates and family (MacDonald 2016). Major midget AAA hockey in Canada can be seen as a site for the changing perceptions of, and attitudes toward, homosexuality in male hockey. Its associated age range (typically fifteen to seventeen) and elite level of play encompass a unique nexus between a sport that has historically excluded homosexuality (Allain 2012; Atkinson 2010) and a generation that is understood to be much more accepting of homosexuality than its predecessors because it is increasingly visible to them on television, the Internet, and among their families and peers (Anderson 2011; McCormack 2012; MacDonald 2016).

The Broader Study

Using a deductive approach involving mixed-methods surveys and interviews, and guided by theories of masculinity and sport, the broader study (MacDonald 2016) enquired into micro-level experiences and expressions of gender and sexuality within the male hockey context. It situates itself within a contemporary body of literature that is divided regarding the current status of homophobia in sport. On the one hand, boys' and men's hockey in Canada is characterized in academic literature as encouraging hyper-masculine or traditionally masculine traits, such as aggression, heterosexism, and mental and physical toughness, along with lack of emotion and anti-femininity (Adams 2006; Allain 2012; Atkinson 2010). The theoretical concept used in the study to describe this hockey-player identity is R. W. Connell's (1987) hegemonic masculinity, which is largely defined by the same traits. On the other hand, there is evidence that sport is not fully responsible for this kind of socialization (Coakley 2011; Eitzen 2012), and some scholars have begun to argue that male athletes are becoming increasingly open to other presentations of masculinity that diverge from stereotypical and traditional ones, and that this includes a cultural decrease in both homophobia and hyper-masculinity among male athletes (Anderson 2011, 2014; McCormack 2012; McCormack and Anderson 2014; Anderson, Magrath, and Bullingham 2016). The theoretical concept used in the study to represent this camp is Anderson's theory of inclusive masculinity (2009, 2011), which states that contemporary men no longer need to be hyper-masculine in order to convince others of their heterosexuality.

The main research question that guided the broader study asked: Within the context of a sport understood to encourage hyper-masculinity and homophobia, how do male major midget AAA hockey players in Canada understand gender and sexuality, and how are their attitudes toward masculinity and homosexuality both shaped and presented in their interactions with others? The research question was answered in three phases: (i) written qualitative and quantitative surveys with ninety-five players and six coaches, (ii) semi-structured qualitative interviews with thirty players, and (iii) a content analysis of seventy-six social-media profiles (those that were searchable among the ninety-five players).[1] Two major themes that surfaced from the player and coach surveys that were relevant to the Twitter analysis included homophobia and a preoccupation with girls and women. In the context of this study, homophobia is defined as any negative attitudes toward homosexuality, including the fear of being or being perceived as gay.[2] First, the study population self-reported in the surveys as fairly open to the idea of homosexuality in hockey, but there were reservations. For instance, 30.6 per cent indicated that they would be upset if they found out a close teammate was gay, and 25.2 per cent did not believe that it is okay to have a gay coach. They also engaged in what Pascoe (2005) calls "fag discourse"—using homophobic language to deride others with no real connotations to sexuality. Second, both the coach and player survey revealed that the players commonly discuss girls, women, and sex. In particular, 79 per cent of the players reported that their teammates often or always discuss girls, women, and sex. Half of the coaches indicated on their surveys that they sometimes hear their players discussing the subject, and one said that he often hears conversations of this nature.

The interviews provided opportunities to build on these two themes. Regarding homophobia, nine of the thirty interviewees indicated that showering with a gay teammate would be a challenge at first, mostly because the players were concerned that a gay teammate would be attracted to their naked bodies. Two players also stated that there was palpable fear in their respective dressing rooms that discussing homosexuality in hockey would result in being ridiculed or accused of being gay. Three players spoke extensively about the use of fag discourse and another added that having a gay teammate would mean that such discourse would have to stop out of respect for said teammate. In his words: "I would think more about what I said. Like, I wouldn't say the word 'gay' and things like that…I'd try to…speak more about other things with him and not make jokes about sexuality. But I wouldn't treat him differently than the other guys, either" (MacDonald 2016, 153). While some players emphasized that their frequent use of fag discourse was not meant to offend anyone, this quotation demonstrates an acknowledgement that perhaps this kind of rhetoric

---

1. The players were not aware that their social-media profiles had been examined prior to the study in order to mitigate researcher bias. This posed ethical questions about the participant risk associated with the researcher knowing and searching for the names of minors who were otherwise supposed to remain anonymous. As such, participants were informed afterwards and given the opportunity to withdraw their information, as per the procedures outlined in Articles 3.7a and 3.7b: Alteration of Consent in the Tri-Council Policy Statement (see Canadian Institutes of Health Research, Natural Sciences and Engineering Research Council of Canada, and Social Sciences and Humanities Research Council of Canada 2014, 35–40).
2. Adapted from Weinberg (1972) and Kimmel (1994).

is socially unacceptable. These fears and apprehensions could be interpreted as homophobia, and the use of fag discourse constitutes a more casual form of homophobia.

The players' preoccupation with girls and women was not a common theme throughout the surveys, with the exception of the aforementioned 79 per cent of respondents who indicated that they often discuss girls, sex, and women. Very little was said on the subject throughout the interviews until two key informants suggested that perhaps the way the players discuss girls and women could be seen as more concerning than their attitudes toward homosexuality. One informant said that he and his teammates obsessively spoke about sex with girls and women, and that this rhetoric was not as innocent or harmless as the homophobic discourse they used. According to him, "It's what hockey players our age say and do. It won't matter what [girls and women] wear or how you look. Guys will be trying to say things over the line. At this age it's all about sex and stories. It's harsh but true" (MacDonald 2016, 188). Another informant echoed these thoughts, adding that the players' conversations would likely be offensive to girls and women. Neither informant was willing to provide specific examples of the content of their discussions after having enthusiastically responded to previous questions, which suggests that said content may be quite problematic where girls and women are concerned.

The Social-Media Content Analysis

A content analysis involves identifying and analyzing texts through systematic description and interpretation (Gratton and Jones 2010). These texts can include written documents, audio recordings or visual material, say. Examples would include newspaper articles, radio shows, print advertisements, television shows, and social-media posts. The analysis takes place through determining the possible messages, meanings, and implications of the texts being examined, including the patterns and relationships forged in the content of the texts. The method is advantageous in the sense that it is typically inexpensive, unobtrusive, and the content under investigation is free from concerns over what a researcher might want or not want to find, otherwise known as researcher bias (Creswell 2014). Disadvantages of content analysis, in this case, included interpretive narrowness because there was only one researcher (although this also contributed to consistency in the analysis) and the limitations associated with interpreting content without having an account of the intended message from the creator (ibid.).

Although scholarship on social-media analysis (Gaffney and Puschmann 2014) suggests several digital data-collection methods, the posts were coded manually because both the size of the study population and the nature of the information being sought were not compatible with available research software. For example, studies of content on Twitter commonly use application program interfaces to analyze the content of tweets (ibid.), but none facilitated a search through specific Twitter accounts. In response to this problem, scholars suggest using a program called Tweet Archivist for saving and analyzing tweets; however, with such third-party programs, it is advisable to manually verify the output (Gaffney and Puschmann 2014). Therefore, the coding was conducted manually.

In the month that the data was collected, the players posted 1,484 tweets, retweets, and likes from fifty-six accounts (seventy-six accounts were identified, however four were locked and sixteen were inactive that month). Coding categories were created through an adaptation of sport-management scholars Katie Lebel and Karen Danylchuk's (2014) study of professional athletes' self-presentation on Twitter. Although their framework was useful, it included elements of professional athletes' Twitter activity that was not relevant to teenage hockey players, such as interactions with celebrity athletes and information relating to endorsement deals. Such categories were thus omitted from the content analysis. Of their coding categories, that which occurred most often in the content analysis was "The Comedian," which signified posts that players shared or created that were meant to be humorous. While coding these posts, special note was taken of those that related in any way to gender and sexuality.

A total of sixty-seven posts out of the 1,484 (4.5 per cent) related somehow to gender and sexuality, and thirty-nine posts of the sixty-seven were coded as The Comedian. They included anything from word puns to commentary on quotidian struggles to videos of people injuring themselves. Of course, this number was generated according to researcher interpretation of what was intended to be comical, which often reflected players' claims in interviews that their humour could be crude at times. Such included posts that could be considered misogynistic. Nonetheless, the limited number of posts related to gender and sexuality may indicate that the subject does not play a substantial role in their online self-presentations. Additionally, only three posts referenced LGBTQ in some way, including one retweet referring to soccer as gay compared to hockey (as per Pascoe's "fag discourse," cited above), one like of a photo of a man screaming with the words "HA! GAY!" superimposed on it (likely also fag discourse), and one tweet asking when people would stop caring about the sexual orientation of others. The analyzed posts could be classified according to the following themes: women's bodies and appearance, sex with women, women who serve or please men, and inferior and emotional women.

Examples of posts related to women's bodies and appearances included: one retweeted video of a monkey grabbing and rubbing his face between a woman's breasts; one like of a photo that placed a super model next to a young woman in a hoodie, the latter with no makeup and disheveled hair, to depict how women present themselves on social media compared to their actual appearance (implying that women mislead audiences by sharing only photos that portray themselves as attractive); two retweeted videos of a woman "twerking" (a dance involving pelvic thrusting in a squatting stance); one retweeted photo of a young, wide-eyed male lurking behind two women, staring at their back sides, with the caption "when the booty game strong," referring to women with attractive posteriors; two likes of a photo of an elderly topless woman with a caption about the photo being a rare nude image of Hollywood actress Jennifer Lawrence; one like of a tweet by a female expressing her concern over her breasts being too small; and, most strikingly, a like of a photo of a heavyset black woman with the caption "The owner of this black suburban please move your vehicle. It's blocking the road." This post, in particular, added a racial layer to discourses of expectations regarding the shape and size of women's bodies, comparing the individual in this image to a sports-utility vehicle while alluding to her race. If we are to extend the metaphor even further, it would suggest that women, like vehicles, are for "riding," which evokes sexual intercourse. Indeed, it quickly became evident that negative attitudes toward homosexuality were much less prominent in the players' Twitter lives than their tendencies to sexualize and objectify women.

Examples of posts depicting sex with women included one tweet about the morning-after pill being a life saver; a retweet about having used the meme "F#$% her right in the pussy!" (originally a hoax video posted online, the "prank" has been repeated by men to disrupt female reporters on live TV); a tweet stating that it is acceptable to have intercourse with ugly women but not to marry them; and a like of a photo meant to depict the difference in vaginal secretions of white, Asian, and Hispanic women through manual penetration. The latter image includes three perspectives of two fingers: one with glitter (white), one with rice (Asian), and one with chili powder (Hispanic). Although there were very few posts of this nature, they are public and can reflect on the players' self-presentations.

The third theme within the context of comedic posts relating to gender and sexuality was that of women as inferior. Examples included the following: one retweet of a post explaining that if "girlfriends are feeling ignored" it is because the latest NHL video game had just come out and not because their "booty game ain't strong" (i.e., their posteriors are not attractive); one like of a tweet about a woman calling herself a trophy wife and then being informed that she was "more like a 7th place ribbon wife"; one retweet of a post about women never achieving equality because men are better than they are; and one like of a tweet by a young woman who said she was worried that her hockey-player boyfriend was going to break up with her because he had moved to another city and was frequenting bars with his teammates, where he would presumably meet other women who would be romantically interested in him. These posts, one of which was created by a young woman, all carry an air of belittlement and allude to women's insecurities and perceived inferiority by men.

The fourth and final theme among the Twitter posts was women who serve or please men. Examples included the following: one tweet referencing "puck sluts" (otherwise known as "puck bunnies" or girls and women who supposedly perpetually seek romantic or sexual relations with hockey players); three retweets of a photo that showed a bin of hockey-player-shaped candies, with the caption "white girls [sic] favourite candy"; one tweet of a photo of a group of young women carrying a player's hockey bag, with the caption "thanks ladies!"; and one like of a video showing a man standing on a dance floor, drinking beer while a woman gyrated around him, with the caption "take notes boys!" These posts, to differing extents, portrayed women as subservient to or preoccupied with men and hockey players. Some posts also made use of race, and some introduced alcohol to the content analysis.

Alcohol factored in eight other tweets. This finding, although not always related to gender and sexuality, is worth mentioning because some underage players posted photos of themselves drinking and made jokes about their inebriation. This could suggest that underage alcohol consumption is not considered taboo in their self-presentations on social media. In any case, an example of an alcohol-related post that fell under The Comedian and contained material related to gender and sexuality was the retweet of a post that claimed beer encouraged stereotypical womanly behaviour, reading, "Apparently beer contains female hormones. After you drink enough you can neither drive nor shut the hell up." All of the posts examined so far demonstrate that the players' sense of humour—and, by extension, their interests and self-presentations—sometimes, but not always, revolve around stereotypical views of women, and that they can also be bound up with race and alcohol consumption. All of this content raises questions about the players' level of social responsibility and awareness given the racialized, sexualized, and occasionally unlawful nature of their Twitter posts.

In order to further investigate how these posts may be related specifically to hockey culture, an inventory was taken of how many had stated in their Twitter biographies that they were hockey players, and that information was then compared to the frequency with which players posted facetious content about girls and women. Biographies are available even in locked accounts, thus allowing access to all seventy-six of the players on Twitter. Just under half of the biographies (44.7 per cent) included self-identification as hockey players, typically noting a jersey number and current team. That less than half of the population made a point to identify themselves as hockey players was further evidence in support that, although hockey is a major priority in their lives, it is not always the pinnacle of their identities. That said, it is not uncommon for players to downplay their athlete status in certain situations. For instance, some junior players (aged sixteen to twenty-one) are forbidden by coaches to wear team apparel to nightclubs so that teams will not be associated with possible negative incidents (MacDonald 2012). This supported an inquisition into whether midget AAA players who did not identify publicly as hockey players would be more likely to post comedic posts about gender and sexuality that may toe the line between humorous and insensitive.

Ultimately, players who did not include their identity as a hockey player in their Twitter biography posted more comedic posts about gender and sexuality. Specifically, ten of the players who did not include hockey in their biographies posted between one and seven times, whereas only five players who did include hockey in their biographies posted the same amount. Put differently, participants who did not identify themselves publicly as hockey players were half as likely to post jokes or images containing sexist connotations. Of course, this is an elementary analysis, and no relationship can be detected between the two based on these numbers, but, as an exploratory study, this finding may be useful in future research on the same or similar subjects.

Indeed, if we are to consider the limited amount of posts on gender and sexuality alongside of which and how many players included hockey in their biographies, the relationship might be relatively insignificant. This would likely be the case because approximately half of the sample population did not include hockey in their biography, but far less than half of that population posted comedic content related to gender and sexuality on Twitter. This suggests that there are likely other explanations for not including hockey in one's biography beyond the potential of not wanting to seek attention for posting misogynistic material on social media.

Discussion

Although the posts related to gender and sexuality were limited, they could be interpreted as harmful reductions of women to inferior, simplistic, sexual objects. On the one hand, this finding is not new; similar studies have established that male hockey players around this age were likely to sexually objectify girls and women (Ingham et al. 1999; Allain 2012. On the other hand, these posts made up such a small part of the whole that they should not be disproportionately viewed as representative of the entire population. What was perhaps most striking was that the players admitted that they frequently engaged in homophobic discourse and conversations about sex with girls and women, yet only one of these themes was evident on Twitter. The unanswered query, then, is why is Twitter a site to ridicule and stereotype women but not homosexuality? Put differently, why are homophobia and sexism against women, two phenomena that are often packaged together under the umbrella of hyper-masculinity, decoupled on Twitter?

One possible explanation for the limited presence of anti-gay humour and fag discourse on Twitter as opposed to misogynistic posts is the players' awareness of homophobia in sport in the media (Anderson 2011) and in their family and social lives (MacDonald 2016). With all of the attention homophobia has received in a sporting context, such as the media coverage of the professional athletes presented in the chapter introduction, it may be clear to the players that humour about homosexuality is only welcome in certain contexts, and that Twitter is not one of them but the dressing room is. This is, perhaps, because many of the players communicated in their interviews that they are not intentionally offending anyone in the dressing room because they do not view themselves as homophobic. At the same time, some interviewees communicated that they do understand that it can be offensive to others, regardless of the context.

Conversely, the players never once spoke in their interviews about women's equality when discussing the following: causes their romantic partners support, such as membership in Gender Identity and Sexual Orientation Alliances; the lessons they learned about gender and sexuality in their personal health and social development classes; or their interactions with parents. This was perhaps because, in many of their eyes, girls and women are equals and the humour that this small group of players uses has been normalized over a long period of time—there may have been little to no effort to educate the players on why such attitudes and actions may have harmful effects on girls and women. The interviewees did, however, communicate their parents' and partners' positions on homosexuality.[3] Within the academy, this can be explained by theorists such as Goffman (1976) and Butler (2004), who argue that the performance of gender is consistently taken for granted because the roles associated with it have been so repetitively played for centuries that it becomes second nature. As a result, others judge us if we do not participate accordingly. Scholarship shows that this judgment is felt by young male athletes, whose hyper-masculinity is highly policed by their peers, sometimes to the point of physical and mental harm (Messner 2002; Adams 2006; Eitzen 2012). This simple yet fundamental explanation of how gender functions in society could be used to explain why there is room for sexism against women on Twitter and not homophobia in the players' lives.

What is most compelling about the social-media content analysis is that a decoupling of homophobia and sexism in the players' public lives represents a break from conventional understandings of hyper-masculinity, which male hockey players have been said to embody for ages, because hyper-masculinity requires both (Connell 1987, 2005; Messner 2007; Allain 2012). The players in this study did not always subscribe to both, and certainly not always in convincing numbers, although this is not to say that limited results are indications of little significance or importance; they are all meaningful in some way.

---

3. The broader study (MacDonald 2016) delves deeper into social and environmental influences on the players' attitudes toward homosexuality, but not how those influences affect their decisions regarding social-media posts.

This decoupling of homophobia and sexism in specific contexts should be probed further. To what extent are homophobia and sexism mutually exclusive? Can they exist separately from one another? Scholars argue that homosexuality has connotations to femininity as the two have historically been associated with weakness and fragility (Connell 1987; Adam 2011). With this argument in view, it would be useful for future studies to examine players' intentions where their digital self-presentations are concerned; are their posts about gender and sexuality intended to make statements about their own sexuality or gender identity? Messner (2002) contends that most young male athletes would participate in such activities because the small dominant group on the team expects it of them, and it is easier to blend in than to be excluded by teammates and have strained relationships.

Conclusion

The presence of homophobia among the study population may provide insight regarding the lack of openly gay players in the NHL. Indeed, homophobia is present among the male major midget AAA hockey players in this study; however, it is limited and operates in compartmentalized and ambiguous ways, depending on the context, such as whether on social media or among teammates, friends, and family. It exists in the players' use of "fag discourse" and the fear of some that a gay teammate would be attracted to them based on nudity, but it is not the virulent and overt homophobia that scholars such as Connell (1987, 2005) and Messner (2002, 2007) once described. At the same time, based on these study results, it cannot be said that the population in question is as open to homosexuality as scholars like Anderson (2009, 2011, 2015) contends. The sample size also limits any ability to make claims about all or even most male major midget AAA hockey players. With that said, the study unquestionably finds itself between the two theoretical camps above. Additionally, Messner (2012) concedes that although attitudes toward homosexuality may be changing in sport, there is still a lot of work to be done before athletes feel safe and included.

Given that the current generation is touted as more open-minded and accepting than its predecessors, it would not be unreasonable to presume that these attitudes also exist in higher levels of hockey. After all, at the end of the 2016–17 NHL season, Ryan Getzlaf (captain of the Anaheim Ducks) was fined $10,000 by the league after having uttered an anti-gay slur on the ice during a playoff game (Chidley-Hill 2017). Both Getzlaf's actions and the consequences demonstrate that although homophobia exists in hockey, it is becoming clear that anti-LGBTQ attitudes are unwelcome. But the NHL may have more ground to cover before players feel comfortable coming out.

The absence of openly gay hockey players in the NHL also poses a conundrum because insistent efforts have been made to express that LGBTQ athletes are welcome, despite the evidence of homophobia in the sport. For example, in order to propagate the message that anti-LGBTQ attitudes will not be tolerated, the Burke family, introduced at the beginning of the chapter, have worked with colleagues and the league to create the You Can Play Project (YCP), to counter homophobia in sports, in honour of Brendan. The organization's mission is to make sport a safe and inclusive space for all athletes, regardless of sexual orientation (You Can Play 2013b). As of 2013, YCP was working alongside sixty NHL players, eighteen Canadian colleges and universities, ten American Hockey League teams, and The Sports Network's (TSN) hockey panel, among others. In fact, the NHL established a formal partnership with YCP in April 2013 as part of a "long-standing commitment to make the NHL the most inclusive professional sports league in the world" (You Can Play 2013a).

What makes YCP unique is that it has joined forces with the Institute for Sexual Minority Studies and Services at the University of Alberta to create a research position meant to explore the reach of homophobia in sport. This will provide an opportunity for academia and the mainstream to collaborate and perhaps identify what exactly it is about hockey that continues to make individuals feel that homosexuality is taboo. Based on this study, boys' and men's hockey culture in Canada appears to be slowly headed in the direction of inclusion; however, the fruit of the labour of activists in the field remains unripe, it seems, until that first player makes himself known. Until then, scholars must interrogate the nature of homophobia in hockey, along with its possible decoupling with sexism against women, and continue to do rinkside research in order to maintain the most up-to-date accounts of both masculinity and sexuality among players at all levels.

Bibliography

Adam, Adi. 2011. "'Josh Wears Pink Cleats': Inclusive Masculinity on the Soccer Field." *Journal of Homosexuality* 5 (58): 579–96.

Adams, Mary Louise. 2006. "The Game of Whose Lives? Gender, Race, and Entitlement in Canada's 'National' Game." In *Artificial Ice: Hockey, Culture and Commerce*, ed. David Whitson and Richard Gruneau, 71–84. Peterborough, ON: Broadway Press.

———. 2011. *Artistic Impressions: Figure Skating, Masculinity, and the Limits of Sport*. Toronto: University of Toronto Press Inc.

Allain, Kristi A. 2012. "'The Way We Play': An Examination of Men's Elite-Level Hockey, Masculinity and Canadian National Identity." PhD diss., Trent University.

Anderson, Eric. 2009. *Inclusive Masculinity: The Changing Nature of Masculinities*. New York: Routledge.

———. 2011. "Updating the Outcome: Gay Athletes, Straight Teams, and Coming Out in Educationally Based Sport Teams." *Gender & Society* 25 (250): 250–68.

———. 2014. *21st Century Jocks: Sporting Men and Contemporary Heterosexuality*. New York: Palgrave MacMillan.

———. 2015. "Assessing the Sociology of Sport: On Changing Masculinities and Homophobia." *International Review for the Sociology of Sport* 50 (4–5): 363–67.

Anderson, Eric, Rory Magrath, and Rachael Bullingham. 2016. *Out in Sport: The Experiences of Openly Gay and Lesbian Athletes in Competitive Sport*. New York: Routledge.

Atkinson, Michael. 2010. "It's Still Part of the Game: Violence and Masculinity in Canadian Ice Hockey." In *Sexual Sports Rhetoric: Historical and Media Contexts of Violence*, ed. Linda K. Fuller, 15–30. New York: Peter Lang Publishing.

Buccigross, John. 2009. "'We love you, this won't change a thing." ESPN. http://www.espn.com/nhl/columns/story?columnist=buccigross_john&id=4685761.

Butler, Judith. 2004. "Gender Regulations." In *Undoing Gender*, 40–56. New York: Routledge.

Canadian Institutes of Health Research, Natural Sciences and Engineering Research Council of Canada, and Social Sciences and Humanities Research Council of Canada. 2014. "Tri-Council Policy Statement: Ethical Conduct for Research Involving Humans." Ottawa: Secretariat on Responsible Conduct of Research. http://www.pre.ethics.gc.ca/pdf/eng/tcps2-2014/TCPS_2_FINAL_Web.pdf.

Chidley-Hill, John. 2017. "Gay Hockey Player Disappointed in Ryan Getzlaf's Apology over Inappropriate Slur." Global News, May 21. http://globalnews.ca/news/3467773/gay-hockey-player-disappointed-in-ryan-getzlafs-apology-over-inappropriate-slur/.

Coakley, Jay. 2011. "Youth Sports: What Counts as Positive Development?" *Journal of Sport & Social Issues* 35:306–24.

Collins, Jason. 2014. "Parting Shot: Jason Collins announces NBA Retirement in his own words." *Sports Illustrated*. https://www.si.com/nba/2014/11/19/jason-collins-retirement-nba.

Connell, R. W. 1987. *Gender and Power*. California: Stanford University Press.

———. 2005. *Masculinities*. 2nd ed. Los Angeles: University of California Press.

Creswell, John. 2014. *Research Design: Qualitative, Quantitative, and Mixed Methods Approaches*. 4th ed. Thousand Oaks, CA: Sage Publications.

Eitzen, D. Stanley. 2012. *Fair and Foul: Beyond the Myths and Paradoxes of Sport*. 5th ed. Lanham: Rowman & Littlefield Publishers Inc.

Francis, Eric. 2015. "Calgary Flames' Brian Burke speaks out about homophobia, cyberbullying." *Calgary Sun*, February 21. http://www.calgarysun.com/2015/02/20/calgary-flames-brian-burke-speaks-out-about-homophobia-cyberbullying.

Gaffney, Devin., and Cornelius Puschmann. 2014. "Data Collection on Twitter." In *Twitter & Society*, ed. K. Weller et al., 55–68. Berlin: Peter Lang Publishing.

Gleeson, Scott. 2015. "Is MLB ready for gay player? First open pro Sean Conroy discusses concerns." *USA Today*, July 21. http://www.usatoday.com/story/sports/2015/07/21/sean-conroy-openly-gay-baseball-player-mlb/30441119/.

Goffman, Erving. 1976. *Gender Advertisements*. London: MacMillan.

Gratton, Chis, and Ian Jones. 2010. *Research Methods for Sports Studies*. 2nd ed. New York: Routledge.

Haudricourt, Tom. 2015. "Brewers minor-leaguer makes baseball history by coming out publicly as gay." *Journal Sentinel*. http://www.jsonline.com/sports/brewers/brewers-minor-leaguer-makes-baseball-history-by-coming-out-publicly-as-gay-b99557156z1-321977731.html.

Ingham, Alan, et al. 1999. "Through the Eyes of Youth: 'Deep Play' in PeeWee Ice Hockey." In *Inside Sports*, ed. Jay Coakley and Peter Donnelly, 17–27. New York: Routledge.

Kimmel, Michael. 1994. "Masculinity as Homophobia: Fear, Shame, and Silence in the Construction of Gender Identity." In *Theorizing Masculinities*, ed. H. Brod and M. Kaufman, 119–41. Thousand Oaks, CA: Sage.

Lebel, Katie, and Karen Danylchuk. 2014. "An Audience Interpretation of Professional Athlete Self-Presentation on Twitter." *Journal of Applied Sport Management* 6 (2): 16–36.

LeBrun, Pierre. 2015. "Patrick Burke: 'NHL is ready for gay player." TSN, November 4. https://www.tsn.ca/patrick-burke-nhl-is-ready-for-a-gay-player-1.388059.

MacDonald, Cheryl. 2012. "'That's Just What People Think of a Hockey Player, Right?': Manifestations of Masculinity Among Major Junior Ice Hockey Players." Master's thesis, Concordia University. http://spectrum.library.concordia.ca/974057/1/MacDonald_MA_S2012.pdf.

———. 2016. "'Yo! You Can't Say That!': Understandings of Gender and Sexuality and Attitudes Towards Homosexuality Among Male Major Midget AAA Ice Hockey Players in Canada." PhD diss., Concordia University. http://spectrum.library.concordia.ca/981103/.

McCormack, Mark. 2012. *The Declining Significance of Homophobia: How Teenage Boys Are Redefining Masculinity and Heterosexuality*. New York: Oxford University Press.

McCormack, Mark, and Eric Anderson. 2014. "The Influence of Declining Homophobia on Men's Gender in the United States: An Argument for the Study of Homohysteria." *Sex Roles* 71 (3–4): 109–20.

Messner, Michael. 2002. *Taking the Field: Women, Men and Sports*. Minneapolis: Regents of the University of Minnesota.

———. 2007. "Gender and Sports." In *Out of Play: Critical Essays on Gender and Sport*, 1–7. Albany: State University of New York Press.

———. 2012. "Reflections on Communication and Sport: On Men and Masculinities." *Communication & Sport* 1:113–24.

Messner, Michael, and Donald Sabo. 1990. "Introduction: Toward a Critical Feminist Reappraisal of Sport, Men, and the Gender Order." In *Sport, Men and the Gender Order: Critical Feminist Perspectives*. Champaign, IL: Human Kinetics Books.

Pascoe, C. J. 2005. "Dude, You're a Fag: Adolescent Masculinity and the Fag Discourse." *Sexualities* 8 (3): 329–46.

Stone, Avery. 2015. "Michael Sam says he's stepping away from football." *USA Today*, August 14. http://ftw.usatoday.com/2015/08/michael-sam-announces-he-is-stepping-away-from-football-montreal-alouettes.

Weinberg, George. 1972. *Society and the Healthy Homosexual*. New York: Saint Martin's Press.

You Can Play Project. 2013a. "NHL and NHLPA Announce Partnership with You Can Play." http://www.youcanplayproject.org/pages/you-can-play-league-partners.

———. 2013b. "Our Mission." http://youcanplayproject.org/pages/mission-statement.

PART V
Rethinking the Pros

Document 6
Maurice Richard : notre icône

Benoît Melançon

Parmi les figures historiques du hockey, une place à part doit être réservée à Maurice Richard (1921-2000), le plus célèbre joueur de la plus célèbre équipe de hockey en Amérique du Nord, les Canadiens de Montréal. Le numéro 9 des Canadiens, celui que l'on surnomme « Le Rocket », a été recruté par son club en 1942. Cet ailier droit ne cessera de multiplier les exploits jusqu'à sa retraite après la saison 1959-1960. Il sera notamment le premier joueur à marquer 50 buts en 50 matchs : cela se passait en 1944-1945 ; il faudra attendre 36 ans avant que pareil exploit ne soit réédité. En nombres, la carrière de Richard se résume ainsi : 1473 minutes de punition, 1111 matchs, 1092 points (dont 626 buts), 18 saisons, 14 sélections au sein de la première ou de la deuxième équipe d'étoiles de la Ligue nationale de hockey, 8 coupes Stanley (emblème du championnat professionnel nord-américain) et 1 titre de joueur le plus utile de la ligue (en 1946-1947). Dans son édition de janvier 1998, le magazine *The Hockey News* le classait au cinquième rang des plus grands joueurs de hockey de tous les temps, derrière Wayne Gretzky, Bobby Orr, Gordie Howe et Mario Lemieux. Quand il sera suspendu pour avoir frappé un arbitre au cours d'une partie de mars 1955 contre les Bruins de Boston, une émeute éclatera dans les rues de Montréal : cette suspension privait son équipe de son meilleur joueur. Beaucoup de commentateurs pressés disent que la Révolution tranquille québécoise serait née ce jour-là.

Cela est facile à expliquer : Maurice Richard n'est pas qu'un joueur de hockey ; c'est un mythe national. À Montréal, où il a vécu toute sa vie, cinq statues rappellent sa présence : devant l'aréna auquel il a donné son nom ; au complexe commercial Les Ailes ; au Centre de divertissement Forum, l'ex-Forum de Montréal, là où s'est déroulée sa carrière ; à côté du Centre Bell, où jouent maintenant les Canadiens ; en cire, au musée Grévin. On ne compte plus les textes écrits sur lui, dans les deux langues officielles du pays : des articles de périodiques et des textes savants, des biographies et des recueils de souvenirs, des contes et des nouvelles, des romans et des livres pour la jeunesse, des poèmes et des pièces de théâtre, des manuels scolaires et des témoignages. On lui a consacré des chansons, des bandes dessinées, des peintures, des films (documentaires et de fiction) et des émissions de télévision et de radio. Son visage a orné des vêtements, des jouets, des publicités, des produits alimentaires, des cartes à collectionner, des photographies sans cesse reproduites, des timbres-poste. On a donné son nom à des lieux publics. Pendant plusieurs années, le billet de cinq dollars de la Monnaie canadienne renvoyait à lui, par l'intermédiaire des premières lignes du conte de Roch Carrier écrit en son honneur : « Les hivers de mon enfance étaient des saisons

245

longues, longues. Nous vivions en trois lieux : l'école, l'église et la patinoire ; mais la vraie vie était sur la patinoire » (*Le chandail de hockey*) (Figure D6.1).

En 1971, le cinéaste Gilles Gascon signait le documentaire *Peut-être Maurice Richard* (Office national du film). On y entendait Richard s'inquiéter de tomber un jour dans l'oubli. Il se trompait. Il ne se passe pas une semaine sans que son nom n'apparaisse dans les médias québécois, et pas seulement sportifs. Près de 20 ans après sa mort, tout le monde se réclame de lui : les joueurs de hockey, bien sûr, mais aussi les représentants politiques et les journalistes. Vous voulez rebaptiser un pont ? Pourquoi pas un pont Maurice-Richard ? Vous voulez refaire la carte électorale (fédérale ou provinciale) ? Pourquoi pas une circonscription Maurice-Richard ? Vous voulez décorer un immeuble du quartier où il a habité ? Pourquoi pas une murale Maurice Richard ? Vous êtes un artiste et vous voulez prouver que vous êtes proche de votre public ? Pourquoi ne pas monter sur scène avec le maillot numéro 9 sur le dos ? Au début du XXIe siècle, il n'existe qu'une icône connue de tous les Québécois, et c'est Maurice Richard.

Quand on a beaucoup travaillé sur lui — c'est mon cas —, quelles leçons peut-on tirer de ses représentations ? Au moins quatre choses. Pour que Maurice Richard soit, selon un sondage du *Journal de Montréal* de 2014, la troisième personnalité la plus marquante du Québec des 50 dernières années, après l'ancien premier ministre René Lévesque et la chanteuse Céline Dion, il a fallu que son image reste présente dans la société sous diverses formes : Richard est l'objet de récits médiatiques, culturels et familiaux — on se le transmet

Figure D6.1 Veste pour enfant inspirée de Maurice « le Rocket » Richard
Montréal (Québec)
Années 1950
Musée canadien de l'histoire, 2002.81.42, IMG2016-0253-0053-Dm.tif

d'une génération à l'autre, tel un héritage commun, un patrimoine. On aurait cependant tort de croire que cette tradition est limitée au Québec ou aux seuls francophones : les autres Canadiens, quelle que soit leur langue, pourraient reprendre la déclaration du commentateur Don Cherry au *Calgary Herald* le 1ᵉʳ juin 2000 : «*People in Quebec loved the Rocket, but he was our hero, too.*» Cela dit, le Maurice Richard de 2018 n'est évidemment plus celui de 1942, quand il a commencé sa carrière : au-dessus de sa photo pour une publicité de l'Année internationale de la famille (1994), on pouvait lire le slogan «La famille. Elle dure quand elle est tendre !», ce qui est une excellente façon de transformer celui qui fut un «dur» en grand-père «tendre». Enfin, une constante apparaît dans les discours sur Richard : même si l'homme pouvait parfois donner une image publique rébarbative, soit par ses déclarations, soit par son silence, il n'est guère possible d'en parler librement, voire de critiquer cette attitude, comme si son image devait être préservée et rester quasi intouchable.

Au Québec comme dans le reste du Canada, Maurice Richard est partout. Celui qui ne fut d'abord qu'un joueur de hockey est aujourd'hui un mythe, une légende, un héros, une idole. Tous ont quelque chose à raconter sur lui. Ce n'est pas près de changer.

Document 7
Joseph Cletus (Joe) Malone, 1890-1969

Marc Durand

(Ce document comprend des extraits de *La coupe à Québec: les Bulldogs et la naissance du hockey*, de Marc Durand avec la collaboration de Jean Provencher, Commission de la capitale nationale du Québec, 2012.)

Surnommé «Gentleman Joe» pour son élégance et son esprit sportif, ou encore «le fantôme» en raison de sa façon d'apparaître au bon endroit, Joe Malone (figure D7.1) est d'abord l'icône du Quebec Hockey Club. C'est aussi un citoyen typique de la capitale: né d'une famille à revenus modestes, il a du sang irlandais et français. Sa mère, Marie-Louise Rochon, a épousé Maurice Joseph Malone, lui-même descendant de la famille Gignac. Il n'était pas le plus rapide ni doté du meilleur tir, mais il décrit ses prouesses offensives en ces termes : «Je n'avais pas le meilleur lancer, mais je savais où la rondelle irait.»

Joe Malone est né à Saint-Colomb de Sillery le 28 février 1890. Son père est *culler* (mesureur de bois), la troisième génération à pratiquer ce métier dans la région. Mais le bois que Joe préfère, c'est celui d'un bâton de hockey.

À Québec (1908-1917, 1919-1920), à Waterloo (1910), à Montréal (1917-1919, 1922-1924) et à Hamilton (1920-1922), il marque 401 buts en 307 parties chez les professionnels, remporte deux coupes Stanley en tant que capitaine du Quebec Hockey Club (les Bulldogs) et quatre titres de meilleur compteur.

Il excelle au hockey, mais aussi à la crosse et au baseball. Il exerce également le métier de *tool maker* (d'outilleur) depuis l'âge de 15 ans, si bien qu'une fois la Première Guerre mondiale déclarée, le Canada le préfère à l'atelier d'armes militaires Ross Rifle de la Grande Allée plutôt qu'en Europe. Au milieu de cette crise, il prend pour épouse Mathilda Power, fille de Michael Power et de Joséphine St-Hilaire, en l'église St. Patrick, le 24 juillet 1916.

Malheureusement, la Ross Rifle ferme ses portes en mars 1917, et un nouvel emploi à Montréal (en compagnie de son coéquipier Jack McDonald) incite le Quebec Hockey Club à cesser ses activités. Loué aux Canadiens, c'est au centre de Newsy Lalonde et de Didier Pitre que Joe Malone connaît une saison légendaire de 44 buts en 20 parties dans la LNH.

La saison suivante, il revient à Québec pour la relance de l'usine et devient «joueur du samedi» des Canadiens, participant à huit parties seulement en saison régulière et ratant la série de la coupe Stanley disputée à Seattle.

Figure D7.1 Carte de hockey de Joe Malone dans l'uniforme du Quebec Hockey Club
Série C57 de l'Imperial Tobacco Imprimée en 1912
Bill Galloway/Temple de la renommée du hockey/Hockey Hall of Fame

Il remporte son quatrième titre de meilleur compteur en 1920 avec le Club athlétique de Québec (Bulldogs, LNH). Le 31 janvier, il inscrit sept buts contre Toronto, un record de la LNH qui tient toujours.

Le club est transféré à Hamilton en 1920 et Joe Malone tarde à s'entendre avec sa nouvelle formation. Lorsqu'il y parvient enfin, le 5 janvier 1921, il patine sur ses propres lames, les «*Joe Malone Special*», des lames tubulaires beaucoup plus légères et rapides. Elles feront la loi pendant plus d'une décennie, portées par des dizaines de joueurs de la LNH, tels Howie Morenz, Aurèle Joliat et Jack Adams.

Le capitaine et entraîneur des Tigers de Hamilton inscrit 55 buts en 44 parties, mais il se fait tirer l'oreille chaque saison à Hamilton. À l'automne 1922, il demande une transaction vers Montréal, où il désire installer sa famille. C'est là qu'il finira sa carrière à titre de joueur de relève. Il raccroche ses patins après un dernier match, le 23 janvier 1924, mais on l'identifie malgré tout comme un membre de l'équipe détentrice de la coupe Stanley.

En 1950, il est intronisé au Temple de la renommée du hockey. La Ville de Québec l'honore le 29 mars 1952, lors d'un match des As, en présence du jeune prodige Jean Béliveau, «un joueur qui me ressemble», dira-t-il. Il demeure un fan de hockey, participant à plusieurs événements officiels, mais discret, effacé et modeste à l'évocation de ses exploits.

Il quitte définitivement la patinoire le 15 mai 1969 d'un arrêt cardiaque, à Montréal.

FAITS D'ARMES
345 buts en 278 parties en carrière en saison régulière
56 buts en 29 parties en séries éliminatoires et tournois
5 buts ou plus à 11 occasions en carrière
4 titres de meilleur compteur (1913, 1917, 1918, 1920)

DÉTENTEUR DE PLUSIEURS RECORDS DE LA LNH
Moyenne de 2,2 buts par match en une saison (1917-1918)
7 buts dans une seule rencontre (1920)
5 matchs de 5 buts ou plus (Gretzky et Lemieux le suivent avec 4 matchs)
Joueur le plus rapide à inscrire 100 buts (en 61 matchs)
Au moins un but à ses 15 premiers matchs en carrière dans la LNH

Chapter 13
Trust and Antitrust: The Failure of the First National Hockey League Players' Association, 1956–1958

J. ANDREW ROSS

On October 9, 1956, the star players of the National Hockey League took to the ice at the Forum in Montreal to show off their skills at the tenth annual All-Star game. In the game format of the day, the reigning Stanley Cup champion Montreal Canadiens played a team of top players from the league's other five clubs. The all-stars were led by "Terrible Ted" Lindsay, "the hard-bitten left winger of [the] Detroit Red Wings," who was making his seventh all-star appearance. George Armstrong shone on a line with his Toronto Maple Leafs teammates Tod Sloan and Dick Duff. Another Maple Leaf, Jim Morrison, stood out on defence, partnered with Bill Gadsby of the New York Rangers. In the match, Lindsay scored a goal, assisted by Gus Mortson of the Chicago Black Hawks, but otherwise his team could not penetrate a Canadiens defence led by Doug Harvey, "who must have stopped almost as many shots as the Habs goalie" (Macleod 1956). Although the contest ended in a tie, according to Baz O'Meara of the *Montreal Daily Star*, "artistically and financially speaking, the game was a huge success" since the record attendance of 13,097 contributed $28,261 more to the National Hockey League Pension Society (NHLPS), the $1.5 million fund that supported NHL players in retirement (O'Meara 1956; *Toronto Daily Star* 1956).

Behind the scenes, however, the players were not content. As the player representatives on the NHLPS board, Lindsay and Harvey had been asking questions about the financial position of the society. Every year every NHL player contributed a hefty $900 per year (as much as 20 per cent of their after-tax salaries) to the NHLPS, and most did not seem clear on the benefits.[1] And there was the question of the NHL's recent television contract with CBS. Would the players be getting a share of the revenue? Feeling the need for collective action, Lindsay and Harvey violated their own competitive instincts—as well as league policy against fraternization with opposing players—and arranged a player meeting in a local tavern after the all-star game. Over beer, they broached the idea of organizing the league's players to get more information about the pension and related issues (*Globe and Mail* 1957a). The pair found an eager audience in their fellow all-stars, who agreed to join the campaign to sign players to a new association. No one breathed a word to club managers

---

1. The average salary in 1956–57 was $8,275; see table III.1 in Ross 2008 (app. III).

or owners until all of the league's players were signed up (save one holdout), and, in February 1957, they held a press conference to announce the formation of the National Hockey League Players' Association (NHLPA).[2]

More than a Game, a Business

To contemporary readers, accustomed to seeing the NHLPA on a more equal footing with the NHL on such matters, it may seem odd that Lindsay and the others felt the need to be secretive. Even in the 1950s, this kind of collective action by labour was widely accepted in North America, and hockey players were not the first major-league athletes to organize. The NHLPA had been preceded by the Major League Ball Players Association (MLBPA) in 1953, the National Basketball Players Association in 1954, and the National Football League Players Association would also form, in the fall of 1957.[3] As a group, professional athletes had come late to the collective bargaining game; their organizing took place at the tail end of a golden age of North American labour, the period from 1936 to 1956, in which union membership grew to record numbers against the background of the Depression, the Second World War, and the emergence of the welfare state.[4] As it was in many areas then, sports were an exception.

Scholars are fond of saying that the meanings of sport resonate throughout broader society, but sport also occupies a special position. In the case of hockey, this idea is encapsulated by the commonplace phrase "more than a game," and in the view that studying the sport can give us special insight into how Canadians experience class, gender, race/ethnicity, language, ability, sexual orientation, and region. One aspect that is often missing, however, is the economic and business framework in which hockey operates. This is particularly curious given that, arguably, the most culturally dominant expression of Canadian hockey, the NHL, is a business. A crucial part of the missing narrative of the business of hockey is the story of its labour force. While the relationship between labour and capital has always been contested terrain, hockey labourers faced special challenges in the 1950s (as they do today[5]): they operated in a monopoly industry that fashioned itself as a cultural rather than as an economic activity; they were both employees and contractors at the same time, but also workers with high incomes and a status that elevated them above the average North

---

2. On the announcement, see *Toronto Daily Star* 1957. The executive claimed to have signed 112 NHL players to the association, all except Ted Kennedy of Toronto, who was soon to retire—see *Globe and Mail* 1957b.

3. See: Korr 2002; "NBPA History," National Basketball Players Association, http://www.nbpa. com/history.php; Condon 1957. There had been several attempts to organize major-league athletes in the mid-1940s; for examples, see Ross 2008 (342–44). To date, there has been no extensive literature on postwar baseball labour issues, with the exception of Korr's work. Paul Staudohar's contention (1996, 3) that labour issues were "not important" until the 1970s needs re-examination.

4. By 1956, just as the major-league unions were finding their feet, general union membership was dropping in both Canada and the United States. Those interested in comparing Canadian and American unionization in this period should consult Lipset and Meltz 2004 (41–44).

5. The current campaign for and against unionizing major-junior hockey players draws on many of the same themes.

American worker; and, significantly, they worked in a transnational enterprise whose very existence was jurisdictionally ambiguous.

This chapter contributes to the narrative of hockey labour by evaluating how the NHLPA struggled to organize the peculiar labour relationships of the players to their teams and the NHL, and adapt to new forces in technology, law, and athlete activism. The question was whether Lindsay and his fellow NHL players would be able to stay united and succeed in reforming the relationship in the face of owner and league resistance. To do so would mean trusting collective action, risking conflict with the paternal beneficence of the owners, and establishing that collective bargaining was the right of all labourers, even those that played a game for a living.

A Resurgence of Athlete Activism

The late arrival of athlete labourers to unionization was due primarily to the peculiar institution that was unique to labour relations within the sports-entertainment industry: a clause in player contracts that "reserved" players to the contracting club even after expiry of the contract, and thus keeping them from moving from team to team. Baseball's reserve clause had been challenged under antitrust laws, but in 1922 the U. S. Supreme Court had concluded, in *Federal Baseball Club v. National League*, that professional baseball was exempt. As time went on, the major league hockey, football, and basketball assumed similar protection.[6] Though it was consistent with a strict interpretation of contemporary antitrust jurisprudence, the *Federal Baseball* decision later came to be understood as having given baseball an exemption based on its cultural status—because the "national pastime" was a sport, not a business. Even though individual clubs were clearly profit-making ventures, the leagues themselves were constructed as non-profit entities, and arrogated to themselves a status of quasi-legal governance bodies for the entire sport.[7] And "the good of the game" could be used to mask the good of the corporation.

Formed in 1917, the NHL had expanded from Canada into the United States in the 1920s, and, like baseball's National League and American League before it, succeeded in suppressing all its competitors to obtain hegemony over both the commercial and amateur versions of the sport by the eve of the Second World War. As such, the NHL became a monopoly that could restrict the number of its members, as well as a monopsony, which could dictate the terms of employment for all professional hockey players, such as reserving the services of stars like Maurice Richard at the discretion of the club (see Figure 13.1).[8] While there were regular bouts of labour unrest in the history of the NHL and its predecessor leagues (Ross 2015, 33, 116–17), by the 1930s the cultural and economic dominance of the NHL solidified the view that its players were not workers in the conventional sense. This was facilitated by the binational nature of the league. The NHL was a Canadian-American

---

6. *Federal Base Ball Club of Baltimore, Inc. v. National League of Professional Base Ball Clubs et al.*, 259 U.S. 200 (1922). For an analysis of how postwar cases misconstrued the decision, see McDonald 1998 and Alito 2009.

7. In baseball, two leagues, the American and the National, were run by a commission. After Kenesaw Mountain Landis became sole commissioner, in 1920, the letterhead he used read simply: "Baseball."

8. For a survey of the issues, see Roberts 1991.

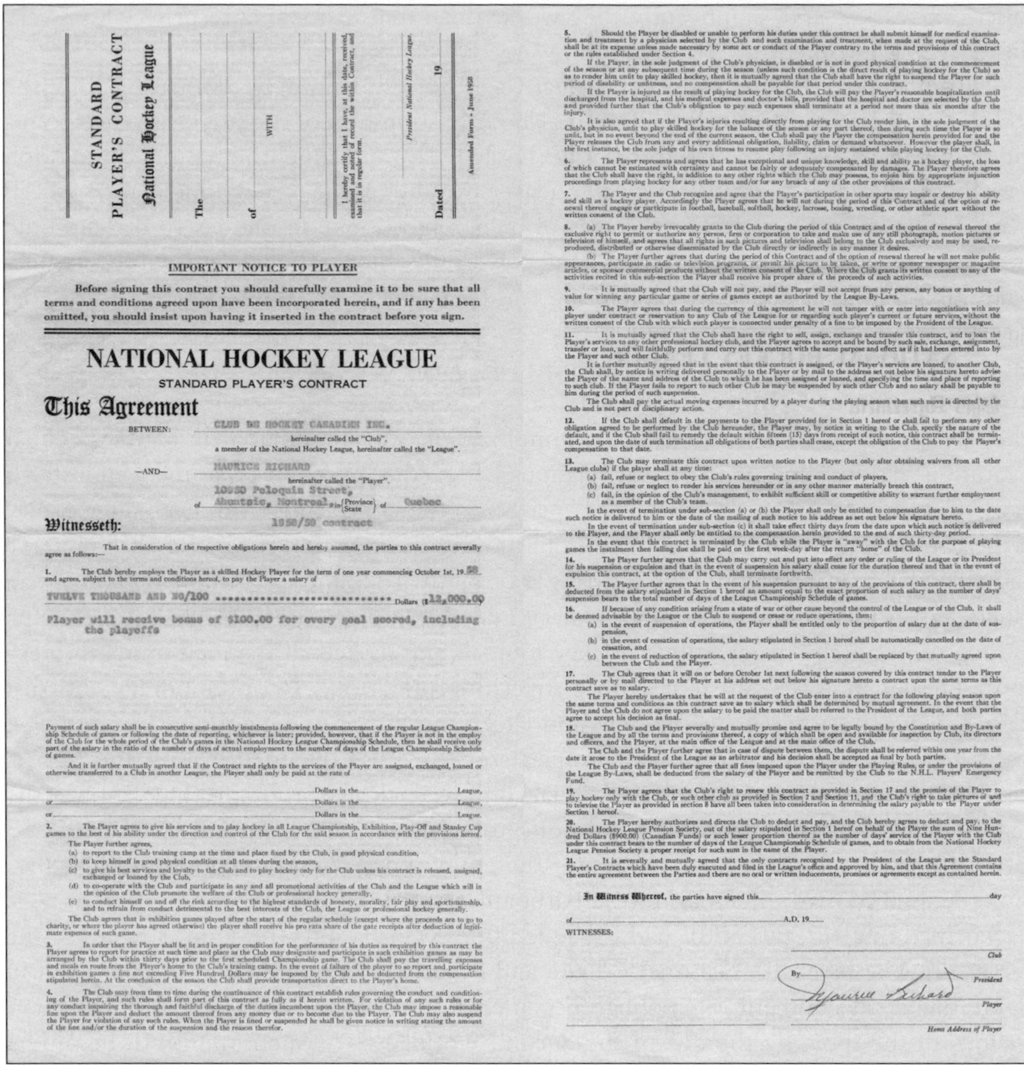
STANDARD PLAYER'S CONTRACT

National Hockey League

IMPORTANT NOTICE TO PLAYER

Before signing this contract you should carefully examine it to be sure that all terms and conditions agreed upon have been incorporated herein, and if any has been omitted, you should insist upon having it inserted in the contract before you sign.

NATIONAL HOCKEY LEAGUE

STANDARD PLAYER'S CONTRACT

This Agreement

BETWEEN: CLUB DE HOCKEY CANADIEN INC.

hereinafter called the "Club",

a member of the National Hockey League, hereinafter called the "League".

—AND— MAURICE RICHARD

hereinafter called the "Player".

10950 Peloquin Street,

of Ahuntsic, Montreal, in [Province/State] of Quebec

Witnesseth: 1958/59 contract

TWELVE THOUSAND AND 00/100 Dollars ($12,000.00)

Player will receive bonus of $100.00 for every goal scored, including the playoffs

Figure 13.1 Maurice Richard's NHL Standard Player Contract from 1958-59
Clause 17 stipulates that "the player…will enter into a contract for the following playing season," in effect reserving his future services to the club.
Maurice Richard's NHL Standard Player Contract, 1958-59
Canadian Museum of History, 2002-H0017.43

league primarily populated by Canadian players and managers but mostly American owners, which produced a confusing and ambiguous legal environment of overlapping transnational, interstate, and interprovincial jurisdictions.

Not Out "to make trouble"

The direct impetus to the formation of the NHLPA was Ted Lindsay and Doug Harvey's frustrations over the lack of information concerning the pension fund. The NHLPS had five directors: two owners, two players, and Clarence Campbell, the league president, as director-at-large. At the beginning of each season, Campbell would visit team dressing rooms and report to the players on the status of the pension. He apparently did not make an effort to make the reports comprehensible, and many players felt intimidated (Ross 2008, 345). As late as December 1953, NHLPS player representative Leo Reise (who was also a trained accountant) had said of the superannuation scheme: "I personally believe it's an excellent plan.... We've never had any trouble with the owners, and they're always happy to confer with our representative" (Moriarty 1953). But by 1956 his fellow director, Lindsay, and Reise's successor, Harvey, were less satisfied (*Hockey News* 1953).[9] They and others wanted to know how the pension fund might benefit from the new American television revenue.

The interest in television came from a baseball precedent. In August 1956, the MLBPA renegotiated its pension agreement and convinced team owners to have it fully funded from all-star game and World Series television revenues (*New York Times* 1956). Since the NHL had just signed its own national television contract in the United States with CBS, NHL players wanted to see if they too could get a share of the revenue (*Globe and Mail* 1956). Lindsay spoke to Cleveland pitcher Bob Feller, who introduced him to the MLBPA's legal advisors, the Lewis & Mound law firm, from New York. With Norman Lewis busy with baseball, the NHL case was taken up by partner Milton Mound, who quickly concluded that the hockey players had "substantial grievances" and should have "the same achievements which have been announced in connection with baseball."[10] (Lewis was more blunt, referring to the NHL as "plain and simple indentured servitude."[11]) Over the fall, Mound met surreptitiously with NHL players to arrange a constitution and bylaws, membership forms, dues collecting, and the election of an executive, which included the 1956 all-stars: Lindsay as president; Harvey, Fernie Flaman, and Gus Mortson as vice-presidents; Jim Thomson as secretary; and Bill Gadsby as treasurer.[12]

At the February 11, 1957, press conference in New York announcing the NHLPA's formation, Lindsay emphasized that the group was not out "to make trouble," and he was emphatic that the group was not a trade union and therefore would not negotiate individual salaries (this was a common athlete point of resistance to unionization). Rather, the NHLPA had been formed simply to request information about the players' pension scheme and negotiate certain changes to the standard player contract (*Globe and Mail* 1957a).[13] In

---

9. It did not help that society meetings were only held once a year. Lindsay had been a society director since 1952, and Harvey since 1955.

10. Summary of Evidence of Milton N. Mound, OLRB hearing, November 23, 1957, Archives of Ontario, F223-3-1-98 (Conn Smythe fonds). (N.B. This source and the Summary of Evidence of Tod Sloane [*sic*] are not official OLRB reports, but rather the notes of Maple Leaf Gardens lawyer Ian Johnston taken at the time of their testimony, and should be treated with due care.)

11. See Cruise and Griffiths 1991 (88); their book, *Net Worth*, has been the main account of the NHLPA to date, and while there are interesting insights from interviews with several of the key actors, it also tends to be tendentious in its interpretation of events.

12. Summary of Evidence of Milton N. Mound, OLRB hearing, November 23, 1957, Archives of Ontario, F223-3-1-98. The constitution was signed on January 31, 1957. See also *Toronto Daily Star* 1957.

13. On the players' reaction to the word "union," see Cruise and Griffiths 1991 (89–90, 92). This was not just a hockey player concern; the word "did not come easily to the vocabulary" of baseball players either (see Korr 2002, 1).

addition to the pension details, the players wanted $35 per day and a meal allowance of $10 for training camp, a no-trade clause after six years of service, payment for exhibition games, a guaranteed minimum salary, and no compulsion to sign contracts after arbitration by NHL President Clarence Campbell.[14]

While no doubt taken by surprise by the announcement, Campbell's reaction was measured and maintained a paternalist view. He told the press that "there was nothing which the players of the NHL could accomplish through a union or association which could not just as easily be secured by direct, informal representations to the League or its member clubs" (*Globe and Mail* 1957c). Others were less temperate. Red Wings General Manager Jack Adams, Lindsay's boss, confronted his players in the dressing room and dared them to voice their support for the new association. Lindsay no doubt did so. Adams then invited local sportswriters into his office and denounced Lindsay, in particular, as "a cancer" and "the ruination of the team," and implied that Lindsay made a salary of $25,000 ($13,000 more than actual) (Cruise and Griffiths 1991, 94).[15] Conn Smythe, the Toronto Maple Leafs owner and chairman of the league's board of governors, was polite in public: "The players on the executive have done a lot for hockey, and hockey has done a lot for them. It's been an even deal up to date." In private, Smythe interrogated players individually about their grievances and consulted his dictionary for the definition of "communist" and "communism."

As a group, the NHL owners saw the NHLPA as a threat for two reasons. One was simply the traditional resistance of a business to collective action by its labour force; but the other was the league's delicate legal position as a virtual monopoly over the commercial hockey industry. The two issues were connected: any recognition of the NHLPA by the league itself could be construed as an admission that it was the league, not the individual clubs, that was the employer. This would leave it open to charges of effecting a monopoly, thus exposing it to an antitrust complaint under American law. (If the clubs were considered the employers, the illusion of "competition" was easier to maintain.) Canadian antitrust law was not at issue since it did not include services like sports, but even having the league head office and two clubs resident in Canada did not protect it from American legal developments that were calling into question the antitrust status of major league sports (Hinnegan 1969, 234–35). Keenly aware of the possible legal implications, the league and clubs carefully avoided giving recognition to the NHLPA so as not to legitimize it as the collective-bargaining representative for the players. At the same time, they began to exploit the binational nature of the league and develop the jurisdictional ambiguities that the league could use to its advantage.[16]

In the meantime, the players entrenched. Mound said he was willing to use the power of U.S. statute, such as the Wagner Act of 1935, which could push the NHL into formal recognition by allowing the laying of charges before the U.S. National Labor Relations

14. They also asked that the Montreal club pay room and board during training and that no new contracts be offered after September 1. See summary of Evidence of Milton N. Mound, OLRB hearing, November 23, 1957, Archives of Ontario, F223–3–1–98.
15. The authors quote Bill Brennan of the *Detroit News*.
16. The NHL had used its binational status to obtain advantages during the Second World War. See Ross 2015 (ch. 7).

Board (NLRB) (*Globe and Mail* 1957c).[17] In the summer following the 1956–57 season, he proposed specific modifications to the standard player contract: restricting club promotional activities and allowing players to make personal appearances without club permission, providing an automatic salary increase of 15 per cent upon renewal of a contract, arbitrating salaries by a third party (not Campbell), and preventing clubs from compelling Leafs players to execute so-called "loyalty agreements."[18] The latter was a response to Conn Smythe's demands that Leafs players declare their "loyalty" to the club before signing for the 1957–58 season. Another new issue was the treatment of Jim Thomson, to whom Smythe had refused to offer a new playing contract, no doubt because of his position on the NHLPA executive. Mound stressed that if the Thomson situation were not "adjusted to the satisfaction" of the NHLPA, the association would lay charges before the NLRB.[19]

Ian Johnston, the lawyer for Maple Leaf Gardens Ltd., the Leafs owner, worried about what jurisdiction the American NLRB might have over the Canadian clubs. Could the Wagner Act conceivably be used to prevent the Canadian clubs from appearing in the United States for games?[20] The reply of the league's American lawyer, Arthur Friedlund, showed the complexity of applying American law to cross-border labour situations, and to sports organizations. He gave the opinion that the players' association could be certified by the NLRB, but that it was highly unlikely the NLRB would designate the league as the employer instead of the individual clubs. This meant that players on a single club could form a bargaining unit and be recognized as a labour union. He doubted the NLRB would take any action to interfere in a Canadian club's activities in the United States, although he cautioned that the U.S. board did have wide discretionary power and that the league had to tread lightly.[21] If the players' association did petition the NLRB to step in, the league could cloud the issue by arguing that the individual clubs were the proper bargaining unit and that Canadian employees must also be allowed to vote in any certification process.

Congress and the Courts

The NHLPA's big stick was American antitrust law. Not since Teddy Roosevelt's trust-busting crusade at the turn of the century had antitrust been so prominent in public discourse, and the U.S. Congress was being pressured to resolve the issues raised in a series of unsatisfying court decisions over the applicability (or not) of antitrust statutes to sports, specifically in the areas of player rights and television contracts. In *Toolson v. New York Yankees* (1953), "without re-examination of the underlying issues," the Supreme Court had adhered to the *Federal Baseball* precedent and held that baseball was still not subject to antitrust

---

17. See also: Memorandum [to Smythe], February 12, 1957, Archives of Ontario, F223–3–1–92.
18. "Summary of NHL Players' Association Requests as Amplified in Conference with League Attorney, June 14, 1957," Archives of Ontario, F223–3–1–94.
19. J. F. Chisholm to Campbell, July 2, 1957, and Mound to Chisholm, May 17, 1957, Archives of Ontario, F223–3–1–92. Chisholm was the NHL's Canadian solicitor.
20. Campbell to Johnston, July 12, 1957, Archives of Ontario, F223–3–1–95; Campbell to Friedlund, July 12, 1957, Archives of Ontario, F223–3–1–95.
21. Friedlund to Campbell, July 18, 1957, and Friedlund to Campbell, August 6, 1957, Archives of Ontario, F223–3–1–95. Friedlund noted that the situation might be changed due to the recent recognition of the NFL Players Association by the NFL commissioner.

laws.[22] However, in 1955, cracks appeared when boxing was included in the scope of the law after the International Boxing Club monopoly of Jim Norris and Arthur Wirtz (the men also owned the Chicago Black Hawks and New York Rangers and their arenas, Chicago Stadium and Madison Square Garden) came under scrutiny.[23] Two years later—and soon after the NHLPA was formed—football was also denied antitrust exemption by the *Radovich v. National Football League* decision. It did not take much inference to conclude that if football was not protected, then hockey and basketball were not either.[24] It seemed that if the U.S. Supreme Court were to rule, no major league would be safe.

The ball was bounced from court to Congress, which had already dropped it several times before. In 1951, the antitrust subcommittee of the U.S. House of Representatives Committee on the Judiciary, known as the Celler committee after its chairman, Representative Emanuel Celler, had investigated baseball and antitrust following *Gardella v. Chandler* (1948), a lawsuit against Baseball Commissioner Albert "Happy" Chandler for his ban on players who had violated the reserve clause to play in Mexico.[25] After the *Toolson, International Boxing Club*, and *Radovich* cases, Celler once again had the political capital to revisit the issue.

The full economic ambiguities of major-league sport came out during the Celler committee hearings in the summer of 1957. Although hockey was a sideshow to the main events, baseball and football, for the NHL the stakes were just as high, and perhaps higher, since the committee testimony itself might provide an opportunity for the NHLPA to force recognition. When Clarence Campbell was invited to Washington in August to testify, the NHLPA was also asked to attend and present.[26]

Before Campbell had his turn, the committee requested that Norris, a target of the boxing case, appear and discuss the hockey interests of he and the Norris family.[27] Norris

---

22. *George Earl Toolson v. New York Yankees, Inc.* (346 U.S. 356) (1953). McDonald discusses how *Toolson* misrepresented the intent behind the Sherman Act. McDonald (1998, 101–02). On the political background of *Toolson*, see Zimbalist 2003 (19).

23. *United States v. International Boxing Club of New York, Inc., International Boxing Club, Madison Square Garden Corporation, James D. Norris and Arthur M. Wirtz* (348 U.S. 236) (1955). In the absence of legislation after the 1953 *Toolson* decision, Norris and Wirtz appealed the decision against them and the district court reversed it. However, on appeal, the Supreme Court sent the issue back to trial (*U.S. v. International Boxing Club*). In 1959, the matter was again in appeal before the Supreme Court, which upheld the district court's decision to order Norris and Wirtz to divest their Madison Square Garden holdings; *International Boxing Club of New York, et al. v. U.S.*, 358 U.S. 242 (1959).

24. *Radovich v. National Football League et al.* (352 U.S. 445) (1957).

25. *Daniel L. Gardella v. Albert B. Chandler*, 79 F. Supp. 260 (1948).

26. The committee was first interested in hearing about the complicated NHL ownership interests of Jim Norris. The previous weeks had seen testimony from baseball, football, and basketball personalities. U.S. Congress, *Hearings Before the Antitrust Subcommittee of the House Committee on the Judiciary, 85th congress, 1st session, June–August 1957* (Washington, DC, 1957) [hereafter Celler Hearings], 1249, 1931–1932. On the American congressional treatment of sports in general, see Lowe 1995.

27. Report on Hearings Before the U.S. House of Representatives Committee on the Judiciary Concerning the Applicability of Anti-Trust Laws to the Operations of Professional Team Sports, Archives of Ontario, F223–3–1–123 [hereafter Campbell's Report on Anti-Trust Hearings].

testified immediately before Campbell, and the committee members showed a special interest in his multiple ownership of NHL clubs (no doubt seeing the pattern of his boxing monopoly reflected). When Campbell came to the table, he assured the committee that the multiple ownership situation was in the best interests of league stability, and he went on to the hockey business model. He submitted a twenty-three-page prepared statement outlining the history of the game, the organizational structure of the NHL, its relationships with the other major leagues, a description of the pension plan, and the NHL's own legislative recommendations. The committee's assistant counsel, Julian Singman, asked if there was a players' association, and Campbell seemed reluctant to admit it, answering, "I believe so, yes. I am quite certain there is."[28] Would it be recognized by the league? Campbell said that this was up to the owners; his own opinion was that players should have "facilities for making their wants or requirements or grievances known," but that he did not know that it should necessarily be "a group medium."[29] He told Singman that the players' demand for representation (i.e., lawyers) was "one of the obstacles" the league had to meeting with the players directly. When pressed, Campbell agreed that the players had a right to be represented by counsel, but he still doubted "whether their interests in the long run will be better served in that manner than if they speak for themselves."[30] When U.S. Representative Peter Rodino emphasized the right to representation, Campbell argued for the special nature of the sports business: "the problem of when you come to negotiate in an organization where the identity of the player and his interest and that of the owner are so intimate, the intervention of someone who is not a party to our business is sometimes a little irritating." Then, in a comment no doubt directed to the players in the audience, he urged hockey players to think carefully, "because both baseball and basketball have decided that they are better represented by their own people."[31]

Campbell was suggesting that sports like hockey were to be treated differently, and not like businesses in the ordinary sense. The underlying sense he tried to convey is that they were more like families, where problems are usually resolved internally, without interference from the state or skilled intermediaries like lawyers. Taken together, Campbell's answers were a consistent defense of hockey's paternalist model of labour-management relations, where player interest were seen to be best met by owner beneficence, without intermediation.

Campbell went on to discuss the very question of whether hockey should be subject to antitrust law.[32] Campbell the lawyer hedged at first, then admitted: "If you are asking me to interpret the effect of the antitrust laws, I would say I don't see how it can possibly be exempted, frankly." Then Campbell the president of the NHL added that the reserve clause and territorial rights were "absolutely essential to [professional sports'] continuance. I don't see how they can possibly survive if you don't have them…all sports would probably be better off if they were completely exempt from the operation of the antitrust laws." Pierce pursued the backtracking, asking Campbell to explain why the purely business aspects of

28. Celler Hearings, 2988 (see note 36).
29. Celler Hearings, 2990.
30. Celler Hearings, 2992.
31. Celler Hearings, 2992.
32. Celler Hearings, 2994.

professional sports were any different than General Motors or U.S. Steel. Campbell admitted the dissonance: "I think I made that clear that logically I can't defend it."[33] Ironically, given his ambivalence—or perhaps as a self-conscious result of it—Campbell concluded by recommending that, whatever legislation was passed, all sports should be treated equally.[34]

After Campbell, it was the NHLPA's turn to show how the prevailing cultural formation that allowed hockey an implicit exemption from antitrust laws had affected labour relations in hockey. Flanked by Lindsay and Harvey, Lewis & Mound associate James Durante spoke of how hockey had been able to create a reserve clause even more restrictive than baseball's.[35] He made tactful recommendations for change (e.g., that the reserve clause be limited to only five years) and argued for the importance of collective bargaining. Without it, he said, the players had not been able to react to changes in the league's business model, including the new CBS television contract, which Durante understood to pay $20,000 per game (it was actually $10,000).[36]

Singman then addressed Lindsay, inquiring as to the chief purpose of the organizing of the NHLPA. Lindsay replied: "I would say right now to better our pension, for security for ourselves and for our families in the future."[37] The association was not just for the older players, as some had contended, but was "trying to get into the position where we can discuss and receive some of the benefits which we are anticipating through television, radio, et cetera, for our game of hockey." When Singman asked if Lindsay thought NHL owners had an "overpaternalistic view toward their players," as in "papa knows best," and if there was an equal bargaining position when players signed contracts, Lindsay explained the relationship. Players started their careers when young, and while some owners took a sincere interest, "then you reach a certain age where you have to start making decisions for yourself. You have to prepare for the future.... We want to be a little bit independent, you might say, but they still kind of want to hold you under that web, you might say. They would like to." Lindsay added that he had never been able to take his own contract home for review, and had received blank copies of the standard player contract from Campbell, but never an executed one.[38]

Doug Harvey took his turn and showed a conciliatory stance typical of professional athletes. Harvey said he agreed that the reserve clause was necessary, but that there should be free agency after six, eight, or ten years.[39] Asked about the Norris situation, Harvey said that the league was lucky to have Norris, especially if a club like the Black Hawks lost $200,000 a year (the deficit claimed by Jim Norris). Lindsay added that fans and the press often asked him about the Norris situation (i.e., monopolism and corruption), and that he defended them against "skeptics who say they think that isn't right for hockey." The NHL

---

33. Celler Hearings, 2995.
34. Celler Hearings, 2995–96. Campbell also wanted any legislation to be "clear and generous enough so that there is no litigation."
35. Celler Hearings , 2998–3002.
36. Celler Hearings, 3000–03. Durante cited *Radovich*, *International Boxing Club*, and also *U.S. v. Shubert* (348 U.S. 222) (1955), where it had been argued that the principle of baseball's exemption should also apply to theatrical performances.
37. Celler Hearings, 3003.
38. Celler Hearings, 3004.
39. Celler Hearings, 3005.

needed six teams, and Norris, he concluded, "loves hockey so much."[40] Even from Lindsay and Harvey, the leaders of the NHLPA, the deference to owners was striking. After all, how many union leaders ascribed owner motives to "love"?

After returning to Montreal, Campbell reported back to the owners that the testimony of Lindsay and Harvey was "certainly not unfavourable to the present pattern of the operation of hockey." In general, he thought hockey had made a favourable impression and he predicted that the tenor of the hearing suggested an intent to maintain antitrust exemption for the reserve clause and other organizational features, but less likely for the "purely business aspects," like broadcasting. It also seemed likely that the legislation would include a specific guarantee of the right of players to bargain collectively.[41]

If the NHLPA thought the congressional appearance had made the league any more amenable to recognition, it was soon disabused of the idea. While Campbell was personally inclined to talk before players reported to club training camps, at Maple Leafs lawyer Ian Johnston's suggestion the league stonewalled. Durante became exasperated and threatened that unless the NHL undertook to bargain with the NHLPA before September 7, he would recommend the association file "unfair labor charges," and that "any consequences detrimental to Hockey and to you flowing from any action by the Association will be solely your responsibility."[42] The league did not reply, and Campbell warned the owners to be prepared for a statement, "possibly explosive," after the September 7 NHLPA meeting.

There was no detonation, because club actions over the summer had struck preemptively to defuse it. In July, Jack Adams had peremptorily traded Ted Lindsay to the Chicago Black Hawks, after thirteen seasons with the Red Wings, and the next month Smythe sent Thomson to Chicago for cash.[43] It was hard to mistake either the message or the timing of the player moves. Although the relationship between Lindsay and Adams had been deteriorating before the NHLPA challenge, Lindsay was a star player who had led the league in assists for 1956–57, and while Thomson's last two seasons had not been among his best, he was the Leafs captain.[44]

With the league playing hardball, the NHLPA carried out one of its threats and, in September, filed charges of unfair labour practices with the National Labor Relations Board, in New York.[45] Then, on October 10, the association pulled out a big gun and filed suit

---

40. Celler Hearings, 3006.
41. Campbell's Report on Anti-Trust Hearings (see note 37).
42. Durante to Chisholm, August 29, 1957, Archives of Ontario, F223–3–1–94.
43. Campbell to Brown, September 4, 1957, Archives of Ontario, F223–3–1–94.
44. Both Adams and Smythe tried to justify the trades, but the union was clearly the issue. In his memoirs, Smythe admitted (1981, 208) this: "I wanted our captain to be concerned with the Leafs and nothing else…. I traded Thomson to Chicago, bang. Ted Lindsay…was traded to Chicago as well. In a sense, we thus isolated the association." Of the rest of the NHLPA executive, Gus Mortson went to Detroit in September 1958, and Gadsby and Harvey were traded in 1961 (to Detroit and New York, respectively), although by that point the connection to NHLPA activities is far from clear. Flaman remained in Boston.
45. Ivan C. McLeod, Regional Director of the Second Region of NLRB, to Respondents in case No. 2–CA–5558, November 16, 1957, Archives of Ontario, F223–3–1–100. For the discussions on the rights of players to broadcasting revenues, see various letters from September 9 to 13, 1957, in Archives of Ontario, F223–3–1–93, F223–3–1–94.

against the NHL and its member clubs in the U.S. District Court in Massachusetts, alleging violations of the Sherman and Clayton Antitrust Acts.[46] Having thrown down the antitrust gauntlet, the association went all out and pursued legal accreditation as a collective bargaining unit in Ontario, New York, and Massachusetts.[47] These attacks on multiple fronts and across the international border meant that, by Christmas 1957, the NHLPA had five legal actions in play in four jurisdictions in two countries. For its part, the NHL owners remained calm, hiring American lawyers to defend the NLRB and antitrust suits, and discussing ways in which the binational aspect of the league could be used to thwart prosecution and the discourse could be changed to further undermine player solidarity.[48]

"Union"

Even as the NHLPA engaged the NHL in legal arenas, member resolve was starting to weaken. Without Lindsay's leadership, players in Detroit wavered and claimed they had not been consulted before the antitrust lawsuit had been filed. The day after the Ontario union-certification application, Lindsay asked for a meeting with the NHL, at which he promised no one from Lewis & Mound would be present.[49] Seeing this as a sign of weakness, the owners were cool to the proposal.[50] After November 1, when Maple Leaf Gardens Ltd. was officially notified of the NHLPA petition for certification in Ontario, another weapon was made available to shake the players' confidence: the definition of the NHLPA as a trade union.

The main battle between the NHL and NHLPA would be joined in Ontario, where the players' association had applied for Ontario Labour Relations Board (OLRB) certification to legitimize it as the collective bargaining representative for Toronto Maple Leafs players. The players would be represented David Lewis, Canada's most prominent labour lawyer, counsel to the Canadian wing of the United Steelworkers of America, and one of the architects of the recently formed Canadian Labour Congress (and future leader of the federal New Democratic Party). The NHLPA needed his expert help. In any other context, a collective-bargaining representative was commonly known as a trade union, but for the NHLPA it was not that simple. While pursuing a common trade—professional hockey— NHL players were paid different salaries and bonuses, and, by virtue of working conditions,

---

46. Specifically, the antitrust complaint alleged that, prior to and in the year 1926, the "defendants entered into an agreement, combination, and conspiracy to dominate, control, and manipulate for their private profit, the professional hockey industry." Complaint, *National Hockey League Players' Association v. Boston Professional Hockey Association, Inc., et al.*, Archives of Ontario, F223–3–1–96.

47. See: *Globe and Mail* 1957d; Ben Aaronson, Examiner of NYSLRB, Southern Regional Office, New York City [to Respondents], December 5, 1957, Archives of Ontario, F223–3–1–94; Petition for Certification, Boston Professional Hockey Associates, Inc., and National Hockey League Players' Association, Massachusetts Archives, Series LA5 430, Labor Relations Case Files, 1950–1967, box 6, file CR2546. There were also rumours of a Quebec certification application. "Players File Certification Application"; Campbell to Walter Brown, December 20, 1957, Archives of Ontario, F223–3–1–98.

48. Campbell to Friedlund, October 17, 1957, Archives of Ontario, F223–3–1–96; Campbell to Brown, October 17, 1957, Archives of Ontario, F223–3–1–96.

49. Referred to in Campbell to Brown, October 22, 1957, Archives of Ontario, F223–3–1–94.

50. Campbell to Brown, October 22, 1957, Archives of Ontario, F223–3–1–94.

were treated more like independent contractors than employees. This created ambiguity, which the league exploited. The players saw the value in an association to act collectively for pension rights and general employment conditions, but they did not want a union to negotiate their individual salaries, which were performance-based and bonus-laden. Not surprisingly, this ambiguity had not been envisioned by Ontario labour legislation, where a union had full rights to bargain on any issue for its members.[51] The OLRB-certification procedure was simply to hold a public hearing to determine whether the applicant was a trade union, decide the scope of the bargaining unit, and then assess how much support for the application existed in the bargaining unit. The apparent OLRB inflexibility on the question of the definition of a trade union and the prevailing player mentality were ruthlessly exploited by Maple Leaf Gardens management in their argument against certification.

At the first opportunity, Conn Smythe went down to the Maple Leafs dressing room to make his case in person to the players. He put his finger on the sore point, proclaiming that the NHLPA was "a trade union" that, if certified as such, would prevent players from negotiating their own salaries.[52] Hearing this, Tod Sloan called Mound in New York to report that the "boys were confused." Mound said he would come to Toronto immediately. Before he got on the plane, he called reporter Jim Vipond of the Toronto *Globe and Mail* to refute Smythe's allegations and promote the association's position: "When Smythe told the players they were forming a union, that was an untruth" (Vipond 1957). The players' association had no intention of negotiating individual salaries.

The next day, in the Maple Leafs dressing room, players voiced conflicting opinions. Swayed by Smythe's talk the day before, some players thought the association would negotiate individual salaries. Others objected to it being called a "trade union," the term actually used to describe the NHLPA in the OLRB application, but just denied by Mound in his interview with Vipond published in that morning's paper (*Globe and Mail* 1957c)! Mound arrived in person to explain, and afterward the players let in Johnston to present the Gardens position.

Johnston spoke for over an hour on a theme of contrast between the suspicious character of the NHLPA's origins and the owners' clear concern for the welfare of their players.[53] He explained that the governors were "convinced that many of their players did not want to be organized into a Union and that they did not consider membership in the Association as being membership in a Union." As a result, the governors did not want to recognize the association as a union and, in so doing, "[commit] their players to becoming members of a Union whether they wished it or not." He reiterated that the OLRB application was in fact seeking accreditation as a trade union, and since all Leafs players were members of the NHLPA, this would make them union members. The NHLPA was trying "to trick" them by denying that it would negotiate salaries for the players, and Johnston planted the idea that Leafs management would need union permission every time it wanted to pay a bonus. Did the players want their opponents controlling their bonuses? Did they want to strike to

---

51. On the OLRB, see Bromke 1961 (27–31, 51–2*ff*).
52. Summary of Evidence of Tod Sloane [*sic*], OLRB hearing, November 23, 1957, Archives of Ontario, F223-3-1–98.
53. "Re: National Hockey League Player's [*sic*] Association," Archives of Ontario, F223-3-1–97.

support the grievance of a player on another team? Or respect other union's picket lines? Ending his peroration, Johnston recited all the things the owners had done for the players in the past, and would do in future. The implied question was: Who did the players trust more, the Leafs owners or the New York lawyers?

In all, Johnston probably used the word "union" over two dozen times. Unbeknownst to him, Mound had already admitted in his own talk that, under Ontario law, the NHLPA would indeed be considered a trade union, strictly speaking, but the players would still be able to bargain above the minimum salary and could ask the OLRB for the right to do so.[54] While some of the subtleties of these arguments may have been lost on some players, they were unanimous that no one should negotiate salaries on their behalf. When Mound assured them that the OLRB certification could accommodate the need to negotiate individual salaries, all the players signed a copy of the application and Mound wrote a letter to the board, saying it was the "unalterable intention" of the association not to negotiate salaries on behalf of the players.[55]

Failing to convince the players they did not want a union, Maple Leaf Gardens now had to persuade the OLRB that a union could not be had. In its official response to the application for certification, the Gardens made a familiar argument: it denied the NHLPA could be a trade union because the hockey business was "a competitive sport only and that for that reason is not an appropriate field for collective bargaining."[56] Maple Leafs Gardens Ltd. lawyers were making an argument arising from the difficulties in placing hockey in the standard labour-relations model. The line of reasoning was not simply legal casuistry, it was rooted in a cultural view that had been internalized to some degree by the owners, the players themselves, and society at large.

From internal Gardens documents, it is clear that even Conn Smythe made a distinction between a business like Maple Leaf Gardens that could have employees, and a sports team like the Maple Leafs, which was composed of independent contractors with no collective rights. After all, in many respects athletes were very different than wage- or salary-earning employees. They did not expect long careers with the same firm, they did not get paid a standard wage, they could be hired and fired at will, and, not least, they played a game for a living. This ambiguous status supported Smythe's paternalist approach to labour relations; essentially, he saw himself as a father figure who was helping to create businessmen. While professing to have their best interests at heart, he and other NHL owners treated their players as juvenile apprentice businessmen. Yet they also refused the players basic rights that would have been available to independent contractors, for example: the right to change

---

54. Mound's interpretation was disputed at the meeting by another lawyer brought along by one of the Leafs players, who advised the team that while it was true that if the association were certified "it would still be possible to negotiate salaries as a minimum and also salaries in excess of the minimum wage," that limited certification "could not be given." Summary of Evidence of Milton N. Mound, OLRB hearing, November 23, 1957, Archives of Ontario, F223–3–1–98; Johnston to Smythe, November 12, 1957, Archives of Ontario, F223–3–1–97; Johnston to Smythe, March 13, 1958, Archives of Ontario, F223–3–1–93.

55. Summary of Evidence of Milton N. Mound, November 23, 1957, Archives of Ontario, F223–3–1–98; Summary of Evidence of Tod Sloane [sic], OLRB hearing, November 23, 1957, Archives of Ontario, F223–3–1–98.

56. Reply to Application for Certification, Archives of Ontario, F223–3–1–98.

employers, to be represented in negotiations by others, to retain copies of all contracts signed, and even to fraternize with their peers.[57] And the paternalism was effective: even Lindsay, the most militant of the hockey players, had acknowledged some beneficence in the system before the U.S. Congress, a tacit admission that NHL players had internalized the idea that they were not regular employees.[58] And the dominance of this ambiguity spoke directly to the issues bedevilling legislators and jurists in respect of other sports: how could the NHLPA be a union if hockey itself was not a business?

Over the course of the fall of 1957, the importance of the Ontario certification decision to answering this question grew, and the survival of the NHLPA increasingly depended on the answer. In mid-November, Jack Adams succeeded in berating the Lindsay-less Red Wings into pulling out of the NHLPA entirely (*Globe and Mail* 1957f).[59] Then the NLRB refused to assume jurisdiction of the unfair-labour-practices charge and asked the players' association to withdraw it.[60] Just after the new year, there was a third blow: Montreal management met with Canadiens players to sound out their grievances and satisfied them to the extent that, in Doug Harvey's words, "we were all out of the union" from that point on (Brown 2002, 159–160). By the time the OLRB hearing resumed on January 7, the continued existence of the NHLPA was in serious doubt.

Acting in his capacity as NHLPA vice-president, Harvey had actually tried to instruct Mound to drop the OLRB application, but rather than do so Mound had gone to the board to press for a quick decision, and the members agreed to sit into the evening.[61] Over a two-day session, in January, the board heard arguments from the labour lawyer David Lewis about the appropriate bargaining unit, its size, and also whether the NHLPA was indeed a union that could be certified.[62] The OLRB decided that all professional hockey players in the employ of Maple Leaf Gardens Ltd were in the bargaining unit, but reserved judgment on the more important union question, delaying its answer for a written report, expected in late January. Sitting in on the OLRB sessions, Ian Johnston concluded it was "too much to hope" that the board would dismiss the unionization application outright, but he advised Conn Smythe that certification votes by players and possible court challenges gave plenty of opportunity to delay the process for a long time to come. In the meantime,

---

57. For Smythe's views on the subject, which were not always consistent, see Smythe to John R. Robinson, January 9, 1958, Archives of Ontario, F223–3–1–97; Smythe to John Bassett, November 29, 1957, Archives of Ontario, F223–3–1–98; and Smythe to Mrs. Frank Williamson, December 17, 1957, Archives of Ontario, F223–2–3–36.
58. For most NHL players, hockey work was seasonal and many had off-season employment, often in their own businesses, which allowed them flexibility. Lindsay himself was in the plastics business with Red Wings teammates Marty Pavelich and Gordie Howe; see Cruise and Griffiths 1991 (76).
59. Cruise and Griffiths describe (2002, 108–09) the meeting between Adams, owner Bruce Norris, and the Red Wings players.
60. Mound's version for press consumption was that the NHLPA did not want to expose the club owners to the stigma of being declared guilty of unfair labour practices, but the withdrawal was not voluntary. See: *New York Time* 1957; Hulse Hays to Campbell, November 21, 1957, Archives of Ontario, F223–3–1–100.
61. Johnston to Campbell, January 9, 1958, Archives of Ontario, F223–3–1–97.
62. Johnston to Campbell.

he advised that the surest strategy was to continue to push the players to break from Mound and the NHLPA as their representatives.

With the Detroit and Montreal players out, Lindsay agreed to meet directly with Black Hawks owner Jim Norris and let him broker a meeting between the owners and one or two player representatives from each team.[63] The best date for such a meeting would be during the NHL's winter meeting in Palm Beach, Florida, February 3–4, but the OLRB was likely to report before then, and if it certified the association then Mound and the NHLPA had to be a part of any negotiations, at least for Maple Leafs players. So Campbell convinced Doug Harvey and Bert Olmstead of the Canadiens, together with Tod Sloan, to get Lindsay to ask for a delay in the publication of the OLRB decision until after the conference with the owners. Lindsay agreed, and his request was granted.[64]

The players and owners met in the swanky boardroom of the Biltmore Hotel in Palm Beach, just after the league's winter meeting. All the owners attended, as did two player representatives from each team and Lindsay, but no lawyers were allowed, which meant that neither Campbell nor Mound was in the room (*Toronto Daily Star* 1958).[65] Over the course of a thirteen-hour meeting that ended after midnight, the owners agreed to concessions on a range of issues. These included: a new minimum salary of $7,000; the paying of player fines directly into the Players' Emergency Fund; clubs were to match player pension contributions dollar for dollar so that players would be guaranteed $5,100 annually at age sixty-five; an increase in the playoff money pool so that Stanley Cup–winning players received $4,000 each; increased hospitalization benefits; limits on the number of exhibition games; reimbursement of moving expenses; a promise to conduct an independent survey of the pension plan with a view to improving it; and agreement that a player would be the sole judge of his own fitness to play (O'Meara 1958b). Last, the owners agreed to form an owner-player council for ongoing mutual consultation. In return for these considerations, the players would drop all pending union-certification applications and the antitrust action.[66] By May, all the legal actions had been dropped. With them, the role of Lewis & Mound was over and the first NHLPA was history.[67]

---

63. Lindsay to Norris, January 17, 1958, Archives of Ontario, F223–3–1–97. This meeting was to be "entirely without prejudice to litigation or labour petitions presently in existence."

64. Madeleine McDonald to Smythe, January 16, 1958, Archives of Ontario, F223–2–4–27. McDonald was Smythe's secretary.

65. All the owners attended, and the players were represented by two representatives from each team, plus Lindsay. "Joint Statement Issued on Results of Owner-Player Conference at Palm Beach […]," February 4, 1958, Archives of Ontario, F223–3–1–93.

66. "Joint Statement Issued on Results of Owner-Player Conference at Palm Beach […]," February 4, 1958, Archives of Ontario, F223–3–1–93. In a familiar pattern, the owner-player council had been borrowed from baseball.

67. The MSLRB dismissed the application at Mound's request in March. Mound to Labor Relations Commission, February 28, 1958; and Harry P. Grages, Chairman of MSLRB, to Boston Professional Hockey Associates, Inc., March 3, 1958; both in Massachusetts Archives, Series LA5 430, Labor Relations Case Files, 1950–1967, Box 6, File CR2546. The U.S. antitrust action was dismissed in May, as was the NYSLRB application.

The End

The owners also held up their end of the bargain, and were happy to do so. In truth, their compromises were relatively few, as most of the concessions were no more than confirmations of existing practices. First of all, the $7,000 minimum salary they demanded was already an unwritten policy of the league.[68] The diversion of player fines into the Players' Emergency Fund, instead of into general league revenues as before, seemed at face value to be in the players' interest, but the payouts to players from the fund had always exceeded the amount of fines imposed anyway, and the league had actually made up the difference from its own revenues.[69] The fact that the players did not know this spoke once again to the poor communication between players and owners. Furthermore, the pension concessions—which addressed an initial *casus belli*—would not be a direct cost to the clubs but would be, as before, mainly funded by the all-star game and playoff surcharges, and the clubs were only liable for a relatively small top-up to match the player contributions dollar for dollar. And the changes made to the existing standard player contract were relatively minor.[70] Even the creation of the owner-player council was an easy concession to make if it killed the NHLPA, and while it provided an official forum for discussion, it had no binding authority over league or club policies. Finally, broadcasting revenues, which had driven the whole affair, were left in the owner's pockets, untouched. These revenues grew from about $500,000 to $1.4 million over the next eight seasons, a period in which gate receipts rose only 80 per cent and player salaries as a portion of gate revenues fell from 27 per cent to 23 per cent (Ross 2008, app. III, VII). The failure of the NHLPA meant that not only had the players failed to benefit from the new revenues, but, in fact, their economic position had weakened.

In the end, NHL players had little to show for their rebellion. Even the communication problem remained. Over the ensuing seasons, the owner-player council did not meet regularly and the cowed players even stopped bothering to ask questions. Paternalism had prevailed. It was not until 1967 that the idea of a union once again gained currency, and a second NHLPA was successfully established and certified, spurred by the impending doubling of the league in the 1967–68 season. That NHLPA endured (Ross 2008, 560–61).

Despite its failure, the first NHLPA provides a compelling narrative in the story of postwar athlete labour organization. It was the only stillborn postwar major-league-athlete collective-bargaining efforts—the NBAPA, NFLPA, and the MLBPA all survived their early years. That the NHLPA was the only association having to deal with members and employers spread over an international border was a congenital defect that was central to its fatality.

---

68. This may have been admitted during the meeting itself. See: O'Meara 1958a, 1958b; Campbell to Smythe, February 8, 1958, Archives of Ontario, F223–3–1–93. Staudohar notes (1996, 148) that hockey's minimum salary was $500 above baseball's.

69. Re: Players Emergency Fund, Statement of Revenue and Expenditures for the Year Ended 30th April 1960, Archives of Ontario, F223–3–1–121.

70. The clubs agreed to pay players a pro-rated share of gate receipts for any exhibition games played after the season started; to pay the players their "proper share" of clause 8 activities (television revenues); to pay to return the players home after the season; and to allow the players to be the sole judge of their own fitness to play. Revised Draft Amendments to Standard Player's Contract Concerning Matters Agreed Upon at Owner-Player Conferences on Feb. 4th and June 3, 1958, Archives of Ontario, F223–3–1–105.

Yet even more fundamental to the NHLPA's failure in 1958 was the issue that was common to them all—whether players were labourers, and whether they could thus form a trade union. Embedded as they were in a postwar cultural moment that defined major-league sports as paradoxically both commercial and non-commercial, a business and a cultural activity, it is not surprising that players felt uneasy locating themselves wholly within either, and the owners were able to use this cultural ambiguity to circumscribe labour autonomy. For its part, the league appealed to the bonds of loyalty and tradition as justifications for retaining the existing economic structure of labour-management relations, long after mainstream industries had accepted the legitimacy of formal, union-led collective-bargaining arrangements.[71]

In other industries, the push to collective bargaining had been forced by legislative statute, but this pressure was noticeably weaker in sports, especially ones like hockey that straddled several jurisdictions.[72] State and federal legislation and regulation were either deemed incompatible or seemed inapplicable. This is evident in the repeated failed attempts by the U.S. Congress to apply antitrust law, leaving the courts to do so in a patchwork manner, and the difficulty labour-relations boards had in accepting sports labour as being subject to trade-union law. In Ontario, where the issues had a chance to be aired, the certification criteria (e.g., interpreting "trade union") seemed ill-equipped to accommodate the specialized nature of athletic employment, where collective salary bargaining was anathema to a pay-for-performance culture. The owners preyed on this, but it also conformed to a general understanding. Players saw the benefits of organizing into an "association" for general work conditions and common benefits, like a pension, but a "trade union" implied fixed wages and seniority perquisites, and these possibilities were actively resisted. Confusing players further, the NHLPA proposed to represent them before the league in group issues such as the pension, but not before the clubs in individual issues such as salary negotiations. Not only were the players not always clear on this, but state and provincial labour boards could not necessarily accommodate this flexibility either (the OLRB might have done so; others likely would not have). Furthermore, even if the NHLPA had been certified in Ontario, the association may have been isolated there—representing players from only one team in a six-team league. Once again, this highlights the obstacles faced in establishing an effective union for a labour force paid by six separate employers in six jurisdictions across an international border.

If the NHL players could not define and reconcile their cultural and business identities, neither the owners nor the state would do so on their behalf. If the failure of the NHLPA had shown anything, it was that unless the players could balance competition and cooperation among themselves and present their common interests as a group—as their employers had learned to do—they would have to continue to trust others to do it on their behalf.

---

71. The National Labor Relations Act (Wagner Act) of 1935 had signaled the sea change in this regard.
72. Staudohar notes (1996, 142) that the state's influence in hockey is less significant than in other sports.

Bibliography

Alito, Jr., Samuel A. 2009. "The Origin of the Baseball Antitrust Exemption: Federal Baseball Club of Baltimore, Inc. v. National League of Professional Baseball Clubs." *Journal of Supreme Court History* 34 (2): 183–95.

Bromke, Adam. 1961. *The Labour Relations Board in Ontario: A Study of the Administrative Tribunal*. Montreal: Industrial Relations Centre, McGill University.

Brown, William. 2002. *Doug: The Doug Harvey Story*. Montreal: Véhicule Press.

Condon, David. 1957. "Pro Football Minimum Wage Deal Approved," *Chicago Daily Tribune*, December 3, C2.

Cruise, David, and Allison Griffiths. 1991. *Net Worth: Exploding the Myths of Pro Hockey*. Toronto: Viking.

Globe and Mail. 1956. "CBS to Televise Ten NHL Games; Dates Announced," July 3, 22.

———. 1957a. "NHL Players' Association Formed, Wings' Ted Lindsay is President," February 12, 21.

———. 1957b. Ted Kennedy Reveals He's Lone NHL Player Not in New Association," February 12, 21.

———. 1957c. "Brass Reacts to NHL Group With Surprise and Caution," February 12, 21.

———. 1957d. "Players File Certification Application," November 5, 16.

———. 1957e. "Maple Leafs to Vote on Group," November 5, 16.

———. 1957f. "Red Wings Quit Players Group," November 13, 1957, 19.

Hockey News. 1953. October 3.

Hinnegan, K. A. 1969. "The 'Services Exemption' under the Combines Investigation Act." *The University of Toronto Law Journal* 19 (2): 234–35.

Korr, Charles P. 2002. *The End of Baseball as We Knew It: The Players Union 1960–81*. Urbana: University of Illinois Press.

Lamoreaux, Naomi, Daniel G. Raff, and Peter Temin. 2003. "Beyond Markets and Hierarchies: Toward a New Synthesis of American Business History." *American Historical Review* 108:419–20.

Lipset, Seymour Martin, and Noah M. Meltz. 2004. *The Paradox of American Unionism: Why Americans Like Unions More than Canadians Do, but Join Much Less*. Ithaca, NY: Cornell University Press.

Lowe, Stephen R. 1995. *The Kid on the Sandlot: Congress and Professional Sports, 1910–1992*. Bowling Green, OH: Popular Press.

Macleod, Rex. 1956. "NHL Stars Tie With Habs," *Globe and Mail*, October 10, 19.

McDonald, Kevin. 1998. "Antitrust and Baseball: Stealing Holmes." *Journal of Supreme Court History* 2:89–128.

Moriarty, Tim. 1953. "NHL Pension Plan Success Realized By Fine Teamwork," *Globe and Mail*, December 23, 15.

O'Meara, Baz. 1956. "Wings' Hall Emerges Outstanding Star as All-Stars Play Deadlock with Canucks," *Montreal Daily Star*, October 10, 54.

———. 1958a. "The Passing Sport Show" *Montreal Daily Star*, February 5, 34

———. 1958b. "NHL Players Agree to Withdraw Lawsuits," *Montreal Daily Star*, February 5, 34.

New York Times. 1956. "Player Pensions Rise in Baseball," August 21, 23.

———. 1957. "Unfair Labor Practice Charge Withdrawn by Hockey Players," November 20, 47.

Roberts, Gary R. 1991. Professional Sports and the Antitrust Laws. In *The Business of Professional Sports*, ed. Paul Staudohar and James A. Mangan. Urbana: University of Illinois Press.

Ross, James Andrew. 2008. "Hockey Capital: Commerce, Culture and the National Hockey League, 1917–1967." PhD diss., University of Western Ontario.

———. 2015. *Joining the Clubs: The Business of the National Hockey League to 1945*. Syracuse, NY: Syracuse University Press.

Smythe, Conn, with Scott Young. 1981. *Conn Smythe: If You Can't Beat 'Em in the Alley*. Toronto: McClelland and Stewart.

Staudohar, Paul D. 1996. *Playing for Dollars: Labor Relations and the Sports Business*. Ithaca, NY: Cornell University Press.

Toronto Daily Star. 1956. "Blake Sees 1–All Draw as Needed Spur to his Champion Habs," October 10, 17.

———. 1957. "See TV as Spark For NHL Players' Union," February 12, 12.

———. 1958. "Drop All Hockey Litigation," February 5, 16, 19.

Vipond, Jim. 1957. "Intimidation by Smythe is Charged," *Globe and Mail*, November 5, 16.

Zimbalist, Andrew S. 2003. *May the Best Team Win: Baseball Economics and Public Policy*. Washington, DC: Brookings Institution.

Legal citations

Federal Base Ball Club of Baltimore, Inc. v. National League of Professional Base Ball Clubs et al., 259 U.S. 200 (1922).

Daniel L. Gardella v. Albert B. Chandler, 79 F. Supp. 260 (1948).

George Earl Toolson v. New York Yankees, Inc. (346 U.S. 356) (1953).

United States v. International Boxing Club of New York, Inc., International Boxing Club, Madison Square Garden Corporation, James D. Norris and Arthur M. Wirtz (348 U.S. 236) (1955).

U.S. v. Shubert (348 U.S. 222) (1955).

Radovich v. National Football League et al. (352 U.S. 445) (1957).

International Boxing Club of New York, et al. v. U.S., 358 U.S. 242 (1959).

Chapitre 14
Eric Lindros et les Nordiques de Québec: deux solitudes[1] ?

L<small>AURENT</small> T<small>URCOT</small>

En cette fin de saison 1999-2000 de la LNH, les Flyers de Philadelphie arrivent premiers dans l'Association de l'Est, ce qui permet aux joueurs d'espérer enfin remporter la coupe Stanley. L'équipe est menée par son capitaine, Eric Lindros, qui a réalisé une saison de 27 buts et de 32 passes en 55 matchs, le grand attaquant ayant manqué plusieurs parties en raison de blessures diverses. Cette récolte est moins bonne que les 93 points qu'il a obtenus l'année précédente, mais cela n'a pas empêché les Flyers de se hisser jusqu'à la finale de l'Association de l'Est et demi-finale de la coupe Stanley, face aux Devils du New Jersey et à leur redoutable gardien Martin Brodeur. Le 26 mai 2000, lors du septième et ultime match, Eric Lindros est en uniforme, mais ne jouera que deux minutes cinq secondes. Le puissant attaquant franchit la ligne bleue et s'enfonce dans le camp adverse, baisse la tête pour contrôler la rondelle, mais n'a pas le temps ou l'occasion de voir arriver en trombe Scott Stevens. Le joueur des Devils assène alors une violente mise en échec à l'attaquant des Flyers en le frappant à la tête avec son épaule. «C'était une mise en échec légale […]» (*La Presse*, 2000), dira plus tard l'entraîneur des Flyers Craig Ramsay. À la suite de ce coup, qu'il soit légal ou non, la tête de Lindros tombe lourdement sur la glace. C'est sans doute sa sixième commotion cérébrale — sa quatrième en l'espace de cinq mois, soulignent les commentateurs sportifs —, et peut-être même la fin de sa carrière. Pour certains, sa valeur marchande vient de chuter brusquement…

La veille, dans le journal *Le Soleil* de Québec, on pouvait lire : «Qu'on l'aime ou non, qu'on le veuille ou non, Eric Lindros est tout un joueur de hockey et, malgré tout ce qu'on a pu dire à son sujet, les Flyers doivent se réjouir de pouvoir compter sur lui pour le septième match de la finale de l'Association de l'Est, ce soir, contre les Devils du New Jersey.» (*Le Soleil*, 2000) Le ton est assez froid, distant, bien loin de celui que les journalistes de ce même journal utilisaient neuf ans auparavant, d'où le fameux «qu'on le veuille ou non». Cette formule fait directement référence à un événement qui a marqué durablement les relations entre les amateurs de hockey de Québec, à l'époque partisans des Nordiques, et le jeune Eric Lindros. En 1991 et en 1992, l'«affaire Lindros» avait défrayé la chronique, plaçant le jeune hockeyeur au centre d'une tourmente. De nombreux commentateurs s'étaient

---

1. L'auteur tient à remercier Michel Vigneault, André Martineau, Mathieu Beauchamp, Caroline Morin et Jacques Beauchamp.

empressés de parler des deux solitudes canadiennes, vécues ici entre une ville francophone et un attaquant anglophone qui ne voulait pas y jouer. Les données du problème semblent simples, mais tout un contexte a alimenté cet épisode. Il ne s'agissait pas que de politique, mais aussi de la place des petits marchés dans une ligue sportive aux salaires surdimensionnés et de la question de la liberté de choisir des joueurs. Que s'est-il passé en 1991 et en 1992?

Certes, l'affaire Eric Lindros doit être replacée dans un contexte singulier, mais on ne saura penser la chose sans faire référence à l'importance symbolique (Turcot, 2016) — culturelle, sociale et politique — qu'a le hockey au Canada, et plus spécifiquement au Québec. Richard Gruneau et David Whitson ont su montrer comment le nationalisme, tant anglophone que francophone, prend appui sur le hockey pour construire un univers mental référentiel pratique (Gruneau et Whitson, 1993 ; Howell, 2011). Benoît Melançon a, de son côté, su montrer que le jeu dépasse la patinoire pour s'incarner dans des devenirs politiques et une identité collective[2]. L'identité canadienne, aux dires de plusieurs historiens (Conacher, 1970 ; Kidd et Macfarlane, 1972), passe en partie par le hockey, vecteur rassembleur, mais aussi événement qui cristallise les tensions linguistiques, politiques et sociales. L'émeute du Forum en 1955 ne serait qu'un épisode d'une longue séquence qui fait du hockey « *more than just a game* ». L'affaire Lindros est donc à considérer dans le contexte brossé par ces historiens, tout comme les méthodes d'analyse employées dans le présent texte, soit l'étude systématique d'articles de journaux (Ramos et Gosine, 2002), pour comprendre les représentations des différentes péripéties entourant les Nordiques de Québec et Eric Lindros.

Un jeune prodige

En 1988-1989, avant même d'être un grand espoir de la LNH, Eric Lindros faisait déjà tourner bien des têtes. Il jouait pour les St. Michael's Buzzers de la Metro Toronto Junior « B » Hockey League. À 15 ans, il est parvenu à marquer 24 buts et à obtenir 67 points, mais aussi à accumuler 193 minutes de pénalité au cours des 37 parties qui lui ont permis d'amener son équipe à remporter la Sutherland Cup, faisant des Buzzers les champions provinciaux. À 16 ans, il devient admissible au repêchage junior de la Ligue de hockey de l'Ontario (LHO) (Ontario Hockey League [OHL]). Les premiers à choisir sont les Greyhounds de Sault-Sainte-Marie, dont l'un des propriétaires, Phil Esposito, s'était promis de repêcher Lindros, comme il l'avait fait avec un certain Wayne Gretzky en 1977. Or, les parents d'Eric n'entendent pas voir leur fils trop s'éloigner du domicile familial, Sault-Sainte-Marie étant à sept heures de voiture de Toronto. On signifie alors aux Greyhounds qu'Eric ne jouerait pas pour eux. Refusant de passer à côté de ce talent pur, l'équipe le repêche malgré les récriminations de la famille Lindros. La réponse est sans appel : le fils refuse de se présenter et se joint à la North American Hockey League pour jouer avec les Compuware Ambassadors de Detroit lors de la saison 1989-1990. Devant le refus de ce qui apparaît de plus en plus comme le « clan Lindros », les Greyhounds se résignent et échangent le jeune prodige aux Generals d'Oshawa contre trois joueurs, trois futurs choix de repêchage ainsi que 80 000 dollars. Cette année-là, Lindros mènera les Generals aux grands honneurs en leur permettant de remporter la coupe Memorial. Lors des passages des Generals à Sault-Sainte-Marie pour affronter les Greyhounds, les partisans de ces derniers s'en donnent à cœur joie, lançant insultes et moqueries à celui qui n'a pas voulu joindre leurs rangs.

---

2. Voir à ce sujet Melançon, 2006 ; Bauer, 2011 ; Guay, 1990 ; Vigneault, 2001 ; Lévesque, 2014.

Certains brandissent même des suces, associant le colosse de six pieds quatre pouces et de 230 livres à un bébé. L'année suivante, en 1990-1991, Lindros marque 71 buts et amasse 149 points en 57 matchs dans la LHO, en plus d'être couronné meilleur joueur junior au pays. Mais l'équipe s'incline en six matchs contre deux devant les Greyhounds en finale : un juste retour des choses, diront les partisans de Sault-Sainte-Marie. Cependant, cette déception est de courte durée, car Lindros sait qu'il sera admissible au repêchage de la LNH au printemps 1991. L'équipe qui semble se diriger vers le premier choix est alors les Nordiques de Québec, équipe qui avait d'ailleurs réclamé le premier choix en 1989 (Mats Sundin) et en 1990 (Owen Nolan). Malgré quelques joueurs de talent dont Joe Sakic et certains autres qui brilleront plus tard, comme Valeri Kamensky, l'équipe a le triste honneur d'être, pour la troisième année de suite, dernière au classement.

La direction des Nordiques de Québec annonce rapidement ses couleurs. Elle entend bien repêcher et recruter Eric Lindros, celui qu'on surnommera bientôt « *The Next One* », en référence à Wayne Gretzky, « *The Great One* ». L'entraîneur et directeur général des Nordiques Pierre Pagé, mais plus encore le propriétaire Marcel Aubut, entendent signer un contrat avec celui qui se présente comme un joueur d'organisation, voire un joueur de ligue. On prend alors pour exemple les Penguins de Pittsburgh : ils attiraient environ 7 000 spectateurs par match en 1983-1984, tandis qu'après avoir réussi à recruter Mario Lemieux, leur premier choix au repêchage, cette moyenne avait augmenté à 15 000 spectateurs, assurant par le fait même le destin de l'organisation dans la ville. Lors du repêchage de 1984, qui se déroulait au Forum de Montréal, les Penguins avaient pris soin d'annoncer leur choix en français pour attirer celui qui évoluait dans la LHJMQ chez les Voisins de Laval. Le geste n'avait pas semblé toucher Lemieux, qui avait refusé de descendre serrer la main des propriétaires et de mettre le chandail : « *I'm not going to put on the sweater if they don't want me bad enough* », s'était confié l'attaquant au micro des journalistes venus l'interroger sur son attitude (O'Shei, 2002, 36). Quelques semaines plus tard, avec un contrat de 700 000 $ sur deux ans, le plus lucratif pour une recrue dans la LNH, Lemieux s'était ravisé, avait mis le chandail des Penguins et était devenu le grand joueur qu'on avait vu en lui. Cette histoire risquait-elle de se reproduire ? Les velléités du clan Lindros à s'associer à Sault-Sainte-Marie se répéteraient-elles à Québec avec les Nordiques ?

Le repêchage de 1991

Au début des années 1990, la ville de Québec est loin de constituer un pôle d'attraction économique. Avec ses quelque 460 000 habitants, elle connaît un taux de chômage de 9,7 %, alors qu'il est de 12,1 % dans la province et de 9,8 % au pays (Ville de Québec, 2016). La ville compte certes quelques grandes entreprises, mais, contrairement à Montréal (une métropole de 3,1 millions d'habitants), elle a peu de sièges sociaux d'importance, comme ceux de la Maison Simons et de Familiprix. À l'époque, Québec n'est pas la seule ville de ce genre dans la LNH. Mentionnons Hartford (Connecticut), qui compte près de 140 000 habitants en 1990, ou encore Winnipeg (Manitoba), où vivent un peu plus de 600 000 âmes. D'ailleurs, toutes verront leur équipe professionnelle de hockey déménager au cours des années suivantes : en 1995 pour les Nordiques, en 1996 pour les Jets de Winnipeg et en 1997 pour les Whalers de Hartford. Avant cette grande vague de transferts, la pression économique qui repose sur les équipes évoluant dans ce qu'on appelle alors les « petits marchés » est de plus en plus grande. Les salaires explosent depuis la fin des années

1970. Les joueurs sont soutenus par une organisation de plus en plus spécialisée dans la négociation. Leurs agents entendent obtenir le maximum d'argent pour ces sportifs dont les carrières professionnelles durent de cinq à dix ans, voire quinze, pour les plus talentueux. Parallèlement, pour soutenir la course aux revenus, les propriétaires veulent rénover les arénas dans lesquels évoluent les équipes. Ce mouvement n'est pas nouveau. Dans les années 1960, les municipalités américaines étaient nombreuses à vouloir une équipe professionnelle et c'était par la construction de stades aux frais des contribuables que l'on tâchait d'attirer les investisseurs (Turcot, 2016). Au baseball, l'Astrodome de Houston avait coûté près de 30 millions de dollars au début des années 1960 et son toit rétractable, qui sera construit cinq ans plus tard, coûtera déjà plus de 45 millions. Le prix du Louisiana Superdome, qui avait été inauguré en août 1975 et qui pouvait alors accueillir 74 000 spectateurs, s'était élevé à 300 millions de dollars, de sorte que les contribuables de la Louisiane devaient s'acquitter d'une facture annuelle de huit millions de dollars. De 1960 à 1980, les gouvernements croyaient nécessaire ce type d'investissements pour les équipes sportives. Dans les années 1980, des 28 équipes constituant la NFL, 26 évoluaient dans des arénas appartenant à la ville ou à l'État (Rader, 1996, 224-225). Cette course contre la montre pour engranger le plus d'argent possible se terminera pour la LNH lors de la saison 2004-2005. À la suite d'un lock-out, on réussira alors à imposer un plafond salarial pour les joueurs de hockey et à ainsi contrôler un peu mieux les dépenses dans ce secteur.

En 1991, le jour du repêchage, nous sommes loin de ces considérations. Il faut avoir les meilleurs joueurs, et pour les attirer et les retenir, on doit leur verser le salaire le plus élevé. Pour la petite ville de Québec, qui fait face à des mégamarchés comme New York, Los Angeles, Chicago ou Washington, le combat est inégal, et le clan Lindros a vite compris que Québec n'a pas et n'aura jamais l'étoffe pour rivaliser avec ces grandes métropoles. Il n'est pas question de victoire sur le plan sportif, mais bien sur le plan des affaires — entendons ici les contrats publicitaires. Carl Lindros, le père d'Eric, comptable sur Bay Street à Toronto, a bien compris la chose.

C'est à Buffalo, le 22 juin 1991, que doit se tenir le repêchage de la LNH. Depuis quelque temps déjà, les Nordiques et Marcel Aubut savent qu'ils ont le premier choix. Eric Lindros apparaît comme le seul choix possible pour cette organisation qui peine à décoller des bas-fonds du classement de la ligue. À Toronto, à quelque 150 km de l'endroit où se déroulera le repêchage et où siège le clan Lindros, la délégation des Nordiques établit ses quartiers pour discuter avec le jeune prodige. Plusieurs rencontres se déroulent, mais aucune ne semble aller dans le sens voulu par Marcel Aubut. Le 15 juin, ce dernier fait venir en renfort le «démon blond», Guy Lafleur, qui vient tout juste de prendre sa retraite sous le maillot des Nordiques. De longues ovations avaient été réservées, à Montréal comme à Québec, à celui qui avait remporté 5 coupes Stanley et passé 17 saisons dans la ligue. Aubut entend se servir de son charisme, mais surtout de l'admiration qu'ont les Lindros pour Lafleur, pour faire pencher la balance du côté des Nordiques. Lors d'une entrevue accordée au journal *Le Soleil* le 14 novembre 1993, Lafleur racontera : «Quand je suis arrivé sur les lieux, je l'ai compris tout de suite, les Nordiques n'avaient aucune chance.» Plus encore, il affirmera :

> Par la suite, on m'a raconté un incident qui se serait produit au cours d'une réunion précédente et qui aurait créé un froid insurmontable. Au moment d'une discussion,

> Aubut aurait échappé une réflexion en français à l'intention de son entourage sans se douter que Bonnie comprend le français. Une réflexion que maman Lindros aurait saisie et qu'elle aurait jugée déplaisante (Hachey, 2015).

Cette version semble véridique, d'autant plus que deux jours auparavant, Bonnie avait déclaré que son fils ne jouerait jamais pour les Nordiques s'ils le repêchaient. Une autre version est celle de Réjean Tremblay, qui affirmera en 2016 :

> Lindros était un géant de six pieds et quatre pouces, mais il était terrorisé par madame. Et Aubut avait piqué une grosse frite dans l'assiette de Bonnie à Buffalo, la veille du repêchage, et elle le détestait. Y avait rien à faire, les frites étaient cuites (Tremblay, 2016).

À ce moment, plus personne ne sait ce qui peut arriver. Eric Lindros a même le choix de refuser le repêchage, ce qui ferait perdre aux Nordiques leur choix de première ronde. Pour ceux-ci, il est hors de question de se résigner. Le président de la ligue John Ziegler, accompagné de Marcel Aubut, de Pierre Pagé et de Guy Lafleur, travaille d'arrache-pied pour éviter l'humiliation d'un refus de repêchage. Rien n'y fait, les Lindros ne bronchent pas. Eric ne veut pas négocier. Le 22 juin, le ciel est gris à Buffalo quand Pierre Pagé se lève pour annoncer le choix des Nordiques. Tous les regards sont braqués sur Lindros. Refusera-t-il d'être repêché ? À l'annonce, celui-ci se lève, un sourire se dessine sur son visage et il se dirige vers l'état-major des Nordiques. Quelques partisans qui ont fait le déplacement applaudissent le jeune joueur. Interviewé avant même de se rendre à la table des Nordiques, il affirme que c'est un honneur d'être repêché en premier, n'évoquant à aucun moment l'équipe de Québec. Devant Pierre Pagé, il prend le chandail qui a été floqué à son nom, mais, contrairement à la tradition, refuse de le porter. Il serre les mains qui lui sont tendues et prend les photos d'usage avant de redescendre de la scène. Les commentateurs sportifs s'interrogent alors : acceptera-t-il ? Marcel Aubut commente la situation : « Il reste maintenant à tout faire pour le [recruter] et on va passer une bonne partie de l'été à faire ce travail-là. » (Radio-Canada, 2016). Pierre Pagé, lui aussi interrogé, affirme qu'il n'a jamais eu l'intention d'échanger son choix de première ronde, comme il n'avait pas eu l'intention d'échanger Mats Sundin ou Owen Nolan les années précédentes.

Un dossier qui se politise

L'effervescence du repêchage passée, le vrai travail commence pour les Nordiques. Réussiront-ils à faire signer un contrat professionnel à Eric Lindros ? Certes, ils ont réussi à éviter l'humiliation du refus de repêchage, mais éviteront-ils celle du refus du joueur de signer un contrat avec les Nordiques ? On connaît bien l'histoire du repêchage de Sault-Saint-Marie, mais personne, chez les Nordiques, ne pense que le scénario se répétera. « C'est une équipe professionnelle », affirment certains. « Ce n'est plus le hockey junior », soutiennent d'autres. L'été 1991 est relativement calme. On « laisse le temps au temps ». Les amateurs de hockey se préparent à profiter de la Coupe Canada qui, du 31 août au 16 septembre 1991, permettra aux meilleurs joueurs du Canada, des États-Unis, de l'URSS, de la Finlande, de la Suède et de la Tchécoslovaquie de s'affronter pour déterminer la meilleure équipe nationale. Toronto, Pittsburgh, Hamilton, Montréal, Chicago et… Québec sont parmi les villes choisies pour accueillir des matchs du tournoi. Alan Eagleson, responsable d'Équipe Canada, décide d'inviter Eric Lindros au camp d'entraînement. Plusieurs lui reprochent de laisser une chance à un joueur qui n'a pas joué un match dans la LNH. Eagleson répond en rappelant qu'il avait fait une erreur, en 1984, en n'invitant pas Mario Lemieux, qui était dans la même situation que Lindros à l'été 1991. Contre toute attente, Eric Lindros réussit à être sélectionné dans l'équipe canadienne, aux côtés de joueurs établis comme Wayne Gretzky, Mark Messier, Paul Coffey et Luc Robitaille.

Le 1er septembre, au lendemain du premier match d'Équipe Canada, auquel a participé Lindros, son agent Rick Curran avise les Nordiques que son client jouera à Oshawa, dans la ligue junior, si Québec refuse de l'échanger. La nouvelle paraît rapidement dans les journaux et ce qui était jusqu'ici un affrontement entre le clan Lindros et l'organisation des Nordiques prendra des proportions qui dépassent le débat purement sportif. Du point de vue sportif, les règles sont claires : si le joueur retourne dans la ligue junior, les Nordiques ont deux ans pour lui faire signer un contrat. Ce délai monte à quatre ans s'il joue en Europe. Rien ne presse. Cependant, le 9 septembre, Eric Lindros et Équipe Canada sont à Québec pour un match les opposant à l'URSS, que la chute du mur de Berlin en 1989 n'a pas encore fait éclater, bien que la dislocation ait commencé en 1990. Le monde qui s'ouvre est neuf, le capitalisme a gagné. À Québec, on se prépare à accueillir le jeune Lindros. Philippe Cantin, du journal *La Presse*, résume bien la situation :

> Le clan Lindros attend avec impatience le match URSS-Canada, présenté lundi pro-chain au Colisée de Québec. Rien ne ferait plus plaisir à maman Bonnie, papa Carl et fiston qu'Eric soit hué à pleins poumons par les fans des Nordiques. Ils auraient ainsi une nouvelle raison de dire non aux Bleus. (Cantin, 1991)

L'affaire Lindros défraie la chronique. On critique l'attitude du joueur, de son agent et de ses parents. Les journalistes francophones comme Claude Larochelle (*Le Soleil*), Claude Bédard (*Journal de Québec*) ou Bertrand Raymond (*Journal de Montréal*) s'en donnent à cœur joie. On s'interroge sur les raisons qui poussent le jeune hockeyeur à refuser de jouer à Québec. On avance l'argument économique, rappelant la difficulté qu'aurait Lindros de trouver des commanditaires s'il jouait à Québec, mais pour certains, il y a plus. Lindros ne fait rien pour aider son cas quand il affirme que trois raisons expliquent son refus de jouer à Québec : les taxes, la taille de la ville et la langue. Sa mère aurait même affirmé à Bertrand Raymond que Québec devrait se pourvoir d'une université anglophone pour que son fils pense peut-être signer un contrat avec les Nordiques (cette rumeur s'est par la suite révélée fausse (Houston, 1991)).

Alors qu'il est à Montréal, le 7 septembre 1991, on demande à Lindros s'il accepterait d'y jouer. Il répond : « Probablement… », mais nuance rapidement son propos : « Entre Québec et Montréal, il y a autant de différence qu'entre le noir et le blanc. » Pour le reste, Lindros est aussi positif à l'endroit de Québec qu'un dépliant touristique quand il affirme qu'elle est « une belle ville à visiter, une belle ville pour sortir… Je n'ai rien contre les francophones, j'aime la culture française, elle donne de la diversité au Canada ». Il poursuit toutefois : « Québec est une ville où je ne veux pas m'établir » (Cantin, 1991). Guy

Carbonneau, capitaine des Canadiens de Montréal, estime que le fameux numéro 88 est allé trop loin dans ses déclarations: «Je suis québécois, je vis ici et je n'aime pas la façon dont Lindros s'y prend», déclare-t-il en ce même jour de septembre 1991. Il enchaîne: «Il a niaisé le monde et ce n'est pas correct» (Cantin, 1991). À la populaire chaîne de radio CHRC de Québec, l'animateur et commentateur sportif Marc Simoneau demande à ses auditeurs d'accueillir Lindros en héros, mieux, de lui réserver une ovation.

Lors du match, Lindros est hué plus qu'il n'est applaudi. Le grand 88 trouve le moyen de marquer le premier but du Canada. C'est assez pour semer la confusion. Doit-on acclamer le but ou huer son auteur? On préfère acclamer. Le lendemain, Réjean Tremblay écrit dans *La Presse*:

> Ce devait être une soirée explosive. Les réseaux de télévision de tout le Canada étaient sur place. Les animateurs de tribunes téléphoniques menaient des sondages pour savoir si les Québécois hueraient ou applaudiraient Eric Lindros. On parlait de fierté, de dignité. On aurait dû parler d'ennui. [...] Les Québécois avaient préparé quelques pancartes pour Eric. Comme dans un film quand le réalisateur veut mettre du visuel à l'écran. Rien de bien méchant. Quelques «Bienvenue Eric» et deux ou trois attaques un tantinet méchantes contre maman Lindros et son «bébé Eric» (Tremblay, 1991).

Plusieurs garderont longtemps en mémoire les suces géantes brandies par quelques amateurs. Serge Chapleau, caricaturiste de *La Presse,* immortalisera la chose (Figure 14.1).

En refusant de signer un contrat avec les Nordiques de Québec, Eric Lindros invoque sa «liberté de choix». Sa croisade est appuyée par de grands joueurs comme Wayne Gretzky et Steve Yzerman. À Québec, le cas Lindros en énerve plusieurs, jusqu'à l'Office du tourisme, qui commence à le trouver moins drôle. Le refus de Lindros de jouer à Québec ternit l'image de la ville au point qu'il devient un peu plus difficile de la vendre aux touristes. Le 9 septembre, Alliance Québec, un groupe qui défend les droits des anglophones au Québec, prend acte de «la réticence de certains sportifs canadiens, comme le jeune hockeyeur Eric Lindros, à s'établir au Québec» et entendent former «[d']ici trois semaines un groupe de travail qui aura la tâche d'évaluer les opportunités d'embauche dans le secteur privé pour les jeunes anglophones québécois» (*La Presse*, 1991). Le dossier ne cesse de se politiser. Le premier ministre du Canada Brian Mulroney, originaire de Baie-Comeau et député de Charlevoix, déclare: «Je comprends mal l'attitude de Lindros, dans le monde, il y a des villes beaucoup moins agréables que Québec, cela je vous l'assure.» Ce à quoi Lindros répond: «Il me semblait que le pays vivait une récession et qu'il y avait des problèmes plus importants que ceux d'un joueur de hockey? C'est une farce!» (Blanchard, 1991)

Si Eric Lindros a raison de ne considérer son histoire qu'à travers le prisme sportif, il oublie de tenir compte du fait que son cas s'inscrit dans une époque de tensions qui opposent le gouvernement fédéral aux forces souverainistes québécoises. Depuis le référendum de 1980, le fédéral avait adopté un *statu quo* en matière constitutionnelle. Le gouvernement conservateur de Brian Mulroney considérait la situation comme étant intenable, d'où l'Accord du lac Meech, négocié en 1987, qui prévoyait entre autres la reconnaissance du Québec comme société distincte au sein du Canada. L'échéance pour la ratification de l'Accord par les provinces avait été fixée à juin 1990. L'opposition avait été forte et l'Accord

Figure 14.1 Eric Lindros, 1991
Caricature de Serge Chapleau
Aquaralle et graphite sur papier
Musée McCord, M996.10.552

a échoué en cette même année. Un vent de nationalisme soufflait sur le Québec, surtout après que Robert Bourassa, premier ministre du Québec, ait déclaré à l'Assemblée nationale le 22 juin 1990 : « Le Canada anglais doit comprendre de façon très claire que, quoi qu'on dise et quoi qu'on fasse, le Québec est, aujourd'hui et pour toujours, une société distincte, libre et capable d'assumer son destin et son développement. » (Monière, 2001, 125) En coulisse, on se préparait, dans un camp comme dans l'autre, à une contre-offensive. Ce sera, dans un premier temps, l'Accord de Charlottetown, rejeté en 1992, et le référendum au Québec, qui se soldera par un refus de l'indépendance en 1995. L'atmosphère qui entoure le cas Lindros cristallise alors les tensions politiques entourant la réforme de la constitution, mais plus encore la possible séparation du Québec. Plusieurs affirment que le jeune Ontarien ne veut pas se retrouver dans une province qui risque de se séparer du Canada. Les propos d'Eric Lindros, comme son refus d'endosser le chandail des Nordiques, apparaissent comme une insulte. Ainsi, le journaliste Claude Bédard donne ce titre à son article du 29 septembre 1991 dans le *Journal de Québec*: «La famille Lindros devrait au moins nous respecter». Le *nous* identitaire, chargé du contexte politique, traduit bien le ressentiment face à un autre, le Canadien anglais, qui refuse d'accepter le Québec tel qu'il est. Réjean Tremblay, en décembre 1991, résume:

> Il faudrait expliquer aux Américains que le fait de voir Eric Lindros dans l'uniforme des Nordiques n'a rien à voir avec l'unité nationale. Et que ça ne changerait rien à la politique de Jacques Parizeau. […] Mais tant que le Québec fera partie du Canada, et tant que le Canada voudra à tout prix exister comme il est présentement, alors ce pays de mal-aimés devra adorer une idole qui a craché son mépris sur ce qui est l'essence même des Québécois. (Tremblay, 1991)

Les deux solitudes semblent vouloir s'incarner de manière puissante dans un narratif du *nous* et de l'*autre* bien trempé. N'en déplaise à Eric Lindros, il ne semble pas qu'il soit ici uniquement question de hockey.

De leur côté, les médias anglophones sont plus mesurés (Ransom, 2014, 73-77). Certains s'attaquent à l'attrait de l'argent qui dévore le clan Lindros:

> *As a proud Canadian, I am very disappointed in the attitudes of such hockey talents as Eric Lindros and Steve Yzerman. After honing their skills in our country on rinks built and maintained with our tax dollars, they are now fattening their bank accounts by avoiding Canadian taxes and moving to the States. Greed!* (Vennema, 1991)

Pour d'autres, il est aisé de faire d'Eric Lindros le bouc émissaire de toutes les tensions politiques: «*And there is always a temptation in the entire province to turn issues into a them-against-us morality play, which in this instance puts Mr. Lindros in the role of [an] English-speaking devil.*» (Simpson, 1991) D'autres encore poussent plus loin l'interprétation en replaçant l'épisode dans la lutte des Québécois pour l'affirmation de leurs droits:

> *Ontarians must now realize that Quebecers want to be their equal partners in this country. Quebecers want recognition, particularly from their economically impressive neighbors, for what they have themselves accomplished. They want to be respected for who they are, not treated just as farmers (or dirty frogs) anymore. Our farming industry has revolutionized and Quebec farmers are now well educated, [shrewd] business entrepreneurs. This, as I see it, is the main problem. Even adolescents like Eric Lindros think that we are still a dirty bunch of frogs.* (Riverin, 1992) (Figure 14.2)

Ils sont cependant plusieurs à relever qu'il ne s'agit pas tant d'une affaire politique que d'une affaire de gros sous. C'est ainsi le cas des journalistes Stephen George et Arnold Keller du *Toronto Globe*: «*Is this 19-year-old athlete just so much meat, or does he have the democratic right to sell his services to the highest bidder?*» (George, 1991). Pourtant, le vernis économique

Figure 14.2 Conseil de Brian Mulroney à Eric Lindros, 1991
Aislin (alias Terry Mosher),
Encre, feutre et pigment blanc opaque sur papier
Musée McCord, M998.48.18

que certains tentent d'apporter à leur argument craque sous la pression du contexte politique :

> *The market dictates that Mr. Lindros is worth a certain amount, he should be free to maximize his earnings in whatever location he finds agreeable. It is farcicle [sic] that so many French-speaking Quebeckers (and a number of self-flagellating English-speaking Canadians) are whining because one individual does not want to work in Quebec. Hundreds of thousands of English-speaking former residents of Quebec would have been content to remain in their native province had it not become so difficult for them to work there. No matter how perfectly they mastered the*

French language, they would never be accepted as members of the so-called "distinct society" with
which Mr. Simpson and his like are so enamoured. (Prendergast, 1991; Simpson, 1991)

L'échange

À partir de septembre 1991, la situation semble bloquée pour de bon. Eric Lindros ne veut
pas jouer pour Québec et demande à être échangé, tandis que l'organisation des Nordiques
ne veut pas entendre parler d'échange. Après la victoire canadienne contre les États-Unis
lors de la Coupe Canada à Hamilton le 16 septembre 1991, Lindros retourne dans la ligue
junior. Rien ne presse pour personne. Marcel Aubut a deux ans devant lui pour recruter
son jeune prodige. Le 22 septembre, ce dernier retrouve la glace d'Oshawa, mais souscrit
auparavant à une assurance vie pour cinq millions de dollars. Le 14 octobre, alors que les
Nordiques enchaînent défaite par-dessus défaite, Marcel Aubut revient à la charge avec une
première option de contrat qui aurait valu à Lindros 55 millions de dollars pour 10 ans. Il
n'aurait pas reçu 5,5 millions par saison pendant dix ans, mais aurait plutôt été rémunéré
sur une longue période. Dans les milieux bien informés, on affirme que son salaire aurait
été étalé sur une période de 25 à 30 ans. Marcel Aubut, à mots à demi couverts, aurait
presque confirmé à des journalistes du *Soleil* que les Nordiques avaient promis à Lindros
de l'échanger s'il les menait à la coupe Stanley. L'offre est alléchante, mais le clan Lindros
ne bronche pas. «Je veux amorcer ma carrière dans une ville où je voudrai passer au moins
15 ans. Je ne veux pas jouer là-bas», dit le principal intéressé en conférence de presse le
2 octobre 1991 (Hachey, 2015).

Le 24 octobre, Lindros rejoint l'équipe canadienne de hockey junior, puis intègre
l'équipe olympique qui représentera le pays à Albertville. Marcel Aubut se rend en France.
Il espère toujours le recruter. Certaines rumeurs rapportent qu'Aubut en aurait profité pour
isoler Carl Lindros, le père, qu'il croyait trop dominé par le choix catégorique de la mère
de ne pas voir son fils évoluer à Québec: «Les deux [Carl et Eric] avaient une peur bleue
de Bonnie», affirmera Réjean Tremblay (Tremblay, 2016). Si l'anecdote est vraie, il n'en
reste pas moins que le résultat est un échec (Bussières, 2016). L'équipe canadienne remporte
l'argent. Peu à peu, Marcel Aubut, mais aussi toute l'organisation des Nordiques, doit se
rendre à l'évidence: Eric Lindros ne jouera pas à Québec. De l'espoir, on passe à la rési-
gnation. Pas question cependant d'aller vite en affaires. On laisse passer la date limite des
transactions pour la saison à venir, soit le 10 mars 1992. Malgré le mauvais rendement de
l'équipe, elle n'obtient que le quatrième choix de première ronde. Cette année là, le repêchage se déroule à Montréal, et Aubut réserve tout un étage d'un hôtel. C'est le terrain où
se déroulent les négociations de ce qui prend l'allure d'un encan. Aubut négocie avec six
équipes en même temps.

Le 20 juin 1992, les Rangers, puis les Flyers, affirment avoir conclu une entente. Dans
les deux cas, l'échange est impressionnant. Les Rangers proposent Doug Weight, Tony
Amonte, Alex Kovalev, le gardien John Vanbiesbrouck, trois choix de premier tour et 12 millions de dollars. Quant à eux, les Flyers offrent Peter Forsberg, Ron Hextall, Steve Duchesne,
Mike Ricci, Chris Simon, Kerry Huffman, deux choix de premier tour (qui deviendront
Jocelyn Thibault et Nolan Baumgartner) et 15 millions de dollars. À la fin de la journée,
personne ne sait qui a les droits sur Eric Lindros. Il faut nommer un arbitre, Larry Bertuzzi,
pour déterminer qui peut négocier avec le joueur. Après deux jours, le verdict tombe:

Eric Lindros appartient aux Flyers. En juin 1992, la saga Eric Lindros se termine à Québec et les Nordiques en sortiront vite gagnants. Lors de la saison 1992-1993, ils amasseront 104 points, soit le double de la saison précédente. Il s'agira de l'un des rebondissements les plus importants dans l'histoire de la LNH. En 1995, Forsberg récoltera 47 points en 50 matchs, une collecte qui lui méritera le titre de recrue de l'année dans le circuit. Hextall sera ensuite échangé contre Mark Fitzpatrick, qui à son tour changera d'adresse en échange d'un choix de première ronde, lequel deviendra Adam Deadmarsh, un futur Olympien américain. En 1995, les Nordiques déménageront au Colorado. Patrick Roy sera acquis en échange de Jocelyn Thibault et en 1996, l'Avalanche remportera la coupe Stanley. Les joueurs impliqués dans l'échange d'Eric Lindros auront grandement contribué à cette réussite. En 2001, ils ajouteront une autre coupe Stanley à leur palmarès. Eric Lindros, lui, comptera 85 buts au cours de ses deux premières saisons avec les Flyers. Il sera le cinquième joueur le plus rapide à atteindre le sommet des 500 points.

★★★

En novembre 2016, le Temple de la renommée du hockey a ouvert ses portes à l'ancien numéro 88, qui a passé sa carrière à Philadelphie, à New York, à Toronto et à Dallas. Lindros a inscrit 865 points en 760 rencontres dans la LNH, mais a aussi raté quelque 300 matchs en raison de diverses blessures, dont de sévères commotions cérébrales qui en ont même fait un cas d'école pour des médecins œuvrant dans le domaine (Echemendia et Julian, 2001, 69-88 ; Cusimano *et al.*, 2013). Encore aujourd'hui, plusieurs s'interrogent sur les raisons qui ont motivé le clan Lindros à refuser catégoriquement qu'il joue pour les Nordiques. Le principal intéressé a eu l'occasion d'aborder la question, notamment en 2014, à l'émission *L'antichambre* du réseau RDS :

> Ça n'avait rien à voir avec la culture francophone. J'ai marié une francophone ! C'était une question de respect de la part de l'organisation, et c'était lié à la direction qu'elle prenait. […] C'était uniquement une décision de hockey et d'affaires. Quand j'y repense maintenant, je suis certain que c'était une décision basée sur le hockey. C'était mon point de vue. L'équipe est maintenant au Colorado et, ironiquement, elle a commencé à avoir du succès quand elle a déménagé là-bas (RDS, 2014).

En 2016, Pierre Pagé ajoutait :

> Depuis l'âge de 8 ans, ses parents savaient qu'ils avaient une vedette entre les mains et ils voulaient aller dans un gros marché. Et ils voulaient gagner. En fait, Québec a gagné au Colorado. […] On lui avait offert 50 millions de dollars. [Mario] Lemieux gagnait 2,5 millions de dollars par année. Et Lindros, il gagnait 3,5 millions de dollars à Philadelphie. On lui avait offert 5 millions de dollars par année pour 10 ans (Agence QMI, 2016).

Un événement a fait réapparaître le dossier Lindros. En septembre 2015, une plainte pour harcèlement sexuel était déposée contre Marcel Aubut. Le 3 octobre de la même année, celui-ci démissionnait de son poste de président du Comité olympique canadien. Quelques jours plus tard, la journaliste de *La Presse* Isabelle Hachey révélait dans un dossier en quatre parties («La chute d'un conquérant», «Le *self-made man*», «Le négociateur» et «Le bulldozer») plusieurs aspects de la carrière houleuse de l'ancien propriétaire des Nordiques, notamment le fait que c'est surtout un conflit de personnalités entre Marcel Aubut et le clan Lindros qui aurait bloqué la route de Québec. Dernièrement, interrogé par le réseau ESPN, Eric Lindros abondait dans le même sens : «La décision de ne pas jouer pour Québec a été prise seulement en raison du propriétaire.» (Agence QMI, 2016)

Il est fort possible que tout cela n'ait été qu'un conflit de personnalités, mais le contexte politique, social et culturel dans lequel baignait la ligue, la province et le hockey ne pouvait que teinter le débat de ce qu'on a appelé l'«affaire Lindros». En 1992, peu de temps après l'échange, le journaliste Daniel Poulin a fait paraître un livre dont le titre à lui seul faisait figure de programme : *L'affaire Lindros — dossier complexe et peu reluisant* (Poulin, 1992). La préface est signée par l'acteur Carl Marotte, qui interprétait le rôle de Pierre Lambert, joueur vedette de l'équipe fictive du National de Québec dans la populaire série télévisée *Lance et compte*, créée par Réjean Tremblay et Louis Caron. Marotte écrivait alors :

> Le débat dépasse de beaucoup Eric Lindros et sa famille. Leur répugnance à vouloir s'associer aux Nordiques et à la ville de Québec découle de l'ignorance crasse et de la peur… Je ne voudrais pas être dans ses souliers pour tout l'or du monde.

Daniel Poulin allait encore plus loin dans les dernières lignes de son livre. Il écrivait qu'Eric Lindros était né un 28 février, tout comme un certain Louis Joseph, marquis de Montcalm, commandant des troupes françaises lors de leur défaite sur les plaines d'Abraham en 1759. Le parallèle ne s'arrêtait pas là :

> Son adversaire, ce jour fatidique, est né la première semaine de janvier 1727, nous apprennent les manuels d'histoire. Officiellement, Wolfe fut le vainqueur de Montcalm, même s'il fut mortellement blessé au cours du combat. Comme par hasard, Marcel Aubut est né le 5 janvier.

Voici comment se concluait le livre. De la glace du Colisée à la bataille des Plaines, pour Daniel Poulin, il n'y avait qu'un pas à franchir. L'historien, plus prudent, y verra plutôt la perpétuelle volonté de faire disparaître le passé tout en faisant de ce dernier un moteur de l'action politique. La portée symbolique du refus d'Eric Lindros est à inscrire dans le vaste débat identitaire et souverainiste qui s'était dessiné dans le Québec des années 1990 et permet de comprendre un peu mieux les tensions qui ont défini les positions politiques dans le Canada post-lac Meech et préréférendaire.

Bibliographie

Agence QMI. 2016. «Le 88 à l'honneur». *Canoe.ca,* 11 novembre. [http://fr.canoe.ca/sports/nouvelles/hockey/lnh/archives/2016/11/20161111-193816.html].

———. 2016. « "Sans l'échange de Lindros, l'équipe qui a déménagé au Colorado n'aurait jamais remporté la coupe Stanley" — Pierre Pagé ». *Journal de Montréal,* 14 novembre. [http://www.

journaldemontreal.com/2016/11/14/sans-lechange-de-lindros-lequipe-qui-a-demenage-au-colorado-naurait-jamais-remporte-la-coupe-stanley---pierre-page].

Aucun auteur. 2000. *La Presse*, mai, G3.

Aucun auteur. 2000. *Le Soleil*, 26 mai, D3.

Aucun auteur. 1991. *La Presse*, 9 septembre.

Bauer, Olivier. 2011. *Une théologie du Canadien de Montréal*. Montréal : Bayard.

Bédard, Claude. 1991. «La famille Lindros devrait au moins nous respecter». *Journal de Québec*, 29 septembre.

Blanchard, Michel. 1991. «Le bluff d'Eric Lindros». *La Presse*, 5 septembre.

Bussières, Ian. 2016. «Lindros en avait contre Aubut». *Le Soleil*, 27 juin.

Cantin, Philippe. 1991. «Lindros, un sauveur incapable de sauver?». *La Presse*, 4 septembre.

———. 1991. «Insulte suprême aux gens de Québec». *La Presse*, 8 septembre.

Conacher, Brian. 1970. *Hockey in Canada : The Way It Is !* Louisville : Gateway Press.

Cusimano, Michael D., Sharma, Bhanu, Lawrence, David W., Ilie, Gabriela, Silverberg, Sarah et Rochelle Jones. 2013. «Trends in North American newspaper reporting of brain injury in ice hockey». *PLoS ONE* 8 (4) : p. e61865. doi : 10.1371/journal. pone.0061865.

Echemendia, R.J. et L.J. Julian. 2001. «Mild traumatic brain injury in sports : Neuropsychology's contribution to a developing field». *Neuropsychology Review* 11 (2) : 69-88.

George, Stephen. 1991. «Right to choose». *Toronto Globe*, 14 septembre, D7.

Gruneau, Richard et David Whitson. 1993. *Hockey Night in Canada: Sports, Identities, and Cultural Politics*. Toronto : Garamond Press.

Guay, Donald. 1990. *L'histoire du hockey au Québec : origines et développement d'un phénomène culturel*. Chicoutimi : Éditions JCL.

Hachey, Isabelle. 2015. «Le négociateur». *La Presse*, 8 octobre.

Houston, William. 1991. «Truth & Rumours». *Toronto Globe*, 20 septembre.

Howell, Colin. 2011. *Blood, Sweat, and Cheers : Sport and the Making of Modern Canada*. Toronto : University of Toronto Press.

Kidd, Bruce et John Macfarlane. 1972. *The Death of Hockey*. Toronto : New Press.

Lévesque, Jean. 2014. «Hockey et politique : jalons pour une historiographie raisonnée». *Bulletin d'histoire politique* 22 (2) : 33-52.

Melançon, Benoit. 2006. *Les yeux de Maurice Richard : une histoire culturelle*. Montréal : Fides.

Monière, Denis. 2001. *Pour comprendre le nationalisme au Québec et ailleurs*. Montréal : Presses de l'Université de Montréal.

O'Shei, Tim. 2002. *Mario Lemieux : Overcoming Adversity*. Philadelphie : Chelsea House Publishers.

Poulin, Daniel. 1992. *L'affaire Lindros : dossier complexe et peu reluisant*, Montréal : Guy Saint-Jean Éditeur.

Prendergast, Hugh. 1991. «Jeff Simpson must be trying to boost his readership». *Toronto Globe*, 28 décembre, D7.

Rader, Benjamin G. (1983) 1996. *American Sports : From the Age of Folk Games to the Age of Televised Sports*. New Jersey : Prentice Hall.

Radio-Canada. 2016. «Affaire Lindros : le refus à tout prix de jouer pour les Nordiques». *Aujourd'hui l'histoire*, 4 novembre. [http://ici.radio-canada.ca/emissions/aujourd_hui_l_histoire/2016-2017/chronique.asp?idChronique=42086]. Consulté le 16 juillet 2017.

Ramos, Howard et Kevin Gosine. 2002. «"The Rocket": Newspaper coverage of the death of a Québec cultural icon, a Canadian hockey player». *Journal of Canadian Studies* 36 (4) : 9-31.

Ransom, Amy J. 2014. *Hockey, PQ: Canada's Game in Quebec's Popular Culture*. Toronto : University of Toronto.

RDS. 2014. «Aucun regret». *L'antichambre*, 7 octobre. [http://www.rds.ca/hockey/aucun-regret-1.1399817].

Riverin, Bruno. 1992. «Quebecers want to be equal partners with Ontarians». *Toronto Star,* 8 février.

Simpson, Jeff. 1991. «Let's say it's cold in Winnipeg, so Lindros won't put on his skates». *Toronto Globe,* 19 décembre.

Tremblay, Réjean. 1991. *La Presse,* 10 septembre.

———. 1991. «Pas du respect, du mépris!». *La Presse,* 12 décembre.

——— —. 2016. «Eric Lindros : honneur mérité». *Journal de Montréal,* 28 juin.

———. 2016. «Le Temple de M. Lindros». *Journal de Montréal,* 15 novembre.

Turcot, Laurent. 2016. *Sports et loisirs : une histoire des origines à nos jours.* Paris : Gallimard.

Vennema, Alan G. 1991. «Players U.S. moves motivated by greed». *Toronto Star,* 27 août.

Vigneault, Michel (2001). *La naissance d'un sport organisé au Canada : le hockey à Montréal, 1875-1917* (Thèse de doctorat). Consultée au https://www.collectionscanada.gc.ca/obj/s4/f2/dsk3/ftp05/NQ65438.pdf.

Ville de Québec. 2016. «*Profil sociodémographique de la ville de Québec,* sur le site du *Service de l'aménagement du territoire, Division de l'urbanisme.*» Ville de Québec, Québec.

Chapter 15
Whiteness and Hockey in Canada: Lessons from Semi-Structured Interviews with Retired Professional Players

Nathan Kalman-Lamb

Recent literature about hockey has productively noted the association between whiteness, hockey, and Canadian national identity (e.g., Abdel-Shehid 2000; Robidoux 2002; Adams 2006; Allain 2008; Norman 2014). In this chapter, I will build on these discussions of hockey, whiteness, and Canadian identity in two ways. First, they will be framed in the context of the nation's prevailing multicultural discourse. Second, I will then proceed to examine how race has been understood by retired Canadian professional hockey players as a simultaneous presence and absence, an ambivalence I argue can be understood as emblematic of Canadian identity. This chapter locates hockey and Canadian identity in the context of multicultural discourse, revealing the tenacity of whiteness as an organizing and dehumanizing category in Canadian hockey culture through the testimony of those who have lived it. This is, I believe, a crucial endeavour because it exposes the disingenuousness of national claims of racial and cultural equity and plurality that function as much to erase structural racism as to mitigate it. Hockey is Canadian identity, and, as such, its failure to accommodate racial otherness reveals the hollow core of the limited-in-its-own-way Canadian liberal multicultural project.

Canada, Multiculturalism, and Whiteness

In the last five decades, Canada has increasingly—and officially—fashioned a multicultural identity for itself through state policy and legislation that emphasizes nominal pluralism through notions of inclusion and toleration. While this multicultural turn has been praised by liberal theorists (e.g., Taylor 1994; Kymlicka 1995), others have framed it as a political strategy to undermine movements for structural change and equity through rhetoric and tokenism (Bannerji 2000). This is because liberalism privileges formal legal and rhetorical equality over the structural equity demanded by anti-racist and anti-capitalist scholars and activists. Liberal doctrine calls for negative rights, such as protections against legal and representational discrimination (hate crimes and hate speech, for instance), but does little to remedy structural conditions such as racialized poverty, for example, through the provision of some form of positive rights that might involve redistribution of wealth and/or power.

Indeed, as I have argued in the past about the Canadian Charter of Rights and Freedoms of 1992 and the Multiculturalism Act of 1988, "despite the rather grandiose rhetoric around equality that…saturates the Charter, the Multiculturalism Act does not lay out any legal or policy obligations upon the state whatsoever" (Kalman-Lamb 2013, 242). For these reasons, multicultural policy and rhetoric can be read as pragmatic moves by the state to retain legitimacy in the context of a global politics increasingly attuned to histories of colonialism. Multiculturalism thus allows the Canadian state to frame itself as a site of cosmopolitanism representative of a globalizing world (Thobani 2007), and confers legitimacy to a state that has its own (legally and politically ongoing) colonial history (Kalman-Lamb 2012). While Canada can rightly be understood as a project of settler colonialism that has wrought centuries of violence upon Indigenous peoples, it is instead perceived through the lens of multiculturalism to be the diverse home of immigrants from around the world: a microcosm for globalization itself. The same multicultural policy and discourse also neatly mask the state's reliance upon a current political economy significantly underwritten by officially sanctioned racialized migrant labour (Sharma 2006). That is, despite liberal claims to equality and protection under the law for Canadian citizens, non-citizens are routinely and systematically brought into the country in order to provide some of the most arduous forms of labour that the political economy demands, such as agricultural work (Basok 2002), yet do not receive the same protections as citizens. Indeed, Eve Haque has convincingly argued (2012, 24) that multiculturalism neatly masks the racialization of labour exploitation by "severing the immigrant body from its labour by designating them 'cultural groups.'" Thus, multiculturalism produces a liberal illusion of parity between diverse cultures in Canada, masking the very real power differentials that exist between whiteness and its multicultures, power differentials that have everything to do with who has access to privileged forms of labour and capital and who is subject to exploitation. This is just one way in which liberal multicultural discourse obfuscates persistent racialized exploitation.

One mechanism the Canadian multicultural project has come to rely on in order to engender consent is the figure of the model minority subject (Kalman-Lamb 2013). The model minority subject is a non-white figure who is celebrated for successfully approximating the prevailing hegemonic norms of whiteness, patriarchy, capitalism, and heteronormativity (Dhamoon 2009). This figure serves a dual purpose. On one hand, they reassure white subjects who fear that an influx of non-white people will overwhelm and absorb "their" identity; that, in fact, non-white people do not pose a threat to white cultural hegemony but will instead work to reproduce it. On the other hand, the model minority simultaneously disciplines non-white subjects by representing to them how they must act in order to be tolerated by the dominant culture (Kalman-Lamb 2013). In these ways, the model minority as a representational construct symbolically instructs Canadians on how to navigate the uncertain terrain of multiculturalism. This is a particularly critical role given the necessity of racialized migrant labour to the political economy of Canada (Sharma 2006).

Sport, Race, and Whiteness in Canada

I have argued that the athlete functions as a particularly important embodiment of the model minority because of the tremendous popularity of sport as a contemporary form of popular culture (Kalman-Lamb 2013, 2015). In order to satisfy the requirements of liberal multiculturalism, in their role as representational figures, most non-white athletes in Canada are compelled to walk the thin line between hero and outcast, model minority and abject failure. There are always two sides to this coin, precisely because precarity exists at the heart of model minorityhood. The non-white subject is never unimpeachably Canadian but, rather, teeters on the brink of symbolic expulsion from the nation through public excoriation. In recent years, prominent athletes in Canada have become more adept at managing this tenuous status, building on the travails of their predecessors. Thus, current Major League Baseball and recent Toronto Blue Jays slugger José Bautista was embraced in Toronto in ways that his much-reviled Dominican compatriot, 1987 American League MVP and member of the Blue Jays during the 1980s, George Bell was not (Kalman-Lamb 2013). Similarly, 1996 Olympic gold medallist (and then-world-record-holder) Donovan Bailey was able to learn from the popular disavowal of his fellow Canadian sprinter of Jamaican descent Ben Johnson, who was infamously stripped of his 1988 hundred-metre Olympic gold medal because he tested positive for the banned steroid stanozolol and subsequently subjected to the ire of the Canadian media (Abdel-Shehid 2005). Despite the complications of this precarious subject position, because of the way that the model minority legitimizes a political economy predicated on migrant labour, there has consistently been a place in nearly all Canadian sport in recent years, particularly high-profile Canadian sport, for athletes who embody the strictures of model minorityhood. All, but one, that is.

Now, before I return to the question of sport, I should acknowledge that the very role of the model minority subject is premised on the fact that multiculturalism as a discourse exists in large part to disguise that, at its core, Canadian identity remains hegemonically white (Mackey 2002). This is a fact that is only laid bare in moments and contexts when the stakes of identity are highest and most personal. One such example was the opening ceremonies of the Vancouver Olympics, in which Canada had the opportunity to present its identity to the world (Kalman-Lamb 2012). What it dramatized was a narrative of white cultural ascendancy legitimized by indigeneity. Indigenous peoples were figured as founders of the Canadian nation who passed the torch of ownership to European settlers. Non-Indigenous, non-white Canadians, and the very notion of multiculturalism itself, were suddenly little more than an afterthought, barely present in any form during this spectacle of national identity.

Similarly, there is one sport that Canadians as a nation have come to prize and associate their identity with above all others: hockey. We need look no further than the testimony of long-serving Canadian Prime Minister Stephen Harper as evidence of this point. In an interview with *Sports Illustrated*, Harper articulated his understanding of the significance of hockey to the Canadian nation through a comparison to baseball in the United States:

> Although there are important sports in Canada—our own football, lacrosse—nothing does compete with hockey. It's on a different plane, to the extent where, rightly or wrongly, people see these sports as deeply reflective of the character of the nation [and] certainly deeply reflective of the sports culture of the nation. And sports culture is an important part of any nation. You can say soccer in many countries [is] just as important but...nobody has a national claim to soccer the way Canada has a national claim to

hockey or the United States has a national claim to baseball. They define the country in a unique way. (Farber 2010)

Central to this passage is Harper's assertion that hockey is "deeply reflective of the character of the nation." Hockey *is* Canadian national identity. Likewise, in his examination of popular Canadian writing about hockey, Gamal Abdel-Shehid quotes (2000, 73) from two path-breaking texts on hockey in Canadian culture, revealing that both present the sport as an essential aspect of Canadian identity:

> Ken Dryden and Roy MacGregor begin their book, *Home Game* (1989: 9), in the following way: "Hockey is part of life in Canada. Thousands play it, millions follow it, and millions more surely try their best to ignore it altogether. But if they do, their disregard must be purposeful, done in conscious escape.... In Canada, hockey is one of winter's expectations," (1989: 9). According to Bruce Kidd and John MacFarlane: "hockey captures the essence of the Canadian experience in the New World. In a land so inescapably cold, hockey is the dance of life, an affirmation that despite the deathly chill of winter we are alive," (1973:4).

For Dryden and MacGregor, hockey is inescapably lodged in the Canadian consciousness. For Kidd and MacFarlane, it is representative of a shared (settler) experience. Both see it is a fundamental aspect of Canadian identity. This framing of hockey as essentially Canadian is crucial when we consider who is permitted or tolerated on the ice. In his book *Breaking the Ice*, Cecil Harris (2003) demonstrates racism is a near-universal reality for Black professional hockey players. In other words, hockey, "the essence of the Canadian experience," is in fact the essence of the *white* Canadian experience.

In the world of professional and semi-professional hockey in Canada, there is little space for the figure of the model minority, because there is little space for non-white subjects of any kind. Canadian hockey is an arena for the unapologetically naked rehearsal of hegemonic whiteness that persists at the heart of Canadian national identity (akin to what Ghassan Hage [2000] has called the "white nation fantasy"). Whiteness, in this context, should be understood to be a shifting socially constructed but structurally and culturally concretized category of power and privilege that is largely invisible in cultural discourse, even as it exists at the heart of ideas about what an "authentic" Canadian identity is, and in relation to which multicultures exist as perpetual outsiders, albeit outsiders tenuously allowed in.

Although the existing literature on race and hockey in Canada is far from exhaustive, research in this area does convincingly document the pervasiveness of racism in Canada's favoured pastime. Harris provides the most thorough empirical study of racism in hockey in *Breaking the Ice*, interviewing an extensive list of current and retired Black National Hockey League players, as well as an assortment of teammates, coaches, journalists, family members, and others, in order to create a portrait of the Black experience in professional hockey. What he found was that "Each black player...has to wage a personal battle for acceptance and respect.... Facing abuse that is verbal, physical or psychological because of their color has been an unfortunate reality for almost all of them" (Harris 2003, 14). Racism in hockey is not confined to the ice. Stacy Lorenz and Rod Murray (2014) argue that, using the case study of former NHL and Ottawa Senators goaltender Ray Emery, non-white, particularly Black, players in professional hockey are subject to excessive regulation and discipline by institutional structures like teams. They additionally contend that Black players are "othered" through media representation that frames them as threatening and different, albeit in the coded language of "new racism." Fan cultures are also implicated in racism toward non-white hockey players in Canada, as blatant instances of symbolic racism have been demonstrated on multiple occasions. Just two of the available examples include, in 2002, when Carolina Hurricanes goaltender Kevin Weekes had a banana thrown at him on the ice in Montreal (CBC 2002), and, in 2011, when Wayne Simmonds of the Philadelphia Flyers had a banana thrown at him from the stands during an exhibition game in London, Ontario (ESPN 2011). Finally, racism in Canadian hockey is not confined to the professional level or to the experiences of Black players alone. Michael Robidoux (2004) examined the experience of an Indigenous community's youth hockey team in southern Alberta and found racism to be prevalent. He shows how members of the Kainai Nation experienced racism on institutional and cultural levels when a Kainai youth hockey team was banned from the local league largely because of the racist attitudes and assumptions of members of the local white communities. The interview testimony that follows in this study can in part be understood as an extension of this and other literature on racism in Canadian hockey culture.

Methodology

In what follows, I draw on interview testimony from a larger project exploring the role of athletic injury in the political economy of high-performance sport and the relation between spectators and athletes. In an attempt to take an intersectional approach to my analysis, I raised questions related to race with my interview subjects and received a range of revealing responses, testimony that I draw upon in this chapter. In this study, I conducted semi-structured interviews with eight former professional hockey players. I did not choose to conduct semi-structured interviews because I believed they would provide entirely com-prehensive answers to the questions I raised, whether they pertained to political economy or race. I am not convinced it is possible for any study—even one that is putatively quantita-tive, and much less one that is qualitative—to provide definitive conclusions about the nature of social phenomena, for the actions and behaviours of human beings remain too varied and complex to be neatly synthesized, particularly through the mechanism of struc-tured lines of questioning, an approach necessary if the sample is to be large enough to be taken seriously as representative. Given these limitations of quantitative approaches, I was much more inclined toward a qualitative, semi-structured interview methodology. What I hoped to achieve from my discussions was not a definitive conclusion about the complex dynamics of race, whiteness, hockey, and Canadian national identity, but rather a meditation upon those themes that would provide greater insight into the racialized dimensions of Canadian hockey culture. This is very much in line with what Dorothy Smith has written about qualitative research:

> The relation of the local and particular to generalized social relations is not a conceptual or methodological issue. The particular 'case' is not particular in the aspects that are of

concern to the inquirer. Indeed, it is not a 'case' for it presents itself to us rather as a point of entry, the locus of an experiencing subject or subjects, into a larger social and economic process. The problematic of the everyday world arises precisely at the juncture of particular experience, with generalizing and abstracted forms of social relations organizing a division of labour in society at large. (1987, 157)

As Smith suggests, the experience of every subject is inherently connected to the broader structures in which they live. An exploration of the experience of any subject is therefore an examination of the contours of the larger system. No individual subject can be imagined as exemplifying the structure as a whole; each embodies some of its elements. Ultimately, this is perhaps the guiding principle of qualitative research: the experiences of every subject are immanently valuable and illuminating in terms of what they teach us about both the particularity of human subjectivity and the interpellating effects of social structure.

All interviews are anonymous and the names and identifying characteristics of the players have been changed. I believe that this anonymity contributed to a spirit of uncommon candour among players accustomed to, and defensive about, media interviews. Players were invited into the study using snowball sampling: I was guided to particular individuals who, in turn, referred me to others. The majority of the players in the study were introduced to me in this manner. One of the players came from a completely different source, referred by an academic in the field. I attempted to contact other players using different gatekeepers and contacts, but was unsuccessful in this effort.

My own subject position, presenting as a white man, may have been a factor in the dynamic produced between me and some of the subjects of the study who identified as white, perhaps producing a greater level of candour. Likewise, it may have functioned to inhibit discussion with a player who identified as non-white and who was considerably more circumspect in his responses than others. Further, while I have experience in locker rooms from my own (limited) experiences as an athlete, it was notable that on multiple occasions, subjects asked me to clarify questions because of overly academic phrasing. This suggests that I may have come across as an outsider, which may have affected their comfort level in disclosing their experiences to me.

Players in the study came from a range of elite hockey leagues, from major junior to European professional to the NHL. This evidently provides a wide range of contextual factors, and limits the ability to make any sort of definitive generalizations. The advantage of this breadth, however, is that it testifies to the relevance of the themes in question.

Hockey, Whiteness, and the Disavowal of Race(ism)

Half of the players interviewed in this study—all but one of whom identified as white— refused to acknowledge the presence of racism in the game. It should be noted that these responses, which I will examine, should be understood in the context of the other half that will follow, each of which suggest that racism is in fact ubiquitous in hockey culture. The refusal to acknowledge racism by the first group is not at all surprising, for I suggest that in the Canadian national imaginary, hockey exists as an essentially white realm. Indeed, the putative racial purity of hockey metonymically comes to represent the pristine whiteness at the core of Canadian national identity itself, beneath the pragmatic veneer of multiculturalism. To acknowledge racism, then, would be to concede that heterogeneity and structural inequality exist within the Canadian nation, a concession that would compromise the legitimacy and sanctity of the nation as imagined (Anderson 1991). The disavowal of racism and racial hierarchy is central to the constitution of whiteness as a position of assumed universal human subjectivity. Whiteness as a mode of identity is premised on the construct that the cultural/social/economic capital accrued by white people is legitimately earned and deserved. Claims of racism disrupt this narrative of self and society by indexing the existence of a system that privileges and empowers white subjects illegitimately through (continued) histories of violence and discrimination. Through the disavowal of racism, then, white subjectivity implicitly denies structural inequality and reasserts its own legitimacy and power. Thus, Darin, an enforcer who played thirteen years in the NHL and in the minor-league American Hockey League (AHL) and identified as white, dismissed the existence of racism in the game:

> Nathan: Did you ever feel like the race or ethnicity of a player affected the way fans acted towards him over the course of your career?
> Darin: I wasn't that familiar with it. I mean, I saw some of the articles and, and news shows that came out, you know, that had that kind of stuff in it, but for me it wasn't, it wasn't really prevalent, but...
> Nathan: It wasn't something you saw first-hand?
> Darin: No, not at all.

Although Darin was aware of a broader discussion in the news media around race and hockey, he denies any first-hand exposure, as if by refusing to acknowledge the presence of race in hockey he can make it disappear. Likewise, for Sean, who played a seven-year professional career largely in the United Kingdom and southern United States, and who identified as Canadian of Irish descent, race was something not to be spoken of in hockey:

> Nathan: Did you ever feel like, during your career...that a player's race, the way that their race, their ethnicity, was perceived affected the way the fans acted towards them?
> Sean: Um, tough to say...you're like, really, is it that bad in Canada? Yeah, I don't know, as, being a, you know, a white guy, you know, but I've never seen anything like that before. But, nothing on the ice, nothing at the rink. Again, if someone said something in a crowd, I don't know, the guys I played with probably wouldn't even bring it up. Why bring attention to it? That's the kind of guys they were, why bring attention to it? So, but nothing, nothing that I've ever been a part of or even experienced on another, a guy on another team or someone on our team saying something, just never, never heard it.

Like Darin, Sean refuses to acknowledge the presence of racism in the game. At the same time, he provides a further window into the culture of hockey by demonstrating the expectation that non-white players would not mention the racist abuse they were subjected to. It is clear from this testimony that a tacit understanding exists that, for non-white players to ply their trade in the game, they must absorb racism without calling attention to it or themselves, or risk becoming the wrong "kind of guys." Much like model minority subjects in other sports, racialized athletes in Canadian hockey typically teeter on the brink of abjection (Kalman-Lamb 2013). Yet, unlike the former, the best non-white hockey players can often hope for is invisibility, the perpetuation of the illusion that they do not exist at all, or, at any rate, have any cultural identity. Sean's sentiment is reiterated by Curtis, who played two and a half years in the NHL and AHL and identified as Canadian:

> Nathan: Did you ever feel like the race of a player that you played with affected the way in which the fans acted towards him?
> Curtis: No, no. We had [a non-white] goalie in [a Canadian city], and he was loved by everybody, fans, players, every-, he was a great guy and there was no, I never thought of that back then either, so it wasn't something that came up.

One question we might ask based on this passage is *why* the subject of race "wasn't something that came up." Curtis suggests that it is because racism was not a factor for fans or players. An alternative reading, however, might be that the goalie in question understood that discussing racism was forbidden in Canadian hockey culture. To do so would be to jeopardize his status as a "great guy." Indeed, precisely what is "great" about him seems to be his consent to participate in the fiction that race and racism do not exist in Canadian hockey—or in Canada itself. Jonathan Long, in a discussion of British cricket, argues that the denial of racism is a persistent feature of sporting cultures in that it "invite[s] black players to become complicit in racialized processes or risk being seen themselves to be the cause of the problem, thereby inviting ostracism from the rest of the game. This may typically mean not just suffering (experiencing and having to put-up-with racism), but even publicly minimizing the level of racism they experience" (Long 2000, 131). Thus, it is perhaps unsurprising that Vasil, who had a lengthy career as a goaltender in the AHL and identified as a Muslim of Macedonian descent, demonstrates a similar adherence to the stricture governing non-white players to deny the existence of racism:

> Nathan: Do you feel like the race or ethnicity of a player affected the way fans acted towards him during your career? Did you ever notice that?
> Vasil: No, that's a good question to ask me, actually, because I'm a Muslim, background, and, so that never really came across anywhere that I played, right, so, especially with my background and my name. To be honest with you, I think it's a little more...race is involved a lot more now than it was back then when I played.
> Nathan: Oh, how so? Can you explain that?
> Vasil: I don't know. I just think just race and a lot of different religions are out there more now compared to back then, so a lot of things like that are a, a big thing especially, you know, even a small little thing said can be a big thing, right? But, with my name [says it and then spells it], it's a different name, and people know that, but never in my career have I ever experienced anything like that.

Vasil denies the presence of racism in his time in the game even as he alludes to the experience of being racialized through his name, while also using the coded language of political correctness to suggest that increased discussion of structural racism is to blame for disrupting hockey culture, as if race is a spectre threatening the bastion of whiteness. For the non-white hockey player, it seems, the only safe discussion of race is a denial that it requires discussion.

Racism and Violence in Canadian Hockey

The fantasy of hockey as embodiment of white Canadian identity, however, is predicated as much on the regulation as the elision of actual non-white people in and from the game. The symbolic expulsion of the racialized other from Canadian hockey culture is evident in the various ways in which spectators and players enact verbal and physical violence upon non-white bodies in the sport. For instance, in the recollections of Lawrence, who had a lengthy career as an enforcer in the NHL and AHL and identified as white, racism was a commonplace occurrence during his time in professional hockey:

> Nathan: Did fans act differently towards players based on their race or ethnicity, in your perception?
>
> Lawrence: Well, I think when we go back to London, Ontario, when they, when they threw a banana peel on the ice for [a player]. I think it says that, yes. So, I think that says a lot.
>
> Nathan: Did you see that first-hand in your own...
>
> Lawrence: I did. I did. You know, there's some, you know, African American guys who played where you heard the N-word a lot from the stands.
>
> Nathan: You did?
>
> Lawrence: Oh yeah. Even on the ice, it was different back then, right? You had players that were prejudiced. They would, you know...I won't mention his name, I played with a player that was prejudiced and there was, I think at the time, three Black guys in the league, and he fought them every game. Every game he went out and fought them.
>
> Nathan: And you felt that was deliberate?
>
> Lawrence: Oh yeah, he made it very clear by his actions, by his words.
>
> Nathan: Do you feel like most teammates accepted that as reasonable, or did most of them sort of think that was problematic behaviour?
>
> Lawrence: Well, back then, you didn't think anything of it because it wasn't..., I mean, like I didn't say anything because I wasn't prejudiced, but when I think now, I'm thinking how wrong it was. Like, for him to talk like that and go right after a guy because he was a different colour was, to me, barbaric when you think of it today, right?

Lawrence is very candid here in this extended meditation on the racial politics of the time. He describes racist headhunting and the general climate the Black players in the NHL were confronted with from both fans and other players. Gladiatorial combat between white and Black players in front of largely white crowds functioned to reproduce the notion of whiteness as heroic even in the climate of a society moving toward liberal multiculturalism. As Hage (2000) has discussed, it produced something of a white nation fantasy that sustains a political economy predicated on racialized, often migrant, labour. Lawrence describes the prevalence of racist culture in hockey as if it is the product of a distant past, yet his career spanned the 1980s and early 1990s.

Luc, a high-profile player in the NHL for over a decade who identified as French Canadian, addresses a different form of racism, suggesting that he was subject to abuse from fans as a result of his French Canadian identity:

Nathan: Okay, so, this question is slightly different, but I'm curious, did you ever notice that fans acted differently towards any players because of their race or ethnicity?

Luc: Uh, yeah, yeah. I... personally felt that and I remember one of the first times I went to Toronto, you know, one fan that was close to the ice, close to . . . the [glass], yelled over the [glass], "Frog!" You know, like, so, I, you know, I heard that, obviously. So, I don't . . . know how much of that actually happens and how much you actually hear. You know, I remember that time, hearing that, and really made me feel uncomfortable.

Nathan: It did, yeah, can you tell . . .

Luc: It's, it's pretty fucking stupid . . . [laughs] for, for fans to, you know, to say such comments. I mean, it's. . . . So, anyway, that's...you know, not that I, you know, that I heard that very often or that I witnessed that stuff very often, but I know it does happen, so . . .

Nathan: And did you carry that with you, sort of throughout your career, the memory of that, of thinking about that?

Luc: Well, if I remember today . . . obviously I did, yeah. I'm talking about something that happened in, probably in, 1993 or something.

He retains a vivid memory of experiencing discrimination as a French Canadian and is confident that many others experienced similar. Indeed, the fact that he uses a profanity when describing the behaviour he was subjected to suggests that it had a significant impact upon him, particularly given that this is the only moment in the interview in which he uses such language. Many scholars have argued that whiteness is a relational, fluid, and complex category representative of existing power relations rather than some sort of fixed biological essence. This means that it is possible for a particular cultural group to be racialized as non-white in one historical moment and later ascend to participate in the privilege of whiteness in another (e.g., Ignatiev 1995; Brodkin 1998). Corrie Scott (2016) has convincingly argued that French Canadians should be understood in these terms. Although French Canadian history can be charted from originary colonial violence to the hegemony of whiteness today, for much of the nineteenth and twentieth centuries French Canadians were a racialized group in Canadian society, subject to discrimination, exploitation, and racist representation. The racist epithet "frog" directed at Luc must be understood in this context. I index this passage of testimony because I believe it reveals how stringent the requirements of whiteness are in the context of hockey culture. No form of otherness whatsoever can be tolerated, even ethnic identities otherwise construed as white in Canadian society.

The interview I conducted with James, a former professional goaltender who played nine years in the AHL and NHL and identified as having a multiracial heritage, was the briefest of the entire set, as he was disinclined to expand on most of his answers. Yet, when I brought up the subject of race, he was quick to acknowledge that racism was a fundamental part of the experience of professional hockey for non-white players:

> Nathan: To what extent do you feel like the race of a player affected the ways fans acted towards him?
>
> James: You know, it wasn't bad for me, but I do have some friends, like, Black friends that play that had bananas thrown at them, like, slurs and stuff. But, I think a lot of the, it doesn't happen too much in the NHL, but it's happened to a lot of my friends and, the fans, and all, but if you go overseas and stuff, like, you'll get a lot more.
>
> Nathan: Okay, so, it's worse overseas, and would you say that most players, most non-white players that you knew had some experiences with racism?
>
> James: Yeah, for sure.

Although he doesn't focus or elaborate on his own experiences with racism in professional hockey, he does acknowledge its pervasiveness.

The following passage from Chris, a former major-junior Ontario Hockey League (OHL) player who identified as Jewish, suggests how deeply ingrained racism is in the world of high-performance amateur hockey. Indeed, this discussion occurred years after the experiences of Lawrence (who believed that the culture had since become less racist) and seems to suggest that racism flourishes today as much as ever:

> Nathan: I was going to ask, to what extent do you feel like the race of a player affected the way fans acted towards him?
>
> Chris: It's not, I mean, if you're not a white Christian, you're like, don't even mention anything else. Don't ask for time off on your holidays, don't bring it up to the team, like, because it just causes some sort, some alternative discourse, and they want the team in military precision, marching, like, it's... I know it's slowly changing, but, I mean, there's, it's, behind the back, especially because you know...over time it will go away, but even so, the people in management now were the people playing before, in the times of racism. Listen, if you can put money in, in the pockets of the owners or the players, they'll have you there. But, if you're just one of those average guys, like, it's just brutal....You know, like, so, you know, a lot of people doing cocaine and stuff, like, it's, it comes with the, you know, like, it's like sex, drugs, and rock and roll kind of attitude. But, it's like, oh, the Black kid does one thing wrong, he's out of here. You know, like, so, and, you don't want to be Jewish, you don't want to be Black, you don't want to be, you *definitely* don't want to be Asian. You know, like, it's whatever the stereotype is: it's like, "Oh yeah, the Asian kid doesn't want to shower. You know, because he, you know, because, like, whatever." You know, the Jew is just like, you know, Holocaust jokes all over the place. The Black is like, the n-word, whatever, like, there's more hate towards, I would say, Blacks....Anything that's not white and Christian. It's like, Catholic is okay, Evangelist is okay, Mormon fine, like, but mostly you want to be, you want to be, like, a Protestant white guy from a farm. And then you're like, "That's the kid we want,

gettin' up early, working hard on the farm, you know, grinding it out, not, like, into excess, not, has no, doesn't fancy education to any extent.

In this extended passage, he demonstrates the depth and breadth of racism in hockey culture, from anti-Semitism to racism against non-white players. What he reveals above all is the way in which whiteness is enshrined as the dominant, desirable subject position for players and the standard against which all others are judged. Note that whiteness is connected to a rural culture; "urban" becomes a code word for racial difference. He goes on:

Chris: I was the only Jew in the OHL that year, so I always saw things a little differently. Someone asked me, first of all, always Holocaust jokes. Like…people would say, "Oh, you should have played for the Osha-witz [Oshawa] Generals," you know? And I was like, "Okay, whatever." Eat it. But, if a younger kid said that, I remember a younger, a rookie, a few years later, said that, and I remember choking him. You know, like, I was really mad and I grabbed him by the throat and he said [he makes a choking sound], I'm like, "Yeah, that's right, you can't say anything, kid." And then I re-, then I realized, "What am I even doing?" Like, so, but that's the kind of jokes, you know. And someone said to me, "That's okay that you're Jewish, you still celebrate Christmas, right?" Like, okay, like, you know, I'm not, like, obviously I'm not, like, very Jewish if I'm playing hockey every Friday night, every Saturday night's a game. Saturday-day, Friday-night game. So, but, my grandfather was in the Holocaust, so, you know, to be called—and he was in Auschwitz, actually—so to be called Osha-witz Generals, like, you know, like, there's just so much racism built in, in the coaches…okay, there was a Black kid on the team, and it was dark in the back of the bus, and the coach was counting and he said to the kid, "Eh, smile," and then, "I can't see you," you know what I mean?

In this passage, Chris sheds still more light on the nature of racism in professional hockey and the impact it has upon players. On one level, he reveals the way in which racialized players are forced to accept the racism directed against them because of the power structure of professional hockey. Chris had to "eat it" when older players and coaches were explicitly racist toward his Jewish ancestry because to resist would be to potentially be branded a locker-room cancer and, with that, risk losing his place. This does not mean he was unaffected, however. The toll of this racist abuse is evident in the way that he lashed out against a younger player who made similar comments. In a sense, this was a displacement of his rage against the institutional racism of professional hockey at the safest outlet: a player with still less power than him.

Ultimately, what this interview testimony suggests is that professional hockey in Canada is a world both rife with racism and utterly evacuated of the very concept of race. This simultaneous presence and absence of race is part of the same project to imagine a Canada that, at its core and through its most precious game, is essentially white. When the fantasy of white homogeneity in hockey crumbles in the face of concrete non-white bodies, it must be replaced by the expurgating violence of racism in order to reproduce an ostensibly authentic, white, Canada. This is a narrative of Canada at once consistent and in complete contradiction with the prevailing discourses and policies of multiculturalism. Such a seemingly paradoxical dynamic is a product of the way in which multiculturalism functions in Canada as an official discourse (Bannerji 2000) designed to manage diversity on behalf of whiteness. Quite simply, multicultural policy and rhetoric do not disrupt the ultimate hegemony and centrality of whiteness in Canada; they merely disguise it. This façade becomes unsustainable in the context of the nation's most sacred cultural practice, wherein a more authentic articulation of identity centred on whiteness returns.

Yet, racial equity is not to be sought in the proliferation of non-white hockey players in the role of model minority subjects as we have seen in other sports. Although such figures do receive much of the adulation and acceptance so often denied non-white hockey players, they nevertheless fulfil an insidious function for the state and nation by enforcing a particular, constraining form of non-white identity. If we are to imagine a more equitable place for hockey in the national imaginary of Canada, it must be as a site for the disruption of normalizations of all sorts. This is something of an elusive vanishing point given the structural imperatives of hegemonic masculinity, whiteness, capitalism, and heteronormativity that currently dominate the way that the game is played, down to its lowest levels. Yet, structures of power and domination are never fully closed systems. Resistance is always possible, even from unlikely places. As non-white people in Canada continue to push back against the logic of whiteness and liberal multiculturalism, a breakthrough is as likely in sport as in any other context. Indeed, National Football League quarterback Colin Kaepernick has recently proven in the United States that it can sometimes take just a single act of symbolic resistance to ignite a national conversation on race, justice, and the nation. If such a radical rebuke to national identity is to take place in Canadian sporting culture, it assuredly must be in hockey that it occurs.

Bibliography

Abdel-Shehid, Gamal. 2000. Writing Hockey Thru Race: Rethinking Black Hockey in Canada. In *Rude: Contemporary Black Canadian Cultural Criticism*, ed. Rinaldo Walcott, 69–86. London, ON: Insomniac Press.

———. 2005. *Who Da Man: Black Masculinities and Sporting Cultures.* Toronto: Canadian Scholars' Press.

Adams, Mary Louise. 2006. The Game of Whose Lives? Gender, Race, and Entitlement in Canada's 'National' Game. In *Artificial Ice: Hockey, Culture, and Commerce*, ed. David Whitson and Richard Gruneau, 71–84. Peterborough, ON: Broadview Press.

Allain, Kristi A. 2008. "'Real Fast and Tough': The Construction of Canadian Hockey Masculinity." Sociology of Sport Journal 25 (4): 462–81.

Anderson, Benedict. 1991. *Imagined Communities: Reflections on the Origin and Spread of Nationalism.* Rev. ed. London: Verso.

Bannerji, Himani. 2000. *The Dark Side of the Nation: Essays on Multiculturalism, Nationalism and Gender.* Toronto: Canadian Scholar's Press and Women's Press.

Basok, Tanya. 2002. *Tortillas and Tomatoes: Transmigrant Mexican Harvesters in Canada.* Montreal: McGill-Queen's University Press.

Brodkin, Karen. 1998. *How Jews Became White Folks and What that Says about Race in America.* New Brunswick, NJ: Rutgers University Press.

CBC (Canadian Broadcasting Corporation). 2002. "Habs won't tolerate racist behaviour from fans." CBC Sports, May 9. http://www.cbc.ca/sports/hockey/habs-won-t-tolerate-racist-behaviour-from-fans-1.331548.

Dhamoon, Rita. 2009. *Identity/Difference Politics: How Difference is Produced and Why it Matters*. Toronto: UBC Press.

ESPN. 2011. "Banana thrown at Wayne Simmonds." *ESPN.com*, September 23. http://www.espn.com/nhl/story/_/id/7007219/fan-throws-banana-philadelphia-flyers-winger-wayne-simmonds.

Farber, Michael. 2010. "Canada's leader on Canada's game," *Sports Illustrated*, February 4. http://www.si.com/more-sports/2010/02/04/stephen-harper.

Hage, Ghassan. 2000. *White Nation: Fantasies of White Supremacy in a Multicultural Society*. New York: Routledge.

Haque, Eve. 2012. *Multiculturalism Within a Bilingual Framework: Language, Race, and Belonging in Canada*. Toronto: University of Toronto Press.

Harris, Cecil. 2003. *Breaking the Ice: The Black Experience in Professional Hockey*. Toronto: Insomniac Press.

Ignatiev, Noel. 1995. *How the Irish Became White*. New York: Routledge.

Kalman-Lamb, Nathan. 2012. "'A Portrait of this Country': Whiteness, Indigeneity, Multiculturalism and the Vancouver Opening Ceremonies." *Topia: Canadian Journal of Cultural Studies* 27:5–27.

———. 2013. "The Athlete as Model Minority Subject: Jose Bautista and Canadian Multiculturalism." *Social Identities: Journal for the Study of Race, Nation and Culture* 19 (2): 238–53.

———. 2015. "Deconstructing Linsanity: Is Jeremy Lin a Model Minority Subject?" In *Killing the Model Minority Stereotype: Asian American Counterstories and Complicity*, ed. Nicholas Hartlep and Brad Porfilio, 203–18. Charlotte, NC: Information Age Publishing.

Kymlicka, Will. 1995. *Multicultural Citizenship: A Liberal Theory of Minority Rights*. Oxford: Oxford University Press.

Long, Jonathan. 2000. "No Racism Here? A Preliminary Examination of Sporting Innocence." *Managing Leisure* 5 (3): 121–33.

Lorenz, Stacy L., and Rod Murray. 2014. "'Goodbye to the Gangstas': The NBA Dress Code, Ray Emery, and the Policing of Blackness in Basketball and Hockey." *Journal of Sport and Social Issues* 38 (1): 23–50.

Mackey, Eva. 2002. *The House of Difference: Cultural Politics and National Identity in Canada*. Toronto: University of Toronto Press.

Norman, Mark. 2014. "Online Community or Electronic Tribe? Exploring the Social Characteristics and Spatial Production of an Internet Hockey Fan Culture." *Journal of Sport and Social Issues* 38 (5): 395–414.

Robidoux, Michael A. 2002. "Imagining a Canadian Identity Through Sport: A Historical Interpretation of Lacrosse and Hockey." *Journal of American Folklore* 115 (456): 209–25.

———. 2004. "Narratives of Race Relations in Southern Alberta: An Examination of Conflicting Sporting Practices." *Sociology of Sport Journal* 21 (3): 287–301.

Scott, Corrie. 2016. "How French Canadians became White Folks, or doing things with race in Quebec." *Ethnic and Racial Studies* 39 (7): 1280–97.

Sharma, Nandita. 2006. *Home Economics: Nationalism and the Making of 'Migrant Workers' in Canada*. Toronto: University of Toronto Press.

Smith, Dorothy. 1987. *The Everyday World as Problematic: A Feminist Sociology*. Toronto: University of Toronto Press.

Taylor, Charlesz. 1994. The Politics of Recognition. In *Multiculturalism: Examining the politics of recognition*, ed. Amy Gutmann, 25–73. Princeton: Princeton University Press.

Thobani, Sunera. 2007. *Exalted Subjects: Studies in the Making of Race and Nation in Canada*. Toronto: University of Toronto Press.

Contributors

Carly Adams is a board of governors research chair (Tier II) and an associate professor in the Department of Kinesiology and Physical Education at the University of Lethbridge. Her research explores sport, recreation, and leisure experiences from the intersections of historical and sociological inquiry, with a focus on gender and community. Her work has appeared in, among others, *The Journal of Sport History, The Journal of Canadian Studies,* and *The International Review for the Sociology of Sport.* Dr. Adams is the editor-in-chief of *Sport History Review.*

Kristi Allain is an assistant professor of sociology at St. Thomas University, Fredericton, NB. Her work examines the intersections of Canadian national identity, gender, aging, and physical culture, highlighting the ways that national identity projects secure some forms of identity as central to the nation—specifically those associated with dominant expressions of gender, sexuality, and race—while often marginalizing those whose identities are considered peripheral.

Jennifer Anderson is an archivist at Library and Archives Canada. She has a master's degree in Central/East European and Russian Area Studies and a PhD in Canadian history, both from Carleton University. While on an Interchange Canada secondment at the Canadian Museum of History, she co-curated the *Hockey* exhibition.

Paul W. Bennett, Ed.D. (OISE/Toronto) is founding director of Schoolhouse Institute and a well-known Halifax author, education professor, and policy researcher. For the past six years, Paul has researched hockey's origins and presented papers to the North American Society for Sports History (NASSH) and the International Society for Hockey Research. He is the author of eight books and many academic articles, most recently in the *Journal of Sports History* on the origins of Canadian schoolboy football.

Marc Durand est réalisateur, animateur et journaliste sportif, travaillant à TQS et Radio Canada, entre autres. Il anime des émissions sportives et couvre plusieurs évènements internationaux, dont huit Jeux olympiques. Il partage plusieurs prix Gémeaux, tant à la réalisation qu'à l'animation. Marc Durand a publié en 2012 *La Coupe à Québec, Les Bulldogs et la naissance du hockey* et en 2017 *Jean Béliveau : La naissance d'un héros.*

Jenny Ellison is Curator of Sports and Leisure at the Canadian Museum of History. Her projects examine the representation and experience of sport, leisure, physical fitness, and health. Dr. Ellison's writing has appeared in *The Journal of Canadian Studies, The Canadian Bulletin of Medical History, The Journal of the Canadian Historical Association*, and the award-winning *Fat Studies Reader.* She is the co-editor of *Obesity in Canada: Critical Perspectives* (University of Toronto Press, 2016). She holds a PhD in history from York University.

Richard Gruneau is Professor of Communication at Simon Fraser University. With David Whitson, he is co-author of *Hockey Night in Canada: Sport, Identities and Cultural Politics* (1993) and co-editor of *Artificial Ice: Hockey, Commerce and Culture* (2006). His most recent book, *Sport and Modernity*, was published by Polity Press in 2017.

Andrew C. Holman is a Professor of History and Director of the Canadian Studies Program at Bridgewater State University in Bridgewater, Massachusetts. He teaches and writes about North American sport history, and about other subjects in Canadian history. He is co-editor (with Jason Blake) of *The Same but Different: Hockey in Quebec*, which was published by McGill-Queen's University Press in August 2017.

Nathan Kalman-Lamb is a lecturing fellow in the Thompson Writing Program at Duke University. He is the co-author of *Out of Left Field: Social Inequality and Sports* (Fernwood Books, 2012) as well as the author of articles on race, multiculturalism, and sport in the journals *Social Identities, Topia*, and *Social Inclusion*, and the edited collection *Killing the Model Minority Stereotype: Asian American Counterstories and Complicity* (Information Age Publishing, 2015). He received his PhD from the graduate programme in social and political thought at York University. His research focuses on labour, race, multiculturalism, gender, and spectatorship in sport.

Denyse Lafrance Horning is a marketing professor at Nipissing University. Her research interests include sponsorship marketing, women in sport, and various aspects of hockey. Denyse is active in hockey as a coach, player, and fan, and was recognized in 2015 with the Hockey Canada Hero of Play Award. Denyse is also a certified mentor with the Coaches Association of Ontario.

Jason Laurendeau is an Associate Professor in the Department of Sociology at the University of Lethbridge. His research explores intersections of gender, risk, embodiment and childhood, and his published work has appeared in such venues as *Sociological Perspectives,* the *Sociology of Sport Journal,* the *Journal of Sport & Social Issues*, and *Emotion, Space & Society.*

Cheryl A. MacDonald is a sport sociologist working as a postdoctoral fellow at the Institute for Sexual Minority Studies and Services at the University of Alberta. She holds a PhD from Concordia University, where her dissertation work was on understandings of gender and sexuality as well as attitudes toward homosexuality among male youth hockey players in Canada. Her secondary research interest lies in the visibility and development of women's hockey, and she frequently has an active study on the subject amidst her other work.

Sam McKegney is a settler scholar of Indigenous literatures and an Associate Professor at Queen's University in the territory of the Haudenosaunee and Anishinaabe Peoples. He has published two books—*Masculindians: Conversations about Indigenous Manhood* and *Magic Weapons: Aboriginal Writers Remaking Community after Residential School*—and articles on such topics as masculinity, environmental kinship, prison writing, and hockey mythologies.

Benoît Melançon, blogueur (oreilletendue.com) et professeur à l'Université de Montréal, est l'auteur de deux livres remarqués sur le hockey, le premier sur le plus célèbre joueur des Canadiens de Montréal, *Les Yeux de Maurice Richard*, et le second sur les mots du sport, *Langue de puck*. Il est membre de la Société royale du Canada et de l'Ordre des francophones d'Amérique.

Joe Pelletier is a hockey writer and researcher from Terrace, British Columbia. He has worked with the NHL, Hockey Canada, *The Hockey News* and the Canadian Museum of History. He has written three books of his own and is the curator of the popular hockey history website www.GreatestHockeyLegends.com

Trevor J. Phillips is Métis from West Jasper Place (Edmonton), a PhD candidate in English literature at Queen's University, a union representative, student support worker, and amateur hockey broadcaster. He is the host of the podcast *At the Edge of Canada: Indigenous Research*. He currently resides in Treaty 1 Territory.

J. Andrew Ross is a portfolio archivist in the Government Archives Division of Library and Archives Canada. He holds a doctorate in history from the University of Western Ontario and is the author of *Joining the Clubs: The Business of the National Hockey League to 1945* (Syracuse University Press, 2015).

Michael A. Robidoux is a Full Professor in the School of Human Kinetics at the University of Ottawa. His first book entitled, *Men at Play: A Working Understanding of Professional Hockey* was a year ethnographic study of a professional hockey team, and was nominated for the Governor General's Award for non-fiction. His second book, *Stickhandling through the Margins*, is anthropological study of hockey played by Indigenous peoples in Canada. Most recently, he has received funding to conduct research on head contact in youth hockey, towards better helmet design.

Robert Rutherdale teaches in the Department of History and Philosophy at Algoma University. He is the author of *Hometown Horizons: Canada's Local Responses to the Great War* (UBC Press, 2004) and co-editor, with Magda Farhni, of *Creating Postwar Canada: Community, Diversity, and Dissent*, 1945-1975 (UBC Press, 2009). He is also the co-editor, with Peter Gossage, of *Making Men, Making History: Canadian Masculinities Across Time and Place* (forthcoming).

Emily Sadler is a Toronto-based writer with a passion for sports. She grew up on a steady diet of hockey and later adopted football as her second love. Her work can often be found on sportsnet.ca. She made her sports-writing debut covering the London 2012 Olympic Games, and has also been published in *Today's Parent* and on House & Home Media.

Tobias Stark is an Associate Professor in the Department of Sport Sciences at Linnaeus University in Växjö, Sweden, where he teaches sport history and sport sociology. Stark is the author of *Folkhemmet på is: Ishockey, modernisering och nationell identitet i Sverige 1920–1972* (The people's home on ice: Ice hockey, modernization and national identity in Sweden 1920-1972) (2010), as well as numerous book chapters and journal articles on Swedish and European ice hockey.

Julie Stevens is an Associate Professor in the Department of Sport Management at Brock University. She examines both macro- and micro-level change through various organization theories to explain the transformation of sport organizations over time. Dr. Stevens has conducted diverse and transdisciplinary hockey research on the governance, development, and structure of hockey that includes topics such as institutional development, large-scale change, innovation, player-development models, and ethics. She is co-author of the book *Too Many Men on the Ice: Women's Hockey in North America* (Polestar, 1997), and has published work on the socio-historical evolution of women's hockey.

Courtney Szto is a graduate of Simon Fraser University's School of Communication. Her doctoral research examined the intersections of race, citizenship, and sport in Canada with a specific emphasis on South Asian experiences in ice hockey. She is also the Assistant Editor of Hockey in Society, a blog that explores critical social issues in hockey.

Laurent Turcot est titulaire de la Chaire de recherche du Canada en histoire des loisirs et des divertissements. Professeur en histoire à l'Université du Québec à Trois-Rivières et membre du Centre interuniversitaire d'études québécoises, il est l'auteur notamment de *Sports et Loisirs, une histoire des origines à nos jours* (Gallimard, 2016).

Hayley Wickenheiser is a five-time Olympic medalist—4-time gold medalist—and seven-time World Championship medalist in hockey. Wickenheiser is passionate about giving back through her work with organizations such as JumpStart, KidSport, Project North, Right to Play, Lace 'Em Up Foundation and "The Canadian Tire Wickenheiser World Female Hockey Festival," among others. She holds a BSc from University of Calgary and is currently pursuing a career in medicine.

John Willis is Curator of Economic History at the Canadian Museum of History. A graduate of Université Laval in historical geography, John Willis is a social historian who has worked on the history of communication, labour, and business. Born in Montreal, he was a Habs fan before he first put on skates, and he will continue to support the *bleu-blanc-rouge* long after the last ice is melted.

Index

The following index is presented in both of Canada's official languages.
L'index qui suit est présenté dans les deux langues officielles du Canada.

MARQUIS

Québec, Canada

Printed in March 2018
by Marquis, Montmagny (Québec), Canada.